Jews of the Pacific Coast

Jews of the Pacific Coast

REINVENTING COMMUNITY ON AMERICA'S EDGE

ELLEN EISENBERG, AVA F. KAHN, AND WILLIAM TOLL

A Samuel and Althea Stroum Book

UNIVERSITY OF WASHINGTON PRESS • SEATTLE AND LONDON

*This book is published with the assistance of a grant from the
Samuel and Althea Stroum Endowed Book Fund. Additional support
was provided by the Lucius N. Littauer Foundation.*

University of Washington Press, PO Box 50096, Seattle, WA 98145, USA
www.washington.edu/uwpress

Library of Congress Cataloging-in-Publication Data
Eisenberg, Ellen.
Jews of the Pacific coast : reinventing community on America's edge /
Ellen Eisenberg, Ava F. Kahn, and William Toll. — 1st ed.
p. cm.
Includes bibliographical references and index.
ISBN 978-0-295-98965-5 (hardback : alk. paper)
1. Jews—West (U.S.)—History—19th century.
2. Jews—West (U.S.)—History—20th century.
3. Jews—California—History—19th century.
4. Jews—California—History—20th century.
5. California—Ethnic relations.
6. West (U.S.)—Ethnic relations.
I. Kahn, Ava F. II. Toll, William. III. Title
F596.3J5K34 2009 979'.004924—dc22 2009027127

For Moses Rischin, who first imagined a western Jewish history

CONTENTS

PREFACE

Jews of the Pacific Coast explores the impact of life in the American Far West on Jews and Jewish communities and the reciprocal impact of Jews on the American Far West. Instead of a comprehensive chronicle of individuals and communities, we have defined our subject by the confluence of two dramatic histories, that of a distinctive western region and that of a distinctive Jewish people. To find a broader meaning in the experience of those Jews who settled there, we sought a new understanding of the historiography. The historiography of the West has been framed by the heroic lore of the frontier, while that of American Jewry has focused on the saga of immigration and assimilation. Regrettably, Jews of the American West have been given very limited attention and no distinctive interpretive mode in either of these historical traditions. Through the 1960s, histories of the West were dominated by accounts of farmers and miners crossing the plains and settling into rural areas, where they were exploited as virtually colonial subjects by the great capitalist enterprises represented by the railroads, the banks, and agribusiness. More recently, scholars of the West have focused on issues of race and gender, with the central theme of Anglo political leaders taking the land from native peoples, exploiting the labor of Asians and Mexicans, and imposing a discriminatory regime on all peoples of color. Jews, though more numerous than one might infer, at first as small-scale merchants and then in more diverse and prominent entrepreneurial roles, apparently—and perhaps mercifully—have found no significant place in either western narrative.

The historical writing on American Jewry has been dominated by accounts of immigration, with its destinations depicted as a collection of disconnected urban settlements. The great cities of the East, especially, of course, New York, where uniquely large and densely settled Jewish communities accumulated, provide the landscape for the intergenerational drama of assimilation. Occasionally midwestern commercial centers like Cincinnati enter the narrative because they have been the site of unique religious institutions or dominant personalities. Jews of the Far West, however, were thought to be so remote from the main drama and so few in number that whatever transpired there could be understood at best as a pale reflection of the main narrative.

In trying to make sense of the thriving Jewish communities along the Pacific Coast, and in regionally connected communities in Nevada and Arizona, we had first to exploit the recently established archives in cities like Seattle, Portland, and Berkeley to recreate any picture of what actually transpired. What our research might amount to has taken longer to appreciate. We knew that San Francisco, as Moses Rischin pointed out thirty years ago, in 1870 held America's second largest Jewish community, with a rich cultural life. We discovered also that by the 1920s Los Angeles had surpassed its northern rival to become the focal point of Jewish—and western—population and cultural creativity. Since World War II new communities in new cities like Las Vegas have surpassed in population Jewish communities in declining cities of the East and Midwest. We wished to explain how and why the population continued to grow so rapidly, why the equilibrium shifted as it did, why communities developed an array of distinctive philanthropic and cultural institutions, and why regionwide connections were established and sustained.

Most Americans know about Levi Strauss, Louis B. Mayer, the Warner brothers, and "Bugsy" Siegel and today read about the achievements of Senators Dianne Feinstein and Barbara Boxer. Jewish scholars have noted the stay of Rabbi Stephen Wise in Portland, the emergence of Rabbi Edgar Magnin of Wilshire Boulevard Temple as "the rabbi to the stars," and the curious career of Shlomo Carlebach as guru of a Jewish commune in the Haight-Ashbury of the 1970s. But could these very different characters, spanning the years from the Gold Rush to the present, be tied together by anything more than the chance that they resided in the same region and were of Jewish ancestry? Were they merely exotic characters, or did they highlight major themes in the evolution of a regional community? As our work proceeded, we uncovered the distinctive roles that Jews have always played in the region, how they created for themselves a set of regional networks, financial, religious, and philanthropic, and how they interacted with non-Jews to create a unique status. Whether our findings will initiate a rethinking of the major themes of western history will be for other scholars to say, but we believe that Jews and their functions can no longer be omitted from the broader narrative. The disproportionate contributions of Jews to the making of markets for commodities, the creation of rural credit, the fashioning of the rule of law, and the shaping of consumer tastes should play a large role in writing a more nuanced view of how the West was settled and how it has emerged as a sophisticated region.

We also believe that the pervasive integration of Jews into the civic fabric of western cities and towns suggests a different relationship with America than does the narrative that focuses primarily on New York and on the other cities of the East and Midwest. The introduction will develop this issue more fully, but we believe that our findings require a reevaluation of the American Jewish narrative that has emphasized the three-generational assimilation struggle. This often guilt-ridden schema, we believe, should be balanced by a story of Jews and Jewish communities recreating themselves as full participants in the civic life of a rapidly developing and very new society. This, indeed, has become a distinctive western regional heritage, passed on from the pioneer women and men to their successors in the twentieth and twenty-first centuries. Jewish communities in the West have not been a pale reflection of a narrative unfolding elsewhere. They were instead pioneers of a new relationship between Jews and America in a distinctive and evolving western landscape. As we observe a growing proportion of American Jewry settling in the West, which is itself in rapid social and ideological evolution very much influenced by the activities of its Jews, we believe that the narrative developed here will describe more and more the creative adjustment that Jews will continue to make to American life.

ACKNOWLEDGMENTS

A book of this scope could not have been completed without the help and consideration of others. Several historians have shared their unpublished work and their opinions with us. We particularly want to thank Karen Wilson for sharing her work on Los Angeles Jewry, Jeanne E. Abrams for sharing archival documents and publishing an important new study of Jewish women in the American West, Alan M. Kraut and Deborah A. Kraut and Mary Ann Irwin for sharing conference papers, Fred Rosenbaum for sharing a chapter of his forthcoming book, and Charles Wollenberg for sharing his knowledge of western history. We also owe a debt to the many scholars, especially George Sanchez, whose papers and panel commentary at the June 2006 Biennial Scholars' Conference on American Jewish History in Charleston reinforced our emphasis on the distinctive regional mentality that developed among Jews settling in the American West. Lee Shai Weissbach and Amy Hill Shevitz have engaged us in dialogues, which have been very helpful in framing the book, while Mark K. Bauman, by challenging our views, has helped sharpen our interpretation. We also are grateful to Lawrence Baron and our colleagues at the Western Jewish Studies Association for providing a supportive forum for the presentation and discussion of preliminary findings over several years. The continuing interest of Jonathan Sarna has sustained our confidence in this project over the half-dozen years this manuscript has been in preparation.

Many archivists have helped us accumulate material for this project. We especially appreciate the work of Susan Douglass Yates of the City of Hope, who contributed a book, documents, photographs, and her time and energy to the publication. Aaron Kornblum of the Western Jewish History Center at the Judah L. Magnes Museum in Berkeley opened the archives for each of us on separate occasions, provided useful research suggestions, and went out of his way to help us obtain significant photographs. Susan Synder of the Bancroft Library, University of California, Berkeley, joyfully provided us personal attention and consideration with both documents and images.

Judith Margles and Anne LeVant Prahl of the Oregon Jewish Museum responded quickly and enthusiastically to our e-mails, conducted archival research, and also sent documents and images. We also wish to thank Lyn Slome of the American Jewish Historical Society for help with documents and images; Kevin Proffitt of the Jacob Rader Marcus Center of the American Jewish Archives for friendly, if long-distance, assistance with documents and images; and Robert Marshall and Jessica Holada at the Urban Archives of California State University, Northridge, for locating and mailing documents. Dr. Grace Cohen Grossman and Mia Cariño of the Skirball Center responded quickly to our many questions and put images at our disposal. Several archivists at the University of Oregon's Archives patiently retrieved the President's Office Correspondence from their temporary and uncataloged shelving.

Much of our work depended on obtaining books and especially Jewish community newspapers from the early twentieth century. We are grateful to the librarians at the Berkeley Public Library, Willamette University's Hatfield Library, and the University of Oregon's Knight Library who assisted us with our many interlibrary loan requests.

We would also like to thank Judith Kahn Gorman, Reuven and Yehudit Goldfarb, Hannah Kuhn, and Frances Dinkelspiel for sharing photographs with us. Harry Stein helped in many ways, especially in locating a photo of a Portland family's store. Rebecca Comhi Fromer and Seymour Fromer took a personal interest in our work; we highly value their thoughts and friendship.

With particular gratitude we wish also to thank Mr. William Frost of the Lucius N. Littauer Foundation for a generous grant to assist in publication and Willamette University for support of our work through the Dwight and Margaret Lear Professorship in American History and through an Atkinson Faculty Development Award.

Several people diligently gathered the material that has made our work possible. They include especially William M. Kramer and Norton B. Stern in publishing *Western States Jewish History*. Without their publication of documents and copious footnotes this project would have been much more difficult. The late Shirley Tanzer of Portland initiated the oral history project through the Oregon Jewish Historical Society, of which Rabbi Joshua Stampfer has been its steadfast support for many decades. Sara G. Cogan completed thorough annotated bibliographies for the Western Jewish History Center.

Safy Nurhussein, a graduate student in the Geography Department of the University of Oregon, patiently prepared the maps for this book to our specifications and those of the press. We also appreciate the personal attention of our editors at the University of Washington Press: Julidta Tarver, Marianne Keddington-Lang, Mary Ribesky, and Jane Lichty.

Finally, we each wish to express to our families that this work would have been impossible without them. We acknowledge Mitchell A. Richman for his patience; Ami, Alex and Ben Korsunsky for their constant love and support; and Junko Iwao Toll for her lifelong commitment to the value of scholarship and the importance of telling the truth.

Jews of the Pacific Coast

INTRODUCTION

Western Landscapes, Western Jews

The Israelites of Marysville [comprise] a large class
of our best citizens. —1853

When Sherith Israel of San Francisco dedicated its new temple in 1904, only two years before the terrifying earthquake that it survived intact, it commissioned a stained-glass window that symbolized not only the experience of its members but the mood of an entire region. Caught in the prism of multicolored lights, Moses descended with the Ten Commandments not from Sinai but from El Capitan. He found himself not on the edge of an unknown promised land but in the midst of a specific landscape already recognized as a national treasure—the great Yosemite Valley. Absorbing the aura of this natural wonder, Jews as pioneers in this new region felt free not only to bring the law as founders of civic life but to cultivate a spirit of innovation that the spectacular landscapes both inspired and required. Starting with the Gold Rush, Jews of the Pacific West were to persist in the creation of a distinctive regional way of life (plate 1).

Since the era of Frederick Jackson Turner, historians have debated the significance of regionalism in American history. More recently, scholars of American Jewish history have raised similar questions.[1] Often the comparison is framed to determine whether Jews in the South, for example, have more in common with Jews elsewhere in the country than they do with non-Jewish southerners. Scholars in the West ask whether the "frontier" has imparted to Jewish settlers a unique western identity, which distinguishes them from Jews living elsewhere. If Jews embraced regional customs and habits by incorporating regional foods into their ritual observance or elements of western landscapes into their synagogue architecture, do we regard these as meaningful variations on American Jewish identity or as merely superficial markers? More generally, should we understand the history of Jews in America primarily in terms of the development of religious ritual and Jewish communal activities? Or should we, by understanding American Jews as a social and cultural group with a religious identity and by reframing history in regional terms, emphasize the ways Jews have persistently redefined themselves and their place in the larger American society, economy, and civic culture?

In examining these issues, we are concerned with two aspects of regionalism. First, we use regionalism as a framework for understanding the interactions among Jewish individuals and communities in a specific geographic area. In the Pacific West—so far removed from the rest of the country—Jewish communities relied on one another, and individuals traveled easily between communities, with San Francisco during the era of early settlement being the clear regional center. The extensive and shifting interaction among communities along the Pacific Coast became a key factor shaping Jewish regional identity. Second, regionalism speaks to the relationship between Jewish individuals and communities and the broader society. In this sense, a regional approach to western Jewish history examines the intersection between American Jewish history and western history, which has its own historiography as America's "frontier," with its own iconic, if not sacred, dimensions.[2] We argue that the timing of settlement and the social,

political, religious, ethnic, and economic climate of the cities and towns in which communities developed profoundly influenced regional identities for Jews as for other westerners.

While we believe that these two aspects of regionalism have been critical to shaping the identities of western Jews, we do not want to suggest that these identities were comprehensive and exclusive. Western Jewish identities, like all identities, have always been multilayered. Individuals could embrace their identities as western Jews while at the same time identifying as Russians, Oregonians, Zionists, merchants, and even former New Yorkers. At the same time, there were variations among western Jewish identities—one could be a traditional Jew, a cosmopolitan, and a San Franciscan or a more provincial Angeleno and still be a westerner. Despite internal variations and points of similarity to the stories of Jews in other regions, particularly those distant from Jewish centers in the Northeast, there is, we believe, a compelling regional history.

Much of the recent scholarly debate about the significance of regionalism in understanding the American Jewish experience focuses on the American South. In 1996, Mark K. Bauman critically assessed the case for southern distinctiveness, arguing that "Jews in the South were influenced by the regional subculture in a relatively marginal fashion" and that many distinctively southern themes actually alienated southern Jews. He concluded, "To a remarkable degree . . . their experiences were far more similar to those of Jews in similar environments elsewhere in America than they were to those of white Protestants in the South."[3] Bauman was one of several scholars whose work shifted the debate about southern Jewish identity and called for a rigorous examination of that identity. He made the crucial point that rather than constantly compare various regional Jewish communities to New York, historians should examine the experiences of Jews in various less metropolitan regions in relation to one another.

The recent literature on southern Jewry provides a helpful starting point for examining the experiences of Jews in the American West. Yet the conclusion of scholars like Bauman and Marc Lee Raphael that southern Jewish distinctiveness has been exaggerated does not mean that the dimensions or locations of regionalism are unimportant in interpreting the American Jewish experience. We argue that the West, compared to other regions of the United States, developed a civic culture—founded in part by Jews—that was particularly welcoming and attractive to new Jewish arrivals. Their embrace of this civic culture shaped the Jewish communities and identities that emerged in the West. This is a notable contrast to the South, a region characterized by the historian Gary Zola as "Jewishly disadvantaged."[4] Historians of southern Jewry frequently set Jewish culture and values against southern ones, using terms like "oxymoronic" to describe "being Jewish in the South." While the editors of a recent anthology argue that "the survival of the southern Jewish community proves that Judaism can endure in the most ominous conditions and still prevail,"[5] historians of western Jewry—and western Jews themselves—have by contrast depicted the West as a promised land.

For a regional approach to hold interpretative power it should explain how unique opportunities proved attractive to particular types of migrants, how social networks and institutions connected specific communities to one another and influenced behavior over time, and how the idea of region attended by specific values or images gave these communities a sense of self-identity and of standing in the larger society. Although Jews settling all along America's developing trade routes in the nineteenth century had similar occupational profiles, attention to regional distinctiveness does help explain how Jews developed a different sense of their personal identity and civic status largely because of where they were settling. As the religious historian Laurie F. Maffly-Kipp argues, "Geographical placement is an important factor in understanding religious behaviors and beliefs. . . . religiously, it matters greatly who one's neighbors are, and who controls the cultural, political, and economic resources of a given region."[6]

America's regions differ in the timing and the lore of their settlement, in their ethnic and racial mixes, and not least in their proximity to the nation's economic, political, and religious centers. Jews, while engaged in similar commercial roles in different regions, could also develop a sense of who they were becoming—as Americans and even as Jews—in part because of when in a region's development they entered, who they encountered as neighbors, and how those neighbors dealt with one another. The historian John Higham observes that in cities where Jews arrived during the early phases of settlement and were viewed as "pioneers," subsequent generations "generally faired better."[7] In the West, this pattern was the norm. The pioneering role of Jews in the region's small towns and larger cities in the nineteenth century laid the foundation for western Jewish identity and community development that is central to this study.

The Jewish experience was shaped by the geography of the region as well as by the timing of its settlement. Along the Pacific Coast, Jewish newcomers understood that they were traveling through vast landscapes far removed from the rest of the nation, encountering different majorities, and facing unprecedented civic challenges. Jacob

Nieto, an immigrant from England and rabbi at San Francisco's Reform Congregation Sherith Israel, wrote ironically in 1911: "The Sierras perform the same kind of unkind office for California that the sea does for Great Britain—we are insular in our prejudices" (plate 2).[8]

The pattern of western development has made the story of western Jewry largely an urban one. Although many Jews in the pioneer generation settled in—and helped to found—small towns, the small town experience was a fleeting one. As Lee Shai Weissbach's recent history demonstrates, small Jewish communities in most parts of the country persisted well into the twentieth century and were reinforced by arriving Eastern European migrants.[9] In contrast, small Jewish communities in the West, while serving early on as important links in regional economic and social networks, dwindled by the turn of the century and often disappeared. In part, this was a reflection of the general history of the region. Mining towns, for example, boomed and then went bust, triggering an exodus by miners and merchants, Jews and non-Jews. More broadly, in contrast to the popular image of the West, the region emerged early in its history as the most urbanized in the country.[10] The relatively rapid movement of Jews from small town to urban center, then, reflected regional trends. Those Jewish families that remained in remote, small town locations even as community institutions stagnated or folded often assimilated into the non-Jewish population.

The experience of Jewish westerners was also shaped by the regional ethnic landscape. The presence of substantial populations of Asian and Mexican immigrants, as well as American Hispanics and Native Americans, made the West the most diverse region in the country. In addition, many of the "white" settlers who came west during the nineteenth century were not Anglo Americans but European immigrants—Italians, Irish, and others— whom many Anglo American easterners considered "not quite white." The West, Patricia Limerick argues, was a "meeting ground" for different ethnicities: "In race relations, the West could make the turn-of-the-century Northeastern urban confrontation between European immigrants and American nativists look like a family reunion."[11]

While race relations in American history have until recently been depicted as the exploitation and depersonalizing of blacks by whites, the Pacific West did not have a significant African American population until the mobilization for World War II. In most of the West, Native Americans, Hispanics, and Asian immigrants were the visible and demeaned "other." The presence of these diverse groups, in conjunction with the region's desperate need for basic services, directly affected the ways in which Jews were perceived. It also created a racial equation that distinguished the nineteenth-century West from other regions. Leonard Rogoff documents in the late-nineteenth-century South a stream of racial thought that called Jewish "whiteness" into question. He concludes that Jews "were accepted as white, but their precise racial place was not fixed."[12] During the same period in the Northeast, the primary "racial" concern was the immigration of Southern and Eastern Europeans. Anglo Americans, who placed themselves at the top of their putative racial hierarchy, saw these "new immigrants" as inferior and "not quite white." Coming from less developed countries, and professing Catholicism, Orthodoxy, or Judaism rather than genteel Protestantism, these immigrants were believed to be less civilized, less cultured, less capable, and less intelligent than Anglo Americans. According to historians of whiteness, it was not until the twentieth-century migration of African

Americans to the North that the diverse European immigrant groups, including Jews, were consistently categorized as white.[13]

While southern, eastern, and midwestern Jews faced heightened anti-Semitism beginning in the late nineteenth century, Jews of the West continued to celebrate their high level of inclusion and civic prominence. In the 1890s, Jews were elected by Protestant majorities as mayors, venerated as town founders, and included in pioneer organizations. While Native Americans were forced onto reservations and the Chinese and then the Japanese became objects of discriminatory state and federal legislation, elite Jews were listed in Portland's and San Francisco's Social Registers. By every measure Jews were accepted as white, though perhaps of a slightly different shade, well into the twentieth century.[14] The journey west could actually transform "not-quite-white" southern and eastern immigrants into "Anglos." As in the South, where antiblack racism served to "whiten" diverse European immigrants, so in the West, Eastern European Jews and Italians were seen as Anglos.[15]

Likewise, Jewish acceptance was fostered by the West's unique religious diversity.[16] Anglo American settlers were confronted by the Catholicism of the resident Mexican Americans, a significant presence of Mormons, and the Buddhism of immigrant Asians. The region was, according to historian of religion D. Michael Quinn, "the inverted image of the Protestant mainstream."[17] In contrast with other regions, "evangelical Christianity did not shape the 'religious character' of the region," and church leaders frequently complained of the region's lack of religiosity.[18] In such a context—and facing the notorious challenges of a newly settled, male-dominated society—early European American religious leaders in the region, both Protestant and Catholic, often saw Jews not as a religious threat but as allies with whom they could "battle together to tame this frontier culture."[19] According to the religious historian Ferenc Morton Szasz, "faced with the virtual absence of any social institutions, pioneer ministers, priests and rabbis all became 'social gospelers' well before the term was created."[20]

These relationships, and the place of Jews in the social structure, became more complex in the twentieth century, primarily because of the vast expansion of population commensurate with the creation of an industrial and then a postindustrial society. As midwesterners flooded into southern California in the early part of the twentieth century, for example, their prejudices temporarily reversed the historic openness of that area. During World War II and in its aftermath, as African Americans came to the Pacific West in large numbers, their presence again shifted the racial/ethnic equation. Far from threatening Jews, the new African American prominence provided an opportunity to create a powerful political alliance. Koreans arriving with skills and capital in Los Angeles in the 1970s and 1980s received a very different, largely positive, reception compared to the Chinese a hundred years before. Mexicans (early immigrants to the West) arriving in large numbers after 1965 have transformed cities from Los Angeles to San Diego, Phoenix, and Las Vegas and have shifted concepts of regional culture and politics.

This book aims to address all of these themes as we explore the regional identity of Jews and the development of their communities along the Pacific Coast and the interior areas connected to it by trade routes. We examine not only how they identified themselves as western "pioneers" but also how the geographic, economic, ethnic, and political dimensions of western life impacted them as Jews. We demonstrate how the changing opportunity structure of the region has shaped the migration streams that have brought Jews to the West, not only during the nineteenth century, but also to the present day. We argue that the social environment of the newly founded Gold Rush San Francisco, or in later years the rapidly growing cities of Los Angeles and Las Vegas, influenced the development of Jewish communities. We contend that the unique ethnic landscape that Jews entered—peopled by Native Americans and Mexicans as well as immigrants from China and Japan—shaped the ways in which they were received by their predominantly Anglo neighbors. The West has changed dramatically over the past century and a half as railroads, highway systems, and the jet plane greatly diminished physical distance and as the movies and television created a more uniform national culture. We maintain that Jews, as they adjusted to such innovations, continued to create a distinctive niche and to see their regional location as formative in their identities. Finally, as reference to the movies suggests, we make the case that Jews as a group have shaped the development of the region and influenced the culture and economy of American Judaism.

The biographies of Ray Frank, Bailey Gatzert, and Joseph Nudelman—nineteenth-century Jewish arrivals—suggest some of the ways in which "region" played out in the lives of individual Jews. Their experiences provide a useful starting point for this exploration, because their early biographies suggest commonalities with their fellow Jewish westerners. The interconnectedness among Pacific Coast Jewish communities as demonstrated by the personal contacts of each of these individuals is one key to understanding western Jewish identity. Furthermore, their stories suggest the characteristics that helped shape a regional Jewish identity.

A native of the West, Ray Frank's early career,

FIG. I.1   *Ray Frank, 1890s. American Jewish Historical Society, Newton Centre, Mass., and New York.*

while exceptional, aptly demonstrates the freedom, mobility, and flexible nature of Pacific Jewish society (fig. I.1). A charismatic speaker and educated Jew, Frank was called the "first woman rabbi," "a female Messiah," and a visionary.[21] Born in 1861 in San Francisco to Polish orthodox parents, she was raised in a traditional home and educated in public schools. After high school, she lived for six years near her sister in Ruby Hill, Nevada, teaching miners' children by day and adults at night. Frank observed the manner and learned from the lectures of the rabbis who often visited the nearby Jewish community of Eureka, where Jewish storekeepers served men trying to strike it rich by finding silver in the Comstock Lode.

In the mid-1880s, Frank returned to Oakland

and enrolled in classes at the University of California, while supporting herself by teaching at the Reform First Hebrew Congregation (Sinai) in Oakland and at the traditional Beth Jacob. At this time, she also began to write for San Francisco and Oakland newspapers and in 1890 went as a correspondent to Spokane, Washington. When Frank inquired about the location of Rosh Hashanah services she was informed that none were scheduled, but they would be held if she would speak. She agreed. A special issue of the *Spokane Falls Gazette* was published to announce that night's religious services. At the Opera House, Frank mesmerized a full house of Jews and Christians. Ten days later, on Yom Kippur, she again attracted a full house.

In a region with few permanent rabbis beyond San Francisco, Frank initiated a career as a traveling Jewish "revivalist." In the fall of 1895, she conducted High Holiday services in Victoria, British Columbia, and lectured in the community. In July 1897 in Portland, seven thousand people—a number considerably greater than the total Jewish population of the entire state of Oregon—gathered for "Ray Frank Day" in Gladstone Park to hear her talks "Nature—the Supreme Teacher" and "The God Idea in Art."[22] In the same way that Protestant women revivalists gained attention for their riveting style and dedication, Frank achieved nationwide notoriety.[23] She garnered praise from both Jewish and non-Jewish audiences, suggesting both the prominent role women were able to play in a region where there was little rabbinic authority and the high degree of interaction between Jews and non-Jews.

While Frank became a regional sensation through the force of her rhetoric, Bailey Gatzert's story illustrates how family-based business networks enabled Jews to move around the region to seek their fortunes. Gatzert, who immigrated to the United States from Hesse Darmstadt (Germany) in 1849, had learned English with a southern accent during three years spent as a store clerk in Natchez, Mississippi. In 1852, he headed west in the hope of finding gold, but instead he found a more practical endeavor, establishing a grocery business in San Francisco. Nine years later, he married Babette Schwabacher, the daughter of a leading Jewish family that operated one of the largest merchandising networks in the West (fig. I.2). Soon Gatzert left the San Francisco trading hub to seek his fortune elsewhere in a region whose settlers hoped to extract raw materials but needed mercantile services in order to do so. He operated a grocery business in Portland and then a general store in Wallula, Washington Territory. By 1869, he had established a general store in Seattle, which was supplied by his Schwabacher in-laws. Over the next two decades, the Schwabacher enterprise, run by Gatzert, became one of Washington's largest businesses and a central part of the state's economy.

As one of the first three Jewish couples to arrive in Seattle, Bailey and Babette were naturally among the founders of Jewish communal institutions, including Seattle's first congregation, Ohaveth Sholum. As a prominent business leader, Gatzert hosted President Rutherford B. Hayes when he visited the city. He was a founder and president of the chamber of commerce, the president of two banks, a city councilman, and Seattle's mayor in 1875. Seattle honored Gatzert by naming a public school after him. Located in the "Central District," the school after 1900 would be the venue for Americanizing the children of Eastern European and Sephardic immigrant families.[24]

Although he never attained the prominence of either Frank or Gatzert, Joseph Nudelman's experience illustrates how migration west was a

FIG. I.2 *Babette Schwabacher Gatzert and Bailey Gatzert, Bella and Abraham Schwabacher, Sara and Louis Schwabacher, and Sigmund and Rose Schwabacher, 1870s. University of Washington Libraries, Special Collections, neg. UW1383.*

self-selected process, usually dependent on family networks. A native of the Odessa region, Nudelman left Russia in 1882 as the leader of a group of Am Olam idealists who hoped to establish an agricultural colony in America. The group included Nudelman's wife, Fanny, and their four children; several of his siblings and their families; and a number of additional families with children. Nudelman and his many companions ultimately exchanged agrarian idealism for entrepreneurial dreams. By the time he set up his grocery and meat market more than twenty years later in Portland, Nudelman had worked on the railroads in Colorado, proved up a homestead and served as a

member of a local school board in North Dakota, tried ranching in Nevada (fig. I.3), sojourned in San Francisco, farmed in two different California locales, and worked in a California orchard. Along the way, he learned to speak English, gained the support of investors, built institutions, marketed goods, and bought and sold real estate—in short, he accumulated the social capital that enabled him to succeed in business and become a community leader in Portland, his final destination.

When Joseph and Fanny moved permanently to Portland, they joined close to fifty relatives who already resided there. Once established, the family operated a network of stores, including Joseph's

FIG. I.3 *Joseph Nudelman and family in Nevada, 1895. Oregon Jewish Museum OJM643.*

meat market, his brother's grocery business next door, and various other relatives' scrap metal, picture framing, dry goods, cartage, and feed stores. The network extended beyond Portland, with family members operating businesses in locales as distant as San Francisco and, in Washington, Spokane and Aberdeen.[25]

The experiences of Ray Frank, Bailey Gatzert, and Joseph Nudelman begin to suggest some of the ways in which the interconnectedness of western cities and towns, the isolation of the West from other parts of the country, and the backgrounds of western Jewish settlers made the region's emerging Jewish communities distinctive. Frank's experience in San Francisco illustrates that city's centrality, particularly during the nineteenth century. The warm reception that she received suggests the scarcity of rabbis in the region, as well as the openness of the region to women in public roles. More important, her popularity with both Jewish and non-Jewish audiences demonstrates the general acceptance that Jews, including women, found in western civic life. Gatzert's story reinforces this theme, further illustrating the centrality of San Francisco, the integral commercial role that Jews played throughout the region, and the civic prominence that successful Jews could achieve. The experiences of Frank, Gatzert, and Nudelman in founding entrepreneurial networks and participating in public life were the norm for large numbers of nineteenth-century Jewish westerners.

Although new western cities were notably open to the immigration of diverse groups of Europeans—particularly those bringing useful skills and experience in trade—the West was not attractive to everyone. In fact, the lack of Jewish infrastructure in much of the region made the lengthy migration self-selecting. Individuals who were inflexible about religious practices, as well as those who lacked family or personal connections, were not likely candidates for westward migration, particularly in the early years. Nudelman's experiences amplify the importance of family in creating secure niches thousands of miles from Jewish settlements, where Eastern European Jews could expect easy acceptance and the space to create their own communities.

A process of self-selection that favored the less insular and the more daring may help to explain why western Jews seemed so amenable to engaging in civic life. People like the Gatzerts and Nudelmans, who expected to live and work among outsiders, opted not for San Francisco but for further isolation, moving to Eureka or Bakersfield, California; to Albany, Oregon, or Spokane, Washington; or even to cities like Los Angeles and Portland that in the 1870s had only five hundred Jews. As

a result of the continued role of migration during the twentieth century—whether from eastern or midwestern Jewish centers or from Israel, the Soviet Union, or Iran—self-selection has remained important in shaping western Jewish communities.

The stories of Frank, Gatzert, and Nudelman also hint at something more: that building community and institutions in these remote locales helped to foster a distinctive identity as western Jews. Engagement and acceptance in civic life led Jewish communities and individuals to embrace regional values and the imagery of natural wonders as part of their Jewish identity. At times this identity, as with that of their Protestant neighbors, was expressed clearly and unambiguously by integrating the landscape into their sacred traditions.[26] This identity, like that of the Mormons who likened the Great Basin to the Sinai desert or of the Unitarian minister who saw in Lake Tahoe the Sea of Galilee, inspired Rabbi Neito and congregation Sherith Israel in San Francisco in 1904 to commission local artist Emile Pissis, the brother of the synagogue's architect, to design the significant stained-glass windows.[27] The use of Yosemite as a biblical theme was popular in mid-nineteenth-century art. Like Pissis, Albert Bierstadt painted Yosemite as part of the Divine, "a biblical Eden on American soil." Writes Kate Nearpass Ogden, "If California was 'a second Canaan for the impoverished and oppressed,' then Yosemite was the symbolic heart of the new Promised Land."[28]

In other cases, becoming a westerner was subtler—a transformation noticed first by outsiders. Immigrant Russian Jews in Portland established synagogues that, years later, they and their children thought of as "traditional." Yet when more recent immigrants arrived, or when visitors came from the East, they found these institutions surprisingly modern. As early as the 1890s, immigrant Rus-

FIG. I.4 *Choir led by Cantor Abraham Rosencrantz, center, ca. 1915. Oregon Jewish Museum OJM31.*

sian congregations in Portland featured sermons in English, choirs and other music, and, in some cases, services on Sunday in addition to the traditional Saturday services. In contrast to the typical Russian immigrant congregation, which appeared cacophonous and disorderly to the uninitiated, Congregation Neveh Zedek in Portland boasted in its newspaper advertisements that it had a "choir of young men thoroughly under good practice and [that] the services will be conducted in good form" (fig. I.4).[29] It can be argued that this degree

of acculturation, coming so early at a new, Eastern European congregation, was a western characteristic, a desire to be proud both of asserting a traditional message and of adapting the enlightened decorum of a modern aesthetic.

Acculturation often went farther. Throughout western history, the region's Jews have been less likely to join congregations than have their coreligionists in other regions of the country. Western Jews have had higher rates of intermarriage and are far less likely to have two Jewish parents than are their counterparts in other regions. Both low affiliation and high intermarriage rates are associated with migration, and self-selection among the migrants is also partially responsible for this pattern.[30] Yet these trends are also reflective of the region. For Christians as well as for Jews, the West has long been the region of the country with the lowest affiliation rates, leading to its reputation among religious historians as "the unchurched belt."[31] The relative secularism of the region both reinforced distinctive patterns of identity and affiliation among Jews and contributed to their acceptance.

Innovation and distinctive patterns of religious practice and affiliation continued to characterize western Jews throughout the twentieth century. Thus Shlomo Bardin chose southern California for his innovative Brandeis Institute (plate 3; renamed the Brandeis-Bardin Institute after his death) because he "saw among the people of postwar Los Angeles a willingness to pioneer . . . to plant their own unique roots."[32] Similarly, the historian Marc Dollinger argues that the California counterculture "revitalized Jewish life" in the state, leading to a plethora of unconventional forms of Jewish worship and expression.[33] The philosophy through which "outreach" to the marginalized among Jews and to ethnic rivals among gentiles was promoted was *tikkun olam*, or "healing the world." Popularized by Michael Lerner in Berkeley, it has become a virtual mantra for rabbis of all denominations in western Jewish communities, where the intermarried are a large minority. Likewise, full inclusion of gays and lesbians was first pioneered in the San Francisco Bay Area. Their integration into the social, economic, and political life of the region has generated new ideas about the meaning of Judaism encouraged in Jewish magazines like *Tikkun* and

in the new Reform and Conservative seminaries in Los Angeles.

Innovation has not been confined to religious expression. Just as nineteenth-century merchants gained stature as pioneers by filling economic needs and supporting civic institutions, later-arriving Jews, like non-Jews, seeking to escape constraints in the East continued to see in the West, rather than the South or Midwest, the best locale for their ideas and their enthusiasm. In the 1910s and 1920s, the movie moguls utilized the year-round sunshine of southern California to escape patent disputes, inclement weather, and high rents in New York. When entrepreneurs of women's clothing joined with movie studio costume designers in the 1930s, they created a sportswear industry that permanently altered women's fashions and made Los Angeles the primary site for domestically produced clothing. In the post–World War II era, Las Vegas was created as an international gambling oasis, in large part by Jewish organized crime. It has since become a population center of almost a million and a half, including more than eighty thousand Jews, and has encouraged gambling in many forms—on riverboats, boardwalks, and Indian reservations—to become a legitimate form of adult entertainment throughout the country. Late in the twentieth century, Jewish—and non-Jewish—scientists and engineers came to campuses of the University of California to promote research in medicine and engineering and to bring that technology to market. Their efforts have transformed the economies of the "Silicon Valley," Los Angeles, and especially San Diego and have also funded Jewish institutions, like the Wiesenthal Center and the Skirball Cultural Center, that offer new national models of education and outreach.[34]

Jews, now numbering close to a million and a

half in the American West, have continued to come to the region largely as entrepreneurs and professionals and have created comfortable niches. Their very increase in numbers, especially in Los Angeles, and their wealth throughout the region have given Jews more political prominence than ever, as their frequent ability to win high office attests. The romance of the pioneer has been eclipsed by the many family foundations—for example, of Mark Taper, Eli Broad, Joan and Irwin Jacobs, Steven Spielberg, Jordan Schnitzer, and Samuel and Althea Stroum—that have given Jews even greater civic visibility. As much as scholars may find similarity in the communal organization and behavior of Jews elsewhere in the country, Jews living on or near the "Left Coast" believe that their lives—secular and religious—and their communities have developed with less friction and greater long-term impact on the regional society than have Jewish communities elsewhere and that they remain quite distinctive.

I   HISTORIES COLLIDE

Jews and the Pacific Frontier

We have here rapid and glorious results.

—Indian Diggings, California, 1855

Drawn by the gold magnet, Jewish men and women joined
thousands in the rush to America's Pacific Coast, a destination that must have seemed to some like the very edge of the
western world. Their lives served as counterpoints to the stereotype of
the free-floating, culturally adrift miner during California's Gold Rush
era.[1] When young Samuel Cohen arrived in California, European Jews—
or even those on the eastern seaboard—worried that it was so remote
that Judaism could not be sustained. To dispel his family's fears, Cohen,
a recent arrival from England, wrote his sister in 1851: "I do not think
that Jews in any part of the world could have kept Passover more strictly
than we did [in San Francisco]."[2]

From Poland carrying his prayer book came the bearded Isaac Goldsmith, who, with his wife, Sarah, and their three children, settled in the
"instant city," San Francisco (fig. 1.1). Older than most adventurers,
Goldsmith provided an essential service as a *shochet*, or ritual slaugh-
terer, enabling men like Cohen to observe kashruth. As a portent of the
status of Jews in the new city, Goldsmith's daughter, Mary, then a child
of five, would become a teacher and the first Jewish woman on San Francisco's Board of Education.

Mary Goldsmith's mentor, Rabbi Julius Eckman, the first rabbi to

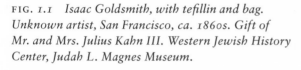

FIG. 1.1 *Isaac Goldsmith, with tefillin and bag. Unknown artist, San Francisco, ca. 1860s. Gift of Mr. and Mrs. Julius Kahn III. Western Jewish History Center, Judah L. Magnes Museum.*

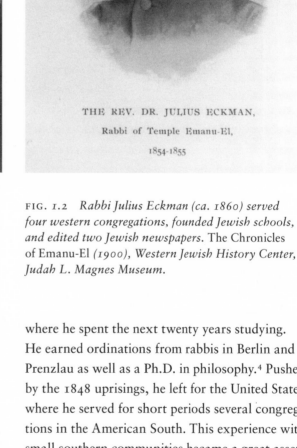

THE REV. DR. JULIUS ECKMAN,
Rabbi of Temple Emanu-El,
1854-1855

FIG. 1.2 *Rabbi Julius Eckman (ca. 1860) served four western congregations, founded Jewish schools, and edited two Jewish newspapers.* The Chronicles of Emanu-El *(1900), Western Jewish History Center, Judah L. Magnes Museum.*

reach the Pacific Coast, also did not seek gold. As described by his close friend O. P. Fitzgerald, a Methodist minister, he was a man of contradictions, with "power and gentleness, child-like simplicity, and scholarliness" (fig. 1.2).[3] Born in 1805, Eckman was raised in Posen, a former Polish province. His father, who traveled widely, buying from and selling to Jews and non-Jews alike, hoped that Julius would enter the family's lumber and grain business. At fourteen, just after the Napoleonic Wars, he was sent to England to learn English and returned after three years. Lacking the temperament of a merchant, he left for Berlin,

where he spent the next twenty years studying. He earned ordinations from rabbis in Berlin and Prenzlau as well as a Ph.D. in philosophy.[4] Pushed by the 1848 uprisings, he left for the United States, where he served for short periods several congregations in the American South. This experience with small southern communities became a great asset in the West, where leadership of Jewish congregations required English fluency, interaction with non-Jews, and the expectation of civic involvement. During his twenty years in the West, Eckman served several congregations, established Jewish schools, and published the *Gleaner*, which both informed the region about world Jewry and carried news of western Jewish communities to the East and beyond.

More typical of the men who journeyed west, young Bernard Goldsmith, a Bavarian-born merchant, emigrated, like Eckman, because of European political turmoil and because "at the time the Jewish people . . . had no civil rights." On his arrival he reflected, "I felt well pleased that I was in a free country."[5] Goldsmith, less than five feet tall, first apprenticed as a watchmaker to a cousin in New York. After learning English, he succumbed to the lure of the Gold Rush and came west in 1850 to satisfy his ambitions. Like so many young Jewish merchants he first traded in California mining towns, then moved to San Francisco to open a store with his younger brother, who had just arrived with supplies from cousins in Boston and New York. When the business failed, Goldsmith moved north, first to Crescent City, then to Portland. There he opened a jewelry store and assay office, began speculating in real estate, and bought land to raise wheat and cattle. In 1869, Goldsmith became the city's first Jewish mayor (fig. 1.3), to be followed in office by his close friend and fellow Bavarian Jewish immigrant, Philip Wasserman.[6]

Bernard Goldsmith, Samuel Cohen, Sarah and Isaac Goldsmith, and Rabbi Julius Eckman all raced west during the Gold Rush. After the Civil War, steamships and railroads brought thousands more to the Pacific Coast to pursue business opportunities along new routes. The Jewish migration to the Pacific West attracted men and women from throughout Europe as well as from New York, New Orleans, Kentucky, and all parts of the United States. Some were single, others married; some were lax in religious practice, while others were observant. Western Jewish communities were characterized by the cultural diversity of their founders,

FIG. 1.3 *Bernard Goldsmith (ca. 1870), Portland's mayor from 1869 to 1871. Oregon Historical Society.*

their commercial experience, and their literacy in English. In this fluid frontier setting, Jews not only became innovative entrepreneurs but also built their own communities, which their gentile neighbors saw as a pillar of civil and commercial society.

Respected as town founders, rather than suspected as subversive interlopers, Jews created a network of stable communities on the Pacific shore, from San Diego to Victoria, British Columbia.

As the gateway to the gold country, San Francisco grew from 850 settlers in 1848 to 35,000 in 1852.[7] In the words of the 1855 *Annals of San Francisco*, it was a "hot-bed that brought humanity to a rapid, monstrous, maturity."[8] It seemed more diverse than any place on earth. In 1852, more than half of San Francisco's population was foreign-born, with immigrants from Ireland, France, Germany, China, Italy, South America, and other locales around the globe.[9] One Swedish miner described it as "a boiling mass of people of all nations and different styles of clothing—Chinese and Turks, Spaniards and Malays, etc. and everything topsy-turvy, but everything one saw was extremely elegant and solid to a degree."[10] Residents proclaimed their diversity and cosmopolitism by quickly erecting an opera house, theaters, restaurants, newspapers, and, like most port cities, a vice district, known as the Barbary Coast. As the commercial hub, San Francisco drew previously isolated places like Oregon (with its timber and wheat) and southern California (with its cattle and hides) into a regional economy. By the 1850s, San Francisco also became the nation's fourth largest port by volume of foreign commerce, exceeded only by New York, Boston, and New Orleans.[11] It became the country's front door to the fur trade in Alaska, the sugar trade to Hawaii, and the importing of tea, silk, and people from East Asia. Pacific Rim trade helped fuel the local economy and led the city to become the headquarters for maritime industry.

Because of the diverse mix of peoples, no dominant culture emerged. Even the Catholic Church, established under Spain and Mexico, was eclipsed in Gold Rush country by the diversity of immigrants producing a "free market" of religious experience. "Cultural mobility and exposure to disparate societies" made this frontier singular, argues Laurie F. Maffly-Kipp.[12] Observed Rabbi Max Lilienthal when he arrived by train in Sacramento on a Sunday in 1876, "No traces of a Puritan-Sunday; people and land are cosmopolitan in the Far West!"[13] Without a Protestant hegemony or established elite, Jews, like the Irish, could easily gain cultural acceptance and middle-class status. In this rapidly growing community, the *Daily Alta California* editorialized, "they [Jews] are Californians. . . . At the bar, in the forum, on the commercial mart, the press, medicine, agriculture, mechanics, and the fine arts, they occupy prominent positions, and have won the respect and esteem of all."[14] Recognized for their business skills, their Euro-American appearance and habits, and their commitment to religion, family, and community life, a Marysville newspaper placed Jews among the town's "best citizens," separating them from the despised Asians, Indians, Mexicans, and blacks, who faced various forms of discrimination.[15] Jewish practice became so integrated into western life by 1858 that the Pacific Mail Steamer delayed its departure until several days after Yom Kippur to allow Jews to complete their business and personal correspondence.[16]

The factors that made San Francisco the major hub of the West Coast made it the regional center for Jewish life as well. Western Jewry developed at a swift pace and with a self-assured style that reflected the region's booming confidence. Between 1840 and 1877, the Jewish population in the United States climbed from just 15,000 to 250,000, while Pacific Coast Jewry grew from a few souls to approximately 20,000, or 5,000 more than the country's entire Jewish population just three decades earlier.[17] The Gold Rush lured young Jewish men and women from England, Alsace, Russia, and the German states, including Württemberg, Bavaria, and Posen, as well as from Australia and the eastern United States.

Instability caused by famines, political turmoil, and long-term economic upheavals fueled by industrialization triggered the migration of Europeans, including Jews, to America. But people undertook the long, dangerous journey west because they saw unique opportunities. At a time when the general migration was heavily male, the trip to San Francisco and beyond was usually undertaken first by siblings, who created migration chains that drew entire Jewish families to the West. After several years in Philadelphia, Polish-born Bernhard Marks, aged nineteen, in 1852 sought his fortune in California. A year later he sent to Philadelphia for his beautiful and strong-willed sister, Hannah, to join him and marry one of his acquaintances. She made the voyage, but refused the match. Instead, Hannah Marks became a teacher in public and Jewish schools and, later, before she married a man of her own choosing, the first and youngest woman principal in the San Francisco school system.[18] Like *shochet* Goldsmith with his wife and children, Hannah Marks's skills supported both the Jewish and secular communities.

After the defeat of Napoleon, emigration by family groups from the German states increased because of the reinstatement of restrictive laws that, in Bavaria and elsewhere, regulated the number of Jews who could live and work in a given town. Although non-Jews also emigrated, because of economic upheavals Jews in Poland and the German states left at a rate almost four times higher than that of their non-Jewish neighbors.[19] Between 1813 and 1861, Bavaria required permits to marry, to establish a household, or even to move from town to town. Such limits made it impossible for many Jews, who often came from large families, to find employment, marry, and establish homes. As a result, between 1830 and 1839 a similar number of Jewish women as well as men left Bavaria for America.[20] From a small village in Württemberg alone, 225 men and women left for the United States between 1845 and 1870. Four of these émigrés eventually reached the Far West. One, twenty-year-old butcher Moses (Morris) Einstein, left Württemberg with his younger brother in 1846. Like many who would follow, Einstein acculturated in the East, where he peddled, learned English, and owned small stores before venturing west in the early 1850s with his new Württemberg-born wife, his cousin Jettle Rosenheim.[21]

Some, like Henry Cohn, fled Europe because of the threat of conscription. Officers routinely oppressed their Jewish recruits. Raised in Dobrzyn, on the Polish-Prussian border, Cohn, a sickly sixteen-year-old, escaped a night raid, carried on his elder brother's back, "wading and swimming" across the Drewenz River into Prussia. He sailed from Hamburg on the two-masted *Lewizow Lelkendorf* for New York. After three years of peddling needles, thread, and necessities to New Jersey farm wives, southern planters, and plantation slaves, Cohn, summoned by a landsman, bought a steamer ticket for California.[22]

The failed revolutions of 1848 and political uncertainty also brought Jews to the United States and ultimately to the West Coast. As the historian Hasia R. Diner observes, "Jews became victims of repeated mob violence, and while few lost their lives, many lost their confidence in the promises of emancipation."[23] Some emigrated because of the depressed conditions in the revolutions' wake, while others were forced to flee. One "forty-eighter," August Helbing, a supporter of liberalizing the German states, swiftly left Europe after the collapse of the revolution. First settling in New York, then New Orleans, Helbing moved west with the reports of the gold finds.[24]

Jewish merchants became key figures among the diverse founders of the newly built towns and cities. As suppliers and sources of credit, they performed an essential function, and they showed their commitment by erecting permanent brick buildings on Main Street. Their prominence as founders led to their civic and political leadership, even in the regional center. Abraham Labatt, a Sephardic Jew from South Carolina, was elected one of San Francisco's first aldermen; Sonorans elected Emanuel Linoberg to their first town council, while Angelenos did the same for Morris L. Goodman.

THE JOURNEY WEST

Stimulated by Jewish newspaper reports, letters, and family visits, Jewish immigration to the Far West increased. Leipzig's *Allgemeine Zeitung des Judentums* reported in March 1850 that "in California, to which many Israelites have emigrated, several congregations have formed."[25] This may have been an overly optimistic account. By 1850, settlers gathered together in benevolent societies and minyanim, or small prayer groups, but it would be a year before congregations formally incorporated. By 1855, however, San Francisco's Jewish community was flourishing. Writing for the *Archives Israelites* of Paris, Luxheim-born and University of Paris–educated Daniel Levy described the scene to potential French immigrants:

> As soon as the first mad excitement of the gold fever had passed, the Jews of San Francisco bethought themselves of the duties that their religious origins imposed on them and as a result, they open places of prayer to observe their religion. . . . Let us add that two beautiful temples . . . are already too small to hold the influx of the faithful on High Holidays. We will also say that a functionary, serving in the three capacities of rabbi, teacher and *hazan*, has been practicing for a year, that kosher meat is available, and that, in other words, all the facilities are here for those who wish to lead a perfectly Orthodox life.[26]

Four years later the *Jewish Messenger* of New York published news of the development of a Jewish community in Portland: "Our attentive correspondent informs us that the Hebrew Congregation of Portland now numbers thirty-three members and is constantly increasing. . . . During the Holydays [*sic*], the Rev. Dr. Bien of San Francisco officiated, and he has now been engaged for a term of one year. . . . The Congregation is enjoying great prosperity which we trust, will be of long continuance. Our co-religionists in the new Pacific States are very enterprising and deserve to succeed in all they undertake."[27]

While newspaper articles and personal letters brought Jews to the West, the most powerful persuasion for making the long journey came from family members returning to Europe, where they told stories of the new promised land. Some men returned to Europe for business, others to see relatives or to find a bride. Technological innovations further encouraged immigrants. By the 1850s, both sailing and steamships left European ports for England and the United States. These ships made crossing the Atlantic relatively safe and affordable for middle-class and lower-middle-class Jews in search of new opportunities. Yet the long journey to the Pacific West, whether by land or by sea, was fraught with danger and was only for the adventurous.

Near Breslau, Fanny Brooks, aged sixteen, had read of the "gold excitement" in the newspapers that in 1853 "were full of wonderful discoveries."[28] These articles reinforced stories told by her future husband, Julius, who delighted his family and friends with tales of his five years in America, where, he said, "money was found in the streets."[29] The two married quickly and made the three-week voyage from Hamburg for New York. When they arrived in August, newsboys were screaming out news of new gold finds. Fanny and Julius agreed, "Why stay in New York when everyone is going west?"[30] After five months in a Jewish boardinghouse, they joined a wagon train in Nebraska and set out for California. Before the completion of the transcontinental railroad in 1869, most Jews traveled by ship, but because Julius suffered from seasickness, they chose to go overland. This route could take almost a year because of the possibility of severe weather and treacherous mountains. The weather turned cold before they reached Salt Lake City, according to Fanny:

> Arriving at the Rocky Ridge near the summit of South Pass the wind freshened into a gale and then a hurricane, howling incessantly for thirty-six hours. . . . Children and women lay in their scanty covering exposed to the blast with no food except bread or biscuit. Tents and wagon tops were blown away and the wagons buried almost to the tops of their wheels in the snow drift. No fire could be lighted. . . . After two days the storm abated and they made their way towards Willow Copse.

The immigrant train followed the Oregon Trail along the Platte River to Fort Laramie and then continued on to Salt Lake City, where Fanny and Julius spent the winter before continuing on to California. It was a difficult trip: Fanny became pregnant and later lost her child. Still, Brooks later described her delight in the journey, telling her daughter, "they were all just like one big family, dividing their joys and sorrows together."[31]

Even for a single man, the overland trip had its hardships. Louis Sloss paid two hundred dollars to join the Turner and Allen Pioneer Train in St. Louis. He had been living in Kentucky since 1845, soon after he left his native Bavaria, and chose to travel overland rather than return east for the ocean voyage. Concerned about arriving safely with the slow, overloaded wagons, where cholera was epidemic, Sloss and two non-Jewish companions left the wagon train and finished the trip by themselves on horseback. Forty-two of the 165 members of his original wagon train died before it reached California, most of cholera.[32] Sloss, a merchant by trade and fluent in English, had worked closely with non-Jews by the time he reached Sacramento in 1849.[33] These experiences enabled him to prosper as a merchant in California.

Jews who chose the overland route like Brooks and Sloss faced not only the physical difficulties common to all such pioneers but also religious challenges. Joining a wagon train meant combining forces with a large group of non-Jewish travelers. Kosher food and other religious requirements like enough men for a minyan did not exist. Clearly, only those Jews who were willing to forgo these would opt to make the overland journey. When Brooks told her daughter that her traveling companions were like "one big family," she revealed her openness to forming close relationships with people of other faiths.

These qualities, beyond making Sloss a good candidate for the journey, shaped his decisions once he arrived in the West. Settling first in Sacramento, Sloss formed a mercantile partnership with his gentile traveling companions. After this venture dissolved, he started partnerships with German-born Jews and lifelong associates Simon Greenwald and Lewis Gerstle, whose sister he subsequently married. After moving to San Francisco in the late 1860s, he and several partners, both Jewish and gentile, founded the Alaska Commercial Company, one of the region's most extensive ventures, with Gerstle as vice president. Beyond its regional enterprises, it did business with suppliers and customers both in the eastern United States and in Europe. Paramount to the company's success was a twenty-year federal lease to hunt fur seals in Alaska. Sloss was having trouble negotiating with the government until former Civil War general John F. Miller joined the firm in 1870 and replaced Sloss as the company's representative in Washington, D.C. Sloss believed Miller succeeded where he had failed because the Treasury would not award the contract to a Jew. Although his identity as a Jew may have affected his dealings with the federal government, it did not limit his success in the West. Sloss and his partners made San Francisco the center of the Far West's fur, fishing, canning, and shipping industries.[34] Given his characteristic openness, it is not surprising that Sloss, like many Jewish business leaders, assumed civic roles, as a Republican elector in the 1868 election, as treasurer of the University of California, and, as a personal "cause," director of the Society for the Prevention of Cruelty to Animals.[35] Always active in the Jewish community, Sloss served as president of Sacramento's young congregation and, later in San Francisco, was prominent in congregation Emanu-El.[36]

While San Francisco grew to be the clear hub of western settlement, Jewish merchants also found success elsewhere in the West and replicated the same pattern of civic engagement. Most Jews who settled in Oregon followed a path similar to Bernhard Goldsmith's, first stopping in California

to accumulate capital before traveling to the north. A few, including Louis (Levi) Fleischner and his brother Jacob, took a direct overland route. The brothers left their home in Bohemia in 1842 and lived in New York, Philadelphia, and Iowa before continuing west with an ox team in 1852 to the termination point of the Oregon Trail and then on to Albany, a commercial center for farmers in the Willamette Valley. During the trek, the Fleischners saw disease kill their cattle, and, as with Sloss, saw cholera spread though their wagon train.[37]

A quicker way to reach the West, although often just as dangerous, was by ship. The majority of Jews had experienced sea travel and chose it rather than a lengthy wagon train trip into a vast wilderness. Ocean travel also presented fewer religious challenges, because travelers brought preserved kosher meats and could eat bread and eggs on the shorter trip (especially by steamship) and could also observe Shabbat. The Newmark family took the longest sea route by sailing around the Horn of South America to reach California. Myer Newmark, aged fourteen, sailed in 1852 with his mother, Rosa (Levy), and his brother and sisters on the *Carrington* from New York bound for San Francisco, where his father, Joseph Newmark, awaited them. Braving high seas and boredom, Myer complained in his diary: "We are now at the extreme point of Cape Horn and the weather is cold, stormy and disagreeable and we all wish ourselves in San Francisco."[38] After four months at sea, the ship arrived in San Francisco on April 20, 1853. The Newmark family soon settled in Los Angeles.

For those who wished a quicker trip, steamships provided a more direct route west. From New York, one boarded a steamship for Central America and then traveled overland at Panama or Nicaragua across the marsh-like isthmus on a combination of small boat, mule, and foot (plate 4). On the western side, travelers hoped for a ship in port, waiting to take them to San Francisco. This trip could take a quick five to eight weeks depending on the length of the wait at the western terminus. When ships failed to appear because of frequent shipwrecks, the delay could be interminable. *Shochet* Isaac Goldsmith and his family chose the Nicaragua route in the summer of 1852. Daughter Mary described her trip across the isthmus:

> Part of the journey was to be by land, part by water along the Chagres River. A native had been hired to carry me, but I was fretful and sick, so father placed me before him on the saddle and we jogged along. By water we were transported in canoes through dense masses of verdure which clogged the streams. Most of the time the natives were in the water dragging and pushing the boat along. Finally we were across and reached the western coast where we waited wearily for the steamer. She came and a thousand passengers were crowded into accommodations intended for four hundred.[39]

The Goldsmiths reached San Francisco on the S.S. *Lewis*, a ship that had come around the Horn, because their steamer had wrecked on its way to the isthmus.

With the completion of the Panama railroad in 1855, this route became a week shorter and safer, though dangers remained. Besides the questionable seaworthiness of the ships, danger lay on the isthmus itself, where diseases were rampant.[40] Leipzig's *Allgemeine Zeitung des Judentums* reported in 1856 that an outbreak of cholera on a steamer from Saint-Jean to San Francisco led to the deaths of one-third of the passengers and crew in twelve days.[41]

Because all routes west proved dangerous, Jewish settlement became self-selective. Most Jews felt forced to leave Europe, but the additional trip west required substantial thought. The timid, the sickly, or the frail probably would not survive the journey. Oregon and the Washington Territory were isolated and attracted only those who were physically strong and willing to be—at least for a time—more religiously flexible. Since San Francisco became established so quickly, it became the logical home for the observant. Only individuals willing to live and work with gentiles and persistent enough to start over, and most times over again, would succeed.

SAN FRANCISCO: JEWISH HUB OF THE WEST

Those who survived the trip found a burgeoning Jewish community. In this new regional metropolis, families enjoyed the benefits of social life and many Jewish institutions. Isaac Markens in his 1888 comprehensive *Hebrews in America* lists by name one hundred Jews who settled in San Francisco between 1849 and 1852.[42] Although the list omitted many known families, it indicates the nationally recognized size and importance of the community. Many of the uncounted young transients traveled in and out of the city, living for short periods in the mining camps and river towns that dotted the region. By the 1870s, San Francisco's Jewish population reached sixteen thousand, making it the second largest Jewish community in the nation, with Jews 7–8 percent of the city's inhabitants, about two percentage points higher than in Cincinnati, until then the primary Jewish center west of New York City.[43] The Jewish community grew in part because of San Francisco's Civil War business boom as the Union war effort required western wool, wheat, and especially gold.[44] Through banking, real estate, or other commercial endeavors Jews accumulated great wealth, which was reflected in architecturally renowned buildings, communal institutions, and newspapers. San Francisco Jewry, once a novelty, now received serious national and international attention. In the 1860s, emissaries from Jerusalem directed their fund-raising appeal to Jews "residing in peace in all the States of gracious America and the magnificent State of California."[45] In 1877, Rabbi Isaac Mayer Wise of Cincinnati, the founder of the American Reform movement and editor of the *American Israelite*, courted congregations to join his Union of American Hebrew congregations. He observed, "As a class the San Francisco Israelites are more prominent than the Hebrews as a class are in any other city I have visited."[46] No longer did American Judaism have only an eastern center: from now on the West would have to be considered.

As Earl Raab noted in an article commemorating one hundred years of Jewish life in San Francisco, "From the beginning the Jews were conspicuous for their sense of community. The first two welfare organizations in San Francisco were set up by Jews."[47] Jewish benevolent, religious, and social organizations developed as soon as the first Jews arrived in San Francisco. Unlike the nation's rural areas, or even New York or Cincinnati just a decade or two before, San Francisco in the late 1850s and 1860s attracted a few learned and ordained rabbis. Often rabbis like Eckman traveled from San Francisco to small towns to lecture and officiate at wedding and funerals. However, because it was a difficult trip to the West, at times congregations had to hire rabbis who did not suit them or else do without. Furthermore, when questions of religious law arose, westerners could not easily seek arbitration because of the great distance

between Jewish communities. For instance, when Cincinnati Jews questioned the certification of a *shochet*, the community sent him to Baltimore or New York for examination; in the West, distance prohibited such a trip.[48] As a result, arguments intensified and schisms developed. This distance led to the formation of congregations with strong lay leadership that reflected the origins and diversity of western Jewish migrants.

Paralleling the "instant" secular city, Jewish life in San Francisco grew just as quickly as did the commercial networks. The new Gold Rush economy brought educated laypeople who built a vibrant Jewish community. As early as 1851, bakers provided Passover matzoth, and by 1857 the community supported at least four kosher butchers. B. Adler advertised that he always had "on hand a good supply of Smoked Meats, Tongues, Sausages, etc.," while Y. Abraham stressed that "orders [would be] forwarded to any part of the City with the greatest punctually."[49] If newcomers did not cook, several kosher boardinghouses could lodge them, including one kept by Mrs. Ellen Heiborn, who advertised that she "keeps an excellent table, and is ready to accommodate boarders on very reasonable terms."[50] Or one could join the gentile Frank Lecouvreur, a bookkeeper for a Jewish mercantile firm, who roomed at the kosher St. Nicholas hotel run by Levy Hess.[51]

In 1849, Jews in Sacramento and San Francisco held worship services on Rosh Hashanah and Yom Kippur. Approximately thirty Jews answered a San Francisco newspaper notice to gather for Rosh Hashanah in Lewis Franklin's wood-framed canvas-covered store on Jackson Street. Word of the service spread quickly among the newcomers: forty to fifty joined together for Yom Kippur.[52] Often men who sold dry goods in mining camps left their dusty mountain homes for "the city" to

More מצות

☞ Owing to the unusual great demand for MATZOS this year, the supply has not been sufficient and I will continue to bake during the Holidays Matzos for general public use.

☞ Also, fresh CAKES and CONFECTIONERY של פסח daily. **I. M. COHN,**

Corner California and Webb streets.

FIG. I.4
Matzos advertisement, Hebrew (San Francisco), April 5, 1871. "More Matzos." Western Jewish History Center, Judah L. Magnes Museum.

join their coreligionists during the High Holidays. Most participants were, like Morris Shloss, recent arrivals to the city, fluent in English and knowledgeable in American customs. Born in Russian Poland, Shloss spent five years in England and then lived in New York until the Gold Rush pulled him to San Francisco. In his later years, he remembered that the men decorated the tent "with tallow candles on Kol Nidre night."[53] Although only one woman attended the 1849 service, in 1850 three married couples listened to the sermon delivered by twenty-nine-year-old Franklin at a service in the Masonic Hall on Kearny Street.[54]

Born in England, the great grandson of the rabbi of Breslau, Poland, Franklin left Liverpool in the 1840s and settled in Baltimore. Word of the Gold Rush brought him to California in 1849. The Kearny Street Hebrew Congregation, as the assembly called itself, heard Franklin emphasize the need to establish a permanent house of worship, to uphold Jewish law and, especially, to keep the Sabbath. Much like the church leaders of the city built on gold, Franklin stressed the hazards of giving in to greed and ignoring religious obligations. He

exhorted the congregation: "How clearly apparent it is that Interest, Wealth, Gold, are the stumbling blocks to the tranquility of the mind, and the rejoicing of the soul. How fleeting and deceptive are the blessings which attend this acquisition of gold."[55] Following the pleas of Franklin, San Francisco Jews sought to form a permanent congregation and build a synagogue. Committees to raise funds for the building and to engage a baker of matzoth for the coming Passover proceeded (fig. 1.4). Yet ethnic diversity and traditions could not be overcome. Although the planning committee decided to appoint a *shochet*, neither the German nor the Polish applicant was acceptable to all, and the meeting disbanded in disarray. This dispute resulted in the establishment of two congregations, Emanu-El and Sherith Israel.[56]

In San Francisco, the instant city, ethnic and liturgical differences between Jews also ignited instantly. Rather than a group of Jews from one part of Europe establishing itself and then being challenged by Jews from elsewhere, Gold Rush Jewry quickly sorted out its inherited provincialisms. Each group wanted a permanent congregation with the stability a rabbi could offer, but each also believed in the superiority of its own liturgy. By 1854 they constructed two synagogues, one seating more than eight hundred and the other more than four hundred.[57]

Although both synagogues were traditionally designed, with separate sections for men and women, the buildings' exteriors did not differ substantially from those of local churches. Where the two congregations differed was in their ethnic makeup, a difference that was reflected in their choice of prayer books. Sherith Israel's members came from England, Posen, and Poland, while Emanu-El's membership hailed from the Rhineland and France. Both congregations also included a number of American-born Sephardim.[58] Sherith Israel followed the Polish *minhag*, or style of prayer, and Emanu-El the German. German became the language of discourse at Emanu-El, while Sherith Israel, dominated by men from England, always used English and would eventually hire clergy from England. The ethnic makeup of the congregations and their diverse origins established the distinct characteristic of western Jewry. Without multiple "waves" of immigrants to create distinctions or hierarchies, these "instant" congregations pushed newcomers into leadership positions and forced them to work with Jews of different origins. Despite their differences, the two congregations worked together for community needs. As the 1854 minutes of Sherith Israel reveal, they joined together to regulate and provide "Israelites with Passover Bread."[59]

Both congregations eventually introduced reforms, Emanu-El more quickly than Sherith Israel. For its first twenty years, Sherith Israel practiced "enlightened Orthodoxy" as observed in England.[60] Its constitution emphasized decorum and adherence to the form of American and British

ish congregations, not those of Poland.[61] When, in 1857, its members hired a rabbi, they chose Henry A. Henry, London-born and educated, who involved himself in secular organizations such as the Masons as well as the workings of the synagogue and the education of its children. Instead of a functionary, the members of Sherith Israel selected an author of several books who Londoners had deemed a "striking exception to the generality of the Readers of the Synagogue on account of his pedagogic talent."[62] Similar to many of the members of the congregations, Rabbi Henry presented himself to both the Jewish and the general community as an English speaker, fully ready to integrate into the wider community.[63]

Emanu-El's members also had valued an English speaker. After employing readers for three years, in the summer of 1854, they hired the region's first rabbi, Julius Eckman. Though he applied in person, Eckman pleased only a minority of the congregation. He had studied in Germany with Leopold Zunz and spoke English, but he did not seem to be a rabbi of the "new school." His insistence on rabbinical authority and traditional Jewish practice put him at odds with a segment of Emanu-El's lay leadership from the beginning. Prior to Eckman's arrival, the lay leadership had made all decisions regarding ritual and observance. Distant from any rabbinical authority by more than two thousand miles, Emanu-El's leaders felt free to make their own decisions about ritual and practice. Like many congregations throughout the United States, Emanu-El's membership was in flux, questioning religious authority and which observances fit with American life. Congregations often hired a series of rabbis until they found one who fit their desires. Although Eckman supported a few reforms, including choirs and an organ, his traditional demeanor clashed with the congregation. He considered it his role alone to approve Emanu-El's *shochet* and published his unpopular choice in the newspaper. Furthermore, he berated members for keeping their businesses open on the Sabbath and holding nonkosher wedding parties. In spite of the work of a few supporters, after a year Eckman's contract terminated, and, temporarily, he left the pulpit.[64]

Emanu-El advertised in the *Allgemeine Zeitung des Judentums* for a rabbi who could bring prestige to the congregation. The congregation also wrote the leader of American Reform, Isaac Mayer Wise, requesting his help in locating a rabbi, stating that they "are much inclined towards the reform style of service."[65] In 1860, the congregation hired Rabbi Elkan Cohn, who accelerated the congregation's move toward reform.

Despite the ouster of Eckman, and the hiring of Cohn, not all of Emanu-El's members embraced reforms. When the congregation in 1864, after years of wrangling over changes in ritual, abandoned the last vestiges of Orthodoxy by rejecting *Minhag Ashkenaz* (the traditional German prayer book) and approving a moderate Reform prayer book that included prayers in German and created a more performance-style service, fifty-five members of the congregation left en masse.[66] Not wanting to cause community discord after breaking with their congregation and friends, members of the new congregation named it Ohabai Shalome (Lovers of Peace), reflecting their desire for harmony. They adopted Emanu-El's original prayer book, *Minhag Ashkenaz*, but allowed some influences of modernity including family seating, a choir, and English sermons.[67] Ritual, however, remained traditional. The constitution called for "the Torah be read entire every Sabath [*sic*] the same as in all orthodox congregations."[68] This departure did not stem from prior ethnic differences or aim at starting a more liberal congregation but was motivated by Emanu-El's many reforms. The break was made after several meetings with the Emanu-El leadership; the final separation took place only when there could be no reconciliation.[69]

Growth came quickly, and within its first year Ohabai Shalome expanded to 125 members (only men were eligible) and built a new synagogue. However, the congregation experienced numerous problems in hiring a permanent rabbi. In 1865, the board agreed to send to Boston for a Rev. M. H. Myers and pay his way. However, because of Civil War interruptions in the overland telegraph system, the message never reached Myers.[70] Although they hired Rabbi Eckman to lead services for the High Holidays that year, it took them another decade to retain a permanent rabbi.[71] Their first permanent rabbi, Hungarian-born Albert (Aaron) Bettelheim, like most western rabbis, previously served congregations in the eastern United States. The split of Ohabai Shalome from Emanu-El demonstrates that even in the West, where Reform Judaism found a welcoming home and adherents achieved notoriety, some still followed more traditional ritual practices. However, neither practice nor membership was completely stable, as families, some still undecided, moved freely back and forth between congregations.

By 1864, San Francisco supported four substantial congregations and a number of more ephemeral ones. Founded in 1860, the traditional Beth Israel had by 1878 swelled to two hundred members, of both German and Polish origin. One small congregation, Shomrai Shaboth (Keepers of the Sabbath), supported a *mikvah* in North Beach and specified that it could supply the public with matzoth that were "prepared according to the strictest requirements of Rabbinical Law."[72] In naming their congregation "Sabbath Observers," members distinguished themselves from the city's other congregations, which they believed desecrated religious laws. This move can be taken as a confirmation of growing reform in the city and/or evidence that Orthodoxy still prevailed in a segment of the population.

Like congregations, Jewish education for children also expanded in San Francisco, where families had several options. One of the most comprehensive programs was run by Rabbi Eckman. After his dismissal from Temple Emanu-El, he established his own day school, afternoon school, and Sabbath school, which found wide praise. The day school, unlike traditional Jewish schools, educated boys and girls together and taught the same subjects as the public schools, "with the difference," according to Eckman, "that it aims at developing the moral faculties simultaneously with the intellectual powers."[73] Based on the new German model, Eckman hoped that his "infant" school, or kindergarten, would "meet with that support which similar establishments have met in Prussia and northern Germany."[74] Schools for young children were new at the time, and Germany was in the forefront of the child development movement. An aunt of one of the students, Helen (Levinson) Newmark, was suitably impressed; she described the kindergarten as having "a live lamb and A*B*C blocks."[75]

Eckman even wrote a prayer book especially for the children.[76] A former student in the afternoon school, Mary Goldsmith Prag, the *shochet*'s daughter, reminisced:

> There we appeared every afternoon, after our daily school hours, got our Hebrew lessons, and on Saturday and Sunday mornings for religious instruction. . . . How anxiously we looked forward to our Sabbath afternoon services which were regularly held there, and in which we officiated, where with all our souls

we sang our "Shemah Yisroal" and "Enkelohenu," our dear Master seated at the organ, and then, how we enjoyed the feast of cake and fruit which was sure to follow if we had done well.[77]

Supplies for religious celebrations were also available in the San Francisco hub, enabling merchants in smaller communities to obtain specialized products that supported Jewish religious life. By 1857, for example, at least three bakeries competed for the region's Passover business. Passover wine was produced, "in accordance with the tenents [*sic*] of our Holy religion" and guaranteed by its vintners to be "the pure article." Furthermore, they "intended using some of it for the ensuing Passover."[78] Steamers regularly traveled between San Francisco and Los Angeles or Portland, as Jews socialized, obtained Passover and other holiday necessities, and acquired locally grown products and manufactured goods to restock their stores. Often the exchanges took place between family members who had stores in several communities. This trade fostered early Jewish communal life beyond San Francisco and kept Jews throughout the West in close contact with the center of the region's religious life. And Rabbi Eckman would be a major conduit along this route.

THE SAN FRANCISCO DIASPORA

The San Francisco hub provided the personnel and supplies not only for the region's vast merchandising networks but also for the emerging Jewish communities. As networks of brothers, cousins, and landsmen spread out to found new stores in remote outposts, they also established Jewish organizations and institutions connected to "the city." The careers of the Franklin family, all English-born descendants of the rabbi of Breslau, illustrate this point. Lewis Franklin, the merchant who led San Francisco's 1850 Yom Kippur service, was soon joined by cousin Selim Franklin, who arrived on the first post–Gold Rush ship to sail directly from London to San Francisco.[79] However, the Franklins did not remain for long. Lewis traveled south to San Diego in 1851, where he established the Tienda California, a general merchandise store supplied by his frequent buying trips to San Francisco. Known as a father of San Diego Jewry, in 1851 Lewis organized High Holiday services in his home, the first such service in San Diego.[80] His cousin Selim settled in Victoria, British Columbia.

Mobility, as the Franklins' travels vividly demonstrate, became integral to western life. During the early Gold Rush years, regional development primarily took place within easy travel distance from the port of San Francisco. Steamers left the Bay for Los Angeles and San Diego in the south and Portland and Victoria in the north. Boats traveled upriver to the cities of Sacramento, Marysville, and Stockton, allowing access to hill towns and mining camps. In 1852, half of California's population of 264,435 lived in the eight mining counties.[81] Jewish settlement followed the general settlement pattern of the region as merchandising networks advanced from San Francisco in ever-larger circles. In 1855 the newly arrived Daniel Levy wrote to his editor at the *Archives Israelites* in Paris: "Among all the areas of the world, California is possibly the one in which the Jews are most widely dispersed. I do not know of one village, one hamlet, one settlement of any kind, either in the North, the mining areas or the South, the region of ranchos, where they have not established themselves."[82] Soon San Jose to the south, Marysville to the north, and the numerous mining towns to the east all supported small Jewish communities. Less than a decade after the Gold Rush, Jewish life was blossoming in the Far West.

Jews, like most others who came west, usually moved several times before they settled. Motivated by boom and bust cycles of the West's volatile economy, the family of Julius and Fanny Brooks first settled in Marysville and then moved to Timbuctoo and later to San Francisco. Then, in 1862, they joined another small wagon train for the two-week trip to Portland, where they bought a store on Front Street. After two years, when a partnership did not work out, they moved on to Idaho, before finally settling in Salt Lake City. Fanny, whose first child died on the way west, gave birth to children in Marysville, Timbuctoo, Portland, and Salt Lake City. A similar pattern of mobility can be seen in the story of Caroline Isaacs Rosenthal. Born in Poland, she came to California with her husband, Lewis, in the early 1850s. They soon left for the northern territories. She gave birth to ten children, two in California, one in the Washington Territory, and seven in Oregon, where they settled on a 160-acre homestead.[83]

Opening branch stores became a further impetus for mobility. Men often brought their brothers or cousins west to clerk until they were ready to run their own stores. As the West's population dramatically increased, so did its need for the manufactured goods that many Jewish merchants could offer through family and partnership supply chains. Merchant Henry Cohn traveled to Marysville and San Francisco regularly to buy rice, clothing, and mining picks for his stores and formed and reformed partnerships with family members as they established stores in Saint Louis, Poker Flat, and a small foothill camp, following the miners to the latest gold find. As Cohn tells of his seminomadic life in a new location: "One summer day in 1858, Poker Flat experienced feverish excitement. A rumor of discovery of rich claims in the near-by-mountain region had been reported. After a number of people moved to this spot from Poker Flat, we decided to open a branch store in this locality. . . . a log cabin was ready within three weeks. Shelves were put up, an iron stove for cooking was procured, and merchandise was brought from a long distance."[84]

Some Jewish merchants named their stores to conjure up images of the faraway places where their merchandise originated. The moniker "New York Store," which signified the latest fashions and value pricing, became quite popular. Philip Schwartz owner of the New York Store on Main Street in the mining town of Columbia, California, promoted himself as "one of the most enterprising business men in the county." As women, as well as men, shopped along the main street of isolated mining towns, Schwartz's advertisements declared that he was "determined, that no other store in his business shall get ahead of him in the way of keeping up his stock—for he has got—All manner of things that a woman can put on the crown of her head or the sole of her foot, or wrap round her shoulders, or fit round her waist."[85]

Nearby, the dusty gold country community of Sonora demonstrates the way in which the San Francisco hub helped to foster Jewish communal development in a remote location. Accessible only by stagecoach or mule train, its population at the height of the Gold Rush reached almost five thousand, approximately one hundred of them Jewish. Prominent in local government, the Masons, and the area's commerce, Jews reported that "there [was] little prejudice" toward them.[86] A benevolent society, founded in 1856, was celebrated locally and nationally. Isaac Leeser, editor of the *Occident*, welcomed their accomplishments: "We are glad to learn that the society of our Jewish fellow-citizens is in a flourishing condition. . . . We offer our good wishes for the continued success of the Hebrew Benevolent Society in its mission of charity and good will."[87]

For several years the community thrived, led by Poland-born merchant Emanuel Linoberg, who joined the miners in Sonora in 1849. Before turning thirty-five, Linoberg became a substantial property owner and served on the first town council and as president of the Hebrew Congregation of Sonora.[88] Through trips to San Francisco and through newspapers, he connected to the larger Jewish world. Sonora did not have a rabbi, so Linoberg, like other Jews in remote areas of the West, addressed questions about religious law to Julius Eckman, who was then the editor of the *Gleaner* in San Francisco. However, he was not wedded to Eckman's opinions and also corresponded with Cincinnati's Isaac Mayer Wise to inform him that he approved of his "advocacy of Reform."[89] Even in remote Sonora, Linoberg participated in current discussions of how Jewish life in the United States should proceed, while at the same time he worked with non-Jews to determine the civic fate of his small town.[90]

Like most foothill residents, Linoberg depended on San Francisco for his business and social connections. There he bought supplies, returning to Sonora with his mule train piled high with merchandise to restock his store, the Tiende Mexicano. On one trip he met Pauline Meyer, his future wife. It is likely that they met in a scene like that described by Harriet Lane Levy in *920 O'Farrell Street: A Jewish Girlhood in Old San Francisco*: "Shopkeepers came to the city from the interior, from towns of the San Joaquin or Sacramento valleys, or from the mining towns, Grass Valley, Calaveras, or Mokelumne Hill to buy goods. Their quest often included a sentimental hope, confided to a downtown wholesale merchant. If a man's appearance was agreeable and his credit good, he would be invited to the merchant's home to dine and meet the unmarried daughters."[91] Emanuel and Pauline married on December 30, 1851, the first recorded marriage at San Francisco's Sherith Israel.[92] A correspondent for New York's *Asmonean* celebrated the marriage and the arrival of Jewish women in the city: "We have been more than usually gay, and the large and constant influx of the fair sex have tended to foster and promote that gaiety. Our people anticipate the pleasure of witnessing tomorrow, a matrimonial ceremony, among the members of 'Shearith Israel' [sic]. The affianced parties are Mr. E. Linaberg of Sonora, and Miss Pauline Myer."[93]

Linoberg brought his bride back to rural Sonora, where other Jews would soon arrive. The Odd Fellows rented the community rooms for Passover and the High Holidays, and they consecrated a cemetery. In nearby Jackson, Jews formed a congregation that followed the Polish *minhag* and built a synagogue in 1857.[94] Some mining town merchants closed their businesses on the holidays, reminding customers in newspaper advertisements to shop ahead of time.[95] Furthermore, some families even kept kosher far from San Francisco. For example, the *shochet* Samuel M. Laski was brought to the mining town of Nevada City so that the whole Jewish community could enjoy an observant Passover.[96]

The German-born Phillip and Caroline Selling, who like the Linobergs also met and married in 1851 in San Francisco, sold goods from the Sonora tent-store that doubled as their home. In 1853, when a fire destroyed their store at a loss of eight thousand dollars, miners passed a hat, filling it with gold dust, to help the Sellings back on their feet.[97] They rebuilt, leaving the foothills only as the

mining economy slowed, and Jews began to move on to other opportunities throughout the Pacific West. Rather than return to San Francisco, the Sellings joined the migration of Californians north to the new city of Portland. Another Sonoran, Poland-born Michel Goldwater, also failed to make a living and, after having "declared himself an insolvent debtor," in 1862 moved south to Los Angeles.[98] He later continued to Arizona, where he found success and, finally, retired to the family home in San Francisco, where his wife and children had stayed while he sought a living in the still-wild desert of Arizona. The city remained the center of his social and business network, the place where he purchased goods for sale, celebrated religious holidays, and his children attended secular and religious schools. An 1877 Arizona newspaper reported that Goldwater "arrived in San Francisco today, where he intends to remain four or five weeks, and be present during the Jewish New Year and participate in the festivities attendant thereto."[99]

The records do not show whether Goldwater received help from benevolent societies. However, his affiliations do illustrate the degree of support available to those in need and demonstrate how, as a western pioneer, one could be an institutional founder without first becoming prosperous. In 1856, the Sonora Hebrew Benevolent Society elected Goldwater vice president. Six years later, having relocated to Los Angeles, he became the founding vice president of Congregation B'nai B'rith (later known as the Wilshire Boulevard Temple). By 1867, Goldwater had become a member of Sherith Israel in San Francisco, where he later served as vice president for eight years.[100] Elected president of San Francisco's First Hebrew Benevolent Society in 1887, he also affiliated with the more prestigious Eureka Benevolent Society and the Hebrew Orphan Asylum. Family ties also solidified Goldwater's pioneer status, as his brother, and later his nephew, married Newmarks, the founding family of Los Angeles Jewry.[101] Within thirty years, Goldwater rose from failed merchant to member of California's Jewish elite.

SATELLITE COMMUNITIES

Migration routes produced regional networks and eventually created permanent communities. After the Canadian gold rush in 1858, Victoria's Jewish community grew rapidly, as itinerant merchants, using their San Francisco ties, supplied gold miners, fishermen, whalers, and the Alaska fur trade. Shop owners like Selim and Lumley Franklin, cousins of San Francisco's Louis Franklin, quickly became civic leaders: Selim was elected to the Legislative Assembly of Vancouver Island in 1860, the first Jew to be elected to a legislature in Canada; Lumley served as the second mayor of Victoria in 1866.[102] Victoria became the center of Puget Sound Jewish life, with benevolent societies, a cemetery, and the observance of religious holidays. Before they could support their own services, Jews in nearby Washington traveled to Victoria. An outpost of the San Francisco Jewish community, men with familiar California names including Sutro, Koshland, and Franklin built stores similar to those of their California relations. According to the Jewish world traveler and chronicler I. J. Benjamin (1818–64), who visited Victoria in 1861, about one hundred Jews lived in the city. He believed that

> the beginnings of the city of Victoria are really due to the Jews. For, no matter how many persons streamed to the island at the outbreak of the gold fever, they scattered again. . . . The Jews, however, held their ground, set up tents for residence and booths for

shops; for they soon realized that this place had a commercial future. This was to be deduced, easily enough, from the situation of the island, which lies between the Sandwich Islands [Hawaii], California and China.[103]

By 1863, the community, now with an estimated 242 Jews, dedicated its own Emanu-El, a structure erected in part with donations from its prestigious San Francisco namesake.[104] The ceremony was a major civic event, attended by spokesmen for St. Andrew's Society and the French Benevolent Society, the Germania Singing Club, Masonic officials, and a band from the HMS *Topaz*. As a port Victoria remained tied to San Francisco rather than to other Canadian cities, and Jews as well as others continued to migrate there in small numbers. The orientation of British Columbian transportation, however, would change after 1886, when the Canadian Pacific Railway completed its trunk line to the new city of Vancouver on the mainland.[105]

Portland, like Victoria, became a satellite of San Francisco, but its economy, based on timber and agriculture rather than on unpredictable gold finds, proved more stable. Unlike San Francisco's, Portland's Jewish community grew slowly, reaching only 135 people in 1860. Yet it played a critical role in the commercial sector: fully one-third of the city's merchants were Jewish. These men did not immediately form a congregation, probably because many had San Francisco connections and were affiliated with its institutions.[106] As most needed to visit San Francisco for business, they could arrange to be there during times of religious significance and thus delay the need to form a Portland congregation. Portland businessmen went to "the city" to purchase merchandise or to find clerks, community leaders to recruit professionals to perform religious rituals, and young Jews, like Emanuel Linoberg from the mining town of Sonora, to find Jewish spouses. Although one could find a minyan of ten Jews as early 1853, only in 1858 did Portlanders form a congregation. While the delay suggests that very few of these individuals committed themselves to attending daily or even weekly services, that they did eventually establish institutions demonstrates that they considered such institutions important.

Founded in 1858, Portland's Beth Israel, the first Pacific Coast congregation outside of California, had strong ties with Emanu-El, whose constitution and bylaws it temporarily adopted.[107] With a Torah and shofar also procured from Emanu-El, and with a similar preference for German sermons, Beth Israel became a sister congregation.[108] As migration patterns indicate, many of Beth Israel's congregants, like the Sellings, started their western life as Californians. Samuel M. Laski, before becoming Beth Israel's reader in the fall of 1858, lived in San Francisco. Probably not an ordained rabbi, but a *mohel* and a *shochet*, he had traveled regularly to the California mining town of Nevada City, where he slaughtered kosher meat and preformed circumcisions for their small Jewish community.[109] Laski officiated at the first Jewish wedding in Portland later that year.[110] By October 1859, he had returned to San Francisco to direct a religious school.[111] His successor, Herman Bien, who pretended he had rabbinic credentials while first at Emanu-El and then in Portland, served only briefly, leaving Beth Israel without rabbinic leadership.[112] Hoping to find a rabbi on the Pacific Coast, the congregation advertised "Minister Wanted" in San Francisco's *Gleaner*.[113] However, Beth Israel was not able to attract an ordained rabbi to its remote community.

Unlike in most western cities, an Orthodox congregation was never formed in Portland; Beth Israel began with desire for reform. When in 1861

the congregation sought a rabbi to consecrate its new two hundred–seat Gothic-style building, it invited Elkan Cohn, Emanu-El's new reformer, to preside. The bespectacled Cohn, who seldom left California, must have felt strong ties with Beth Israel's membership to make the long trip up the coast. So important was Cohn's presence at the ceremony that the steamship line held its ship in port for twenty-four hours so that Cohn could officiate before returning to San Francisco.[114] Two years later, failing to obtain the services of a rabbi with the prestige of Cohn, Beth Israel invited Rabbi Eckman to lead High Holiday services and then asked him to remain. Just as Eckman had not been a good fit for Emanu-El, neither was he a match for Beth Israel, whose leaders sought a rabbi to steer them toward reforms in their worship services and probably one who would submit to laity control. Eckman did have some success in Portland: as in San Francisco, the congregation's school flourished under his leadership.[115]

By 1869, Portland's Jewish community had grown sufficiently to support two congregations. Beth Israel became increasing divided between its South German majority and its steadily increasing Posener, or Prussian, minority.[116] When ethnic and ritual discord separated members of Portland's Beth Israel, those who withdrew adopted, like San Francisco's Ohabai Shalome, the name Ahavai Shalom (Lovers of Peace) to symbolize the tranquility that they hoped would now reign at least among themselves. The members of Ahavai Shalom wanted a congregation that kept more elements of traditionalism than did those who remained at Beth Israel. Similar to Ohabai Shalome, Ahavai Shalom introduced English sermons and retained family seating and a choir.[117] They became know as the "Polish" congregation, but the label was inaccurate. German Jews, bringing their European

prejudices with them, often used "Polish" to con-
note a class they considered "less cultured," that
is, those whose parents may have spoken Yiddish
rather than the more refined German. Although
members of Ahavai Shalom may have been born in
former Polish provinces, many hailed from Posen,
a province rapidly undergoing Germanization in
the nineteenth century, and they did not practice a
Polish form of Judaism. Their split from Beth Israel
was not over ritual (*minhag*), as had occurred in
San Francisco more than a decade before. Rather,
Poseners by 1869 simply had enough numbers to
create their own congregation. Ahavai Shalom
adopted the German rather than the Polish *minhag*,
illustrating a deep grounding in German-Jewish
practice and a disinclination to see themselves as
Polish. Most came from towns, not rural areas,
and valued traditional Jewish education and piety,
yet they were attracted to the more cosmopolitan
Germans.[118]

The members of Ahavai Shalom brought Rabbi
Eckman again to Portland, where he finally found
a congenial pulpit; it mirrored his origin, education, and religious values.[119] Eckman, familiar to
his new congregants as editor of the *Gleaner* and
the *Hebrew Observer* and a former rabbi of Beth
Israel, not only reflected the religious outlook of
Ahavai Shalom but also could address the congregation and the community at large in English.
By hiring Eckman, the congregation reinforced its
choice to become a singular Prussian congregation,
stressing its ethnic ties and American point of view.
After three successful years, Eckman returned to
San Francisco, where in his final years he served as
headmaster at San Francisco's Sherith Israel Sabbath school.[120]

By the 1870s, Ahavai Shalom's parent congregation, Beth Israel, still had not found peace. Like
congregations throughout the United States, Beth

Israel "oscillated" between continuing Orthodoxy
and instigating reforms.[121] In fact, in 1873, their
new rabbi, Moses May, accused the congregation
of wanting to follow "*Minhag* Portland," alluding
to its practice of picking and choosing reforms that
temporarily suited the majority of the congregation.[122] May, in his early twenties and apparently
arrogant, sought ideological consistency rather
than pastoral peace. He arrived at Beth Israel in
1872 believing that the congregation should follow
the ritual of the "land we are living in." He sent a
letter to the board of directors requesting to officially adopt *Minhag America*, and the congregation took his advice. However, by 1879, May had
accumulated enemies in the congregation, some
of whom made defamatory charges against him.
They accused him of "outrageously slandering and
blackmail[ing] several members of the Congregation; condemning himself, by his own actions, as
an immoral man and an unbeliever in the doctrines
of Holy Writ; acting as a libertine and rake during a visit to San Francisco"; calling congregants
names; opening the mail of congregational officers;
and "threatening to join the Unitarian Church in
the event Mr. Philip Selling were re-elected President." A committee of the board, including former
mayor Bernard Goldsmith, Sigmund Blumauer, and
Solomon Hirsch, exonerated him of all charges,
though it averred that he had made indiscrete
remarks about the ignorance of the congregation and had an "inclination to insult people with
ease."[123] San Franciscans were brought into the
fray. Rabbi I. A. Messing traveled from "the city"
to speak at a congregational meeting, where he
"emphasized the need for keeping the peace among
the members."[124]

The argument between the rabbi and some
members of the congregation over reforms continued. May used the Reform prayer book and

continued to make enemies of congregants who held more traditional views. Adolph Waldman, the chairman of the religious school committee, a man in his mid-fifties, complained to the board that Rabbi May refused to follow rules laid down by his committee. All came to a peak in September 1880, when Waldman and the rabbi had a fist fight on the streets of Portland. Rabbi May produced a pistol from his pocket and tried to shoot Waldman, who was fined for assault, because he first attacked the rabbi. May argued that the fight had started over long simmering arguments about religious practice and concluded that he would teach not the religion of the congregant but "that of Moses."[125] Under these bizarre circumstances, the congregation forced May to resign, though he received a settlement of twelve hundred dollars, the equivalent of eight months' salary. More than a year later, when May applied for a position elsewhere, the board wrote a letter attesting to his fidelity in carrying out duties as a hazan and teacher for nine years and noting that "he can make his services interesting and is a man of considerable erudition."[126] But May's leaving did not change the battle over reforms. The congregation would continue to vacillate in its prayer book and practices until the end of the century.[127]

Unlike Jews in Portland, those in Los Angeles quickly organized home-based Shabbat and holiday observance. Early Jewish observance revolved around extended family and business networks. In 1851, just a year after the city's incorporation, Shabbat services took place regularly at the home of the Greenbaums, who had come from Poland.[128] Tina Greenbaum, twenty-one, operated a boardinghouse, while her twenty-three-year-old husband, Ephraim, ran a store.[129] The Jewish population remained small (in 1850, before the arrival of women, it comprised only eight unmarried men—in a total population of 1,610). The opposite of the "instant" San Francisco, Los Angeles retained the feel of a small Spanish town for decades. Although many ties to San Francisco Jewry proved important, distinct characteristics shaped the evolution of the Los Angeles community.

In the mid-nineteenth century, the Jews of Los Angeles were directed in their religious practice primarily by their patriarch, Joseph Newmark. From the day of his arrival in the city in 1854 until his death in 1881, Newmark provided a focal point for organized Jewish observance in Los Angeles. Like many other early western Jews, Newmark had considerable experience organizing American Jewish communities. He came to the United States from Prussia in 1824 and lived in New York, Somerset (Connecticut), St. Louis, Dubuque (Iowa), and San Francisco before finally settling in Los Angeles, where he joined his cousin J. P. Newmark and his nephew Harris.[130] In many of these cities and towns, he took leadership roles in the founding of synagogues and benevolent societies.[131] With this considerable experience, Newmark, a *shochet* and the grandson of a Polish rabbi, became the young community's Jewish authority. Until Rabbi Abraham Edelman joined the community in 1862, Newmark officiated at most Jewish occasions.

The entrance of Joseph Newmark finalized all the requirements for establishing a Jewish community as set down by Cincinnati's renowned rabbi Max Lilienthal. These included ten men to form a minyan, a "religious feeling" caused by the arrival of the High Holidays, a nearby community to supply advice, provisions for observance of Jewish life, and a "committed leader" to encourage others.[132] Newmark became in effect the community's lay rabbi. The Hebrew Benevolent Society was purportedly formed at his home, and he led High Holiday services.[133] In 1859, to ensure that the community could strictly observe Passover, Newmark arranged for a Catholic baker, Louis Mesmer, the same baker who would supply bread to government troops, to prepare matzoth under his close supervision.[134]

In 1859, the *Los Angeles Star* reported on the community's observance of *Yom Kippur*: "This, we believe, is the most solemn holiday of the Jewish ritual, and is strictly observed by all members of the church. It is a sacred fast-day, and is devoted exclusively to religious services. All business is suspended, even the most common household duties being dispensed with."[135] This practice was continued at least into the late 1860s, when it was reported in 1867 that, on Yom Kippur with Jewish businesses closed, Los Angeles "looked like Sunday in a New England village."[136]

By the 1860s, the community desired a permanent rabbi and congregation, so it started a search for an appropriate man. Luckily for Los Angeles, San Francisco had been nurturing such an individual. In 1862, Newmark and Moritz Morris induced twenty-seven-year-old Abraham Edelman to lead their new congregation. The son of a Polish merchant, Edelman spent eight years in the eastern United States before he and his wife settled in San Francisco, where he taught Hebrew, worked in a dry goods firm, and, most important, studied with Sherith Israel's scholarly Rabbi Henry A. Henry.[137] By the time Edelman assumed the rabbinate of B'nai B'rith, he had learned from Rabbi Henry the art of leading an American congregation, was fluent in English, and had become known as a "fine public speaker . . . almost without an accent."[138] Edelman, like many of his congregants, soon became fluent in Spanish, thereby earning the title "Jewish Padre" from Spanish-speaking Angelenos.[139] Soon he also became the *shochet* for the community, selecting meat daily for slaughter.[140]

That year, a kosher meat market opened, making it possible for observant Jews to be comfortable there.[141]

Edelman served the newly founded Congregation B'nai B'rith for twenty-two years, though he may not have rigidly followed Newmark's desire for an Orthodox congregation. Isidore N. Choynski, a San Francisco correspondent for the *American Israelite*, reported that Edelman's wife cooked on the Sabbath, while otherwise keeping kosher.[142] Furthermore, like Beth Israel in Portland, the congregation engaged in several practices that were not Orthodox: men and women sat together, it had a mixed choir, it held confirmation ceremonies for girls and boys, and it used an organ during services.[143] In fact, Edelman, like Rabbi May in Portland, may have been quicker to adopt reforms than was his congregation. According to an 1873 report in the San Francisco *Hebrew*, which carefully followed the progress of its sister city, "Rev. Edelman tried to introduce some innovations on the first day of the New Year, which were not well received."[144] It appears that Congregation B'nai B'rith experimented with reforms well before it formally became a Reform congregation in the 1880s.

Unlike Beth Israel's German founders, Poles constituted the majority of B'nai B'rith's founders. Of the twenty (of twenty-four) founders of B'nai B'rith whose origins can be documented, seventeen were Polish, or Poseners; two were Bavarian; and one French.[145] B'nai B'rith's first rabbi was of Polish origin, and the congregation followed the Polish *min-hag*. However, the prominence of several Bavarians, including the very successful Hellman family, led to the assumption that German Jews established the Los Angeles community.[146] This misconception may have been perpetuated by an upwardly mobile congregation that wanted to eradicate its Polish origins. By the 1870s, the well-respected Bavarian banker Isaias W. (I. W.) Hellman assumed the presidency of the congregation, which now sought a more prestigious, German rabbi. Soon B'nai B'rith would fully embrace Reform.

The congregation migrated for ten years, meeting in civic buildings and hired halls. The 1860s had been an especially difficult decade for Los Angeles: the city was infected with a smallpox epidemic, a three-year drought destroyed much of the city's agricultural economy, and the Civil War disrupted development. All of these factors may have delayed the building of a synagogue. By the 1870s, however, the railroad from San Francisco reached the city, and Los Angeles's population reached 5,728, of whom Jews made up an impressive 5.76 percent, numbering 330.[147] Fund-raising for synagogue building in most western cities relied primarily on male merchants, but Los Angeles turned to its women, who had already raised money for Jewish and non-Jewish institutions alike. The women formed a building committee in 1872 and in just six months raised the funds for the synagogue, which included one thousand dollars from San Francisco merchants. On August 18, 1872, the first cornerstone was laid. Hellman presided over the dedication of B'nai B'rith's first building, which fulfilled the wish of Rabbi Edelman for a "suitable place of worship" and provided the foundation for an elaborate community structure that would follow.[148]

Social life in Los Angeles had also matured. By the 1860s, the city's Jewish festivities rivaled San Francisco's, although it still depended on the hub. In one especially grand celebration in 1867, Joseph Newmark performed the marriage ceremony for his daughter, Harriet, and the French-born merchant Eugene Meyer.[149] The bride wore a dress of satin and lace, trimmed in "the latest style" with California's famed orange blossoms and sewn with material brought from San Francisco. Silk, hats, leather boots, gloves, and wedding presents of the finest china and silver came from Europe by way of San Francisco. Guests included not only extended family but also some of the leading citizens of the state such as I. W. Hellman, Governor John Downey, and the French consul. The lavish wedding supper featured ice cream, something new in the city.[150]

Compared to California and Oregon, the Washington Territory, which at first yielded no gold, developed more slowly, and its Jewish community organized gradually. Although Jews had lived in the Washington Territory since at least 1853, when it was separated from Oregon, its population remained small. In the 1880s, when San Francisco's Jewish population reached sixteen thousand, Seattle's Jewry numbered about one hundred out of a total population of thirty-five hundred, and other Jewish families were scattered throughout the towns around Puget Sound. Unlike Los Angeles, few sought Sabbath services.[151]

The life of Bailey Gatzert highlights the growth of the Seattle community. Born in 1829 in Germany, Gatzert came to the United States in 1849, first settling in Natchez, Mississippi, then for brief intervals in Nevada City, San Francisco, Portland, Wallula, and Seattle.[152] In San Francisco, he married Babette Schwabacher, and as a business associate of her brothers he opened the Schwabacher's store in Seattle. Abraham Schwabacher bought stock in San Francisco for the Seattle store, which advertised "San Francisco Prices." Gatzert played a major role in Seattle's commercial and civic life, serving as Seattle's sixth mayor in 1875.[153] Because Seattle lacked a Jewish population large enough to establish welfare organizations, Gatzert retained his membership in Portland's Jewish communal institutions, though both he and his wife were buried in San Francisco because of her family affiliations.[154] Before Seattle's first congregation was formed in 1889, Jews could choose to celebrate Passover and other holidays in San Francisco, Portland, or Victoria. Often Jews traveled to Victoria for weddings and burials and brought men from that city to Seattle to lead services. Others traveled to Portland and San Francisco to attend life-cycle ceremonies, to be introduced to potential marriage partners, and to buy merchandise for their stores. The 1880s brought changes to the community: the transcontinental railroad reached Seattle, and with it came reduced transportation costs and a larger Jewish population. Before then, only Olympia had a Jewish cemetery and a Hebrew Benevolent Society, both founded in the mid-1870s.[155]

As the Jewish communities in the Far West grew, they maintained their connections to San Francisco. Although Jews in smaller towns started their own Jewish institutions, San Francisco remained the primary source for marriage partners, clergy, and religious supplies. Before the 1870s, if one wanted a Jewish life that included a variety of synagogues and social organizations and a large cosmopolitan secular community, only the hub of San Francisco would do. Thus when the Schwabacher brothers married, their wives told them that they wanted "big Victorian houses in San Francisco," not life in the Washington backwater.[156] When Michel Goldwater went off to Arizona to recoup his fortune, his family remained in "the city."

A SENSE OF COMMUNITY

In cities along the Pacific coast, especially San Francisco, Jewish life was sustained by a variety of fraternal and self-help organizations. Men and, separately, women joined to provide insurance for one another and care for the poor in time of need. As Hasia R. Diner emphasizes, "Communal service came to be the common denominator of American Jewry. Though Jews could not always—or indeed ever—agree on matters religious, they could, in literally thousands of community organizations, agree on their common obligation to provide assistance to Jews in need."[157]

In the West as elsewhere, the Jewish community first created self-help benevolent associations. Following 1849's first High Holiday services in the candle-lit tent on Jackson Street, some of the same men, principally from Posen, Poland, and England, who would two years later establish congregation Sherith Israel, formed the First Hebrew Benevolent Society. The first of many such associations in the region, its primary goal entailed providing for "the indigent, the needy sick, and the burial of the poor, of the Jewish persuasion."[158] Like other societies, to raise funds it organized elaborate balls that advertised music and mirth, highlighted by dancing and suppers. For the society's ninth anniversary in 1858, its annual Purim ball was held at the city's Musical Hall, the location of many elegant parties.[159]

A year after the founding of the First Hebrew Benevolent Society, a second men's benevolent society formed in San Francisco, foreshadowing the separation of the community into two groups divided by ethnic origins. Although the First Hebrew Benevolent Society formed first, the Eureka Benevolent Society became larger and the longest lived. While the boundaries on occasion became porous, predominately Bavarian and French Jews created the Eureka Benevolent Association in 1850. Unlike the First Hebrew Benevolent Society, where English was the language that united its diverse membership, the Eureka Benevolent Society's language remained German until the mid-1870s.

Founded by "forty-eighter" August Helbing, the Eureka Benevolent Society by the late 1850s grew to three hundred members, the largest Jewish association in the region. Before the construction of San Francisco's wharves, members met incoming ships in small boats and brought Jews, often ill from the long journey, to the port and helped them recover and acclimatize to the West. The society became both a mutual aid society and a philanthropic organization, with membership open only for men between ages eighteen and fifty, so that there would not be an immediate drain on its coffers.

The Eureka Benevolent Society helped those in need remake their lives. Helbing believed "that mere alms-giving is more likely to degrade than elevate the poor, while the advancing of a sufficient sum to elevate those reduced to penury, to make a new start, imparts new hope and leaves the recipient his or her self-respect."[160] Before the formation of women's associations in the mid-1850s, the society took responsibility for women and children. When a widowed man died in the explosion of his San Francisco–bound steamboat, the society cared for his young son and established the boy in a trade.[161] The growing need to care for children led the Eureka Benevolent Society in 1858 to establish a widow's and orphan's fund, which evolved, with the help of B'nai B'rith, into the Pacific Hebrew Orphan Asylum.

Benevolent societies also provided a social network, bringing men together for communal activities. Helbing remembered, "We had no suitable way of spending our evenings. Gambling resorts and theaters held no attraction. We passed the time in the back of our stores, disgusted and sick

from loneliness." The Eureka Benevolent Society rented a room where they could gather and hold their meetings and the sick could be nursed back to health.[162] For its first twenty years, the society's members, many of them bachelors, personally took care of one another. By the 1870s, most members had married and had families to care for them, so society committees took responsibility for securing help for the sick, burying the dead, and performing obligations that previously belonged to the group as a whole.

Another German-language association, Chebra Berith Shalom, took care of its members beyond San Francisco's borders. In fact, the association assumed Jewish men would travel through the region and included in its constitution a provision for the care of ill members living temporarily outside of San Francisco: "A member taking sick out of town, but within the State of California, Oregon and Washington Territories, shall be entitled to a weekly benefit of seven dollars and fifty cents, if free in the Book, and having notified the Recording Secretary of such a removal, and by sending a weekly attest from the physician attending him relating the sickness and its origination, and certified by the authority of the place."[163] When Chebra Berith Shalom was only eight months old, it had 105 members and one thousand dollars in its treasury.[164] This quick growth may be attributed to the extensive geographical area it covered. The organization's first president, the satirist Isidor N. Choynski, found the provisions for travel especially important.[165] In 1863, Choynski, twenty-eight, and his father-in-law sought to strike it rich at a new gold field. In a letter to his wife, Choynski wrote, "I too have been sick, and only left my bed this afternoon; the chills, stomach and headache have played the very deuce with me."[166] Chebra

Berith Shalom's arrangement ensured that, whether residing in San Francisco or mining, peddling, or delivering merchandise to a business partner in Portland, a sick man or his widowed wife and children would be comforted by the society.[167] Despite the society's recognition of the peripatetic nature of their lives, members who ventured beyond the Pacific states were not covered. Through their constitution, the members of Chebra Berith Shalom reinforced the concept of regional identity and the interconnection between San Francisco and its satellite communities.

Reliance on the benevolence networks based in San Francisco is also suggested in the case of Prussian-born Selig Ritzwoller. In 1869, Ritzwoller committed suicide in his Sonora dry goods store. He left a note in German stating that he was in debt to his brothers-in-law and asked the San Francisco Hebrew Benevolent Society to take "pity on his poor wife and children."[168] Ritzwoller may have been unable to afford to join the Sonora society (just more than half of the men in Sonora belonged), or, possibly, he was a member of the San Francisco society. Another possibility is that he may have simply put his faith in its reputation for aid, since San Francisco had become recognized as the center of Jewish charity.

The Los Angeles Jewish community also benefited because of its proximity to San Francisco. The Sephardic Labatt family helped create Jewish community life in both cities. Henry Labatt had served as the secretary of San Francisco's First Hebrew Benevolent Society in 1853.[169] His brothers, Samuel K. and Joseph, settled in Los Angeles, where they became agents for their father's San Francisco dry goods business. Samuel complained of the lack of Jewish social and intellectual pursuits in the city in an 1854 letter to Isaac Leeser, the editor of the *Occident*:

Being a Resident of this small town, and as it is only a small city we have naturally more time for reading than we would have in a large and Bustling city and therefore, we as a club through your humble servant, wish to become subscribers to your valuable work [the *Occident*] as we feel confident that it will not only serve as a source of amusement but as a medium of obtaining much knowledge of our People, that we would otherwise be ignorant of.[170]

Men like the Labatts, who had lived in New Orleans and San Francisco, were not used to isolation. Samuel had been a member of the New Orleans Hebrew Benevolent Association and was anxious to form a similar society in Los Angeles to "act as a burial society, a social-fraternal club, a Jewish philanthropic agency, [and] a general charity." With twenty-nine Jewish men, Samuel founded the Hebrew Benevolent Society of Los Angeles in June 1854.[171] Present at the formative meeting, and maybe an instigator of the event, was the famed painter and photographer Solomon Nunes Carvalho, who had just crossed the Rockies as part of Colonel John C. Fremont's fifth expedition west.[172] Previously, Carvalho had been instrumental in establishing Jewish benevolent societies in other cities.[173]

Becoming the first charitable organization of any kind in the city, the Hebrew Benevolent Society hosted religious services until the formation of the congregation and also constructed a fenced cemetery. The latter may have been a first for the community, as the *Los Angeles Star* took note, advising Protestants to follow suit: "We hope this example of the Hebrews will be an incentive to Protestants to take into consideration this important subject."[174] Judaism requires a consecrated burial ground, so it was not surprising that the construction of a fenced cemetery was the society's first act.

It received similar attention in Stockton, where the *San Joaquin Republican* commented that "the Jews have stolen a march on the Christians."[175]

Women also formed benevolent societies. Like the men's organizations, they provided for the sick, for the dead, and for widows through mutual aid. In San Francisco, the first women's associations, the German-speaking *Israelitishe Frauen Verein*, and the Hebrew Ladies' Benevolent Association, both founded in the mid-1850s, attest to the number of Jewish women in the city. The societies were affiliated with Emanu-El and Sherith Israel, respectively. I. J. Benjamin praised the associations in 1860, but also commented that there was "no claim upon [the associations' funds] for there are very few poor Jewish women in San Francisco."[176]

As with men's organizations, the associations brought together like-minded women. Initially, men served as the officers of many of these associations. In Portland, the First Hebrew Ladies Benevolent Society first met in 1874, twenty years after the San Francisco organizations. This Portland society "regularized the female responsibility of visiting the sick and caring for children by empowering the vice-president to recruit members for the task."[177] The Ladies' Hebrew Benevolent Society in Los Angeles, founded in 1870 with thirty-nine members, from the beginning had female officers. Similar to other benevolent societies, its goals were "to administer relief to the poor, the needy, the sick; to prepare the dead for interment; and to see that the dead receive every honor and rite the Hebrew religion accords."[178] The society worked with other non-Jewish organizations to provide for the city's needs. Many of its members also belonged to other charities, which was not unusual, since in the latter half of the nineteenth century, women's sphere of influence expanded outside the home to include caring for children, the sick, and the poor of all faiths.

Outside of caring for local Jews, westerners supported the poor of Jerusalem as early as 1859 and later formed Ohabai Zion (Friends of Zion) societies to institutionalize the charity.[179] The San Francisco society led by the rabbis of Emanu-El and Sherith Israel and the *Gleaner*'s Eckman was founded after a visit from an emissary from Jerusalem in 1861. Although San Franciscans held different views on reform practices, they could agree on the tradition of caring for their coreligionists. When an emissary visited again in the 1870s, his goal was a "mission to U.S. of America and California." This special connection between the golden land and the Promised Land foreshadowed continued interest between Jews who shared a similar climate and geography, if not always the same religious outlook.[180]

Beyond religious and benevolent associations, Pacific Jews founded fraternal organizations and social clubs. In the larger cities, social clubs provided more facilities and grandeur than benevolent societies could offer. The Concordia Clubs in San Francisco and Portland catered to the German elite. Although many Concordia members were merchants, wealth in the "egalitarian" West was not the only criterion for membership; ethnicity was also critical. As was common throughout the country, social clubs like Concordia restricted membership to Germans, although Poles, Poseners, and Bavarians could mix fraternally at B'nai B'rith meetings.[181]

B'nai B'rith and Kesher Shel Bazel (Band of Iron)—like the Masonic organizations to which many Jewish men also belonged—were national, enabling men to join chapters and feel at home as they moved across the country or within the region. Since most western members first joined in the East, many had leadership experience when they settled in the West. David A. D'Ancona, president of the District No. 4 (western) Grand Lodge of B'nai B'rith commented in Los Angeles during a tour of the region's lodges in 1877, "[Mr. Jessie Goldsmith] was formerly a member of Manhattan lodge in New York. He is the right man in the right place, and under his able management Orange Lodge is sure to prosper."[182]

The first western lodge of B'nai B'rith met in San Francisco in 1855. Soon the organization spread throughout the region. By 1863, Sacramento and the mining community of Grass Valley established lodges. San Francisco alone had four lodges by 1865 with a combined membership of 390.[183] Portland boasted one lodge by 1866 and another by 1879. Los Angeles formed its first lodge in 1874, and Oakland in 1875, while Washington did not organize a lodge until 1890.[184]

Out of the "utmost necessity," so that "the Order might be promulgated more rapidly," the six California lodges in 1863 sent a request to the Constitutional Grand Lodge in New York for permission to form a district grand lodge on the Pacific Coast.[185] The western members stated their case: "The Order of the B'nai Berith [sic] having advanced very rapidly for the last year, and our geographical position being so distant as to render a delay of decision detrimental to the progress of the Order on this Coast, your honorable body cannot fail to perceive the necessity of granting our prayer."[186] The new Grand Lodge in San Francisco would end the delays that consulting the East entailed. The New York lodge granted their request, and soon men met for lodge meetings in Portland and throughout the West. In 1870, the District Lodge began to raise funds for the Pacific

Hebrew Orphan Asylum, B'nai B'rith's first western institution. Lodges from Los Angeles to Portland and from San Francisco to Reno all sent funds to establish this new regional institution.

The region's newspapers facilitated the spread of B'nai B'rith and other regional associations. Jewish newspapers welcomed new arrivals to the San Francisco hub, informed Jews up and down the coast and in the interior of Jewish events worldwide and in their new hometowns, and advertised goods and services available to sustain religious and communal life. From goose fat to rum and wine, San Francisco markets sold a variety of "Kosher for Passover" products. Beyond local offerings, San Francisco's *Weekly Gleaner* advertised "Pure native California Wine," supplied by Newmark and Kremer of Los Angeles.[187]

Often two, three, or four Jewish newspapers could be purchased in San Francisco. This selection, second only to New York's and greater than Cincinnati's, contributed to San Francisco's reputation as a very comfortable city to live in as a Jew.[188] Jews in outlying areas also benefited from the active San Francisco press, particularly from the *Weekly Gleaner*, which Rabbi Eckman published for eight years. Written primarily in English, with occasional Hebrew advertisements and commentary, the *Gleaner* attracted readers in San Francisco and Sacramento and in small towns including Humboldt Bay, Olympia, Placerville, Eureka, and Deer Creek.[189] Often republished in eastern papers including the *Jewish Messenger*, Eckman's commentaries instructed his readers on regional, national, and international news and informed easterners and Europeans about the evolution of Jewish life in San Francisco and the region.[190] Through advertisements and letters, people in small mining camps, river towns, and developing cities communicated with one another. At the same time, Eckman sought to educate his audience: "We shall endeavor to render the *Gleaner* a medium for the free interchange of thought from whatever source it may emanate—and its columns will always be open for the temperate discussion of all questions connected either with our own as with the public well being."[191] As one of the few rabbis on the West Coast, Eckman spoke authoritatively to readers living in far-flung parts of the region, giving himself a virtual congregation of thousands. For example, in 1857, Sonoran Emanuel Linoberg wrote to Eckman to ask whether a Jewish man who had married a non-Jew and was buried in a Christian cemetery could be reburied in a Jewish cemetery. The members of the Sonora Hebrew Benevolent Society wanted to decide this divisive issue the American way, by a vote. Eckman advised them instead to "submit" to his rabbinic authority.[192] Likewise, in 1859, Abraham Blackman of Victoria described the difficulty of having baby boys circumcised on the eighth day after birth.[193] Eckman responded that the Jews in Victoria "may either do as Moses did, while traveling with his people through the wilderness; where expediency, probably danger, caused him to postpone the rite till the arrival to Canaan; or, if observances are worth observing, they ought to be worth a sacrifice."[194] By this statement Eckman probably meant that either the community should bring a *mohel* to Victoria or the parents should bring their child to a *mohel* in Portland or San Francisco. Until these Jewish services were more widely available, newspapers like the *Gleaner* served as a critical link for Jews who had chosen to live far from large Jewish centers.

The international news not only educated readers but kept westerners, Jews and non-Jews, apprised of world events. For example, during the Mortara affair, in which the Papal Guard kidnapped a young Jewish child in Italy because he had been baptized by a Catholic family servant, Eckman published twenty-four articles about the case and called for a mass meeting.[195] Demonstrating the power of the *Gleaner*, three thousand San Franciscans, Jews and Protestants, turned out to protest the abduction, one thousand more people than had attended a similar protest in New York. Not only Jewish but also Protestant leaders spoke for the release of the child. The shared stage illustrates the good relationship between local Jews and Protestants. However, there were strong American political undercurrents to the protest. Although Rabbi Eckman insisted that the gathered "must not identify Catholics with Catholicism," the anti-Catholic Know-Nothing Party and the new Republican Party, created with Protestant support, used the Mortara issue to curry favor with Jews.[196] Local Protestants may have flocked to the demonstration to voice their anti-Catholicism.[197] The *Gleaner* published the proceedings of the meeting so that they could be read throughout the region.

When Eckman was called to serve Beth Israel in Portland in 1863, the masthead of the *Gleaner* changed to read "San Francisco and Portland."[198] The impact of Eckman's *Gleaner* cannot be exactly measured, but the historian Robert E. Levinson believed it let easterners know that Jewish communal life existed in the Far West, and it gave western Jews a spiritual outlet and a Jewish identity when no other regional institution existed.[199]

FROM RUSH TO MATURITY

Here [in San Francisco] are congregated Israelites from all parts of the world—from the States, from

FIG. *1.5* *Congregation Emanu-El, San Francisco, Sutter Street, ca. 1867. San Francisco History Center,*
San Francisco Public Library

England, Holland, Germany, Hungary, Russia, Spain, Africa, and Australia—and they are found in every trade, profession and calling. There are Jews as tailors and bootmakers, hatters and furriers, jewelers and watchmakers, tinsmiths and plumbers, painters and glaziers, printers and engravers, lawyers and sailors, clerks of court and teachers of music. The papers come to us from a Jewish newsvendor, and our butter from a Jewish dairy. The editors of the chief newspapers here are Jews. The principal of the largest public school is a Jew.

Jewish doctors will attend you if sick, and a Jewish astrologer takes your money if you are a fool.
—DAVID A. D'ANCONA, 1876

As the London-born D'Ancona, president of B'nai B'rith's western district lodge, recognized, western Jews could not be stereotyped.[200] By the end of the 1870s, a large, diverse Jewish community had grown to maturity in the Pacific West. With San Francisco as its hub, Jews built social, religious, and business networks that flourished up and down the coast. Clergy achieved national recognition for their modern views, and Jews participated actively in civic and ecumenical life. Just as Rabbi Eckman had kindled a friendship with a Methodist minister, his successor at Emanu-El, Elkan Cohn, maintained a friendship with the renowned Unitarian minister Thomas Starr King, and their congregations shared their "ethical universalism."[201] Bernard Goldsmith, Phillip Wasserman, and Bailey Gatzert served as mayors of western cities, and Jews including Solomon Heydenfeldt sat on the California Supreme Court. San Francisco had constructed synagogues that were on par with any in the eastern United States or, for that matter, in Europe.

San Francisco's new Temple Emanu-El exemplified western Jewish success (fig. 1.5). According to the congregation's historian Fred Rosenbaum, "The grand scale of the Sutter Street temple indicated [not only] that a Jewish commercial elite had crystallized in San Francisco . . . [but that it had done so] within a shorter time than anywhere else," only fifteen years after the founding of the congregation.[202] Situated on top of a hill, adorned by two distinctive bronze-plated domed towers about fifteen stories high, the temple was one of the first buildings visitors saw as they approached the city by sea. From the east, the domes could be seen as far away as the Berkeley Hills.[203] This was not only a place of worship but also a symbol of elite status. Designed by the renowned church architect who built Thomas Starr King's Unitarian church, it had the features of both a Gothic medieval cathedral and a synagogue replete with Jewish symbols.[204] Stained-glass windows filled with Stars of David could be viewed from a distance, while the tablets of the law graced the front of the building. Both contemporaries and later historians agreed that it was "the West's most renowned Jewish edifice."[205] As San Francisco's *Daily Alta California* described it, "In point of architectural beauty and grandeur the synagogue not only surpasses all churches in the State, but excels the great majority in the United States. . . . It is a chaste and elegant ornament to our country, and reflects credit on California talent in its construction, and does honor to the taste and liberality of our Jewish fellow-citizens."[206]

This was the congregation of the region's elite families; its membership list included the names Sloss, Gerstle, Schwabacher, and soon Hellman. The wealth of these men came not just from their businesses in San Francisco but also from their investments throughout the Pacific West. And, in turn, congregations in Portland, Victoria, and other cities benefited from the generosity of Emanu-El's members, who had siblings throughout the West and contributed to their support. This network of families and wealth would become even more significant as the region developed and prospered.

2 A BIRTHRIGHT OF ELITE STATUS

The Shrine Auditorium is . . . a matter for especial pride
to the Jewish community of Los Angeles because the
President of the Board of Trustees, . . . Mr. Louis Cole,
is perhaps the best beloved . . . leader in the Los Angeles
Jewish community.—1926

In San Francisco on March 26, 1930, public business came to a halt
as a special meeting of the Board of Supervisors, with many honored guests, eulogized the late Rabbi Jacob Nieto. For more than
thirty-five years Nieto had used his rabbinate as a platform to advocate
for social justice in his adopted city. Born in 1863 in England, he held
his first post as rabbi and Sunday school principal at Sheffield Hebrew
Congregation.[1] After a brief tenure in New York, he was called in 1893
to Sherith Israel to succeed the late Falk Vidaver and his predecessor,
Henry Vidaver, both of whom had been known primarily for their scholarly interests.[2] Nieto (fig. 2.1), however, would embody Reform's "Mission of Israel" by integrating Judaism into a civic movement for social
reform and even physical reconstruction after the horrifying earthquake
and fire in 1906.[3]

Among Jews, Nieto in the late 1890s reached beyond his own congregation to create the Educational Alliance Sunday School in the rooming
house district locally known as "South of Market." Here he hoped to
bring Torah ethics to children whose parents he accused of neglecting
their duty to educate their children Jewishly. To accommodate members
of his own congregation unable to attend on the Sabbath, he initiated a

47

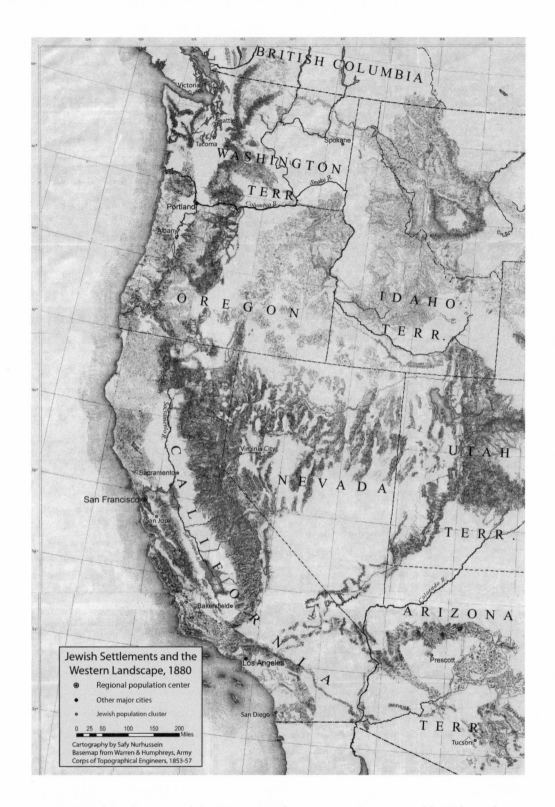

MAP 1. *Jewish Settlements and the Western Landscape, 1880. Map prepared by Safy Nurhussein.*

Sunday lecture series to which all San Franciscans were invited.[4] Far more important in a predominantly Catholic city, he extended his vision of Jewish ethics to the Irish and Italian working class by supporting strikes by organized labor, despite the objections of many of the merchants in his own temple.[5] A resolution of the San Francisco Central Labor Council on December 29, 1921, called him "a true friend of the toiling masses." The Board of Supervisors noted that he had been identified with "the civic life of our community for nearly forty years," and supervisor Andrew Gallagher, after pointing out Nieto's general support of labor, added that "to the cause of the Irish he was also a friend." Longtime mayor James Rolph, after recalling a lifetime of personal friendship with Nieto that included many visits to Sherith Israel, observed that "his death has created a great void in the life of San Francisco." Supervisor and future mayor Angelo Rossi added, "Above all, he was a democrat. He was a civic leader."[6]

Ten months later, on January 15, 1931, the Oregon legislature in Salem adjourned, and in Portland flags flew at half-staff to mourn the passing of Ben Selling, who was groomed virtually from birth for civic leadership. Selling was born in San Francisco in 1852 to the Bavarian immigrants Phillip and Caroline Selling, who had begun their careers on the Pacific Coast with an ill-fated store in Sonora. During the Civil War the family moved to Portland, where Phillip built a successful importing business. On Phillip's retirement in 1882, Ben, with two partners, started a wholesale boot and shoe business, while on his own he opened a men's clothing store and supplied a network of young Jewish merchants stretching to Oregon's remote eastern corners.[7] In 1886, Portland's mayor recruited Selling and other prominent men to defend the Chinese from vigilantes. Selling saw this

FIG. 2.1   *Rabbi Jacob Nieto soon after his arrival in San Francisco, ca. 1893. Western Jewish History Center, Judah L. Magnes Museum (1969).*

service as the duty of leaders to maintain order, while also defending vulnerable populations. He explained to a friend: "We have been threatened with serious trouble on account of the Chinese agitation. At Oregon City the Anti-Coolie Club drove the Chinamen out of town during the night. The better class of citizens deprecate this, and here in Portland have enrolled about two hundred deputy sheriffs. I am one and have done patrol duty two nights. . . . I think the organization of citizens will prevent any riot, but if there is one, somebody is going to be hurt."[8]

EVERYBODY KNOWS WHERE BEN SELLING STANDS.

FIG. 2.2
*Ben Selling campaign poster,
1912.* Oregonian, *March 12,
1912. Selling won the Republican primary for the U.S.
Senate but narrowly lost
the general election. Oregon
Historical Society.*

Selling was also known for his attachment to a country whose physical beauty symbolized its ability to accept Jews as equals. In 1893, just after he and his wife, Tillie Hess of San Francisco, had taken the grand tour of Europe, Egypt, and Palestine, he told friends that Oregon still was "the chosen land of this age."[9] He was subsequently elected to both houses of the state legislature several times,

and in 1912, when his friend and fellow member of Temple Beth Israel, Joseph Simon, served as Portland's mayor, Selling lost a close race for the U.S. Senate (fig. 2.2). With his son, Laurence, launched on a medical career that included a professorship at the fledgling University of Oregon Medical School, the elder Selling committed most of his income to philanthropic ventures in his Pacific Northwest paradise. Selling supervised for the B'nai B'rith every detail of the resettlement in Portland of men and families sent across the continent by New York's Industrial Removal Office, he participated in every major Jewish fund-raising effort in Portland, and in the 1920s he also served on the board of directors of the newly organized community chest.[10] In the 1920s, he underwrote a loan fund that enabled thousands of local students, mostly non-Jews, to enroll in Oregon's colleges.[11]

On a visit to Los Angeles in 1924, the B'nai B'rith lodge honored Selling with a banquet presided over by Rabbi Edgar Magnin and highlighted by testimonials from Portland friends who now lived in southern California. Selling then urged his listeners to participate vigorously in politics, in order "to show the American people what the Jews really stand for."[12] In 1928, the Portland Realty Board named him Portland's First Citizen, a title celebrated in Jewish newspapers from Seattle to Los Angeles. The *Oregonian*, describing his memorial service at Beth Israel, noted, "Governor Meier and Mayor Baker were there, along with members of the Japanese and Chinese colonies, negroes and Italians and Jewish immigrants from lands of oppression across the seas."[13]

Selling and Nieto solidified the status of the Jewish community by bringing to the nation's most remote region new dimensions of philanthropy, social responsibility, and support for unpopular causes like labor unions. While men like Nathan Straus, Jacob Schiff, Louis Brandeis, and Rabbi Jacob Krauskopf received greater publicity for innovative civic roles in New York, Boston, and Philadelphia, on the much smaller stage of the Pacific Coast men like Selling and Nieto became even more conspicuous. They highlighted the extraordinary integration of second-generation Jews into regional leadership, and for their efforts the broader community gave them the highest recognition.

The elevated status of Jews in all large cities in the region is evident as early as 1880. In that year, the federal manuscript census demonstrates that several thousand Jewish merchants, presiding over large, multigenerational households, resided in the most desirable residential areas of San Francisco, Portland, and Los Angeles. Well-established Jewish fraternal, religious, and philanthropic institutions constructed architecturally prominent buildings that made their status visible to their gentile peers. The B'nai B'rith District Grand Lodge No. 4, with headquarters and an orphanage in San Francisco and with an annual convention drawing representatives from cities throughout the region, provided a convivial and philanthropic focus for community leaders. Throughout the Pacific West hundreds of Jewish men obtained high office in Masonic lodges and in local government, leading to their perception as pillars of the struggle for order.[14]

Jews did face some early legislation such as Sunday closing laws in California that represented an effort by transplanted New England clergymen to transfer their culture to the Pacific Coast. But by the early 1880s the courts, juries, and the legislature had overturned them. As the *San Francisco Chronicle* commented in 1883, "The bitterness of sectarianism, which is so often found in eastern communities, is absent here, because we are more cosmopolitan, and therefore more tolerant of all beliefs."[15] Despite the exclusion of individual Jews from social clubs established by gentile elites and occasional concerns about anti-Semitic opinions,[16] by the early 1890s Jewish Concordia clubs, with a list of their members, were included in social registers in Portland and San Francisco.[17] Jewish wives and daughters, organized after 1900 through sections of the National Council of Jewish Women in Portland, Seattle, and San Francisco, belonged to secular federations of women's clubs, which they often represented at national meetings.

TABLE 1. Jewish population estimates, Pacific states

State	1877	1907	1917	1927
California	18,580	42,000	63,652	123,284
Oregon	868	6,000	9,767	13,075
Washington	145	5,500	9,117	14,698

SOURCES: *American Jewish Yearbook*, 5675 [1914–1915], 352; *American Jewish Yearbook*, 5701 [1940–1941].

As the population of major western cities grew rapidly after 1900, and both religious bodies and city and state governments expanded social services, Jews conspicuously sponsored social welfare activities and became professional administrators. Between 1900 and 1912, Reform rabbis like Jacob Nieto, Stephen and Jonah Wise in Portland, and Samuel Koch in Seattle joined elite Protestant ministers in making public responsibility for social welfare a major component of a new "progressive" agenda. Governors from 1902 on routinely appointed rabbis and prominent Jewish merchants, like Adolph Wolfe and Charles F. Berg in Portland and Simon Lubin in Sacramento, to state boards overseeing activities like immigration and social hygiene.[18] In the mid-1920s Louis Newman, who as a protégé of Rabbi Stephen Wise had come from New York to serve as rabbi at Emanu-El, wrote that "the high standards of philanthropy in San Francisco are due in large measure to Jewish contributions of money and intelligence."[19]

As had been the case in the pioneer generation,

western Jewish leaders continued to believe that they enjoyed a higher status among their gentile neighbors than existed for Jewish communities elsewhere. Thousands of Eastern European Jewish newcomers arrived during these years and established their own synagogues, lodges, and benevolent societies, many with women's auxiliaries. Members of San Francisco's Emanu-El Sisterhood for Personal Service might have been repelled by Eastern European immigrants who, they believed, were begging on Market Street "as if they were in Warsaw."[20] Nevertheless, the leaders of established Jewish institutions integrated newcomers into philanthropic federations so that the Jewish community as a whole would retain its respectable cachet. By the 1920s, consolidated B'nai B'rith lodges recruited the sons of Eastern Europeans and Sephardim; these lodges were to become the largest in the country.[21]

SAN FRANCISCO:
REGIONAL METROPOLIS

In 1870, San Francisco had the second largest Jewish population in the United States. National Jewish journals marveled at its institutions, while local Jews proudly noted their rabbis, merchants, bankers, playwrights, actors, and artists. By 1880, as Eastern Europeans settled in large numbers in the industrial cities between Boston, New York, and Chicago, San Francisco lost its position as American Jewry's "second city," though local leaders remained quite satisfied with their regional hegemony. As individuals moved to pursue business opportunities, as rabbis and social workers from Spokane or Portland were called to more prominent positions in San Francisco and later in Los Angeles, a sense of Jewish regional coordination and prominence was reinforced. What happened two thousand or more miles to the east seemed not to matter.

In the thirty years after 1880, as had been true since the Gold Rush, economic and social life in the Pacific West focused on San Francisco. By 1880, not only did San Francisco hold 21 percent of the population of the Pacific region, but also its merchants, including many Jews, handled 99 percent of the region's imports.[22] When Rebekah Bettelheim arrived as a child in 1875 to join her father, Rabbi Albert Bettelheim, she was amazed to find that "it was the most cosmopolitan city of America. One could see members of almost every nationality on the streets. . . . Chinatown was squalid and Barbary Coast sinister, but San Franciscans preferred that attention be given their art-galleries and libraries, their flourishing social and literary clubs, and their public school system, which ranked third in the United States."[23] Rabbi Bettelheim wrote for the local newspapers, and his home became a gathering spot for men of vision like the flamboyant entrepreneur Michael Reese, future mayor Adolph Sutro, the renowned artist Toby Rosenthal, the impresario David Belasco and the aspiring actor and future U.S. Congressman Julius Kahn.[24]

As the city became a manufacturing center, many of the city's Jewish pioneers reinvested their commercial profits in light industry to produce items like shoes, men's clothing, woolen cloth, cigars, brushes, and paper products, all of which would find outlets in markets they had already developed. S. Reinstein had manufactured men's clothing on California Street since the 1860s, but Levi Strauss created the region's signature apparel.[25] Beginning as an import merchant in the 1850s, Strauss supplied denim from New Hampshire to tailors, like Jacob Davis of Reno.

When Davis needed capital in 1872 to patent and manufacture large quantities of cotton work pants with a unique system for reinforcing the seams, he went into partnership with his more affluent supplier, Strauss, and moved to San Francisco to supervise the cutting-out procedures. When their conventional process of production could not meet demands, they acquired a larger four-story building, recapitalized their factory, and hired women to sew up the garments. As they sought new markets by producing more expensive lines of pants, they acquired the local Pacific Woolen Mill to provide the lining.[26] Straus, Reinstein, and their colleagues helped San Francisco produce more goods than the other twenty-four cities of the region combined.[27]

The career of yet another early merchant, I. W. Hellman, illustrates how Jews and gentiles, starting separately as merchants and suppliers, became integral partners in creating credit infrastructure and innovative industry into the twentieth century.[28] After succeeding with his brothers, cousins, and other partners in general stores and a small bank in Los Angeles, in the early 1870s Hellman recruited more than a dozen investors to start the much larger Farmers and Merchants Bank (fig. 2.3). Among the board, key managers, and other employees were both Jews and gentiles, as there were among Hellman's later partners in real estate investments and electric street railways. By 1880, Hellman already had sufficient prestige to be named a trustee of the University of California, on whose board of regents he served until his death in 1920.[29]

In 1890, the Nevada Bank in San Francisco, whose capital had derived from the silver mines in the Comstock Lode and on whose board of directors Strauss served, needed reorganization. Colis Huntington, a former Sacramento merchant and partner in the Southern Pacific Railroad, suggested

FIG. 2.3   *I. W. Hellman in his office at Farmers and Merchants Bank, Los Angeles, ca. 1905. Courtesy of Frances Dinkelspiel.*

Hellman, who found new investors in New York, London, Los Angeles, and San Francisco. In 1905, Hellman, now living in San Francisco, merged the Nevada Bank into the Wells Fargo Bank, and his access to capital is given credit for helping San Francisco rebuild after the earthquake and fire of 1906. Retaining a major stake in Los Angeles, Hellman, his son, and various relatives served on the boards of dozens of Los Angeles banks. With Huntington's nephew, Henry Huntington, Hellman financed the interurban system on which the development of the vast Los Angeles basin depended.[30]

Hellman also lent capital to the more imaginative Italian immigrant investor Amadeo Giannini, whose Bank of Italy in San Francisco not only sought immigrant depositors that larger banks

shunned but recirculated Hellman's money among
Jews in a virtually endless interethnic chain of
capital stretching into the mid-twentieth century.
Giannini's brother, Attilio, who ran the Bank
of Italy's subsidiaries in New York, lent venture
capital to motion picture pioneers Marcus Loew
and Jessie Lasky (a San Francisco native) to open
studios in Brooklyn. When the studios proposed
to build new production facilities in Los Angeles
after 1916, the Gianninis lent more money. The
quick profitability of the studios led Giannini to
appoint "moguls" like Louis B. Mayer and Joseph
and Nicholas Schenk to the bank's local advisory
boards.[31] By the mid-1930s, Giannini's bank, now
called the Bank of America, also joined Benjamin
R. Meyer's Union Bank & Trust Company in Los
Angeles in lending money to men's and women's
clothing manufacturers like Joseph Zukin and
Fred Cole, who created the predominantly Jewish
sportswear industry.[32]

Jewish bankers had their counterparts in
regional politics, where Jews played major roles
as party organizers. San Francisco politics in
the 1890s was dominated by a struggle between
organized labor and a commercial elite, and Jews
played major roles on both sides. A decade before
Rabbi Nieto gave a Jewish voice to the needs of
labor, Adolph Sutro returned to San Francisco with
the fortune he accumulated from building a tunnel
to ventilate and drain the mines at the Comstock
Lode at Virginia City, Nevada (fig. 2.4). Acquiring
a vast tract called the Western Addition, he built
a mansion there, far from the city's established
gentile and Jewish elite who had built their homes
on Pacific Heights.[33] On the hills overlooking the
ocean, Sutro laid out extensive public gardens,
and at the water's edge he installed a series of salt
baths (plate 5). When the Southern Pacific Railroad charged a high fare on its trolley line to the

FIG. 2.4 *Adolph Sutro with the pick he used to strike
the first blow on the Sutro Tunnel, 1869, London.
Nevada Historical Society.*

baths, Sutro earned the public's trust by building a
parallel route and forcing the railroad to lower its
rate. In the depths of a depression in 1894, Sutro,
still identified with miners and skilled labor, was
elected the city's mayor on a Populist ticket. Upset
by the acrimony of politics, he declined to run for
reelection after his two-year term and died shortly
thereafter. Rabbi Nieto, in keeping with both his
religious duties and his identification with organized labor, presided over the private funeral.[34]

More in sympathy with the Jewish mercantile
mentality, the German-born Julius Kahn first

gained local fame in the 1880s as an actor. After practicing law in the 1890s, he entered politics and was elected to the House of Representatives, where he served for twelve terms as the city's Republican congressman.[35] Allied to conservative interests, he gained national prominence by promoting military preparedness and authoring the Selective Draft Act (1917) for Democratic president Woodrow Wilson, when congressmen from Wilson's own party would not. For his leadership two thousand members of the St. Cecile Lodge of Masons in New York City honored him in May 1918 with "Julius Kahn Day" at their clubhouse. After World War I, under a Republican administration, Kahn authored legislation that reorganized the military establishment. At his death in 1924 he was succeeded for six terms by his wife, Florence Prag Kahn (fig. 2.5), the granddaughter of Gold Rush *shochet* Isaac Goldsmith. While her Republican politics often mirrored those of her husband, her sharp wit and assertiveness won her wide respect among her congressional colleagues.[36] Behind the scenes, Hellmans, Levisons, Fleischackers, Haases, and Brandensteins, all from the same clique, played prominent roles as officers of banks and insurance companies and in appointive positions. Through the 1920s, two Jews served at various times on the city's board of supervisors, and the retired teacher, Mary Goldsmith Prag, the mother of Congresswoman Kahn, held one of two Jewish seats on the school board.[37]

The Bavarian-Jewish merchants at the heart of San Francisco's social and economic network expressed their collective pride through Temple Emanu-El. Though damaged during the earthquake and fire in 1906, and substantially repaired, the congregation replaced the temple in 1926 with an opulent structure costing more than one million dollars and located on Lake Street in the Western Addition.[38] By 1905, when Moses descended

from El Capitan at Sherith Israel, San Francisco boasted eight synagogues.[39] One had been Rabbi Bettelheim's Ohabai Shalome, which was graced by an interior that the city directory as early as 1879 described as having "a beautiful appearance and the entire arrangements are appropriate and imposing."[40]

By the 1890s, the congregations in San Francisco, as befitting the regional metropolis, employed an impressive group of rabbis, each with distinctive skills, and all of whom would remain in their pulpits for many years. In addition to Sherith Israel's Jacob Nieto, Beth Israel (the "Turk Street shul") hired Meyer S. Levy to succeed the deceased Rabbi A. J. Messing. An Englishmen like Nieto, Rabbi Levy had served during the 1870s (when still in his twenties) as the first full-time rabbi at Congregation Bichor Cholim in San Jose. In 1881, he accepted the pulpit as the first rabbi at the First Hebrew Congregation of Oakland and remained for ten years. Shortly after coming across the Bay to Beth Israel, his congregation built a new synagogue on Geary Street near Octavia, where the Reverend Levy, according to Jacob Danziger, became "the most popular minister among the Jews."[41] His popularity no doubt rested on his flexible personality, as he presided over congregations whose founders espoused Orthodoxy but whose congregants by the 1890s desired less traditional rituals. His strong support for Rabbi Nieto's Educational Alliance further suggests a man able to see the value of adjusting education and ritual to the interests of his constituents.[42]

Temple Emanu-El had a series of influential rabbis, including by 1890 Jacob Voorsanger, a friend and literary collaborator of Isaac Mayer Wise. Before becoming Elkan Cohn's assistant in 1886, Voorsanger had developed a strong interest in Jewish journalism and held cantorial positions in

FIG. 2.5 *Congresswoman Florence Prag Kahn, the first Jewish woman to serve in Congress, when she was acting Speaker of the House of Representatives, 1926. Western Jewish History Center, Judah L. Magnes Museum (1975).*

Washington, D.C., and Providence, Rhode Island, and a pulpit in Houston, Texas.[43] Though, like Wise, never formally ordained, he was accepted as the temple's rabbi at Cohn's death in 1889. Voorsanger was more a scholar than a community activist and fancied himself an intellectual interpreter of Reform Judaism.[44] According to Danziger, "Timely and well put expressions have made Doctor Voorsanger popular."[45] As a student of German biblical criticism, Voorsanger volunteered to teach Hebrew at the University of California and served as professor of Semitic languages from the posi-

tion's inception in 1894 until his death in 1908. He also taught occasionally at Stanford University and in 1895 played his most important regional role by founding a weekly newspaper, *Emanu-El.*

Within his congregation, Voorsanger borrowed the idea of "personal service" from Temple Emanu-El in New York and mobilized the temple's women to assist Jewish immigrant families. The Emanu-El Sisterhood for Personal Service, founded in 1894, rented a large building on Folsom Street, south of Market, where temple women organized clubs to bring new ideas on child rearing and adolescent care to young immigrant mothers and their children.[46] Voorsanger's vision of social service also led him to support Rabbi Nieto in 1897, when the latter organized the Jewish Educational Society, which met at Sisterhood House. Though never joining Nieto in supporting organized labor, Voorsanger did engage in public debate by forthrightly expressing controversial views, like criticism of American imperialism in the Philippines and opposition to political Zionism.[47] When Danziger in 1895 wrote a piece for the prestigious *Overland Monthly* on the contribution of Jews to the city, he saw the preeminence of local rabbis as only one of many sources of pride. He concluded that "the question, 'What have the Jews done for San Francisco?' might be answered by a counter question: 'What have they not done that others have?'"[48]

THE ICONS OF MAIN STREET

By the 1880s, many Jewish merchants had left depleted Gold Rush towns for San Francisco, but some remained in farming and ranching territory much longer. From Ellensburg, Washington, to Tucson, Arizona, many Jews enjoyed the provincial intimacy and social prominence that pioneer towns afforded. Jewish men supplied farmers and ranchers on credit during the growing seasons and in exchange took gold nuggets, grain, cattle, wool, and hides, which they shipped on to relatives in larger cities who acted as exporters and commission merchants. The British humanitarian Norman Angell, who spent part of his youth in the early 1890s in the Tejon Pass area of southern California, was encouraged to study law by the Weil brothers, who kept a general store in Bakersfield. The Weils, he later wrote, "were the type of Jew[s]

who represented at that time in the new country the most cultured and civilized element of the community."[49]

In the towns of central Oregon, the search by the Durkheimer brothers for mercantile success and the civic leadership that followed illustrates how Jewish men continued into the early twentieth century to work their way into the social fabric of the region's most remote districts. Just after the Civil War, all three brothers obtained apprenticeships in Portland to trades like printing and bookkeeping.[50] Julius Durkheimer, the most adventurous brother, went to Baker, Oregon, in 1874, to clerk for two Jewish merchants and took a decade to acquire his own store. By 1887, he apparently sold it and moved his own operations about forty miles to Prairie City, Oregon. He then quickly branched out to Canyon City and Burns, installing either a bachelor brother or another Jewish clerk to manage his satellites. When Julius married Delia Fried, the daughter of a Portland Jewish merchant, in 1889, he sold the Canyon City store to three Jewish businessmen and sold the Prairie City store to his brother Moses, who remained there as storekeeper and mayor until his accidental death in 1919. Julius operated the store in Burns and was also elected its mayor. The winter snows, however, kept eastern Oregon isolated from the Willamette Valley for at least four months, and Jewish life must have been extremely difficult to sustain. In 1896, Delia Durkheimer insisted that the family, which now included two sons, return to her home community in Portland. Using his savings, Julius bought into Portland's leading wholesale grocery, while Delia quickly found a social outlet as an officer in the Ladies' Hebrew Benevolent Society.[51]

The network of cousins and friends, and their ability to work their way into the social infrastruc-

TABLE 2. Jewish population of selected western
towns, 1880

Town	Total Population	Jewish Population	
Portland	17,577	508	2.9%
Albany, OR	1,867	72	3.9%
Seattle	3,533	98	2.8%
Los Angeles	11,183	420	3.8%
San Jose	12,567	242	1.9%
Virginia City, NV	10,917	146	1.3%

SOURCE: Data gathered from U.S. manuscript census returns,
1880.

NOTE: Most persons are identified as Jews from records of synagogues, benevolent associations, or B'nai B'rith lodge minutes.
Others are added from the 1880 federal manuscript census
returns, as their social characteristics suggest that they, too,
were Jews.

ture of remote towns, is further illustrated in the career of Sampson H. Friendly, who had come in 1863 from New York to San Francisco, where he worked for a firm owned by Martin and Moses Heller. After acquiring business experience for two years, Friendly took a position as a clerk for Wells Fargo, the regional express and gold transfer company, which sent him to the remote farming town of Eugene City in Oregon's Willamette Valley. In a frontier economy starved for currency and credit, Wells Fargo provided both, though it opened and closed offices as business required.[52] Young Friendly, apparently desiring to remain in the small town, must have acquired the confidence of farmers and merchants, because he explored other business opportunities. He also came to know a young cousin of the Hellers, a man named Lauer, who was then working as a clerk in Portland. By 1869 Lauer had also relocated to Eugene, opened a gen-

eral store with Friendly, and subsequently married Friendly's sister. Under various permutations and partnerships, Friendly continued to operate a business that sold retail merchandise, supplied farmers on credit, and sold their hops and grains through a relative, Charles Friendly, in Portland.[53] Sampson H. Friendly served on Eugene's city council and as mayor and for many years was on the fledgling University of Oregon's Board of Trustees. As a measure of the university community's affection, shortly after his death in 1915, the trustees named the first dormitory in his honor and the city named a major street for him between streets named for Presidents Monroe and Adams.[54]

As commercial farming, timber, and light industry came to dominate the region, the sons of Jewish immigrants coordinated their business careers with life-cycle transitions and reinforced their image as pillars of civic stability. The chain of migration that had drawn their parents from Central European villages in the 1850s and 1860s now launched them on mercantile apprenticeships around the region, from larger cities to smaller towns and back. Almost always they remained within the region, seeking business opportunities where they could. Harris Newmark, whose narrative of Los Angeles Jewry provides so many details about communal life, represented the sales and exchange link in a family business coordinated by his brother in San Francisco. As a measure of the interlocking relationship of the firms, when his brother spent several years in New York, Harris moved his family to San Francisco to oversee the business's distribution hub. As opportunities to supply farmers and ranchers continued to expand, men like Ben Selling provided the stock for half a dozen general stores staffed by younger relatives and friends in Oregon towns like Bend, The Dalles, and Pendleton. Others like Sig Lipman, who had a general store in Virginia City, saw a better opportunity in Portland in partnership with Adolph Wolfe. Lipman moved and, with Wolfe, built the most prestigious department store in the city.[55] In 1881, just as Lipman left Virginia City for Portland and Adolph Sutro left for San Francisco, the Hamburger brothers headed south for Los Angeles, where in 1905 they built a five-story department store, at that time the largest in that growing metropolis.

An even more remote and forbidding inland frontier of the California hub, the Arizona Territory's commercial development accelerated with the completion of the transcontinental railroads and the distribution of irrigation water for commercial development. Here Michel Goldwater, his three brothers, and his several sons played prominent roles as merchants and civic boosters. At various times they operated stores at Ehrenburg, Gila City, La Paz, and Prescott. At Phoenix, where an irrigation system enabled farmers to grow grains and later cotton, the firm of Aaron Barnett and Benjamin Block signed the articles of association for the town site in 1870, and the firm of Hyman Mannasse of San Diego had already opened a short-lived branch. Commercial farming continued to attract Jewish merchants like Michael Wormser, who parlayed grain trading into large real estate holdings. Other firms, like Goldman & Company, founded by four Goldman brothers in 1875, came to specialize in groceries and farm implements, while Hyman Goldberg and his sons built the town's leading men's furnishing store.[56]

As the railroad expanded into the territory, Goldwater, like the Durkheimer brothers in Oregon, moved his stores to keep pace with new settlements. He acquired government contracts to supply forts and used his earnings to establish stores in what he hoped would be new railheads.

When Michel, at age sixty-six, retired to San Francisco in 1886 to take an active role in Sherith Israel, his son, Morris, remained at Prescott, where he was elected mayor, served in the legislature, and became grand master of the state's largest Masonic lodge. Further railroad expansion allowed Morris to open a new store in Phoenix, where his younger brother, Baron, became manager. Having spent much more time with his mother in San Francisco, Baron had acquired a feel for elegant clothing and sophisticated marketing typified by department stores like the Weil brothers' Emporium, City of Paris, and I. Magnins. As Phoenix grew to support more affluent residents, Baron brought his marketing ideas to the desert town, where they soon made Goldwater's the most successful retailers in the territory.[57]

Jewish merchants became thoroughly integrated into civic life throughout the region. In Phoenix in the late nineteenth century, Emil Ganz served twice as mayor, and Goldmans, Goldbergs, and others sat on the city council and represented the town in the territorial legislature. They contributed to the Sisters Hospital and subscribed to the Young Men's Christian Association (YMCA).[58] In nearby Tucson in 1883, the citizens elected Charles Strauss mayor, and he promoted the construction of a city hall, fire station, and library. Selim Franklin, who followed the burgeoning economy from British Columbia to Arizona, represented Tucson in the territorial legislature and acquired the University of Arizona for his town, as part of an allotment of new state institutions, including a prison at Yuma and a mental hospital at Phoenix.[59]

Almost fifteen hundred miles to the north, at Ellensburg, Washington, Henry Kleinberg had joined his elder brother, Sam, in the hay and grain business. Pleased to see his social status rise with his commercial prosperity, Henry acquired farmland, contributed to the building fund for the YMCA, and helped finance downtown street lamps. He reluctantly consented to move to Seattle after World War I, when his wife insisted that the children needed Jewish companionship and religious instruction. His fellow Jewish merchant, a man named Kreidel, remained in the small town, where he was elected mayor.[60]

In Portland, Fleischner-Mayer and Company grew into the largest supply house in the Northwest, and the various partners, including Sichels, Sellings, and Hirsches, adorned their business success with civic prestige. As a smaller, more tightly knit contingent than in San Francisco, Portland's Jewish merchants became the core of an influential Republican clique. In a state where the Democrats represented skilled workers, some small businessmen, and southern Oregon's small farmers, many of whom had supported the Confederacy, to be a Republican meant to promote the expansion of railroads and river shipping and the sanctity of the Constitution. In the early 1880s, Solomon Hirsch, who sat in the state senate, was nominated for the U.S. Senate, but he lost the election in the legislature by one vote—his own. Instead, he accepted an appointment from President Benjamin Harrison as ambassador to the Ottoman Empire. He remained a cog in the national Republican apparatus by distributing campaign largesse for Senator Mark Hanna of Ohio, the chairman of the national Republican Party and mentor of President William McKinley.

Hirsch's younger associate, Joseph Simon, became a partner in Portland's most influential corporate law firm, whose gentile senior partners were frequently elected by the legislature to the U.S. Senate. From the late 1870s on, Simon served as chairman of the Multnomah County Republican Central Committee, and in 1898 the legislature elected

him to the U.S. Senate. After serving one term he returned to Portland, where he was elected mayor in June 1909. Hardly a "Progressive," he nevertheless supported the famous "Oregon System" that incorporated the referendum and recall into the process of governance.[61] As a lifelong bachelor, he ignored a campaign to eradicate prostitution, but he did encourage Portland to join the "City Beautiful" movement, with its plans for city parks, wider streets, and a formal civic center.[62]

Even later arriving immigrants could follow a similar pattern, pairing new economic opportunities in western outposts with civic leadership. Samuel Fox, for example, came to New York at age eighteen in 1881 and spent four years learning English and retail skills before seeking better employment prospects in San Francisco. In 1885, he moved to Los Angeles and, a year later, to the much smaller town of San Diego, where he and several other Jewish merchants played key roles in obtaining the federal subsidies to link their town to the transcontinental rail system.[63] There, at the crest of the first southern California land boom, Fox opened a realtor's office and developed business practices that assured steady if not spectacular income. Like his many Central European Jewish predecessors, once he had established a business he married the sister of a local Jewish clothier, inherited the store at the latter's death, and built a business that appealed to a more affluent clientele. And like many others, he augmented his real estate and mercantile pursuits with public efforts to promote the economic growth of his city. In addition to serving on the board of Reform Temple Beth Israel and directing its fund-raising for increasingly larger structures into the mid-1920s, he served as city water commissioner, a member of the board of directors of the chamber of commerce, and a primary organizer of the community chest.[64]

FIG. 2.6   *Hyman Steinbock's House of a Million Bargains store and Cherry Parade float in Salem, Ore., 1915.*
Oregon Historical Society.

The prominence of individual Jewish merchants reinforced their continuing collective visibility (fig. 2.6). This was particularly true in Spokane, where the clustering of Jewish businesses in the 1920s became even more conspicuous than in Albany, Oregon, or Virginia City, Nevada, in 1880. In the mid-1920s, members of Spokane's Reform Temple Emanu-El included forty-three who owned jewelry, clothing, and furniture stores clustered on six consecutive blocks of three parallel downtown business streets. Very few other Jewish businesses were located anywhere else in the central business district. Only four blocks to the south, the temple and the Orthodox synagogue stood a block apart,

and the vast majority of these store owners resided within walking distance. While Jews owned only a small segment of Spokane's stores, their narrow lines of merchandising, the close proximity of their stores and homes, and their cohesion in synagogues and fraternal lodges created the image of an intense community integral to the city's commercial success.[65]

Although the Jewish merchants in smaller communities throughout the region achieved prominence as civic leaders, they had difficulty sustaining congregations, erecting buildings, and retaining religious functionaries, let alone attracting the kinds of prominent rabbis who were such a key presence in San Francisco. Perhaps men with less interest in sustaining a pious life ventured into remote towns, or perhaps the limited funding available from small populations made the employment of a rabbi seem unimportant. In small towns the emphasis on the temple as social center outweighed the interest in providing formal spiritual guidance or education for the children. A cluster of merchants in an agricultural marketing center like Albany, Oregon, for example, organized a congregation to preside over a cemetery. They met annually at Passover—in conjunction with a few members from nearby towns like Eugene and Corvallis—to conduct business, and they apparently had no wider expectations. They planned no structure, and no rabbi was ever invited to conduct religious services. As membership declined because children sought opportunities in larger cities, the congregation reluctantly allowed widows to join, and by 1920 the cemetery was entrusted to the Masons for maintenance.[66]

In larger towns, the desire to construct a building marking the Jewish presence outweighed the desire to pay salaries that might make religious leaders want to stay. With a mortgage to be met, congregational meetings continued to reconsider the length of the rabbi's contract and his salary. In 1892, while sufficiently aware of innovations in Judaism to want a Reform temple, Jews in Spokane and Tacoma had priorities similar to the frontier congregations of California thirty years before. For them, the temple had to provide a permanent meeting space and a symbol of their secure status more than it did a center for piety or even for religious instruction. The twenty-two men who met to create Spokane's first synagogue wanted a Reform temple rather than a synagogue whose worship service followed an Orthodox European *minhag.* The founders of Temple Emanu-El immediately incurred a

debt to build a synagogue, but they offered their first "minister," Dr. Emanuel Shreiber, who had previously served Congregation B'nai B'rith in Los Angeles, only a one-year contract. The board of directors must have been men of strong opinions, because in June 1892, the one-year renewal of Shreiber's contract accompanied a resolution "that no member shall dictate to Dr. Schreiber in what manner he shall lecture." He soon left, and in 1895 the board hired a Dr. Farber on a series of annual contracts. Distressed by the national depression, the board struggled to pay the mortgage and let Farber go after the High Holy Days in 1897.[67]

In Tacoma the seventy-five men who organized Temple Beth Israel in 1892 also desired a Reform congregation even before such a group had been organized in nearby Seattle. They also went into debt to erect a wood-frame building, but they sought formal religious leadership only on the High Holidays. They contented themselves with students from Hebrew Union College or a retired hazan from Portland. In 1903, they hired Rabbi Montague N. A. Cohen, but within a year he too had left, for a meandering career as rabbi and religious journalist in various western cities and military outposts.[68]

In the late 1890s and the early years of the twentieth century, congregations in Los Angeles, Portland, and Seattle felt large enough and sufficiently prominent to follow the lead of San Francisco's oldest synagogues by hiring Reform rabbis who would bring Rabbi Nieto's activist spirit to their cities. In 1896, for example, Congregation B'nai B'rith in Los Angeles accepted a Reform prayer book and in 1899 brought Rabbi Sigmund Hecht from Milwaukee. Hecht wanted to develop an institution that could promote the Jewish community's role in civic philanthropy. To this end he persuaded the B'nai B'rith lodges to consolidate into one lodge and to relinquish their insurance functions in favor of fund-raising for more general welfare needs. By 1910, between sponsorship of the B'nai B'rith and the philanthropy of the Newmark family, the Jewish community completed a new home for orphans at Montabello and the Kaspare Cohn Hospital, where Rabbi Hecht gave the dedicatory address.[69] In a region where Catholic Sisters had provided the bulk of hospital care and Protestant churches increasingly emphasized personal spiritual healing, Jewish philanthropy was especially conspicuous.[70]

In 1899, Portland's mercantile elite also sought a man who could become their spiritual spokesman to the larger city. Solomon Hirsch and Ben Selling met young Stephen Wise of New York when he was visiting his brother, Otto, in San Francisco, and they quickly raised five thousand dollars for an annual salary to persuade the dynamic twenty-five-year-old to become their rabbi.[71] In Portland, Wise quickly increased Beth Israel's membership from 130 to more than 200 families, much to the delight of his board. But Wise also wanted the Jewish elite to take communal rather than individual responsibility for social reform.[72] He got the city's largest B'nai B'rith lodge, No. 416, to examine the problems of organized labor, and he opened his pulpit to spokesmen for women's suffrage and unions. With the assistance of his wife, Louise Waterman Wise, a trained social worker, he virtually merged Temple Beth Israel's alter guild into the local section of the Council of Jewish Women and had Ben Selling raise more than five thousand dollars to build a new Neighborhood House that would provide the base for settlement work.[73]

Noting that no Reform temple within five hundred miles of Portland had a full-time rabbi, Wise himself took a more visible role in public service. His focus on social reform led him to develop a close friendship with Portland's Unitarian minister, the kindly Thomas Lamb Eliot. Wise met frequently with Protestant ministers wherever he went, and in Salem he spoke to prisoners and boys in the reform school. At the invitation of Sampson H. Friendly he even visited Eugene, where he spoke to both townsmen and students at the university.[74] In recognition of his dynamic personality, the governor appointed Wise to the state board of charities, the first rabbi in Oregon ever to hold such an office.

After only six years in Portland, Wise in 1906 returned to New York, partly because of his health, but largely because of a notorious conflict with his board over the freedom of his pulpit. His public visibility, however, had created a regional legacy for the Reform rabbinate. His successor at Beth Israel, Jonah Wise, the son of Isaac Mayer Wise, was expected to be equally active in civic life.[75] During his almost two decades in Portland, Jonah Wise had an even greater visibility than his more vocal predecessor. He was appointed to state boards that monitored controversial innovations like sex education in the public schools and the use of psychologists in the juvenile courts. By serving on such boards with Jewish businessmen, lawyers, doctors, and social workers, he projected a much more sophisticated image of Portland Jewry as a community willing to provide professionally informed civic leadership. Even President Prince Lucien Campbell of the University of Oregon recruited him to liberalize moral instruction in higher education by introducing a course on Judaism at the public university's Portland branch.[76]

Just as Stephen Wise was leaving Portland, Temple De Hirsch in Seattle brought young Rabbi Samuel Koch (fig. 2.7), a Hebrew Union College graduate, from Pensacola, Florida, to preside over its growing synagogue. Within a little more than a decade Rabbi Koch had become embedded in the city's civic elite by marrying the socially prominent Cora Dinkelspiel, joining the Scottish Rite Masons, serving on the board of virtually every social service agency in Seattle, and becoming "instrumental in organizing the Central Council of Service Agencies."[77] By 1914, he had been named president of the state conference of charities and corrections and had an excellent relationship with President Suzzalo of the University of Washington. Like Stephen Wise, Koch voiced political opinions that differed from those of the majority of his board or his B'nai B'rith lodge, especially his support of world peace and his consistent opposition to political Zionism.[78] Considering himself, like Nieto and Wise, a friend of organized labor, he nevertheless criticized union leaders for condemning Protestant churches, many of whose clergymen, like many rabbis, according to Koch, had defended the union movement.[79] But unlike Stephen and Jonah Wise, he never contemplated leaving (no doubt because of his wife's family) and remained at Temple De Hirsch until his retirement because of illness in 1941.[80]

FIG. 2.7 *Rabbi Samuel Koch, Temple De Hirsch, Seattle, 1906–42. University of Washington Libraries, Special Collections, neg. UW1583.*

THE EARTHQUAKE CRISIS

The Jewish philanthropic infrastructure along the Pacific Coast that had been rejuvenated at the turn of the century would be tested by the region's primary ecological catastrophe of the twentieth century, the earthquake and fire in San Francisco on April 18–21, 1906 (plate 6). In its aftermath San Francisco's Jewish elite not only provided emergency leadership but also created a professional approach to social welfare that gentile civic leaders within the region learned to emulate. The self-sufficiency with which San Francisco Jewry managed its recovery, and the professionals who came to the city in its wake to reorganize philanthropic institutions, created a cadre of experts that became a model for the region. While the efficient organization of philanthropy had been under way nationally for perhaps twenty years prior to San Francisco's disaster, the event itself spurred action for reform all along the coast.[81]

San Francisco's calamity initially destroyed five square miles of industrial sites, as well as working-class and more exclusive middle-class housing on both sides of Market Street. While at the time officials put the death toll at about five hundred, scholars now believe that at least twenty-five hundred people perished, many of them Chinese whom no official wished to count.[82] During the first day, the reporter James Hopper toured the spreading fires for his paper and noted in horrific detail how it had destroyed the largest new hotels and even the new steel-framed skyscrapers in the financial district.[83] But in July the *Overland Monthly*, reflecting the promotional views of business leaders, carried an article demonstrating how the city was already rebuilding.[84] I. W. Hellman privately assured his business associates that "San Francisco is in ashes but will rise again greater than ever. The insurance companies will most all pay up and money will then become very plentiful. . . . My banks are solid and safe and are certainly considered among the best in the country."[85] So sure was he of his ability to orchestrate the city's reconstruction that he and his friend, the railroad magnate E. H. Harriman, assumed they would select the banks to hold federal and other funds contributed for reconstruction.[86]

The fire, nevertheless, left the poorest Jewish families homeless and destroyed the Emanu-El Sisterhood building, where many had received social services.[87] It also gutted Emanu-El's iconic temple on Sutter Street (fig. 2.8) and consumed middle-class Jewish housing on Bush, Geary, and O'Farrell streets.[88] About ten thousand Jews, like more than two hundred thousand of their neighbors, sought shelter with friends, often beyond the city in Alameda or in Oakland, or in tents in Golden Gate Park. An estimated eight hundred Jews from the immigrant district established an emergency camp along San Bruno Road, probably the beginning of Jewish settlement in the area.[89] The city's Jewish elite, men as well as women, mobilized to restore the Jewish community and to assist in rebuilding their city. Rabbi Voorsanger immediately organized a food supply for the Young Men's Hebrew Association (YMHA), and Mayor Schmitz appointed him to head a subcommittee on relief of the hungry.[90] When San Francisco's Committee for Reconstruction selected a five-person subcommittee to advise the governor on an agenda for a special session of the legislature, it included E. S. Heller, a son-in-law of I. W. Hellman.[91]

Sherith Israel's new temple, with its stained-glass testament to California, had been spared, and the city temporarily located its superior courts there, while Rabbi Nieto organized much of the emergency sanitation, water supply, and food relief efforts in the area. As he informed Mayor Schmitz,

> I organized a substation at the corner of Bush & Webster for the purpose of giving food to the people in the six blocks between Laguna and Fillmore. . . . This substation has been supplying 350 families with food during the past week. . . . At the present time I have established my office in my temple . . . for the purpose of having people of the Jewish community who are homeless, register their whereabouts with me, so that I may be able to reply to the numerous telegrams for information which are reaching us almost every moment.[92]

By the fall, perhaps thirty thousand people were still homeless, so the city, taking responsibility largely for women and children, erected fifty-six hundred wooden cottages in Golden Gate Park and at the Presidio, along with buildings for kindergartens and meeting rooms.[93]

Congregations in Portland and elsewhere offered their assistance, though Rabbi Voorsanger asked them to wait until he could assess needs more specifically.[94] When Jewish philanthropists in New York sent San Francisco–born Rabbi Judah L. Magnes and the eminent welfare professional Lee K. Frankel to evaluate conditions, Rabbi Voorsanger complained that their estimate of needs was

FIG. 2.8 *Emanu-El after the earthquake and fire, April 1906. Western Jewish History Center, Judah L. Magnes Museum (1967).*

niggardly. In the end, San Francisco leaders preferred to raise their own funds to rebuild institutions like the Orphan Asylum and the Old Peoples' Home, which had been destroyed, and Mount Zion Hospital, whose wooden structure was obsolete.[95] A committee at Emanu-El that included I. W. Hellman and Marcus Koshland raised the funds to restore the Sutter Street Temple and to assist other synagogues as well.[96] Professor Jessica Peixotto of the University of California, who studied the relief work two years after the earthquake, noted that

the Hebrew Board of Relief wished to care for the Jewish poor apart from the city's Associated Charities. Her report does not indicate how many Jews the city may have assisted, but she does note that 3 percent were "Russian or Polish," which may be taken for a rough surrogate.[97]

Despite the prominent role of Jews in the city's relief and rebuilding, the political reaction to earthquake recovery also exposed an undercurrent of anti-Semitic rhetoric, which Jewish leaders had usually ignored. A small segment of the gentile business elite led by ex-mayor James D. Phelan and the "sugar baron" Rudolph Spreckels made Abraham Ruef a scapegoat for their ambitions. Ruef, an honors graduate of the University of California and its Hastings School of Law, like Joseph Simon in Portland, had used his exceptional intellect to build a successful law practice, from which he launched an ambitious political career. But while Simon made himself an "insider" by working within the Republican Party, Ruef, whose family belonged to Sherith Israel, reflected Rabbi Nieto's interests by helping to reorganize a Union Labor Party. In 1901, the party offered a union musician, Eugene Schmitz, as its successful mayoral candidate. Under a new city charter in 1905, Mayor Schmitz could appoint members of various city commissions, and Ruef, quite mindful of the ethnic basis of Labor's support, followed a policy of appointing Protestants, Catholics, and Jews to each one. He also solicited financial contributions from contractors and protection fees from houses of prostitution and gambling dens, all in the guise of legal fees. His machinations were already the object of a privately funded investigation prior to the earthquake.[98]

In the wake of the disaster, Phelan and Spreckels, aided by the ambitious editor of the San Francisco *Bulletin*, Fremont Older, amplified these charges to gain control of the extralegal Emergency Board and the volunteer committees overseeing reconstruction. Their journalistic advocates invoked the imagery of working-class ignorance and Jewish venality to make Ruef's greed the rationale for their seizure of power.[99] An article by George Kennan in *McClure's Magazine* in September 1907, for example, after describing acts of bribery in great detail, lumped Jews as a group with brothel and saloon keepers, gamblers, and prizefight promoters as Ruef's constituency.[100] In November, an anonymous "Q," in a lengthy article

in the *Overland Monthly*, referred to the "cunning of the Asiatic" to account both for the "noble leaders" Jewry had historically produced and for Ruef's venal behavior. "The Jew," Q wrote, "is a problem of centuries, and there must be somewhere in his makeup an element so terribly at variance with the rest of mankind that throughout countless ages he has been accounted an offending enigma."[101]

With the rising rhetoric of anti-Semitism, Rabbi Nieto tried to salvage the good name of the Jewish people through a highly publicized and dramatic effort to induce Ruef to confess. Disassociating themselves as much from his labor constituency as from the "Boss" himself, prominent Jews expressed little sympathy when Ruef served a four-and-a-half-year term in San Quentin. How deeply anti-Semitism affected the political choices made by Phelan is hard to say, because he had no difficulty appointing prominent Jewish bankers and merchants with Republican credentials to the various boards managing the reconstruction. Furthermore, when the de Young family, owners of the San Francisco *Chronicle* and of Jewish descent, and prominent Jewish department store owners pushed for a rapid recovery of business largely along established routes, Phelan and his friends accepted without apparent recriminations this deviation from their desire for a "City Beautiful."[102]

GENDER, JUDAISM, AND CIVIC REFORM

Women, with Jewish women playing a conspicuous role, made the nurture of poor families as important a subject for civic reform as male reformers had made the initiative, the direct election of U.S. Senators, and the advent of the professional city manager. By 1910, the National Council of Jewish Women's sections in Portland, Seattle, and San

Francisco expanded their volunteer work to include more demanding intervention with public agencies. As women's suffrage was again placed on the general political agenda in Oregon, Washington, and California, Jewish women along with Protestant peers in women's clubs expanded their demand that public agencies deal more fully with the needs of the poor, especially immigrants.[103] Julia Swett, who would succeed her husband, Isaac, as director of Portland's Federation of Jewish Charities in the mid-1920s, informed Oregon's citizens in 1916 that Portland's Council of Jewish Women, "through our Civic Committee, have affiliated ourselves with practically every move for a city beautiful and city wholesome."[104] Volunteers in effect became social workers by speaking to administrators of neighborhood schools on behalf of immigrant households to arrange for medical services and to establish after-school playgrounds. Even more ambitiously, several women became volunteer caseworkers for the new juvenile courts, where they gained supervisory powers over Jewish children placed in Jewish foster homes.[105] As late as 1924 in Los Angeles, Judge Harry Archibald of the juvenile court attended a council meeting to praise the work of its children's bureau, which then had sixty-seven girls in its charge.[106]

Jewish women's activism bringing new social services to immigrants was only part of an effort to make Jewish welfare services conform to progressive ideas about how to assist the poor. As a consequence, women even more than men moved Jewish philanthropy from the pioneer era when benevolence was based on a sense of personal obligation to an era when professional training would determine how support would be dispensed and who would speak for the Jewish community in the burgeoning social service network.[107] In addition, the new coalition of community leaders would recognize the social mobility of newcomers, both as members of new boards of directors and in the activities that Jewish philanthropy would sponsor. As the B'nai B'rith lodges consolidated and as the various welfare institutions were federated for fund-raising and budgeting, a new elite, still based in part on pioneer families, came to organize Jewish communal affairs. The elite, however, was inclusive, because assertive men and women among Eastern European immigrants, as well as welfare professionals, assumed leadership positions. But the more the federation of Jewish philanthropy and the professional training for leadership along the Pacific slope came to resemble larger communities in the East, the more local leaders felt they were reinforcing a regional distinctiveness because of the leadership that Jews provided for the broader community.

In cities like Chicago, Boston, Philadelphia, and even New York, non-Jews provided much of the leadership in settlement work and philanthropy. But on the Pacific Coast, Jewish Neighborhood Houses, working girls homes, innovative orphanages, and individual social workers set the regional standards.[108] As William Blumenthal, executive director of the Los Angeles Jewish Federation, noted in his annual report in February 1924, the Los Angeles community chest had finally been organized, largely through the efforts of the local Jewish community. "In making the community chest a success," he noted, "more will be expected from us than from any other group, and we will have to respond in the spirit of noblesse oblige." As a story in the next issue of the *B'nai B'rith Messenger* noted, the Jewish community "has long been held up as a model by the leaders of charitable work in the city of Los Angeles."[109]

The process of modernization began with the consolidation of the many small B'nai B'rith lodges.[110] The cities of the American West spawned hundreds of Masonic lodges, and Jewish merchants, as a statement of their personal interests and of their high social status, were elected to high office in the most prestigious. But as young men with families, they also initiated B'nai B'rith lodges for basic welfare benefits and for conviviality. By the 1860s San Francisco had more than half a dozen small B'nai B'rith lodges, and by the 1880s Portland had three and Los Angeles at least two. The San Francisco lodges took the lead to create District Grand Lodge No. 4, and in the early twentieth century local lodges sent delegations consisting of the most prominent businessmen, Reform rabbis and other professionals to the annual regional conventions.

As the pioneer generation passed away and as their sons acquired life insurance from national carriers, the B'nai B'rith nationally eliminated its life insurance function, thus making it easier for lodges who had members in different age brackets to coalesce. To promote its new emphasis on benevolence, fund-raising for regional orphanages, sanitariums for tubercular patients, and resettlement work for immigrants, the national headquarters officially recommended that the many small lodges in large cities consolidate. When District Grand Lodge No. 4, following national guidelines, eliminated its insurance pool, a new lodge absorbed the two older lodges in Los Angeles. The new lodge constructed its own building and attracted younger men who did not care about the old insurance feature. New rabbis Hecht and Myers joined, and the lodge followed the philanthropic program of the national headquarters by paying dues to a new local Jewish hospital and by sponsoring families sent west by the Industrial Removal Office and the Galveston Project. In 1910, Lodge No. 487 succeeded in attracting young businessmen and

became the largest in the District Grand Lodge.[111]

In Portland, the process of consolidation was somewhat different, but the consequence of attracting men of various social backgrounds to support modern communal philanthropy was the same. In 1910, Portland still had four B'nai B'rith lodges, when a core of sixty men formed the B'nai B'rith Building Association to construct a new community center for social and educational purposes. The board of directors consisted of fifteen successful businessmen from both the Reform and Conservative synagogues. Their new building, completed in October 1914, was located midway between the central business district and a middle-class residential neighborhood where many members owned homes. It featured a swimming pool and showers, a gymnasium, meeting rooms, and a large hall for entertainment. As its executive director, Harry Kenin, noted in the mid-1920s, "Unlike settlement houses it is not imposed by the well-to-do on the poor; it is to be democratic and self-governing."[112] By 1914, three of the four Portland lodges had coalesced into a consolidated Lodge No. 65, and by 1919 the last holdout had joined.[113] In early 1921, District Grand Lodge No. 4 voted to allow only one lodge per city, and by January 1922 the two lodges in Seattle finally consolidated. Only San Francisco still had more than one, though within a few years they too merged. This belated settlement of petty differences in San Francisco led Rabbi Louis Newman of Temple Emanu-El to chastise the new lodge for depriving the community of a much-needed building similar to the community center in Portland.[114]

Like the consolidation of B'nai B'rith lodges, the formation of welfare federations was promoted by visitors from cities like Chicago and New York but had the consequence of enabling local philanthropic leaders to create an even wider sense of community cohesiveness, self-reliance, and a need for professional management. In January 1910, Dr. Martin Meyer returned to his native San Francisco to succeed the late Jacob Voorsanger as rabbi at Emanu-El. Meyer was known for his philanthropic and civic work in Brooklyn, where he especially worked to create a federation of Jewish welfare organizations. Within six months, and with the support of Rabbi Nieto, he had persuaded the heads of the Eureka and First Hebrew Benevolent Societies, the Emanu-El Sisterhood, Mount Zion Hospital, a Free Loan Society, and the many women's benevolent societies to federate for fund-raising and for an equitable distribution of the proceeds. Under the leadership of Judge M. C. Sloss, an initial annual income of $135,000 was assured.[115] In 1911, Judge Julian Mack of Chicago urged Los Angeles's Congregation B'nai B'rith, whose members were then the largest supporters of Jewish charitable institutions like the Kaspare Cohn Hospital, to consolidate its fund-raising through a subscription list, as had just occurred in his home city.[116] By 1912, Los Angeles had also created a federation of its many welfare institutions.

When war broke out in Europe in September 1914, fund-raising for devastated Jewish communities, and then for Zionist projects in Palestine, substantially increased, and local leaders felt pressured to further rationalize fund-raising. After observing prolonged competitive efforts to raise funds for Jewish communities in Europe, for Yishuv projects in Palestine's Jewish settlements, and for local immigrant families, a consolidated Jewish leadership in Oakland and in Portland in 1920 had created federations, as did Spokane in 1922. Now participating agencies had to submit monthly reports and annual statements and make the case for their operating budgets.[117] In Portland a subcommittee headed by Ben Selling from the

Portland Committee on Relief of Jewish War Sufferers drew up a constitution for a federation that included the various men's and women's benevolent societies, the B'nai B'rith Building Association, Neighborhood House and the Portland Hebrew School. By January 1920, Federated Jewish Societies, with support from the owners of the leading department stores, as well as Eastern Europeans like Nathan Director, David Nemerovsky, and Orthodox rabbi Isaac Faivusovitch, initiated a campaign to raise fifty thousand dollars and quickly joined the community chest. Isaac Swett, a lawyer of Russian descent who was well known for his interest in issues of unemployment and immigration, was named executive director. By 1921, the component agencies had a budget of thirty-five thousand dollars.[118] Seattle's Jewish charitable organizations joined the local community chest but did not manage to organize a formal federation until 1925. With due pride Philip Tworoger, who wrote a weekly column for the *Jewish Transcript*, noted that "there is a movement on foot to form a federation of Protestant Charities patterned after the Federation of Jewish Charities. Imitation is the sincerest form of flattery, assuming that flattery ever can be sincere."[119]

The federation process not only made remote communities feel modern but also promoted an internal succession of communal leadership. Eastern European Jews like the Shemanskys and Sierotys, who had made new fortunes by creating a chain of low-priced clothing stores, the Directors and Mosessohns, and the movie moguls Louis B. Mayer and Harry Warner gained prestige as key fund-raisers. Within welfare agencies professionally trained administrators introduced national standards and emerged as knowledgeable new spokesmen. As a cadre of men, including Irving Lipsitch and Samuel C. Kohs, moved their expertise from city to city, they created standards of professionalism and a network of contacts that tied the Jewish communities of the region more tightly together. While many of their ideas about fund-raising, management, and social work strategies may have been brought from New York or Chicago, their ability to work with descendants of pioneer bankers and department store heirs, as well as newcomers growing wealthy from motion pictures, scrap metal, or clothing manufacture, helped a new generation of the philanthropic leaders coalesce. Using innovative forms of entertainment, they were able to raise unprecedented sums and especially in Los Angeles to erect new civic landmarks.

The intersecting careers of Kohs and Lipsitch illustrate how the local elite came to look to secular professionals for communal leadership and how the communities, as they shared the federation experience, came to coalesce as a distinctive regional entity. Kohs, originally from New York, came to Stanford University, then a leading institution in developing intelligence testing, to earn a doctorate in psychology. In 1918, he became an assistant professor at the new Reed College in Portland, where the juvenile court soon hired him as a consultant. His reputation led the governor to appoint him to a state-funded committee with Rabbi Jonah Wise, Adolph Wolfe, and Charles F. Berg to promote sex education in the public schools, and he was hired by the University of Oregon to teach advanced psychology courses through its Portland extension program. In addition, his commitment to Zionism and his membership in the newly consolidated B'nai B'rith lodge made him a frequent speaker and fund-raiser in the Jewish community. By 1924, Kohs had moved to the Bay Area as the superintendent of the Jewish Federation of Oakland. There he supervised the construction of a community center with a modern gymnasium and large meet-ing rooms, much like the B'nai B'rith building in Portland. He was welcomed by the director of the Emanu-El Sisterhood Home in San Francisco, Ethel R. Feineman, who invited Kohs and his wife for Shabbat dinner with the young ladies, followed by a brief talk about his work.[120]

In the Bay Area, Kohs found, in addition to social work professionals, Rabbi Rudolph Coffee of Temple Sinai of Oakland, who, like Kohs, held an academic doctorate as well as a rabbinical degree from the Jewish Theological Seminary. Coffee championed many causes, including world disarmament, birth control, and prison reform, and he headed the statewide Jewish Committee of Personal Service that ministered to Jews in state prisons. In January 1924, the governor of California appointed Coffee to the State Board of Charities and Corrections, with responsibility for overseeing state prisons. When he left Temple Sinai in 1933, he became chaplain at San Quentin.[121]

Irving Lipsitch directed San Francisco's Eureka Benevolent Society and was also the superintendent of social services for the federation. When Lipsitch moved on to Los Angeles, where the rapidly growing population expressed an even greater need for fund-raising, Kohs moved across the Bay to succeed him in both positions.[122] Kohs, an outspoken Zionist, developed a distinctive philosophy of social work, which emphasized that respect for Jewish cultural continuity should provide the basis for a communal responsibility binding the donors to the recipients of philanthropy. In the Bay Area, he came to believe that both the federation's wealthiest contributors and most social workers ignored the potential of Jewish cultural education in assisting Jews who might need social services. He found the Board of the Eureka Benevolent Society ignorant of professional "best practices," with some members openly hostile to the cultural foundations of his program. "One of these members is a person who believes that she knows everything that requires to be known about social work, is very sarcastic and bitter in her remarks and is an assimilist [sic] of the first order."[123] Pursuing his vision in what he felt would be a more congenial climate, he left in 1928 to head the Brooklyn Jewish Federation.[124]

The fluid situation in Los Angeles created an attractive position for a coordinator and chief fund-raiser for the growing federation's many welfare services. Boris Bogen, who had gained a national reputation as the superintendent of the Jewish Federation in Cincinnati and then as director of the Joint Distribution Committee work in Russia, for family reasons accepted an offer to direct the Jewish Federation in Los Angeles in 1924. There he organized an unprecedented campaign to raise one million dollars to build a new home for the Kaspare Cohn Hospital, new cottages for the orphanage at Vista Del Mar, and a YMHA and several Talmud Torahs for Boyle Heights. He expressed rather fulsome praise for the old Jewish banking elite for supporting new federation work, but he was also careful to recruit the new Hollywood and garment industry wealth (many like himself brought as children from Eastern Europe) as presidents of fund-raising campaigns.[125] He induced the Jewish Welfare Federation to join the community chest, before leaving in 1926 to become executive director of the national B'nai B'rith.

Lipsitch, as Bogen's successor, was already well known among the social elite on the boards of the various Los Angeles welfare institutions, and he set about expanding fund-raising and serving on a plethora of committees. Campaigns were then under way to relieve the debt of the Consumptive Relief Hospital, to build a new home for incurables and an innovative orphan's home, to replace the obsolete Kaspare Cohn Hospital, to expand a Jewish Aid Society for Boyle Heights, and to create a series of community-supported educational institutions; and Lipsitch was involved in every one. He took an equally active role in raising funds to meet the Los Angeles quota for displaced Jews in Poland under the United Jewish Appeal, for Zionist projects in Palestine, and for all manner of B'nai B'rith fund-raising.[126] One following his activities in the *B'nai B'rith Messenger*, reading his reports for the federation (also printed in the *Messenger*), and following accounts of parallel work in San Francisco and Portland could see how Jewish communities along the Pacific Coast tried systematically to bring transparency to their budget process and to include the interest of all segments of local Jewry in their philanthropy.[127]

And philanthropy, now managed by a professionally trained rather than a patriarchal elite, had become virtually the definition of what the community did. As Rabbi Louis Newman noted in early 1929: "In the Far West we . . . have endeavored to finds points of emphasis by which Jewish life might maintain its vigor. The high rank of western Jewry in the general commonwealth is taken for granted. The officially chosen leading citizens of at least two of our coast cities are Jews. It is edifying to behold that the very leaders of prominence in the general community are at the same time the foremost Jewish spokesmen, communal workers and philanthropists."[128]

Although San Francisco's earthquake and fire rebuilding called attention to established rabbis, bankers, and leading merchants, the other major cities of the region grew at a more rapid rate, and the center of gravity for the region and for its Jewish communities moved elsewhere. Seattle surpassed Portland in population in 1910, and both cities continued to show steady growth through the

1930s by intensifying the development of timber, ranching, and farming along rail and water routes into the interior.[129] With the discovery of petroleum and the availability of abundant new sources of water, Los Angeles by 1910 had acquired the possibility for dynamic growth. By 1920 its population surpassed San Francisco's, and by 1930, with huge federal subsidies for harbor development and the passage of ships through the Panama Canal, its economy soared and its population exceeded one million, making it more than twice as large as San Francisco and the country's fifth largest city.[130] Jews were instrumental in the expansion of Los Angeles by creating a new industry, the motion pictures, as well as starting an innovative clothing industry with close ties to the fashions popularized by the movies' glamorous stars.[131] From the rebuilding of San Francisco to the establishment of the Hollywood studios, regional Jewry believed that they were building on their pioneer heritage, further demonstrating their civic leadership and innovative entrepreneurship. As Los Angeles eclipsed San Francisco as the center of the region's continuing growth, Jewish capital and the Jewish community continued to be major innovators and conspicuous players. But the majority of the new Jewish population and most of the new business venturers were newcomers, who traced their roots to Eastern rather than to Central Europe.

3 EASTERN EUROPEANS, SEPHARDIM, AND THE BELATED CREATION OF JEWISH SPACE

He has been self-supporting and desires
to have his wife and children sent out here.

Early in 1882, Kayla Lauterstein joined a group of at least twenty families from Odessa, Russia, aiming to establish a Jewish agricultural colony in the United States. Kayla, her husband, Hirsch, and her four children traveled with her two brothers and their families and three of Hirsch's siblings. By 1883, they were among the forty families that had filed homestead claims in Painted Woods, North Dakota (fig. 3.1).

While several of the families stayed on at Painted Woods through the end of the decade, Hirsch's sudden death ended Kayla's venture in farming. She took her children to Bismarck, where the oldest son worked and Kayla took in boarders. Two of them, Israel Bromberg and his son Harry, were related to Painted Woods settlers. Within a few years, Kayla and Israel married, boarded the train with their newly merged family, and headed west to Portland, where they subsequently had five more children. There, they became pioneers for a vast network of relatives and former colonists who settled in Portland over the next two decades.

The Brombergs, the first of their extended family to arrive in Portland, were in the vanguard of Eastern European migrants, most of whom did not reach western cities until after the turn of the century. The Brombergs' early arrival, along with the experience and skills they had gained during their sojourn in North Dakota, launched them into

75

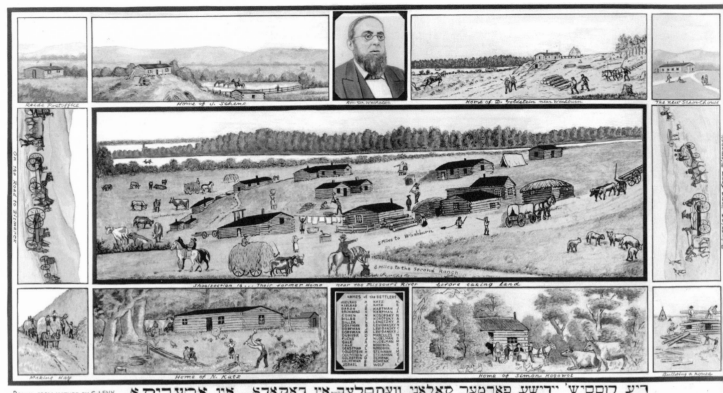

DRAWN FROM NATURE BY S. LEVY   אין אמעריקא   די רוססיש ידישע פארמער קאלאני וועקסלער אין דאקאדא

THE RUSSIAN JEWISH FARMER SETTLEMENT WECHSLER
BURLEIGH COUNTY DAKOTA TERRITORY.

COPYRIGHTED BY T. W. INGERSOLL

FIG. 3.1   *Kayla Lauterstein Bromberg and Israel Bromberg (ca. 1880s) immigrated to the United States as part of a group that established the Painted Woods agricultural colony in North Dakota. The pair met in North Dakota, married, and relocated to Portland, Ore., where Bromberg became a community leader. Jacob Rader Marcus Center of the American Jewish Archives, Cincinnati.*

positions of communal leadership. Israel, for example, helped organize the Portland Hebrew School and became a leader in Zionist circles.[1]

In western cities like Seattle, Portland, and Los Angeles, coreligionists from the Mediterranean soon joined Eastern Europeans like the Brombergs. Newcomers like Solomon Calvo and Jacob Policar from Marmara, a Turkish island near Istanbul, and Marco Franco, a native of Rhodes, became the founders of substantial Sephardic communities,

which in the context of smaller West Coast communities loomed more significant than in the East. Franco, who arrived in Seattle in 1909, was part of a chain migration that brought Sephardic Jews to the Pacific Coast beginning in 1902. Initially, the young men constituted a bachelor society tenuously connected to an established community of Ashkenazic Jews who viewed them as alien. The Sephardim, in turn, felt more comfortable in Seattle's Greek coffeehouses than in the established

Jewish shops and institutions. By the time Franco brought over his wife, Rosa, in 1910, a number of the bachelors had married. Their extended families joined them, and the community soon established institutions including three small synagogues based on regional groupings, from Rodosto, Marmara, and Rhodes.

Like so many of his colleagues, Franco began as a bootblack. In 1911, he joined the ranks of Sephardic small businessmen, when he opened a produce stand in the Pike Place Public Market. Franco maintained his stand until 1938, while expanding his business to include approximately fifteen additional grocery stores and delis in locations from San Francisco to Bellingham.[2] He also became a leader in the emerging Sephardic Jewish community, helping in 1914 to found Ezra Bessaroth, a congregation of immigrants from Rhodes, and served terms both as president of the congregation and as head of its Talmud Torah. Like a number of other Sephardic immigrants, Franco also joined the Reform Temple De Hirsch, in approximately 1920. As his son, Albert, explained, "I think it was part of what he considered to be the Americanization process. He himself never attended [Temple De Hirsch]—he went to the Sephardic synagogue. Thinking back and knowing my father, he wanted his children to have contact with other segments, outside of the Sephardic community. He saw this as a way, I believe, of giving his children a broader community perspective."[3]

Decades after Kayla Lauterstein Bromberg's arrival in Portland and Marco Franco's arrival in Seattle, Gershon Einbinder—known to his readers by his pen name, Chaver Paver—arrived in Los Angeles. Born in Bessarabia in 1901, Einbinder had immigrated to New York in 1924. By the time he relocated to Los Angeles sometime in the 1930s, he was a well-known Yiddish author of short stories,

novels, children's books, and plays. Although the Los Angeles Jewish community developed late—it numbered only twenty-five hundred in 1900—by the time Einbinder arrived in what he called "America's Paradise," the city had been transformed into a vital immigrant Jewish center, rich with Jewish culture and boasting a network of Yiddish writers, speakers, and theatrical productions. Einbinder vividly conveyed a sense of the cultural world that he found in Los Angeles when he wrote of the arrival of one of his characters, Zalmen the cobbler, in the city: "On Brooklyn Avenue we got to a trolley-car into which we had to climb a few ladder-like steps. It was filled, homey, and noisy with many Jews speaking Yiddish, much as in their own homes. From what I heard, I gathered many of them were going down-town to a Workmen's Circle meeting and many others were on their way to the lecture to which Noah and I were going."[4] Just as the fictional Zalmen finds ample opportunity to attend Yiddish lectures and theater, Einbinder found an eager audience for his talents, writing and adapting a script for a Federal Theater Project production in 1938 and writing a screenplay for a Yiddish film produced in 1937. The Jewish Angelenos who formed the Chaver Paver Book Club enthusiastically supported his activities by publishing several of his works, beginning in the 1940s.

The stories of Bromberg, Franco, and Einbinder suggest the distinctive patterns that characterized the stream of Jewish migrants who arrived in the Pacific West during the late nineteenth and early twentieth centuries, after the pioneer generation had already consolidated their business, civic, and fraternal networks. As the story of the Bromberg suggests, the route that Eastern European Jewish immigrants took was often circuitous, particularly for those who arrived in the West before the turn of the century. Like Kayla and Israel, these migrants often lived in America for several years prior to finding their way to the Pacific Coast. Sojourns in places like North Dakota that were far removed from eastern immigrant centers allowed them to become acclimated before their arrival in the Pacific West. In contrast, for Sephardim like Franco, direct immigration was typical. While Sephardim who arrived during the colonial period are recognized as America's first Jews, historians often overlook the arrival of immigrants from the eastern Mediterranean in the early twentieth century, in part because they were so few compared to the flood of migrants from Eastern Europe. Yet in several Pacific Coast cities—particularly Los Angeles and Seattle—the new Sephardim were quite visible and made these Jewish communities uniquely diverse. Still, the Jewish migration to western cities was far smaller than in the East, and the emergence of visibly Jewish communities like that celebrated by Einbinder was delayed in the West. Los Angeles provides an exaggerated example of this pattern: a small Jewish mercantile settlement at the beginning of the twentieth century, the city's Jewish community would become the country's second largest by mid-century.

The mass migration of Jews from Eastern Europe, beginning in the 1880s, has long been considered the major turning point in American Jewish history. Newcomers overwhelmed northeastern and midwestern Jewish communities, and established members of these communities often regarded the immigrants with a mixture of pity, disdain, and a modicum of responsibility. Arriving from Russia and other Eastern European countries belatedly experiencing the dislocations of industrialization, the new immigrants came from a milieu in which Yiddish was the lingua franca and religious ritual was relatively untouched by reform. Many had congregated in industry rather than trade,

and those who had moved to cities like Vilna and Bialystok had been influenced by radical ideologies and trade unionism rather than by the bourgeois values embraced by established American Jews. Unlike the Reform establishment, which regarded America as their promised land, many of the newcomers embraced Zionism. While northeastern and midwestern Jewish communities experimented with strategies to divert the immigrants or acculturate them to American norms and values, the numbers were simply overwhelming. They reshaped Jewish communities in the East and Midwest quite rapidly and in profound ways.

Although new immigrants also had an impact on Jewish communities in the Pacific West, their arrival was far less divisive, in part because it was more gradual. Because few opportunities for industrial employment existed in the West, the region attracted immigrants who, like their predecessors, generally engaged in trade. Differences of wealth and culture did mark western Jewish communities, but they were less frequently felt as *class* conflict between owners and employees than they were in eastern and midwestern communities. The distinctive Jewish ethnic mix in the West also helped to mitigate the gap between newcomers and pioneers, because established Jews from Posen, with their mixed German and Polish identities, bridged the gap between old-timers and newcomers. In addition, the influx of Sephardim diverted attention from tensions between Germans and Eastern Europeans. More broadly, the unique racial diversity of the West, where Jews had long been accepted as pioneers and in a more abstract way as "white," alleviated concerns about anti-Semitism that in eastern cities had shaped the response of Jewish leaders to Yiddish-speaking immigrants.[5] Although such problems were not entirely absent, western Jews pointed with pride to their good fortune. As a turn-of-the-century chronicler of Spokane's rapidly growing Jewish community boasted, "Anti-Semitism, inequality, or distinctions between [Jews] and . . . the other nationalities is entirely unknown here."[6] Such perceptions molded both the responses of existing Jewish communities to the newcomers and the identity of the new migrants and encouraged the development of communities that were relatively open and less insular than their eastern counterparts.

GRADUAL MIGRANTS:
EASTERN EUROPEANS

Eastern European Jewish immigrants came to the Far West later and in far smaller numbers than they did to the East (fig. 3.2). While New York's Jewish population grew between 1880 and 1900 from eighty-five thousand to five hundred thousand, growth in the West, although impressive in percentage terms, was numerically far less dramatic.[7] Los Angeles's Jewish community grew from just more than three hundred individuals in 1878 to twenty-five hundred in 1900.[8] Between 1896 and 1906, only about six thousand Jews came to San Francisco, despite its status in the 1870s as the second largest Jewish community in America.[9] The Hebrew Sheltering and Immigrant Aid Society of America reported that among the 66,577 Jews arriving in American ports in 1915, more than 80 percent were bound for northern and central Atlantic states and less than 1 percent for the West. Even among those who entered through Galveston, Texas, under a program designed to divert the flow of immigrants away from the East, fewer than 10 percent planned to settle in the mountain or western states.[10] As New York's Jewish population inched toward one million in 1910 and Chicago's passed one hundred thousand, San Francisco Jews still numbered only about thirty thousand, and no other West Coast city was over the ten thousand mark.[11] Although the influx seemed substantial to local Jewish leaders, the total number of immigrants in nearly every western city remained relatively small.

The influx was also gradual. In Portland, the Jewish community grew by four thousand (counting both new arrivals and natural increase) between 1878 and 1910 and by only seven thousand more by 1927; in Oakland, the population increased by approximately seventeen hundred between 1878 and 1910 and by four thousand more by 1927. Seattle's Jewish community took until 1940 to top ten thousand.[12] As early as 1900, immigrants made up four-fifths of the total Jewish population in New York, but in 1906 they comprised only one-fifth of the San Francisco Jewish community.[13]

Even this modest growth was limited to the larger Jewish communities. Lee Shai Weissbach has demonstrated that the mass immigration of Eastern Europeans did not dramatically increase the size of many small Jewish communities. His figures suggest that the migration had only a limited effect on small western communities founded in the mid-nineteenth century, many of which dwindled or vanished despite the "mass migration." Jewish populations in California towns like Novilland, San Bernardino, and Santa Cruz shrank or even disappeared in this period, as did Oregon pioneer Jewish communities like Roseburg, Jacksonville, and Baker.[14] In the South, by contrast, Weissbach demonstrates that Eastern European immigrants contributed to the growth of existing small communities and even founded new Jewish centers.[15] Although the later migrants did establish new communities in western cities like Spokane and Belling-

SOUTH-דרום

FIG. 3.2 *Yiddish map of the United States, published in a 1912 guidebook for Jewish immigrants. John Foster Carr, Guide to the United States for the Jewish Immigrant, American Jewish Historical Society, Newton Centre, Mass., and New York.*

ham,[16] the Jews who came West during the period of mass migration more likely settled in one of the region's few major cities than did either their counterparts in the South or their predecessors who had arrived in the West between 1849 and 1880.

The general pattern during the period of mass migration, then, was one of slow and relatively late growth and overwhelming concentration in the four major cities of Seattle, Portland, San Francisco, and Los Angeles. Although the mass immigration of Eastern European Jews to the United States is usually dated to the 1880s, its first impact on the West was delayed until the 1890s and, in some cases, after 1900. In San Francisco, Oakland,

and Portland, the earliest arriving Russians joined existing congregations and did not establish their own institutions until the early 1890s.[17] Seattle's Chevrah Bikur Cholim, founded in 1891 as a mutual aid and burial society, began holding services during the 1890s. It did not become formally incorporated as an Orthodox congregation until 1900, a year before the first Orthodox synagogue in Spokane.[18] In Los Angeles, the first traditional Eastern European shul was founded in 1899.[19] A history of the Los Angeles Jewish community notes the impact of an influx of Protestant midwesterners in the 1890s but fails to mention the immigration of Eastern Europeans as an issue until after the turn of the century.[20] Indeed, according to Max Vorspan and Lloyd P. Gartner, "The first surge of able-bodied East European Jews to Los Angeles seems to have taken place in 1904."[21] A distinctive Jewish neighborhood did not emerge there until the early 1920s.[22] The pattern in the West was distinctive: while Jewish immigration to the eastern cities peaked in 1906–7 and restrictions drastically reduced the number of newcomers in the 1920s, the greatest growth in Jewish population in the West took place *after* 1920.

One explanation for these patterns is the indirect route many of the migrants took. Early-twentieth-century records for Jewish communities along the West Coast demonstrate that immigrants rarely entered the country directly through western ports. Prior to their arrival in the West they often sojourned for months or years elsewhere in the United States or Canada. Of 122 identifiable Jewish immigrants who completed their naturalization in Seattle between 1907 and 1914, only 13 entered the country through that port, suggesting that the overwhelming majority had taken some overland route to the Northwest. A majority (66 percent) first arrived in eastern ports, most often

New York. One found his way from Galveston to Seattle, while 24 (20 percent) apparently sojourned in Canada.[23] Not until World War I made travel across the Atlantic dangerous because of German submarine attacks did western ports become a significant source for Jewish arrivals. In its annual report for 1916, the Hebrew Sheltering and Immigrant Aid Society of America noted the establishment of new branches in San Francisco and Seattle and expressed the hope that "directing the immigration current through the Pacific Coast" would lead more newcomers to settle in the West. Yet even during the war years, when Jewish immigration became "unusually active" on the Pacific Coast, the society reported the number of entries through these western ports was in the hundreds, not the thousands seen in the East.[24]

Families not only commonly entered the country via eastern ports or through Canada but also spent years living in North America, often in places quite distant from Jewish centers, prior to their arrival in the Pacific West. Among eighty-three Russian Jewish families who arrived in Portland during the 1890s, for example, at least thirty-one sojourned in other western or midwestern states before their arrival in Oregon.[25] This number includes eighteen families, like the Brombergs, who joined Jewish agricultural communities in the Dakotas during the 1880s and early 1890s. Census and immigration records provide evidence of such sojourns by listing the children born in the American hinterland. Immigrants filing naturalization papers in Seattle had children born in places as diverse as Duluth, Minnesota; Trinidad, Colorado; Des Moines, Iowa; and Winnipeg, Manitoba.[26] Early Portland arrivals sojourned not only in the Dakotas but also in places as diverse as New Jersey, New Mexico, and Missouri.[27] In the southern California city of Venice, an ocean-side suburb of Los Angeles, Amy

Hill Shevitz found that four out of five immigrant Jews in the 1920 census had been in the United States for more than twenty years and that "their sojourns on the way to California had taken them through a variety of American settings, several in the East (New York, Pennsylvania) but also in the Midwest (Ohio, Illinois, Wisconsin, Missouri) and the West (Colorado, Oregon). Several families of Russian origin came down from Canada . . . several families had lived in Nebraska."[28] Eastern European migrants to Oakland, notes Fred Rosenbaum, "penetrated the vast American West only gradually."[29] Vorspan and Gartner argue that although the increase in Los Angeles's Jewish population in the 1890s and early 1900s coincided with the mass migrations, "very few immigrants came directly from the ship to southern California."[30]

Oral histories confirm this pattern, with immigrants often recounting lengthy stays in eastern cities, in rural areas, or in Canada. Julius Shafer, who arrived in Seattle in 1890 as a teenager, first sojourned in Kansas and Texas, working for uncles who had migrated earlier.[31] Rachel Silverstone, whose family left Romania in 1898, spent about two decades living in Montreal and then Toronto, before moving to Everett, Washington.[32] Likewise, Sol Krems, a Polish immigrant who became editor of Seattle's *Jewish Voice*, learned the printing trade in London and lived in both Montreal and Vancouver prior to his arrival in Seattle in the early 1900s.[33]

While many of these immigrants, like their predecessors in the pioneer generation, had worked as peddlers during their sojourns, others had moved to the hinterland to try their hand at farming. Train routes that linked the Dakotas to the Pacific Northwest made Seattle and Portland natural destinations for families like the Brombergs and the Nudelmans, who had first settled in Jewish agricultural colonies on the northern Great Plains. The Nieder family farmed in Missouri and Illinois and joined the gold rush to Alaska, before settling in Seattle during the first decade of the twentieth century.[34] Fanny Heppner remembered that her father homesteaded in Barber County, Kansas, as part of a group of approximately twenty Jewish families who set out from Pittsburgh. After giving up farming, the group relocated to Wichita and "then, one by one, they came to San Francisco in 1888. Only two or three of them stayed there [in Kansas]."[35]

Not all aspiring farmers abandoned their agrarian dreams before arriving in the Far West. Idealists of the Am Olam movement, aiming to establish a network of communal agrarian settlements in the United States, created New Odessa in southern Oregon in 1883. Traveling together from Odessa, Ukraine, to New York and then on to Oregon, the group of about fifty, mostly men, recruited an experienced gentile communitarian to guide them and established a colony where they practiced vegetarianism, engaged in mutual criticism, and worked at "perfecting and development of physical, mental and moral capacities of its members [*sic*]."[36] After five years, a fire and disagreements over leadership tore them apart. A few returned to New York, but several New Odessa colonists remained in the West, some settling in or near Portland.[37]

Western Jews who had sojourned in agricultural colonies, independent farms, or the smaller towns of the Midwest or West ultimately congregated in the region's major cities. As Weissbach notes, the tendency of American Jews "to gravitate toward the country's more important urban centers" was particularly pronounced in the West.[38] Like the Jewish agriculturalists who left North Dakota or southern Oregon for Portland, nearly all of the twenty-five Jewish families that had homesteaded in Republic, Washington, relocated to Seattle during the first two decades of the twentieth century.[39] Such migrations, while consistent with national Jewish settlement patterns, also reflect the western context: in a region that is often associated with homesteading and other frontier activities, as early as the 1880s, the West was "the most urbanized" region in the United States.[40] For Jewish immigrants, an important exception to this pattern would develop when the rural settlement of Petaluma, California, became in the 1920s a community of chicken ranchers.[41]

Circuitous migrations were characteristic of immigrant Jews who were lured to California by its healthful climate. Vorspan and Gartner found that "a high proportion of Los Angeles' arrivals consisted of the health-seeking group, unfortunate consumptives who made their way to the Pacific Coast in search of healing."[42] Careful study of death certificates, records of children born in Colorado (which, like southern California, was often recommended to those with tuberculosis, or T.B., and other respiratory diseases), and Jewish women's childbearing patterns led the historian Mitchell Brian Gelfand to conclude that "the search to recover the health of a family member prompted a significant number of Jews to come to Los Angeles."[43] For example, Russian-born Fanny Jaffe Sharlip reached Los Angeles around 1900 after contracting T.B. in the sweatshops of Philadelphia. With her husband, Ben, she joined others seeking a cure in the California sun.[44]

By the 1920s, when the community grew most rapidly, immigrant health seekers had been replaced by American Jews, and the typical newcomer was "an acculturated European immigrant or his grown sons [and daughters] who had some resources and were allured by Los Angeles' economic opportunities and not indifferent to its climate."[45] As early as 1900, half of Los Angeles's Eastern European Jewish immigrants had lived in the United States for at least fifteen years, and roughly 80 percent of them had already obtained American citizenship.[46] In other words, it is important to think of these newcomers not just as Jewish immigrants but as *American* Jews, who, like other Americans, were attracted to the West by its spectacular economic growth and its mild, healthful climate.

Throughout the West, the migration of already acculturated immigrants persisted. A 1922 study of the Jewish immigrant district in Seattle found that in the neighborhood most heavily populated by Jewish immigrants, the overwhelming majority of grammar school students—80 percent—were born in the United States. While approximately 240 of these students reported that Yiddish was their parents' native language, only 138 reported speaking Yiddish at home.[47] Immigrants who had lived for several years in rural America not only were likely to be conversant in English but also had valuable experiences that greenhorns lacked. Homesteaders, for example, had dealt with government agents, bankers, and local authorities. In some cases, they had even held public office, as was the case with several North Dakota colonists who served as members of the school board before relocating to Portland.[48] Such experiences proved invaluable in the creation of new congregations and other community institutions and in the establishment of immigrant-run businesses (fig. 3.3). With few manufacturing jobs available, most immigrant Jews to the West entered the trade sector (fig. 3.4).[49] As small-scale merchants, peddlers, and junk dealers, these newcomers—unlike their garment-working counterparts in cities like New York—had to be able to interact with a clientele that was not Jewish.

FIG. 3.3 *Dora Levine with her daughter Esther in front of her Portland fish market, ca. 1910. Levine, in an interview confided, "I had to attend one year eight hundred pounds carp to sell myself and cut salmon, halibut, black cod, white fish" (Lowenstein, Jews of Oregon, 96). Oregon Jewish Museum OJM265.*

FORMING ETHNIC COMMUNITIES

In addition to easing the transition into western communities, the indirect route to the West likely reinforced a less than traditional religious outlook among early arriving Russian Jewish immigrants. In discussing the mass migration of Eastern European Jews to the United States, Jonathan Sarna writes,

Those who departed were by no means a microcosm of those left behind. It is too much to claim, as one expert did in 1904, that "the most enterprising, the most robust, the better off or the least wretched, alone succeeded in leaving"; and it is likewise an exaggeration to assert, as a more recent scholar did, that "only the poor and the not very learned came." What can be said with certainty is that fervently religious Jews and those who sought to spend their days engaged in Jewish learn-

FIG. 3.4 *Mosler's Bakery (ca. 1936) became a Portland institution. Oregon Jewish Museum OJM641.*

ing immigrated much less frequently than those more temperate in their beliefs and more enterprising in their ambitions.[50]

Eastern European Jews who entered the country through New York and tarried in places such as North Dakota, Manitoba, or Kansas had twice made the decision to leave a place with a strong Jewish infrastructure for one with little or none. In discussing Jewish immigrants in general, Sarna suggests that the process of migration itself "loosed

East European Jews from their religious moorings, or, alternatively, that the immigrant stream included a disproportionate number of those who had abandoned their faith years earlier." Sarna concluded that "both propositions are likely correct."[51] If such trends are evident in the migration from Eastern Europe to the United States, migration from the East to the Pacific West—and the various sojourns in between—likely magnified them.

Certainly, living in rural America often signaled

a willingness to compromise or abandon traditional practice. Although oral histories and personal accounts show that some Jews made heroic efforts, it was exceedingly difficult to maintain traditional religious requirements in isolated locales. Families unwilling to compromise on dietary laws and ritual observance were unlikely to relocate to communities where rabbis, *shochatim*, and synagogues were unavailable. As Reva Clar writes in her memoir of Jewish life in the San Joaquin Valley in the early twentieth century, "Like many of the Jewish families who arrived in the small communities of the Far West . . . my grandparents abandoned the practice of *kashruth* for practical reasons."[52] Whether due to self-selection or the effects of living in remote locations, these trends among Jews were emblematic of their adopted region, which sociologists have labeled "the unchurched belt."[53]

When immigrants arrived in western cities, local Jewish philanthropic organizations fostered the tendency away from religious traditionalism, by communicating a message that to be "modern" and "American" would require dispensing with at least some rituals and garb. Sponsored primarily by second-generation women from the elite and well-integrated pioneer families, local sections of the National Council of Jewish Women, and, in San Francisco, the Emanu-El Sisterhood for Personal Service, offered programs aimed at teaching the newcomers "American" social norms and, in some cases, Reform Judaism.[54]

Such messages were reinforced by organized migrations. Groups of Russian immigrants dedicated to the formation of agricultural colonies in the West—and elsewhere in rural America—attracted women and men with radical ideas, many of whom had rejected a traditional Jewish life. Their goal of "normalization" required a search for new lifestyles and the capacity to adapt to America's new opportunities.[55] Similarly, philanthropic organizations like the Industrial Removal Office (IRO), which aided Jewish immigrants willing to leave the congested neighborhoods of New York, targeted people for relocation in the West if they had some expectation of succeeding there and if they could be assisted by relatives who were already acclimated to American life. Thus nearly two-thirds of the immigrant New Yorkers whom the IRO relocated to other parts of the country between 1908 and 1914 had resided in New York for more than three years.[56] Believing that those who were less Orthodox would adjust more readily to life in midwestern or western cities, the IRO selected immigrants who seemed adaptable. The Pacific Northwest was by no means a major target of the IRO, which sent 907 immigrants to Washington and 858 to Oregon, out of a total of more than 73,000 individuals "removed" between 1901 and 1917. Still, given the small Jewish populations of these states—and the fact that once relocated, those who had been removed served as "magnets" attracting family and friends to follow them—the IRO's impact proved significant.[57] Its importance is most clearly visible in California, which received 4,850 migrants, including approximately 2,200 who arrived in Los Angeles, most between 1904 and 1914. With the Jewish community in Los Angeles numbering only 2,500 in 1900, and with each of the single, male immigrants drawing several additional family members or friends, "the historic importance of the Industrial Removal Office's activities [in Los Angeles] would be hard to overestimate."[58]

Indeed, the late growth of many western Jewish communities can be attributed in part to such chain migrations. Those venturing west early were followed by relatives and townspeople who migrated more directly. In Bellingham, Washington, for example, the Jewish community was made up largely of families from Skopishok, Lithuania, who followed Eli Schuman and his family to the Northwest after the turn of the century.[59] Edward Glazer, whose immigrant parents spent approximately five years in New Haven, Connecticut, before following a relative to Bellingham, recalled that everyone was "more or less related to each other directly or indirectly."[60] Similarly, a cluster of families from Russia's Volhynia Province settled in Portland, all following an uncle.[61] In such cases, while the initial migrant had not come directly to the West, the friends and relatives who followed him often did. Immigrant aid societies, such as the West Coast branches of the Hebrew Sheltering and Immigrant Aid Society, fostered such chain migrations once the initial immigrant proved he was self-supporting. For example, Lucius L. Solomons, president of the Roumanian Relief Society in San Francisco and past president of B'nai B'rith's District Grand Lodge No. 4, wrote several letters in 1901 urging support for the migration of family members of individuals who had settled in that city. In an August 1901 letter, Solomons urged eastern authorities to send west the family of T. Goldstein, "one of the Roumanian immigrants who arrived in San Francisco several months ago." He indicated that Goldstein "has been self-supporting and desires to have his wife and children sent out here."[62] Similarly, in Portland, most of the cases evaluated by volunteer IRO agents like Ben Selling were requests for family reunification. When resident family members were self-supporting, Selling was willing to recommend that the IRO assist in family reunification—or even to lend his own funds for that purpose.[63]

That early arrivals had often spent years in the United States prior to settling in the West and that the friends and relatives who later followed them were more likely to migrate directly had important impacts on the development of Eastern European institutions and neighborhoods. Among the most striking is the fact that the first institutions established by Eastern European newcomers to western cities were often not small shuls built on *landsleit* connections, as one might expect based on the New York or Boston model, but synagogues open to the more democratic demands of western families. The first two Russian Jewish congregations founded in Portland during the 1890s advertised sermons in English and German, the participation of well-rehearsed choirs, and even, on occasion, instrumental music during the service.[64] As early as 1900, Portland's Russian congregation Neveh Zedek had adopted mixed seating.[65] Not until *after* the turn of the century did traditionalists break off *from* Neveh Zedek congregation to form the Orthodox Shaarei Torah.

Similarly, in Los Angeles, Vorspan and Gartner note, "unlike most eastern congregations of immigrant origin, new groups were not based on a common European home town. Los Angeles Jews from Eastern Europe had made too many stops en route to organize upon a *landsleit* basis. Most congregations were organized, simply enough, by neighborhood."[66] But in addition to their eclectic membership base, they were also open to untraditional leadership. While many characterized these congregations as Orthodox, they were not immigrant shuls. Beth Israel and Congregation Sinai, the "predominant traditional synagogues," were clearly more modernist than this label implies. Likewise, Beth El, which labeled itself "Conservative," chose as its rabbi Moses ("Michael") Solomon, the former rabbi of Congregation B'nai B'rith, the Reform-leaning congregation of established Angelenos.[67] Solomon was a Posener who had studied in Berlin and New York and was ordained at

Hebrew Union College in Cincinnati. His decision to move to Beth El signaled his desire to practice in a more traditional fashion. Still, had the immigrant congregants of Beth El hoped to create a traditional, Yiddish oriented shul, Solomon would not have been a logical choice.[68]

Likewise, Congregation Sinai, founded in 1906, also failed to fit the stereotype of an insular, immigrant shul and found leadership in Rabbi Isadore Myers, who came to California from Eastern Europe—by way of Australia. Longtime member and honorary life president L. G. Reynolds described Rabbi Myers's background as that of "a happy blend of a famous East European Yeshiva and an up-to-date Australian University. A fine Talmudical scholar, and accomplished Hebraist, a master of the finest English and other secular literature, a keen wit and humorist, he combined all the elements which made him a most interesting lecturer, sermonizer and teacher."[69] Beginning with its dedication in 1909, the congregation reached out to Jews and non-Jews in the Los Angeles area, following the practice of established pioneer congregations of inviting leading Jews and Christians to make speeches. While presenting itself as traditional, Sinai was quite modern—with practices that some described as lacking "religious clarity" and others as "conglomerate ritual."[70] Myers himself described the congregation as "Conservative, that is, Rabbinical Judaism," yet the use of an organ, Friday night sermons, and English language all suggest a quite *American* congregation.[71] According to Vorspan and Gartner, "All in all, Conservative Judaism at Sinai was distinctly for acculturated Jews and their children, aiming to accommodate traditional Judaism to their general environment."[72] Other immigrant congregations in Los Angeles characterized themselves as "'modern orthodox,' like Shaaray Tefila, or 'traditional,' or 'in conser-

vative form,' like Rodef Shalom." The "outright Orthodox" Breed Street Shul was more exceptional than typical, and its late establishment—in 1905—is consistent with the pattern of the relatively late founding of traditionally observant congregations in the West.[73]

This is not to say that Eastern European Jews who arrived in the West easily abandoned traditional religious practice. Seattle's Congregation Bikur Cholim had evolved from a mutual aid society into an Orthodox congregation during the 1890s and steadfastly retained its Orthodox identity in the twentieth century, even as some of its number joined the breakaway Congregation Herzl, which slowly moved toward Conservative Judaism. The struggle between traditionalists and reformers at Bikur Cholim is suggested in their evolving constitution and bylaws. For example, although earlier constitutions did not characterize the congregation as Orthodox or address in detail religious practices, its 1921 constitution was very explicit: "The name of the association shall be Congregation Bikur Cholim, a religious congregation professing strict adherence to the principles, customs, usages and practices of traditional Orthodox Judaism." To amplify its Orthodox intent, the constitution provided considerable detail:

> To maintain a house of worship, or Synagogue, wherein services are to be conducted *Al Pi Nusach Ashkanaz*, and in accordance with the laws, rules and regulations expounded in the "*Shulchan Oruch.*" That during such services men and women shall be seated separately, as required by Orthodox Jewish law and tradition. No law shall be enacted in future changing this requirement. The Congregation shall also maintain a *Mikveh* for the purpose of ritual immersion in accordance with Jewish law.[74]

Yet at Bikur Cholim, determination to hold fast to orthodox ritual did not indicate a lack of acculturation. It was clearly an *American* congregation. Among those members identifiable in the 1910 census, the overwhelming majority (fifty-three out of fifty-six) spoke English, owned a business (forty out of forty-six), and had lived in the United States for more than a decade (thirty-one out of forty-six).[75] When Polish immigrant, skilled printer, and Bikur Cholim leader Sol Krems founded Seattle's *Jewish Voice*, he could have used the "cases of handmade Yiddish type" that he brought with him, but he chose instead to print it in English. As his son recalled, "I think he decided to print it in English because most of the population of Seattle spoke English[;] it may have been accented but it was [English] . . . [They] spoke and read English."[76]

While Bikur Cholim maintained separate seating and other Orthodox practices, it aspired to "modern" forms as well. Thus the congregation's January 1912 minutes indicate that the "matter of a modern Rabbi was taken up," and in the congregation's 1916 contract with Cantor Solomon Tovbin, the shul mandated that the cantor form a self-sustaining choir to assist him in services.[77] The program for a fair and bazaar, held in 1917 to raise money to support the completion of a building opened several years before, is a testament to the level of acculturation in this Orthodox shul. Printed entirely in English, the program demonstrates that the synagogue valued its prominence not only within the Jewish community but also in greater Seattle. The week's events included elements common to dedications at pioneer synagogues decades earlier: performances by orchestras and other musical groups, dances, and addresses by Washington's governor Ernest Lister and Seattle's mayor Hiram Gill, as well by both male and female congregational leaders.[78] Such documents make

clear that the small businessmen of this congregation wanted both to retain traditional practices and to reach out to the larger Seattle community, as they had three years earlier when "all prominent people of Seattle were present" at the dedication of their (then only partially completed) new synagogue.[79]

In contrast to earlier Eastern European immigrants, who often arrived in western cities already acculturated and established congregations that reflected innovations in ritual, later settlers were more likely to arrive directly from Europe and to be the force behind newer but *more* traditional Orthodox congregations. In Portland several Orthodox congregations were established in the first two decades of the twentieth century. The largest was Shaarei Torah (also known as the First Street Shul), founded in 1902. The congregation's first president was Joseph Nudelman, a man well acculturated to America, after years spent in North Dakota, Colorado, California, and Nevada. Yet when the congregation finally settled on a long-term rabbi in 1916, they turned to an immigrant, who like many of his congregants had come directly from the Old Country.[80] Portland's Orthodox organized two additional Ashkenazic congregations in the 1910s, Linath Hazedek in 1914 and a splinter group at Kesser Israel, in 1916.[81] Unlike Portland's earlier congregations, Linath Hazedek appears to have organized along *landsleit* ties—and was known as the *kazatzker shul*. Both congregations attracted Yiddish-speaking congregations.[82]

A similar pattern can be seen in California. For example, in Los Angeles in 1900, Congregation Kehal Adath Beth Israel (known as the Olive Street Shul), was created through a merger between the Conservative People's Synagogue Beth El and the Orthodox Kehal Yisrael and other congregations, all of which "consisted of Russian and Polish

FIG. 3.5 *Boyle Heights, Workmen's Circle school class, ca. 1935. Shades of L.A. Archives, Los Angeles Public Library.*

Jews, besides a few native Jews out of accord with Reform Judaism." This merged congregation "long retained its character as an immigrant synagogue, consciously preserving the Judaism remembered from Eastern Europe."[83] In Oakland, several small, "ultra-Orthodox" congregations, catering to newly arriving, Yiddish-speaking immigrants, joined earlier established Orthodox synagogues in the second decade of the twentieth century.[84] Although some congregations moved toward Conservative Juda-

ism, others remained Orthodox, in part by continuing to absorb new, Yiddish-speaking immigrants. Fred Rosenbaum writes of Oakland's Orthodox congregation Beth Jacob (founded 1893) that in the mid-1920s, "most of the membership were only a few years removed from Eastern Europe, as can be gleaned from the broken English and frequent misspellings of the secretaries' reports."[85]

As with Orthodox shuls, identifiable Jewish neighborhoods eventually coalesced in all of the major West Coast cities, but they emerged quite late in comparison to their northeastern and midwestern counterparts. New York, Chicago, Philadelphia, Boston, and Baltimore all had "dense enclaves of eastern European Jews" by the turn of the twentieth century.[86] In Los Angeles, some concentration began in the 1910s and 1920s, with immigrant Jews beginning to cluster in the Boyle Heights section and creating a "large-scale Jewish environment" with distinctive Yiddish culture (fig. 3.5).[87] This critical mass seems to have attracted newcomers. With a population of fewer than two thousand Jews in 1920, Boyle Heights grew to a Jewish community of more than ten thousand by 1930, and by 1940, despite the Depression, had became the largest Jewish neighborhood west of Chicago.[88] Oral histories recalling the 1920s and 1930s describe a strong Jewish atmosphere in the neighborhood, which many compared, however metaphorically, to a shtetl. Although the neighborhood became in truth quite heterogeneous, with significant populations of Japanese, Chinese, Mexicans, and later some African Americans, many Jews focused on their own institutions and specialty stores and imagined it to be largely Jewish.[89]

With far fewer people than Boyle Heights, Seattle's Yesler/Cherry Street area in the Central District emerged as the center of that city's Jewish community in the first decade of the twentieth century. Housing more than 86 percent of Seattle's Jewish community by 1910, many within the community regarded the Central District as "Seattle's distinctive Jewish neighborhood," even though Jews never accounted for more than 15 percent of its population.[90] A study of residential patterns indicates that the Central District reached its peak of more than ten thousand Jews in 1940, another indication of the lateness of community development in the West.[91]

By the 1910s, the Central District boasted all of Seattle's four congregations, and several kosher butcher shops competed for rabbinic approval as "strictly kosher," catering to separate Sephardic and Ashkenazic clientele.[92] Its vibrant Jewish cultural life included synagogue-based celebrations and Yiddish musicals at the Workmen's Circle Hall.[93] In 1912, W. K. Sickels, a non-Jewish, Republican candidate for county clerk, made an effort to appeal to Jewish voters in the Central District with posters in Yiddish (fig. 3.6). The posters, printed by the firm of Jacob Kaplan, a leader in the Orthodox Bikur Cholim congregation, testify not only to the increasing number and importance of Yiddish speakers in Seattle but also to their rapid acculturation. Although printed in Yiddish lettering, the poster was made up largely of transliterated English phrases, such as that proclaiming Sickels "an up-to-date man."[94] Ironically, while Sickels made this appeal in Yiddish script, Seattle's major Orthodox congregation functioned almost entirely in English.[95]

In San Francisco, not surprisingly, given its importance as the regional Jewish center, the Eastern European ethnic district formed earlier, in the 1890s, among rooming houses south of Market Street. In part because the district was populated not by families—like Boyle Heights or South Portland—but by footloose Irish and German laborers, Rabbi Nieto feared for the safety as well as the Jewish education of its immigrant children. Since only one shul was known to exist in the area, he established the Educational Alliance to provide religious schooling, while Rabbi Voorsanger's Emanu-El Sisterhood for Personal Service saved immigrant Jewish children from the streets by establishing the first Jewish settlement house in the West in the district.[96]

Yet after the earthquake and fire destroyed that

נייעס נייעס   וויכטיגע נייעס   נייעס נייעס

ווער פון אייך האט ניט געהערט דעם נאמען די. קיי. סיקעלם,
דער קאונטי קלוירק? אללע וויסען פון זיין ערליבקייט און אלם פריינד
פון יהודים, איין ריכטיגער „אוהב ישראל" ער האט שטענדיג געטריים
זיין בעסטם אז אידען זאלען ארבייטען ביי עם אין אפים און אויך יעצט
וועט איהר ביי עם געפינען אידען ארבייטען.

ווען ער איז געלאפען פאר קאונטי קלוירק מיט 2 יאהר צוריק
האט ער נאר קיין אפאזישאן געהאט און ער איז איין שטימיג ערוועהלט
געווארען, ליידער קען ער מעהר דעם אפים ניט אנהאלטען ווייל די
קאנסטיטושאן זאגט אז מעהר וו 2 מאהל קען ער ניט זיין אין דעם
אמט, דערפאר האבען אלע אויפגעשטעלט אלם קאנדידאט פאר דעם
זעלבען אמט זיין אייגענעם זוהן אויך איין ערליכער מאן און א פריינד
פון יהודים, ווייל די „עפיל פאלט ניט ווייט פון בוים" זיין נאמען איז

ו. ק. סיקעלם

ער וואהנט צוויישען אייך זיין אדרעסע איז
19-302 טע עוועני סא. קאר. מיין סט.

ער איז געהאדעוועט געווארען מיט אייך צוזאמען און ער וועט
געווים זיין א קרעדיט פאר דער שטאדט, ער פערשפרעכט צו זיין ווי
זיין פאטער און פיליכם בעסער ווייל ער איז א יונגער מענש און א
אפ-טו-דייט מען.   עם איז די פפליכט פון יעדען איינעם אפ צו געבען
זיערע שטימען און אויך צו רעדען זיערע פריינד, עם מאכט ניט אוים
צו וועלכער פארטי ער בעלאנגט, פערגעסט ניט

דיענסטאג דעם 10 טען סעפטעמבער זאלען אלע ווי
איינער ארויסגעהן און ארבייטען פאר אייער פריינד
ו. ק. סיקעלם וועלען מיר איהם עלעקטען מיט א גרויסע
מאזשאריטי.

I have served you faithfully in a subordinate position and now ask for promotion

W. K. SICKELS

Republican Candidate for Nomination for

Primaries Sept. 10, 1912   **COUNTY CLERK**

קאפלאן פרינטינג קא. 709 פערטע עוועני. סיאטעל. וואש.   Kaplan Printing Co., Seattle, Wash.

FIG. 3.6
Campaign ad for W. C. Sickels (1912), candidate for city clerk, in Yiddish lettering but containing several English phrases. University of Washington Libraries, Special Collections, neg. UW27643z.

area in 1906, it took years before the Fillmore District became the major Jewish immigrant neighborhood. In this period, some perceived a decline in observance. For example, Lilian Gertrude Cherney, daughter of Eastern European immigrants who had sojourned in a "real Jewish neighborhood"

in St. Louis during the 1890s, found Jews in San Francisco less likely to follow traditional practice and perceived the trend to be away from tradition in the years following the earthquake: "Not many Jewish people—a few, until 1906, 1908—observed *michik-flashig* [*sic*] [the separation of dairy and meat required under dietary laws]. But after 1908, 1910, no. You got away from it. In the first place, the Jewish meat was much, much more expensive, and the children . . . became more broadened in their thinking of associating when they went to school with goyish children."[97]

As in other parts of the West, the more traditional and insular San Francisco Jewish neighborhoods were founded after the turn of the century as the first Eastern European immigrants were followed in chain migrations by their less acculturated relatives and landsmen. Just as Cherney's family "got away from it," an influx of immigrants buoyed traditional institutions and helped found new, Orthodox synagogues. In 1908, when Rose Hartman Ets-Hokin's intellectual family arrived in San Francisco from Hungary after a three-year stay in New York, they quickly moved away from the immigrant district because "there were too many immigrant, ghetto-type people moving in. My mother was quite an aristocrat."[98]

New Jewish neighborhoods formed in the years following the 1906 earthquake, first "Out the Road," on San Bruno Avenue, and later in the Fillmore District. The former offered a "full range of Jewish organizations and services," during its heyday between 1907 and 1940.[99] The latter, which became the major immigrant Jewish neighborhood, was not at its height until the 1920s. There "shoppers poured into the busy food stores and markets on Fillmore and McAllister Streets on Saturday nights and Sundays. There they bought kosher meats and chickens at the butcher and poultry counters."[100] During this period, Raye Rich's parents ran Wall's Grocery and Delicatessen, on Fillmore Street, where she worked behind the counter. Rich remembered that people came from all over to purchase her mother's homemade pickles, potato salad, and coleslaw. "Even the Russian priest that

used to be on Green Street" would come in for the food and for Russian conversation, she recalled in an oral history.[101] Although Rich and journalist and neighborhood chronicler Jerry Flamm shared recollections of the Jewish atmosphere, they differed on specifics like Sabbath observance, with Flamm writing that "on Saturday nights, stores opened after sundown when the twenty-four hour Jewish Sabbath ended and stayed open until eleven o'clock," while Rich recalled working on Saturdays with the store only closing on the first day of Rosh Hashanah, Yom Kippur, and three hours on Good Friday, "out of respect for the Russian Church."[102]

In addition to the immigrant Jewish neighborhoods in the city, Petaluma, a country town, also emerged as a distinctive Jewish settlement between World War I and the 1930s. Petaluma attracted mostly Yiddish-speaking, leftist immigrants who, like colonists settling New Odessa, Oregon, or Painted Woods, North Dakota, decades before, had agrarian, cooperative aspirations. Russian-born David Soren, for example, moved to Petaluma in 1927 after spending a decade and a half working as a cap maker and union organizer in Toronto, Los Angeles, and San Francisco. Although before visiting the settlement he had never considered leaving the union or the cap makers' trade, he recalled, "I liked Petaluma when I came in here and saw all the Jewish community here—what they were doing. And then economically I liked the difference—they were raising baby chicks. Some of them were egg producers too. I liked it!" (fig. 3.7).[103]

Petaluma's former factory workers, according to the community historian Kenneth Kann, "established a vibrant political community that combined socialist and Jewish internationalism with the parochialism of an ethnic minority in small-town America."[104] By 1925, with approximately one hundred Jewish families settled there, Petaluma

FIG. 3.7 *Petaluma chicken ranch, 1925. Sonoma Public library.*

established a Jewish community center that served as the hub of a vital cultural and political life, hosting an active Yiddish theater program, a folk chorus, and lectures by nationally and internationally known leftist activists, intellectuals, and artists. Unlike many other small-town western communities, where ideological and religious differences had to be glossed over in order to sustain institutions, Petaluma's Jewish population was sufficiently large and committed that the kinds of ideological divisions that were more characteristic of New York City were played out in this small California town.[105] In one of several disputes over the community center, some radicals refused to join, because "there was a *shul* in the building. They thought religion is the opiate of the people."[106] Despite rivalries between Socialists and Communists, the religious and nonreligious, Yiddishists and Hebraicists, and among Zionists of various stripes, Petaluma's Jewish community continued to grow through the Depression and beyond. In contrast to the dwindling experienced by most rural Jewish communities— particularly those in the West— Petaluma's Jewish population, while losing its distinctive socialist tradition, continued to grow through the mid- to late twentieth century as it evolved from country town to San Francisco commuter suburb.[107]

The immigrant Jewish culture of Petaluma and all the Jewish enclaves in the West Coast's major cities bustled with Zionist activity. Like Eastern European immigrants to other parts of the country, many newcomers to the West brought Zionist inclinations with them from Europe. Sonia Myers Wachtin, one of the early members of Seattle's first Hadassah chapter, founded in 1923, recalled that, even in Russia, her family had a *pushke* (collection box) for Zionism. Similarly, Laura Berch, also active in Hadassah in Seattle, recalled, "I think I was born a Zionist."[108] Seattle's Congregation Herzl, which split from Congregation Bikur Cholim in 1906, included Zionism as a principle in its articles of incorporation, stating in article 3: "This congregation shall always be in favor of the principles of Zionism as set forth in the Basle Programme."[109] Orthodox Zionists in Seattle, mostly members of Bikur Cholim, were active in Mizrachi and Ladies Mizrachi by 1916, while Hadassah became established in the early 1920s.[110]

Although immigrant Jews confronted anti-Zionist contingents in some western cities (most notably San Francisco and Seattle) Zionist groups actively raised funds in every major West Coast city by the 1910s.[111] A decade later, a report on Zionist activity in Los Angeles proclaimed that "the progress of Zionism here has been steady and substantial" and that Zionist activities "have been as varied as the population and all embracing as the city boundaries."[112] In Portland, the Modern Hebrew School by 1910 had developed a curriculum that promoted both Americanization and Zionism.[113]

Although immigrant Jewish neighborhoods offered a full array of Jewish services and goods,

they were "more limited in scale than in the East," and the "ties with the Old Country were weaker."[114] Weaker ties to the homeland can be seen in the fraternal organizations created by immigrant Jews in the West. In contrast to large eastern communities, where organizational membership reflected local village, city, or provincial ties, most immigrant Jewish organizations in the West became much more inclusive. Thus, Chevrah Bikur Cholim, the first mutual aid organization established by immigrant Jews in Seattle, attracted Eastern Europeans regardless of their home region but specified in its articles of incorporation that officers be citizens of the United States and residents of Washington for at least one year.[115] In communities like Los Angeles, where the population was eventually large enough to support a number of welfare organizations, Jews usually associated themselves according to national rather than regional or town origin. Los Angeles Jewry boasted a Hungarian American Club, a Roumanian Aid Society, and a Jewish Polish Society, but not an *Anshe Zhitmir* or *Anshe Elizovetgrad*.[116] Later migrants, however, did found a Chicago Club, perhaps modeled after the Iowa or Kansas clubs that Protestant migrants from the Midwest were fond of organizing for picnics and recreation.

The pattern of step migration to the Pacific West, with the early arrival of relatively acculturated immigrants and the late emergence of traditional institutions and concentrated neighborhoods helped to lessen the dichotomy between the pioneers and the Eastern European immigrants. In Tacoma, for example, while immigrants set up their own shul rather than join the temple, the two groups "mingled" in a single B'nai B'rith lodge and in most other community activities, though intimate friendships were within their own group.[117] Certainly, the separate congregations, fraternal organizations, and social networks that emerged in all of the major West Coast cities, and even disagreements over fund-raising and social welfare projects, indicate that the differences between Eastern European immigrant Jews and their predecessors, as elsewhere, were clear and important. Yet Vorspan and Gartner's observation that "the lines between the primarily European Jews and the highly acculturated older settlers were not nearly so sharp in Los Angeles as elsewhere" can be applied to the other major West Coast communities, except San Francisco.[118]

Portland, where the early Russian immigrants were particularly acculturated, provides a striking example. In that city, the early arriving Russian immigrants established English-speaking, modernist congregations, with acculturated rabbinical leadership. Indeed, the gap was sufficiently narrow that the more traditional of the two established congregations, Ahavai Shalom (founded 1869) and the immigrant Russian congregation Neveh Zedek, actually merged briefly in the mid-1890s.[119] Similarly, the men of the pioneer families served together with the early arriving, acculturated Russians on the board of directors of the Free Loan Society in Portland.[120] Although there were certainly social divisions between the established Portland elite and the newcomers—evidenced, for example, in the late-nineteenth-century in separate B'nai B'rith lodges—they were less profound than in the East. Within a generation, the separate German, Polish, and Russian lodges unified, as the sons and grandsons of German Jewish pioneers worked together with Russian immigrants and their sons in organizations like the B'nai B'rith Building Association.[121]

Differences between the daughters of the pioneer generation and later arriving Eastern European immigrant women kept their respective organizations separate longer. Unlike the B'nai B'rith, which bridged the ethnic gap among men, the Progressive local chapter of the National Council of Jewish Women continued to be the province of Reform temple women well into the twentieth century. It was not until as late as the 1930s that Hadassah emerged as the first organization in Portland to unite Jewish women from both groups and propel women of Eastern European origin into positions of leadership.[122]

The strong presence of Poseners among the established Jews in the West revealed something of the subterranean cultural struggles among Jews and also helped to bridge the differences between the old timers and the new arrivals.[123] Among immigrants who believed that acculturation to German standards carried the cache of modernization, those from Posen, which had come under Prussian influence in the nineteenth century, believed that they had absorbed highly valued norms that masked their backward "eastern" origins. As a group, Poseners did generally display more affinity for traditional practice than did Jews of Bavarian origins, and so they could serve as intermediaries between the westernized German Jews and the Eastern European newcomers. Congregations with substantial Posener populations, like Sherith Israel in San Francisco and Ahavai Shalom in Portland, were well established by the time the Russians began to arrive. Like their Bavarian counterparts who belonged to Emanu-El and Beth Israel, the members of these congregations also tended to be upwardly mobile merchants eager to engage in local affairs. Though they encouraged their rabbis to reach out to the larger community through sermons in English and participation in public events, they encouraged retaining traditional ritual practices and supported the newcomers' emphasis on studying Hebrew and supporting Zionism.

The blend of community engagement, acculturation, and tradition appealed to some of the early arriving Eastern Europeans, and Ahavai Shalom attracted several of the Russian immigrants. Once Russian immigrants organized congregations, Ahavai Shalom continued to play an "in between" role, seen most vividly in its brief merger with the Russian's Neveh Zedek in the 1890s.[124] In cities where Poseners had not created their own congregations, they sometimes left the Reform-oriented, pioneer congregations to join Russian congregations established by newcomers. In Los Angeles, for example, Rabbi Solomons along with some of his congregants left Congregation B'nai B'rith for Beth El.[125] Although Russian immigrants formed new congregations rather than join San Francisco's Sherith Israel, Poseners played intermediary roles in other ways. Marcus Rosenthal, who publicly chastised Emanu-El's Rabbi Jacob Voorsanger's anti-immigrant position as "exceedingly reprehensible and under the circumstances positively cruel," was born in "Prussian Poland," likely in Posen.[126]

CREATION OF SEPHARDIC COMMUNITY

Just as the presence of the Poseners created a cultural middle ground and leadership cadre, the diversity infused into these communities by the influx of Sephardim also served to diffuse potential conflict between the pioneers and the Eastern European immigrants, though for different reasons. This was particularly true in Seattle and Los Angeles, home to the most substantial Sephardic communities. A few Sephardic families of Portuguese descent, like the Peixottos and Solis-Cohens, had been part of the migration west from the start. But after the turn of the century, groups of relatively poor Sephardim immigrated directly from Turkey and Rhodes. Seattle's Sephardic community, which has been called the "mother colony of Sephardic life on the West Coast," grew through chain migrations from two pioneers in 1902, from six hundred in 1913 to more than two thousand by the 1920s.[127] This growth made Seattle the second largest Sephardic community in the country, after New York.[128]

The customs and, apparently, the appearance of Sephardic and Ashkenazic Jews seemed so different from one another that the Ashkenazim initially had a hard time believing that these newcomers—with whom they shared no common language—were Jews. Gershon Rickles, a leader of Congregation Bikur Cholim, actually wrote to Jewish authorities in New York in order to verify the claims of the Sephardim that they were Jewish.[129] For their part, the Sephardim at first preferred to socialize with local Greeks than with Ashkenazim. For the Sephardim, even the divisions among the three major groups, from Marmara, Rodosto, and Rhodes, were difficult to bridge, and they—unlike their Ashkenazic counterparts— set up separate congregations and mutual aid societies based on the equivalent of *landsleit* ties.[130] The three groups did work together in establishing a Young Men's Sephardic Association and a unified Sephardic Talmud Torah— though the latter was only sporadically supported. Although they too resided in the "Jewish" Central District and, like the Ashkenazim, started small businesses (fig. 3.8), the Sephardim remained socially, culturally, and religiously separate. Nearly all their socializing took place within large family circles or through the synagogues. Even philanthropy was handled internally, with needs met through a "secret fund" rather than through the established Jewish communal organizations that used more formal practices.[131] In addition, in contrast to Seattle's Ashkenazi Bikur

Cholim, which appears to have functioned from an early period primarily in English, the Sephardic congregations, like Ezra Bessaroth, did not provide English-language sermons until the 1930s. A 1922 neighborhood survey reported that 57 percent of the children whose mothers' language was Yiddish ("Jew") spoke Yiddish at home, while more than 90 percent of children whose mother tongue was Ladino ("Spanish") spoke that language at home.[132]

The same study repeatedly lamented the self-imposed segregation between Ashkenazim and Sephardim, suggesting reluctantly that separate dances should be provided for the community's youth since the two "do not mix well at social functions."[133] Children from the two groups reportedly called one another names based on their respective cuisines, with Ashkenazic children labeling Sephardim "olive oil," and Sephardim responding with the epithet "shmaltz [chicken fat]." Although the Eastern European community—and particularly Bikur Cholim's Rabbi Hirsch Genss, who virtually adopted some of the early Sephardic immigrants—initially offered aid, the Sephardim ultimately developed more ties with the Reform community. Yet these were largely philanthropic rather than social ties. Temple De Hirsch's Rabbi Koch was instrumental in moving his congregation to help raise money for the Sephardic synagogue-building campaigns and in opening his Sunday school to Sephardic children—but even those who attended did not socialize with Ashkenazic children.[134]

Even though the economic gap between Eastern European immigrants and the Sephardim was smaller, there was greater alienation between these two groups. Marco Franco's son, Albert, recalled,

> Well, interestingly enough, the friction was not so much between the German Jews and the Sephardic

Jews as between the Eastern European Jews and the Sephardic Jews. But it wasn't real friction. I think it was just kind of a normal lack of communication. Here you have immigrants that came from different cultural backgrounds just as different as night and day. They spoke a different language. They had a different cuisine; they had a different history; they were physically different in many ways. And the only thing they had in common actually was a long Jewish history which is very important. But in the American milieu where there were other forces that were imposing themselves on these two societies, there was kind of a tendency for them to draw away from one another and maybe each [was] drawn a little bit toward the American society around them, but certainly not towards each other.[135]

Elazar Behar, while confirming the separation between the two communities, denied reports of friction:

> There was a closeness with the Ashkenazic neighbors. We had different lifestyles. We spoke a different language. You got to place yourself in a different time frame entirely. Like for example, someone like Leni and myself, if we were down the street and we saw another person, an older person especially, we'd be speaking in Spanish and the Ashkenazic kids would be speaking in Yiddish. They went to their synagogue and we went to ours. We were Jewish and we celebrated the holidays together. In school there was a kind of bond because we were the Jewish kids, and the others were the Japanese kids and the white kids. As far as mixing, the communities were pretty much separated. As far as having any feeling, there was absolutely no bad feeling.[136]

Certainly, the impact of their shared experiences in public schools, and frequently also in the temple

FIG. 3.8 *Sephardic shoeshine men in front of stand at Yesler Way, between First and Occidental avenues, Seattle, ca. 1918. Left to right: unknown, Raliamin Calderon, Edward Tarica, Sam Amon, Ralph Policar, unknown, Albert Ovadia, and Isaac Eskenazi. University of Washington Libraries, Special Collections, neg. UW1085.*

Sunday school, did erode the distance between the groups, but only gradually. Sephardim who came of age in the 1920s, like Mary Capeloto, recalled spending much time at Neighborhood House, just like their Ashkenazi peers. Still, according to Capeloto, her decision to join the National Council of Jewish Women and Hadassah made her an exception among Sephardic women of her genera-

tion.[137] Second-generation Sephardic Jews, who began entering university in the late 1920s and early 1930s, found that while the Jewish fraternities at the University of Washington pledged Eastern European immigrants, they excluded Sephardim—a practice continued until the World War II period.[138] The social distance between Sephardim and Ashkenazim, coupled with a relatively small pool of potential Sephardic partners, helps to explain the finding in a 1939 study that Sephardim were four times more likely to marry non-Jews than were Ashkenazim.[139]

The other major West Coast Sephardic communities can be linked directly to Seattle and developed along similar lines: "Seattle Sephardim formed the nucleus of the Portland community and it is estimated that a large segment of the LA community consists of Seattle Sephardim."[140] In Portland, young men like Ezra Menashe and Isaac Hasson arrived around 1910 and started bootblack and cigar stands, as well as fish stores near the produce market on Yamhill Street. They resided near their work downtown rather than among the Ashkenazi immigrant families of South Portland. Because the community was too small to support multiple congregations, the families from Marmara and Rhodes maintained a unified congregation, Ahavath Achim, which met in the B'nai B'rith Building until finally building its own synagogue in the early 1930s. Like their relatives in Seattle, they too sought the support of Ben Selling and the Reform Temple Beth Israel rather than that of fellow immigrants from Eastern Europe.[141]

The Los Angeles Jewish community, which began to form in the same years, quickly became "one of the largest centers of Rhodeslis outside the island." By 1913, twenty-five families from Rhodes had arrived and established ties with a second group of Sephardim from Turkey, while having only "limited" contact with the established Jewish community.[142] The Sephardim settled near one another between Sixth and Pico Boulevard and created fraternal groups and religious congregations to maintain their distinctive identity.[143] As in Seattle, efforts to maintain pan-Sephardic institutions often failed, with the separate groups forming institutions based on home region. The immigrants

from Rhodes, for example, left the unified Avat Shalom to form the Peace and Progress Society. By 1919, there were three very small, separate congregations: the Sephardic Communidad, the Haim Vaheset, and the Yacov Tovee—some of which later merged again.[144] Similar to their Seattle brethren, Sephardic immigrants coming directly to Los Angeles lacked both the capital and the language skills to open "sedentary" businesses and instead entered the economy in "street corner" jobs, such as selling flowers and produce or shining shoes.[145] As in Seattle, Los Angeles Sephardim followed the tradition of confidentially providing assistance to those in need through "el fundo secreto" and tended to avoid established Jewish philanthropies.[146]

WHITENESS AND THE "NEW" JEWISH WESTERNERS

The establishment of visible Sephardic communities that maintained separate institutions, traditions, and languages, along with the significant presence of the Poseners, created a subtle layering of western Jewish communities instead of the dichotomy between established Jews and Eastern European immigrants so common elsewhere. In addition, the peculiar regional ethnic landscape, in which the presence of nonwhite "others" helped to reinforce the acceptance of Jews as "white," continued to play a role in counteracting anti-Semitic discrimination. While Jewish businessmen like Ben Selling were aware of stereotypes and prejudice against Jews, it was understood as an aberration in the experience of western Jews, at least prior to the 1920s. This complex texturing of Jewish communities and the limited concern for anti-Semitism compared to other regions of the country helps to explain the mostly muted response of established

Jews to the arrival of Eastern European and Sephardic immigrants.[147]

Although historians have demonstrated that Jews and other "new" European immigrants were not fully accepted as whites in America during the period of mass migration, Jews in the West had long functioned as part of the "Anglo" community to an unusual degree.[148] In addition to their prominence in civic affairs, Jews found acceptance even in groups like the Native Sons of Oregon and California's Native Sons of the Golden West, both of which were notoriously nativist organizations dedicated to honoring white history in the West.[149] Sol Blumauer served as a founding trustee of the Oregon organization and was elected to its presidency at the turn of the century. Blumauer, his wife, Hattie Fleischner Blumauer, and at least six other Jewish Oregonians were recognized as native sons or daughters and honored with pictures and/or biographical profiles in the inaugural volume of the organization's publication *Oregon Native Son*.[150] Brothers Meyer and Henry Lissner and David Edelman, son of Los Angeles's first rabbi, were among the mostly Jewish founding members of the Corona Parlor (no. 196) of the Native Sons of the Golden West in 1896.[151] Inclusion in Native Sons is vivid evidence of Jewish acceptance as whites, and profiles of Jewish members, sometimes including mention of their service to Jewish organizations and other achievements, contrast sharply with the stereotype-laden treatment of groups perceived as nonwhite.[152]

The avoidance of anti-Semitic rhetoric by the Ku Klux Klan during its heyday in Oregon in the early 1920s also illustrates the degree to which some Jews at least were recognized as members of the region's founding generation. Given their acceptance in organizations like Native Sons, it was difficult for Klansmen to portray Jews as a group as

"other." Both Temple Beth Israel and Ahavai Shalom suffered arson attacks within a few weeks of each other in 1924, and individual Klan spokesmen occasionally targeted Jews, but the highest Klan official in Portland criticized those attacks on the grounds that there were "so many Jews in Portland who are . . . widely known as this state's finest citizens."[153] A major Klan initiative in Oregon (a state with a miniscule black population) was a 1922 ballot measure mandating public school attendance aimed at Catholics. Although the initiative would not have affected supplementary religious schools or the Portland Hebrew School, Jewish communal leaders played an active public role in fighting it, and the Jewish community seemed to suffer no retaliation.[154] A Klan effort to use a boycott of the Meier and Frank department store to protest the appointment of Julius Meier to a state committee in 1925 failed after the *Oregon Voter*, the state's leading public affairs journal, condemned the action.[155] By 1926, the Klan in Portland, as in most cities throughout the country, was rapidly disintegrating. Four years later, Meier, running as an independent, was elected governor of Oregon in a landslide, winning more than twice as many votes as either his Republican or his Democratic rival.

In California, when the opening of the Panama Canal led to fears of an influx of immigrants, Simon Lubin, the California-born son of a prominent, Gold Rush–era, Polish Jewish merchant, designed the response of progressive governor Hiram Johnson and became the first head of the California Commission on Immigration and Housing (CCIH) in 1913. Rather than advocate restriction, the commission focused its efforts on improving housing and employment conditions and providing education. Yet progressive policies focusing on Americanizing and protecting immigrants were reserved for "white" immigrants, and "the Commission's tolerance had virtually no effect on Californian's on-going campaign against Asian immigrants, primarily the Japanese." California enacted its Alien Land Law the same year that it established the CCIH.[156]

The secure Jewish position in the Anglo community becomes most vivid when their experience is compared with that of Asian immigrants. While Jews played leading roles in all aspects of western civic life, Asians were widely considered irredeemably alien, a threat to Anglo civilization, and denied access to the naturalization processes, even though their children born in America were citizens.[157] Rabbi Voorsanger of Emanu-El himself believed that the Chinese were "a non-assimilative race," unable to "mix with Caucasians," and Congressman Julius Kahn played an active role in the Asiatic Exclusion League.[158] In all three Pacific Coast states, the anti-Asian hysteria that had led to the Chinese Exclusion Act in the early 1880s continued to spawn racist legislation well into the twentieth century. The most notable discrimination took the form of alien land laws, which prevented "aliens ineligible to citizenship" from purchasing land.[159]

The western focus on Asians as aliens diffused prejudices expressed so strongly against Jews and other Southern and Eastern European immigrants in other parts of the country. As Rosenbaum notes, "It was the Asians who were abused during these years of turmoil; they and not the Jews became the scapegoats."[160] When the Abe Ruef trial stirred anti-Semitism, *Emanu-El*'s editors maintained, "There is practically no race prejudice in the West. Anti-Semitism has not the slightest foothold here."[161] Historians differ on the extent to which anti-Semitism underlay the affair, but they agree that it had no local impact on the ability of Jews to be elected or appointed to public office and

relatively little on Jewish access to employment or housing.[162]

Hostility toward the Asian (and, in southern California, the Mexican) other played an important role in reinforcing Jewish acceptance as whites. The western Jewish press did not participate actively in the stigmatizing of Japanese immigrants after the turn of the century as it had in the anti-Chinese movement several decades earlier. But only rarely did a Jewish community leader directly criticize such prejudice, as did Rabbi Emanuel Jack of Stockton in 1920.[163] Yet even as the Jewish community avoided involvement in the volatile anti-Asian politics of California, the issue facilitated its acceptance. As the historian Frank Van Nuys argues, "Racial constructs aided in the categorization of immigrants and minorities as either unassailably white and thus possessed of proper citizenship qualities, or decidedly nonwhite and therefore undesirable as possible citizens."[164] While both the established Jewish community and state agencies like the CCIH emphasized the importance of fostering Americanization, Jewish immigrants were welcomed as whites who would help to shore up civilization against Asian "invaders."

IMMIGRANTS AND THE WESTERN ECONOMY

The economic structure of the western economy created different opportunities for Jewish migrants than they would find elsewhere in the country. Mass employment in the garment and allied industries that predominated among immigrant Jews in New York or Chicago did not exist in the West. But timber, ranching, and farming continued to expand, as did trade with East Asia, so western cities continued to afford opportunities to merchants, whether as pawnbrokers or secondhand furniture dealers along the Seattle and Portland waterfronts or as jewelers in Spokane. While growing southern railheads like Norfolk, Richmond, or New Orleans also provided opportunities for Jewish grocers and owners of secondhand stores especially serving the new black working class, western cities seemed more dynamic and offered a healthier social atmosphere.[165]

The funneling of Jewish newcomers into merchandising also meant that, despite differences in wealth, western Jews never saw one another across a class divide. The Jewish labor and socialist movements, which were so significant in the urban East, had only a shadow existence in western cities, where working-class sensibilities substituted for shop-floor solidarity. Clara Gordon Rubin, whose father, Solomon Alexander Gordon, was a union activist, first in Dallas and later in Seattle, remembered the Seattle Workmen's Circle largely as a cultural and educational organization. While her father participated in the labor movement—most notably in the Great Strike of 1919—she recalled that about half of the Workmen's Circle's members were small business owners, not laborers.[166] Even with its mixed membership, the organization remained tiny: a 1922 survey of Jewish life in Seattle found only twenty-five children attending the Workmen's Circle's Modern School.[167] Even for a union activist like Gordon, class antagonisms were generally not directed at established Jews. Gordon worked as a machinist in the shipbuilding industry and later as a streetcar operator—not for Jewish employers—and he opted to send his daughter to Sunday school at the Reform temple in the hope that she would "make the social contacts."[168] Among the forty-six members of Seattle's Orthodox Bikur Cholim congregation whose occupations are identifiable in the 1910 census, forty were busi-

ness owners (of these the largest number, thirteen, were clothing merchants). Only one was listed as a laborer and two as tailors who did not own their own shops.[169]

Similarly, in Oakland, which offered few opportunities to garment workers, the majority of Eastern European immigrants

would not sell their labor at the marketplace, but rather a line of goods, and they dealt in everything from fruit—like Shapiro, "the Watermelon King"—to jewelry, sold by men with names like Riskin, Shane, Goldstein, and Samuels. Those less fortunate were peddlers, a common sight still in the late 'twenties on the state's dusty back roads. . . . Most typical were those who bought and sold used merchandise. Immigrant Jews were the city's pawnbrokers, appraisers, auctioneers, and junk dealers; by the 1920s, they ran almost a hundred surplus and second-hand stores in the East Bay.[170]

Immigrants commonly moved from peddling to establishing retail and wholesale shops, and it was not uncommon for their children to enter the professions. The economic distance between the pioneer generation and the Eastern Europeans— never a classic class divide—had begun to dissipate by the 1920s.

Los Angeles became something new in the constellation of western cities because after 1900 it experienced a unique combination of public investment in infrastructure and private investment in oil exploration that created a large industrial working class.[171] The dramatic growth was then supplemented by Jewish investment in the movie industry and also in a specialized garment industry that attracted some Jewish workers. Earlier in the century, Jewish immigrants in Los Angeles were as heavily concentrated in trade as they were elsewhere in the West.[172] Mitchell Gelfand demonstrates that "Eastern European Jews not only achieved a singularly high degree of residential stability and occupational success, but persisted in Los Angeles and climbed the occupational ladder at a greater rate than the city's previously more integrated non-Jewish groups."[173]

By 1920, however, as many as one-third of Los Angeles's Jews could be classified as workers or artisans, while more than 50 percent held white-collar positions and another 17 percent were salesmen.[174] As the city's middle class expanded dramatically in the 1920s, its disposable income combined with the unique climate to generate a new demand for women's sportswear. Jewish pattern makers, cutters, and other skilled workers came from New York and readily found employment in the new industry.[175] Such newcomers fed local Yiddish, socialist culture that developed to a degree not found elsewhere in the West. As Gershon Einbinder's writings suggest, Jews could attend Yiddish clubs, lectures, theaters, and literary events, read Yiddish newspapers, even as traditional religious observance and Jewish study declined markedly.[176]

This expansion of a Jewish subcommunity with a working-class consciousness, if not necessarily artisan employment, took place within a larger context of diversity. Although the Amalgamated Clothing Workers had a sporadic presence, with Jewish cutters in the men's garment industry, Mexican women dominated the labor force in the large women's clothing sector by the early 1930s.[177] Identification with the cause of labor and the Yiddish cultural milieu that accompanied it persisted and were evident in the proliferation of socialist clubs and Yiddish literary events celebrated by Einbinder. But for Jews, industrial employment was generally fleeting. Relatively low start-up costs enabled many to become proprietors and eventually move to more expensive, and far less ethnically conspicuous, neighborhoods.[178]

RESPONDING TO THE MIGRANTS

Although regional migration patterns, ethnic landscapes and the steadily expanding economy all fostered relatively good relations between newcomers and established Jews, the influx, and particularly the development of concentrated neighborhoods, did arouse concerns that echoed those in the East. Despite their own high status and apparent lack of social stigmas, established Jews feared that an influx of immigrants with strange dress, language, ritual, and culture might excite an anti-Semitic backlash. In addition, they worried that new arrivals might lack income and sap the resources of the existing community. Community leaders offered aid to their coreligionists to help family members escape Russia for the United States in the wake of the pogroms in 1906 and 1907. But in Los Angeles and elsewhere, they did not advocate relocating these unfortunates to the West Coast.[179]

Not surprisingly, the most vocal opposition to immigration was expressed in San Francisco, where the numbers of immigrants were, at first, largest. As early as 1890–91, Emanu-El's Rabbi Voorsanger became involved in efforts to settle the migrants in agricultural colonies, but, according to Rosenbaum, "he rarely offered his own state for this purpose" and even raised money to send colonists back east. Voorsanger's alarm about the immigrants was rooted in his belief that Russian traditionalism was a "retrogressive force," that the immigrants would be unable to adapt, and that "an invasion from the East [would] threaten to undo the work of two generations of American Jews."[180]

Motivated by fear that the concentrated settlement of poor immigrant Jews in the South of Market area would become "another one of the reeking pestholes," he actively supported immigration restriction, putting him at odds with most national Jewish leaders and organized groups.[181] Yet, despite his influence as founding editor of *Emanu-El* (1895–1908), "there is virtually no indication that his views were accepted by his congregation and his readers."[182] Marcus Rosenthal, who had reached the pinnacle of western Jewish leadership by serving as president of the West's B'nai B'rith District Grand Lodge No. 4 in 1902, publicly castigated Voorsanger's anti-immigrant position as unrepresentative.[183] Voorsanger's successor, Rabbi Martin Meyer, who returned to his native San Francisco in 1910 to serve Emanu-El, was more concerned about the "weakening ties" of his congregants to Judaism than about any threat to a more general Jewish status posed by the newcomers.[184] For this reason, Meyer tended to view the immigrants' traditionalism rather positively, even expressing the belief that "the future of the Jew in America will be in the hands of the Russian-descended contingent . . . because he is conscious of his Jewish affiliations and anxious to perpetuate the traditions of his people."[185]

Similarly, the correspondence of Simon Lubin reveals considerable sympathy for the immigrants among California Jews. In the spring of 1914, Lubin received letters from a group called the Judeans of Oakland, who expressed their desire to "help care for and distribute Jewish immigrants" and assured him of their "energy and enthusiasm" for this work.[186] In his capacity both as head of the California Commission on Housing and Immigration and as a national director of the Hebrew Sheltering and Immigrant Aid Society of America, Lubin corresponded extensively with individuals throughout the country who were sympathetic to immigrant needs.[187] His reputation as a champion of immigrants was based in part on his work to expose the exploitation of rural laborers and improve the housing and educational opportunities of urban newcomers. But even more, he depicted immigrants as potential contributors to a cosmopolitan American culture rather than as drains on the local economy or threats to cultural norms. A series of articles he wrote with a colleague for the *Survey* in 1920 argued, "Only by adapting the national spirit in the stranger to the new environment can he be made a helpful influence in the new nation; and only by developing the national spirit of stranger and native combined can this new nation itself be developed."[188]

Even Voorsanger's most prominent congregant, Congressman Julius Kahn, who, like the rabbi, strongly supported Asian exclusion, joined national Jewish groups in opposing immigration restrictions such as the literacy test that would limit the influx of Europeans. Since many westerners viewed virtually any restriction on immigration as a step toward the popular goal of Asian exclusion, support in the region for the literacy test was very strong. Despite Kahn's staunch opposition to Asian immigration, he was the only member of the western delegation to refuse to support the literacy test when it passed over President Woodrow Wilson's veto in 1917.[189]

Supporters of open immigration like Lubin and detractors like Voorsanger could agree on the need to create institutions to foster their rapid acculturation. Relatively quickly, the San Francisco Jewish establishment came to terms with the challenges presented by the influx of Russian Jews. In his 1906 presidential address to District Grand Lodge No. 4, San Francisco's Ben Schloss, reflecting the lodge's recent decision to drop its insurance function, urged the membership to reorient the organization toward "higher aims," including the recognition that "to advance the cause of our emigrant and Ghetto co-religionists requires much money. To seek in California homesteads to relieve the congestion of the Eastern seaport towns."[190] When Schloss made this plea, the district already had a functioning committee on immigration, which worked with the Industrial Removal Office. Portland and Seattle formed similar committees, and the B'nai B'rith operated employment bureaus in these cities as well. These committees agreed to assist only those individuals—and reunite only those families—who were demonstrably self-supporting. Thus Portland's Ben Selling recommended assisting the migration of friends and relatives of individuals who had repaid loans for their relocation, but he recommended against subsidizing the travel of a man whose family had failed to provide all they were able to for the cost of relocating. On that occasion Selling wrote, "This community can get along very nicely without him."[191]

Established communities extended a variety of services to the newcomers. Reform temples offered Sunday school education to immigrant children, and the women of these congregations, like their counterparts across the country, volunteered their time and money to support settlement houses. While established Jews and immigrants in the West generally avoided the workplace-based conflicts prevalent in the East, newcomers still faced paternalistic attitudes, which they recognized and resented. Immigrants and their children might utilize settlement house services, but they took exception to the paternalistic attitudes that infused them. Jean Braverman La Pove, who attended the kindergarten at the San Bruno settlement house in its early years, recalled that her mother resented the assumption by house sponsors that her daughter's

good manners were due to the settlement workers' influence. "My mother said 'we weren't taught by them. This is the way we really are.' She resented being patronized."[192] In Portland, where immigrant Jewish newsboys encountered dangerous and exploitative working conditions, local National Council of Jewish Women member and civic activist Mrs. Isaac Leeser Cohen helped to lobby for protective legislation. But when she attempted to merge the newsboys' independent clubhouse into Neighborhood House, the newsboys felt no need for the increased supervision and rebuffed her.[193]

A 1922 survey of neighborhood needs for the Seattle settlement house recognized the tension over paternalism, noting "the stigma that the Center now bears for many of the neighbors—that of being [a] 'superimposed institution with a patronizing atmosphere.'"[194] In the more controlled space at Emanu-El Sisterhood's home for Jewish working girls in San Francisco, the resident social worker, Ethel R. Feineman, brought progressive social skills to "her" young women, some of whom had been released from the Jewish orphanage or had come to the city to find work. The smaller rooms in the building housed classes where the girls could study homemaking, dietetics, home nursing taught by Jewish women doctors and nurses, stenographic skills, and English composition. But one former resident wrote to Miss Feineman: "At times you played Lady Bountiful to me and very poorly, at times you were unkind and cruel. . . . You don't understand me or my family nor how to help us."[195]

Certainly, there was often conflict or at least a gap between the personal goals and manners taught at home by immigrant parents and what was conveyed at settlement houses like the Clubhouse in San Bruno. As Vivian Dudune Solomon recalled,

[At the Clubhouse] we had another mother figure. We had the Eastern European parent figures whose values were what they brought from Europe and they were Orthodox. We had the second parent figure in Miss [Grace] Weiner, whose ambitions for us were higher education, to be very ambitious and go on to college. She nudged and pushed and nagged and looked very disapproving. We were all afraid of her disapproval, so we excelled because of her. We would have excelled of course because of our parents, but we would have been directed in different areas of life.[196]

Similar issues surrounded the religious education programs. Both the American-born and many immigrants generally regarded traditional Jewish education, based on the model of the heder, as culturally narrow and pedagogically archaic. Those planning new schools also tacitly accepted the view that education for Jewish identity in America should be available equally, to girls as well as boys. Both sexes would be educated in the same subjects in the same location at the same time, just as they were in public schools. With immigrant congregations often unable to support stable religious schools, and many immigrants reluctant to send their children to Reform Sunday schools, the established communities in many cities formed educational alliances that offered Jewish education to immigrant children outside of the synagogue structure. Often operating at settlement houses, these schools tended to function best where the established Reform community—which usually provided much of the funding and volunteer teaching—succeeded in overcoming its paternalism and working in tandem with immigrant leaders.

At one level Jewish educators seemed to be working against the grain of the Americanization campaign that gentile educators in western states felt compelled to promote. State governments in the region feared the disruption that mass immigration had brought and wanted the public schools and state agencies to prepare immigrants for complete loyalty to the United States.[197] Jewish educators, however, saw no contradiction between loyalty to America and teaching their pupils about their cultural origins. Jewish learning, Jewish educators believed, would anchor the new immigrants in an ethnic culture that had much to contribute to American life. Simon Lubin and promoters of Zionism in cities like San Francisco and Portland believed implicitly in the "cultural pluralism" expressed by the philosopher Horace M. Kallen, who argued that only by respecting the differences among groups would America sustain the emotional stability of its immigrants and win their loyalty.[198] The location of most Hebrew schools in settlement houses reinforced the view that Jewish education encouraged rather than obstructed integration into American life. As state and federal funding for Americanization waned in the 1920s, settlement houses persisted with a pluralist approach toward integrating immigrants.[199]

Not surprisingly, given their successes in cooperating on other projects and the generally harmonious relations in the city, the Portland Hebrew School was among the most successful. There, the early Russian Jews became the driving force behind the school, which had been started sometime around 1900 as a Talmud Torah. By 1913 it had been formally established at the Council of Jewish Women's Neighborhood House in South Portland. Although Jews like Ben Selling provided the principle financial support, its modernist bent was driven by Russian immigrants like Israel Bromberg. Unlike a traditional heder, the school did not emphasize rote learning and Torah study, but became "a vehicle for instilling in their children and grandchildren an appreciation for a culture that could contribute to their moral stability in a very mobile secular culture."[200] Its innovative principal in the 1920s, Bert Treiger, employed "Ivrit B'Ivrit" (a method of Hebrew instruction) as his pedagogical method. The graduates, according to Conservative rabbi Herbert Parzen of Ahavai Shalom, had a knowledge of bible, rabbinics, and modern Hebrew. Treiger taught with sufficient thoroughness that local universities gave graduates of the school credit for the Hebrew language, just as they gave applicants from public schools credit for French or German.

Similarly, Seattle's Modern Hebrew School, established in 1913 as a citywide school with the cooperation of both Reform and Orthodox congregations, was committed to "make the word 'modern' of real meaning" and included study of contemporary Jewish history and modern Hebrew. Yet discord among immigrant congregational leaders over the curriculum prevented the establishment of a stable, unified school, and the Modern Hebrew School disbanded in 1917. It was replaced by an afternoon Talmud Torah in 1920 that also reflected contention among the Orthodox and proved equally fractious.[201] In 1922, only about half of the Ashkenazic and one-fourth of the Sephardic children living in the immigrant district attended religious school, with only two hundred attending the Talmud Torah—even though its facilities could accommodate three hundred. Only two dozen attended the Modern School, run by the Workmen's Circle and offering a socialist, Yiddish curriculum. About one hundred more attended either the Sephardic or the Ashkenazi Orthodox Sunday school.[202]

In contrast to Portland, Seattle's Educational Center did not have a religious education program to accompany its many vocational, cultural, and social programs. The center's goal of Americanization—and its assumption that Orthodoxy would dissipate as immigrants became acculturated—was evident even as it reached out to its clients through tradition. Its 1922 report suggested:

> There ought to be little difficulty in drawing parents to the Center if they are frequently invited to see their own rich heritage portrayed and interpreted anew by their children. The parents coming with pride to enjoy the religious pageants, festivals, plays, that portray their traditions, given by their own children, can easily and quite naturally become a nucleus of a parents' club. And here the Center finds its opportunity to foster respect between parents and children that are growing apart. Here is the opportunity to remind children of loyalty to their heritage in spite of the disappearance of religious orthodoxy, and to teach them to respect and preserve the best in the traditions of the older generation.[203]

In San Francisco, Reform Jews led various efforts to provide religious education, beginning with the Jewish Education Society founded by Rabbis Voorsanger (Emanu-El), Nieto (Sherith Israel), and Levy (Beth Israel) in 1897.[204] Yet given the greater gulf between immigrants and the established community, it is not surprising that their efforts met with less success. Initially focusing on "the history, religion and literature of the people of Israel," the society operated free schools for immigrant children who were not served by synagogue religious schools. The society's founders argued that the nonaffiliated schools filled a need because many of the immigrant congregations did not have adequate educational programs, and "children attending their schools would not attend the Sunday schools affiliated with the various [non-Orthodox] congregations on account of their parents' opposition to the curriculum given there."[205] In 1918 the Jewish Education Society opened a "modern Hebrew school," which offered daily (weekday) instruction at a main campus and at several branch locations. This feat occurred only after compromise by both sponsors and clients, according to Moshe Menuhin, who became principal in 1918: "The rich had to be convinced that Jewish education is not in conflict with Americanism, that it is constructive, that even they and their children are in need of it. . . . The orthodox had to be awakened and made to understand that this *metziah* of disposing of your Jewish duties in a 'quick lunch' manner through a bar mitzvah speech and *broches* [*sic*] was not Judaism."[206]

Students attending such schools often found the same gap between what was taught at home and at school as those partaking in cultural and social programs sponsored by the established community. Vivian Dudune Solomon, who attended religious school at the San Bruno Clubhouse, recalled a conflict between what her parents taught her and the education she received from Cantor Reuben Rinder, "which was Reform and patterned after Temple Emanu-El." The gap was particularly large, noted Solomon, when the students from the Clubhouse were brought for special occasions, like Sukkoth to Temple Emanu-El: "It was very interesting. Except when we came home, our lives were orthodox."[207]

Without the close cooperation seen in Portland, immigrants often found themselves choosing between schools financed and operated by Reform volunteers and poorly funded and unstable schools run by immigrant congregations. In Los Angeles, for example, the Council of Jewish Women supplied educational programs to the immigrants through their settlement house, and the B'nai B'rith Temple created "short-lived daily Hebrew school in the poorer Jewish district" in 1912. But conflict with parents led it to close down.[208] Despite the struggles over curriculum at these schools, some immigrant parents—either because they had no viable alternative or because they believed that it would lead to valuable social connections—enrolled their children at the Reform congregations' Sunday schools. While just more than half of the fifteen hundred children enrolled in Jewish educational programs in Los Angeles in 1923 attended a Talmud Torah (the largest number at the Orthodox Breed Street shul), roughly one-third attended the temple's Sunday school, and nearly a tenth attended Yiddish folk school.[209]

Despite the efforts of both established congregations and new ones, Jewish educational programs for children remained inadequate, according to critics. In San Francisco, by 1926, Menuhin found that only about 40 percent of Jewish children (two thousand of five thousand) were getting any Jewish religious instruction at all, and among those who were, 75 percent were enrolled only in weekly Sunday schools at one of the Conservative or Reform congregations. Only five hundred children, roughly 10 percent of the total number, attended the daily modern Hebrew school run by the society.[210] While local critics like Menuhin bemoaned these figures, they compare favorably to statistics available for large Jewish communities. For example, in Baltimore's immigrant district in 1920, only about 35 percent of children received any Jewish education. In Brooklyn in the 1920s, the figure was just 12 percent, and in New York City in 1924, it was 17 percent.[211] The western stories of local variations suggest how tightly knit the smaller communities of the Pacific Coast were. They also demonstrate how personally men like Bromberg, Treiger, and Menuhin could express their commitment to bridging the gap between Jewish traditions and life in a modern, pluralistic culture.

Differences between immigrants and established Jews over curricula commonly reflected not only contrasts in how Jewish and American identities were to be blended but also the two groups' differing orientation toward Zionism. Reform Jews, in their 1885 Pittsburgh platform outlining the movement's guiding principles, had officially rejected nationalist sentiments, so one might expect, given the strongly Reform orientation of the established communities, that this conflict would be particularly sharp in the West. However, there was considerable variation, and, in general, tensions over issues like Zionism were often tempered by communities that were relatively small and, as the period wore on, becoming increasingly tight-knit.

Outright opposition to Zionism was strongest in San Francisco, where the classical Reform rabbis Voorsanger and Nieto expressed categorical opposition to a Jewish state in Palestine.[212] But Rabbi Voorsanger's successors, Rabbis Martin Meyer and Louis Newman, were protégés of Stephen Wise and active Zionists, as were some prominent members of Emanu-El like Otto Wise, Rabbi Stephen Wise's older brother, and long-serving cantor Reuben Rinder. This suggests that there was considerable flux, even at Emanu-El in the early decades of the century, and that positions were not completely polarized and fixed.

Rabbi Meyer was instrumental in setting up the San Francisco Zionist Bureau office in 1916, and there was sufficient Zionist sentiment in that period to raise thirty-five thousand dollars at a 1915 meeting, the "largest sum ever raised for a Jewish cause in San Francisco up to that time." In the same period, Hadassah established a San Francisco branch, which met in the Rinder's home and was led by the cantor's wife, Rose.[213] From its first year, 1925, San Francisco's Jewish National Welfare Fund—the unified fund-raising federation for national and international Jewish causes—supported a variety of Zionist organizations, including Hadassah, the Jewish National Fund, and Mizrachi.[214] Although Rabbi Nieto through the 1920s remained an opponent of political Zionism, after a visit to Palestine in 1927 he too embraced many Zionist projects. Nevertheless, the Reform community in San Francisco retained a reputation as staunchly anti-Zionist, and this likely contributed to the greater rift between the immigrant and established communities in that city than elsewhere in the West.

Seattle's Reform community also had anti-Zionist leadership in Rabbi Koch, who served Seattle's Temple De Hirsch from 1906 until 1941. According to Sonia Myers Wachtin, the founding president of Hadassah in Seattle, "You couldn't mention Zionism in there [Temple De Hirsch]." Nevertheless, Rabbi Koch, true to his commitment to "freedom of speech," opened his pulpit to a sermon by visiting rabbi Louis Newman, who came to Seattle to raise funds for the ZOA.[215] In 1919 the Seattle section of the Council of Jewish Women "went on record as being opposed to the project of a National Zionistic Home in Palestine, expressing themselves as being opposed to Palestine being organized as a Jewish State."[216] At the same time, however, Seattle's major Jewish newspaper, the *Jewish Transcript,* had a Zionist orientation and reported on a wide array of Zionist activities by the 1920s. Despite the opposition of Rabbi Koch and some of his congregants, Seattle's ethnic Eastern European community aligned itself enthusiastically with Zionism and expressed optimism that even temple members could be swayed. As Felix Frankfurter wrote in a letter to Bikur Cholim leader Solomon Prottas in 1917, "Just keep at it, and if the work of organization can be increased and carried on in a systematic way, I am sure a great portion of Dr. Koch's congregation would join us. They must; it is inevitable."[217]

Opposite Rabbis Voorsanger, Nieto, and Koch stood Portland's Stephen Wise. During his time in Portland, Wise emerged as a leader in the Reform and Zionist movements; he had helped found the Federation of American Zionists in 1897 and had attended the Second Zionist Conference in Switzerland the following year.[218] Wise's articulate and ardent Zionism helped to win much support for the movement among his Reform congregants.[219] Active laymen like Zack and Isaac Swett and Moses Mossessohn also played a key role in promoting Zionism in Portland. In the 1920s, Bert Treiger and Rabbi Herbert Parzen of Ahavai Shalom made Zionism a central component in the program of the centralized Hebrew school and in community-wide public discourse.

The experience in Los Angeles, especially as it grew into the region's largest city and largest Jewish community, seemed closer to Portland than to San Francisco. Vorspan and Gartner argue that local leaders were mostly "hostile or indifferent to Zionism."[220] But Kramer and Stern seem closer to the truth about popular opinion in Los Angeles when they write that "both Eastern European and Germanic Jewish families supported the building up of the Holy Land, as the cause developed in the West."[221] Although Rabbi Edgar Magnin, unlike many other Reform rabbis in the West, did not take a strong stance on either side of the Zionist question, the reporting of fund-raising and rallies by Labor Zionists and Mizrachi leaders and the reports on visits to the Holy Land by rabbis suggest a broad public consensus in support of Zionist projects.[222] The largest circulation Jewish newspaper in Los Angeles, one with strong links

to the Wilshire Boulevard Temple, actually called for the organization of a Zionist group. A number of Zionist organizations were active in the city as early as 1912, and, not surprisingly, the influx of Jews to the region after World War I led to significant growth in the movement.[223] By 1927, Zionists in Los Angeles proclaimed, "It has been said that no longer are there Jews who label themselves anti-Zionists, who flaunt an alleged super-patriotism as a vain excuse for their lack of Jewish consciousness and who attack on this score the attempts of their fellow Jews to rebuild the ancient homeland. The present attitude of the Jewish community of Los Angeles would seem to be prima facie evidence that such a statement is substantially correct."[224] Reporting on the Arab riots in August 1929 led to overwhelming public support for Zionism.[225]

Variations in the degree of community cooperation over issues such as religious education and Zionism demonstrate that the early-twentieth-century influx of newcomers had created cleavages within western Jewish communities. Yet those variations within the West seem less significant than the ongoing differences between the West and other regions. In contrast to the East and Midwest, where the persistent flood of immigrant Jews at least through 1915 completely transformed existing communities, the migration to the West was more gradual and the change less profound. Even in comparison with regions of the country like the South, the pace and pattern of migration, regional economic development, and the ethnic landscape of the West all served to make the transition smoother and the gulf between the newcomers and the pioneers easier to overcome. Although immigrant neighborhoods and institutions analogous to those in the East emerged in the West, they were late in their development and less culturally insular and the established Jewish communities had an easier time adjusting to their presence. This sense of consolidation was central in shaping western Jewish communities as they responded to new challenges in the 1930s and 1940s.

Although the impact of immigration on communities in the Pacific West was less profound than in other parts of the country, the arrival of the Eastern Europeans and Sephardim created new needs. While Jewish communities had tried to assume responsibility for local Jewry since the earliest days of settlement in the West, the newcomers challenged the existing philanthropic institutions. Jewish philanthropy, central to community organization and identity, would be transformed to meet these challenges.

4 FROM CHARITY TO PHILANTHROPY

A Regional Model, 1870s–1930s

If you have one lung or two wives
you go to California. —YIDDISH APHORISM

It is recorded in the lore of the San Francisco Jewish community that Lewis Gerstle saved the Emanu-El Sisterhood for Personal Service from failure. In dire need of money for its new settlement work, the sisterhood called a meeting to formulate a fund-raising plan. When no plan gained group support, Gerstle told the women, "Leave the matter to me," and sent a twenty-five hundred dollar check.[1] San Francisco's Jewish social service institutions benefited from the region's rapidly growing economy and the rising status of Jewish settlers. The mutton-chopped Gerstle was a cofounder of the highly successful Alaska Commercial Company, which hunted seals in western waters and prepared the fur for market. A member of B'nai B'rith, he helped sponsor its Pacific Hebrew Orphan Asylum, and as a member of Temple Emanu-El, with his wife, Hannah, he supported the Sisterhood for Personal Service, which took the assistance of immigrants and especially working girls as its grand project (fig. 4.1). Although benefactors like Gerstle supported these institutions, reflecting the developing social stratification of the Jewish community, they did not follow the earlier practice of providing care to the beneficiaries personally.

Portland's energetic Ida Loewenberg, though from an elite family, proved an exception to this rule by working much more closely with

FIG. 4.1 *Lewis Gerstle with his wife, Hannah, and their family. Western Jewish History Center, Judah L. Magnes Museum (1967).*

the new Jewish immigrants. Loewenberg at first volunteered at Neighborhood House, but enthused by the work, she studied in Eugene, Chicago, and New York to become one of the region's first professionally educated social workers.[2] Though Ida's father made a great deal of money and she was educated at private schools in Portland and Germany, her life changed when her father lost his fortune in the depression of 1897 and died two years later. To support themselves, Ida and her sisters sought

FIG. 4.2 *Loewenberg sisters: Ida and Zerlina, front row; Rose L. Goodman, back left; and Laddie G. Trachtenberg, right rear, 1946. Oregon Jewish Museum OJM1580.*

FIG. 4.3 *Peter M. Kahn, right, with Julius Bisno, left, in the Los Angeles Jewish Community Library, ca. 1950. After Kahn's death, the name was changed to the Jewish Community Library of Los Angeles—Peter M. Kahn Memorial. Courtesy of Judith Kahn Gorman.*

careers, not jobs. Ida chose social work, while her sister Zerlina became a librarian (fig. 4.2). For more than thirty years, Ida Loewenberg directed South Portland's Neighborhood House; she raised funds for an adjoining building with a swimming pool, took women to doctors, and involved herself in the lives of Jewish, Italian, African American, and other community residents and of the volunteers who served with her.[3]

Part of the established Jewish elite, Loewenberg and Gerstle felt that charity was both their Jew-ish and civic duty, a demonstration of strongly felt American pride and their general community leadership.[4] By the early twentieth century, however, a new kind of Jewish philanthropist emerged, first in Los Angeles's rapidly expanding Eastern European community and then in other western cities. Immigrants like Peter M. Kahn who shared origins with the communities they served quickly moved from newcomer status to become leaders and founders of community institutions (fig. 4.3).

Before reaching the United States in 1904 at the

age of twenty-six, Kiev-born Kahn had an early career as a revolutionary.[5] Tall, he appeared to be a "western farmer or explorer for California oil."[6] After four years in St. Louis, the Kahn family settled in Los Angeles, drawn west like many other health seekers. Kahn, an asthma sufferer, sought relief in the southland's healing climate, where he climbed the occupational ladder from fruit peddler to wholesale broker, to farmer, and finally to store owner. But like other successful Russian immigrants, he remained loyal to the values of his socialist youth. He joined the Workmen's Circle, the American Jewish Congress, the Labor Zionist Histradut, and the Hebrew Free Loan Association.[7]

As the Pacific West's Jewish population increased, so did the number of philanthropic institutions founded by Russian immigrants such as Kahn. He became identified with the Jewish Consumptive Relief Association of Southern California (the forerunner of the City of Hope hospital), the Jewish Community Council (later the Jewish Federation), the Orphans Home, Mount Sinai Home for Chronic Invalids (later Mount Sinai Hospital), the Community Library, and Jewish educational institutions. On his death in 1952, Kahn was eulogized by Rabbi Jacob Kohn as "the father of the city," but, more correct, Kahn fathered the institutions that defined the mid-twentieth-century Los Angeles Jewish community.[8]

Philanthropy gave focus and public identity to western Jewry outside of the synagogue. In a region where religious observance and membership in religious organizations for most ethnic groups were usually less common than elsewhere, charitable activities were critical.[9] Philanthropists reflected the changing duties of community leaders, regional ethnic landscapes, and interlocking systems of community control. They controlled more than

charity; their visions affected relationships with new immigrants, the religious orientation of institutions, community reputations, and the ability to attract continued funding. An examination of a Jewish community's philanthropies and charities not only chronicles institutions but also reveals the complicated relationships between leaders and community members.

Central to this story is a theme common to Jewish communities in other parts of the country: the transformation of mutual aid charities into professionally run organizations. Between the 1870s and the 1930s, the general and Jewish populations in the Pacific West grew at an unprecedented rate. Western Jewish immigration, however, peaked later than in the East and never overwhelmed the established communities. As Los Angeles replaced San Francisco as the regional center, in both cities settlement houses and community federations superseded mutual aid and benevolent societies. But in the West, the needs of communities changed as the "health rush" of the late nineteenth century brought the sick, who believed that the golden land would cure their ills.[10] The style and substance of philanthropy altered; acts of kindness toward neighbors with shared cultures gave way to donor-sponsored institutional care from professional social workers. All development was governed by a community's demographics, the local urban milieu, and the degree of civic control by pioneer founders.

LAYING THE FOUNDATION

Throughout the Pacific West, benevolent societies had provided the first form of philanthropy. Men created benevolent societies in San Francisco (1849, 1850), Los Angeles (1854), Oakland (1864),

Portland (early 1870s), Olympia (1873), and Seattle (1895). Women formed parallel societies, and in one unusual case, Seattle's Jewish women's organization predated the men's by three years. For both men and women, benevolent societies regulated the visiting of the sick and care of the needy.[11]

Most societies raised their entire budgets from small monthly dues and the occasional entertainment benefit or dance. In 1892, the Ladies' Hebrew Benevolent Society in Los Angeles celebrated that in its first twenty-two years it gave twenty thousand dollars to men and women in need. Yet support was so abundant that the women held only "four public entertainments for the benefit of [its] relief fund."[12] In their formative years, men often assisted as officers or counselors for women's organizations, instructing their wives in the proper conduct of meetings and directing their investments. Men served as officers of the First Hebrew Ladies' Mutual Benefit Association in San Francisco during the 1870s, and three men from the Los Angeles Hebrew Benevolent Society counseled the parallel ladies' society. But usually within a decade the women led their own organizations.[13]

These benevolent societies occasionally extended charity to the non-Jewish poor. The Los Angeles women's benevolent society prided itself on its ability to work with other sectarian benevolent associations and respond to "public calamity."[14] But benevolent societies became less important or obsolete as fraternal organizations, congregations, professionals, or family members took responsibility for charity. Younger men often joined the B'nai B'rith, while women joined sisterhoods and national organizations such as the National Council for Jewish Women (NCJW), which helped those in need by providing services as well as aid.

Just as individual Jews circulated from one western community to another, so did philanthropic funds and initiatives, especially after a catastrophe like the San Francisco earthquake and fire in 1906.[15] Portland and Seattle particularly benefited from their close proximity, with Portland, the more established community, available to help Seattle with advice and trained leadership. Through repeated visits, the women of Portland affected both the founding and policies of Seattle's NCJW. In 1900, Blanche Blumauer of Portland's NCJW traveled to Seattle to instruct women on meeting procedures and charter provisions, and as late as 1927 Seattle's Hebrew Benevolent Society hired Portland's Mae Goldsmith (daughter of its former mayor) as its paid director.

When growing Jewish populations made it necessary for communities to expand their scale of care, they did so based on regional as well as local needs. The oldest, wealthiest, and largest, San Francisco, developed a multiplicity of organizations well before the early-twentieth-century influx of newcomers. Portland and Seattle created fewer, more modest endeavors. When Los Angeles faced explosive growth, it quickly transformed its social services from elite-organized benevolence to a dynamic multi-location system of social welfare organizations.

San Francisco, the hub of settlement in the nineteenth century, provided the region's first social service institutions. By the mid-1870s, the Eureka Benevolent Society had stopped requiring members to visit the sick and organize funerals and instead offered more institutionalized support, while B'nai B'rith men sought to build a Jewish orphan asylum and an old age home. The Protestant Orphan Asylum had opened in 1851, and the Roman Catholic Orphan Asylum in 1852. However, not until 1870 did the western District Grand

Lodge No. 4 of B'nai B'rith organize the Hebrew Orphan Asylum and Home Society, which would house children from the entire region.[16] The 1870 call for funds read: "The time has at length arrived to put into effective being the hopes and wishes which have long been cherished in your hearts. Of the many communities of Israel in America, none have proved their claim to the promptings and deeds of charity more than those dwelling on the shores of this Western Ocean. . . . We need—we must have—in San Francisco—for the benefit of the Pacific States, a JEWISH ORPHAN ASYLUM AND HOME."[17] By 1878, the asylum employed two public school teachers, a matron and her husband.[18] Volunteer doctors, women who sewed, and men who offered a variety of professional services contributed to the home's success.[19] Jewish families and communities throughout the region relied on the orphans home for the care of their children, so the smaller western cities did not have to worry about building their own institutions for many years. Los Angeles's Jewish orphans were sent to the San Francisco institution until the local Ladies' Hebrew Benevolent Society opened its own home in 1909; Seattle sent children to San Francisco until 1925.[20]

In the smaller communities, benevolence persisted in part because the gap between founding families and later immigrants was narrower. With fewer Jewish institutions, founders and new immigrants often recognized one another, even if they did not socialize. However, even smaller communities like Seattle shifted away from personal care after the turn of the century, in response both to a substantial increase in the number of immigrants and to the national trend to professionalize social work. Because benevolent societies had formed later in cities like Seattle, the time between elite

leadership and professionally run organizations was compressed, and the second generation completed the professionalization process.

TRANSFORMING PHILANTHROPY

Western women often led this evolution toward professionalism. Elizabeth Herr observed that "the unique characteristic of the frontier is that its newness loosened the constraints under which women lived in more established areas and offered them a variety of opportunities."[21] This differentiated them from southern Jewish women, who, like other southern women, were tied to traditional patterns and slow to move outside the home to work with others in public roles.[22] In the West, Jewish women, like women in general, embraced leadership roles in organizations that cared for and educated newcomers. As Jeanne E. Abrams points out, "An emphasis on voluntarism and celebrated individualism that has come to be associated with the West placed the burden of caring for the needy squarely in the private arena."[23] Jewish women had helped build the West's first charitable infrastructures both in cosmopolitan "instant" cities and in remote small towns. This gave women not only experience but also confidence in their organizational and interpersonal skills. Jewish women in San Francisco were so organized that by 1909 they had founded fifteen social service associations, almost as many as in New York City.[24]

Unlike in the East, where the new women's organizations at the end of the nineteenth century "transformed the idea of women's religious work by drawing it from home into the public realm of organized charity," western women by necessity had always been involved in communal life.[25]

Throughout the West, Jewish women learned skills that allowed them to establish social services and train "themselves in the rudiments of professional expertise."[26] By the early twentieth century, they used these skills to take simple benevolence into the political realm.[27] For western women, suffrage (in Washington in 1910 and in California and Oregon in 1911) well in advance of their eastern counterparts facilitated their activity, especially in the areas of immigration, settlement, child welfare and the building of modern and safe institutions and hospitals.[28] Jewish organizations worked with non-Jewish clubwomen for secular, civic, and political causes that concerned the community as a whole.

As the Progressive movement created fundamental changes in the way society treated children, the poor, and the sick, philanthropy with its social scientific connotations became the modern term for charitable work.[29] Women and men trained in the new field of social work led the movement. Jane Addams and Lillian Wald, prominent reformers, emphasized women's moral authority to address public problems considered an extension of a woman's sphere, "the home." The "home," including the care of children and the sick, extended to encompass the entire community and redefined gender roles.[30] In this new environment, it became proper for women to take care of others by establishing settlement houses and hospitals and by working with the rapidly expanding public schools.

Rationalization became crucial to this new reform movement. New institutions stressed efficiency, coordination, and especially expertise. Social work quickly emerged as a valued profession with set principles and procedures. Immigrants and children often became the focus of reformers' attentions. Settlement houses, milk stations, city parks and beautification, public baths, juvenile courts, and Americanization programs all became part of these new reform endeavors.[31] In her study of western women, the historian Peggy Pascoe argues that female moral authority had its "origins in a 'women's culture' rooted most firmly among white middle-class women, its use of the female values of that culture to strengthen the social authority of women, and its assumption that those values applied (or should apply) to women of ethnic minority groups as well as to white women."[32] Western women, mostly Protestants, expressed their voices with confidence and authority and sought to exert moral authority over the less fortunate, less white, and, usually, not Protestant women in rescue homes.

Some aspects of Pascoe's thesis apply to Jewish middle-class women as well. Many of the wives and daughters of Jewish community founders believed that their station in society gave them the moral authority to instruct immigrants, especially women. These reformers believed that when immigrant women adopted American Jewish ideals, as well as modern ideas about child rearing, they would reinforce rather than jeopardize the standards of the Americanized Jewish community. They concurred with the idea of protection and rescue but retained the view that men should exercise authority in family life. Many Jewish female reformers saw their goal as preparing girls for marriage and training married women to become efficient managers of a modern Jewish family. For them the transformation to a modern, yet still Jewish, family proved paramount, and philanthropy became part of their Jewish identification.[33]

The stability of western Jewish pioneer families provided the foundation for the communities to care for immigrants and others in need. On the Pacific Coast, families like the Hellmans, Newmarks, Schwabachers, Gerstles, Hirsches, and Sellings could always be counted on to support communal institutions with their time and money. By the early twentieth century, these dynasties, based on family and business networks, accepted the Progressive Era's ideology of outreach to create new programs. Unlike their Protestant peers, Jewish women were not rebelling against male dominance but extending female authority based on their mothers' pioneer experience in benevolent societies.[34] Although not formally educated in social work, Mae Goldsmith led a social service agency in Seattle based on charitable values she had learned from her mother, Emma (Froham) Goldsmith, who had served for many years as president of Portland's Hebrew Ladies Benevolent Association.[35] The way in which Jewish westerners cared for their community would continue to be reinterpreted again and again as social work and services modernized.

FROM CHARITY TO MODERN MEDICINE

The first western hospitals were either charitable institutions or small house facilities run by doctors for paying patients. Catholic orders such as the Sisters of Charity and ethnic groups such as the German and the French supported early hospitals.[36] Indeed, Catholic charitable orders were responsible for the first hospitals serving the general public in virtually every major city in the West. Western Jews, like Jews elsewhere, built hospitals that "reinforced the culture of separatism;" they celebrated their American civic identity, yet built Jewish institutions apart.[37] Similar to Catholics, Germans, and others, Jews "saw their [medical] institutions as symbols of community identity and responsibility."[38] These institutions grew at a

time of increased immigration and were Jewish in funding, management, and identity, although not always religiously observant.

Responding to both increased population, which taxed charities, and the development of modern medical practices, late-nineteenth-century western Jews began to organize hospitals. Some worried that charity wards in non-Jewish hospitals could subject Jewish patients to pressured deathbed conversions, a common practice of evangelical Protestants.[39] In addition, as medicine was professionalized, many Jewish doctors chose to work and train in Jewish hospitals to avoid discrimination or outright exclusion from sectarian or public hospitals.

Although western communities were substantially younger than those in the East, their hospitals soon became their equals, by incorporating the new Progressive scientific ideology.[40] The elite founders of San Francisco's Mount Zion, the Pacific West's first Jewish hospital, expressed this ethos as a natural extension of their paternalism and dedication to community care. Instead of providing doctors for home care, as had been the practice in benevolent societies, they now would support professionals to care for the sick in modern institutions.

When Mount Zion opened its doors in 1897, its aims, funding, leadership, and religious practices illustrated how elite San Francisco Jewry continued to control community institution building well into the twentieth century. Precipitated by concern over increased immigration, the perceived need for a hospital with a Jewish atmosphere, and the poor quality of care in the public hospital (it had been condemned as dangerous by the Board of Health), forty-three people, including one woman and rabbis from the four largest congregations, met in 1887 to discuss building a Jewish hospital.[41]

Rabbi Jacob Voorsanger of Emanu-El believed that "the Jewish sick should have a home of their own . . . where medical skill and religious care and scruple may join their beneficent hand and cure the stricken and the ailing."[42] Voorsanger, however, was not envisioning an Orthodox institution, with kosher food and religious observance, but a modern, medical facility under Jewish auspices to care for the indigent sick and provide a high standard of medical care for the community.

It proved difficult to forge a community-wide consensus on the hospital's orientation. Minute books note the lack of "cooperation from our co-religionists" and an "under current . . . at work to belittle this noble work."[43] As in other American cities, controversy raged about whom the hospital should serve.[44] Some believed that the Jewish community was too small to support a hospital; others thought that a Jewish hospital should serve only Jews.[45] The ultimate founders believed that, unlike benevolent associations, the proposed hospital should be "for the purpose of aiding the indigent sick without regard to race or creed, to be supported by the Jewish community."[46]

However, the charity orientation did not preclude the founders' original aims of also providing hospital care for those who could pay. Unlike Christian hospitals that could count on church support, American Jewish hospitals were supported by a combination of donations and fees from those who could pay. Jews in San Francisco, like those in Newark, New Jersey, believed in the "twin impulses of philanthropy and self-help."[47] And the founders themselves wanted to insure that they could obtain the best possible medical care.

In its first decades, Mount Zion's patient profile varied widely. While charity patients were an important part of the hospital's mission, they were not always the largest contingent. In 1899, sixty-eight patients entered the hospital for at least one night, and only three paid for their care.[48] Three years later, the numbers had changed drastically; there were now 272 paying patients and 186 free patients.[49] The nativity of patients also helps explain the community's composition. In 1899, more than half were foreign-born.[50] By 1903, the majority of free patients were American-born, followed closely by immigrants from Russia and Germany.[51] The predominance of free patients born in the United States, Russia, and Germany reinforces the fact that the West, unlike the East in this period, was not overwhelmed by Eastern Europeans but may have attracted migrants hoping for a better climate to cure their ills.

Mount Zion hospital did treat a small proportion of non-Jews. In 1899, the hospital cared for eight gentiles, and ten years later, fifty-five, when the City and County Hospital had been intentionally burned to the ground because of plague-infested rats.[52] Although the concept of a free hospital for all was an important part of the hospital's creed, non-Jews never flocked to Mount Zion. Still, when the staff reported that the city of Oakland was sending its Jewish poor to Mount Zion for care, the board realized it had become a regional medical center, but only a local charity.

Besides donations and payment for services, Mount Zion was supported by memberships. Unlike nationally funded T.B. facilities, Mount Zion, like the B'nai B'rith's Orphans Home, maintained that "the membership shall be confined to the Jewish people of the Pacific Coast."[53] In 1888 alone, men in Sacramento and Honolulu took out subscriptions, and three New Yorkers with strong connections to the community joined. Soon the hospital had members in Spokane, Seattle, Olympia, and Reno.[54] Beyond membership, regional families including the Hellmans and the Schwabachers generously contributed, as did non-Jewish elites like Jane Stanford, whose husband, Leland, founded Stanford University.[55]

Hospital leadership and the control of charity continued to rest in the hands of San Francisco's Jewish elite who also supported the Hebrew Orphan Asylum and the Emanu-El Sisterhood for Personal Service. Organizational meetings were held at Temple Emanu-El, and its members were encouraged to support the hospital and served on its board of directors and on the ladies auxiliary. Volunteering for the hospital became an expected duty. For example, Joseph Brandenstein, the father of the founders of M.J.B. Coffee and Tea, was Mount Zion's president from 1893 to 1899 and also the former president of the German Benevolent Society and Hospital and a director of the Pacific Hebrew Orphan Asylum.[56] This consolidation of leadership meant that Eastern European immigrants were not asked to join hospital committees or the board and were kept out of decision making.[57] However, the overlapping leadership did have its benefits; Mount Zion doctors oversaw the Orphan Asylum, the Emanu-El Sisterhood's clinics, and a clinic established at the NCJW's settlement house. It was even suggested that orphan girls be trained as nurses, which would benefit all four institutions.[58]

In all of these institutions, women's support proved essential, as was the case in other Jewish hospitals. The historians Alan and Deborah Kraut point out that women's participation "was consistent with the enthusiasm of many for Progressive reforms."[59] Since the Mount Zion Hospital Association was founded at the same time as western women's clubs, the Emanu-El Sisterhood for Personal Service, and the NCJW, women anticipated that they would have a role in hospital leadership. Here, Victorian women's tradition of

caring for the sick would be extended to articulate moral authority over the vulnerable in the most modern of settings. Like women in other hospitals, they volunteered their labor and donated food and necessities, bypassing the "board and budget process."[60] Nevertheless, women of Mount Zion for three decades had to fight male dominance for leadership roles.

Women volunteers raised funds and provided for patient comfort. Soon after the hospital began to accept patients, the Ladies Auxiliary Society formed to help with the running of the hospital. First president of the auxiliary (1897–1908) Esther (Neugass) Hellman, the wife of I. W. Hellman, was characterized as "smart, shrewd and compassionate" by family members. She was followed in office by her daughter-in-law Frances Hellman (1908–28), so for thirty years women's leadership was held by one of the most prominent families in the region.[61]

Although the women involved themselves in the hospital's household chores, like purchasing and mending the linens, managing the kitchen, and making "the non-paying patients as happy and comfortable as possible," they did not sit on the hospital board.[62] These volunteers, most of whom were the wives and daughters of members of the board of directors and officers of their own charitable organizations, approached the board asking to contribute to the hospital's welfare beyond housekeeping chores. This perplexed the board:

> The suggestions made by the Ladies Committee have been discussed as well as complaints made and we find ourselves in rather an embarrassing position for the reason that we are not clear as to the duties of the ladies and the position which they occupy in the hospital. A careful examination of the constitution and by laws fails to give us any information and we

therefore respectively suggest that a communication be sent to the Ladies asking them what their own ideas are as to their duties and position. . . . We would state, however that we would not approve of a condition whereby anything relating to the management of the hospital proper would be taken out of the hands of the Executive Committee.[63]

The Ladies Auxiliary Society threatened to disband unless they were given responsibilities beyond visiting and mending. They were given the job of organizing a "Grand Ball," whose proceeds allowed the hospital to expand.[64] Now, the women also demanded a say in how the money was spent.[65] In October 1907, the auxiliary again asked for opportunities to carry out the "betterment of the domestic arrangements of the Hospital." When the board was soon reorganized, governing committees were enlarged, with representatives of the auxiliary composing a fourth to a third of most committees.[66] Only on the membership committee did the women almost achieve parity, demonstrating how important they were to the hospital's growth. Members of the ladies auxiliary served on every committee except the powerful finance committee, from which they were barred.[67]

The chairman of the board, not without condescension, later evaluated the board decision: "When these ladies were first taken into our administrative work there were some who feared a clash of authority or lack of cooperation, and others who prophesied absolute failure. After two years of experience we can say the experiment has been a complete success in every particular. The ladies have been of inestimable assistance in all committee work, and have absolutely silenced all apprehension as to the result of what was considered by some a hazardous experiment."[68] Although committee members, it would still be almost two

more decades before women became board members.[69] The men kept a tight reign on hospital spending. However, during much of these decades, women gained control of the day-to-day operations that were outside the purview of the doctors.[70]

Like Jewish hospitals in Denver, Chicago, and New York started by Reform Jews, Mount Zion was neither kosher nor supportive of Jewish rituals.[71] Capturing the city's Jewish identity, the hospital was led by a Reform elite that expressed a paternalistic attitude toward more religious Jews. Requests for kosher food were denied as an unnecessary expense. The board did inquire how questions of kashruth were handled in eastern hospitals, but it did not establish a kosher kitchen. Reluctantly, the administration allowed a *mohel* to perform circumcisions, but he was required to conform to modern cleanliness standards and wear a doctor's gown and gloves. Patients had to organize their own religious observances. They lit Sabbath candles in the wards and conducted religious services among themselves. Autopsies, against Orthodox interpretation of Jewish law, were a source of disagreement with the hospital's medical staff.[72] However, patients remembered their hospital and clinic experiences as distinctly Jewish. A doctor on Mount Zion's staff recalled that the hospital from his boyhood was "by, for, and with the Jews." Speaking of his 1915 hospital stay, he reminisced, "All of the other patients on the ward were Jewish, and all on the free clinic service. . . . [At the clinic] I remember it being somewhat crowded, with Yiddish the resounding language throughout the clinic. There was no question at that time as to the Jewishness of Mount Zion Hospital."[73] In addition to most of the patients, all of the doctors were Jewish.[74]

Mount Zion became pivotal for demonstrating the civic leadership of San Francisco's Jewish elite.

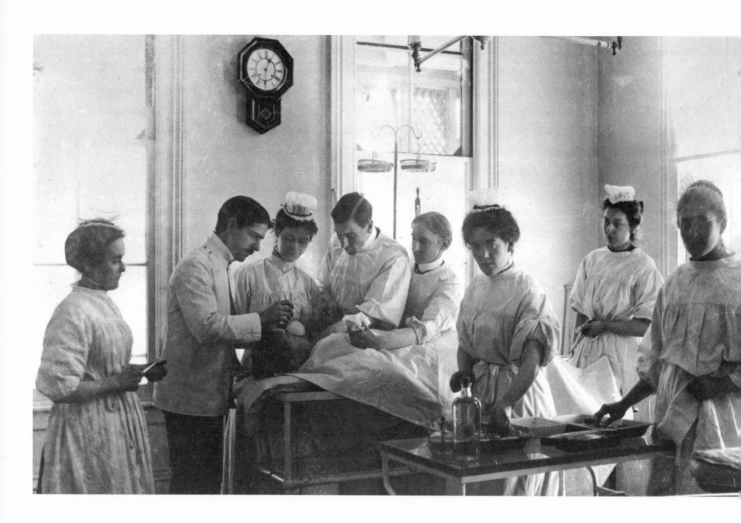

FIG. 4.4 *Surgery at Mount Zion Hospital, San Francisco, ca. 1900. Western Jewish History Center, Judah L. Magnes Museum (1992).*

With the help of bond sales and large donations, especially that of I. W. Hellman, a cornerstone was placed in 1912 for a prominent building.[75] Once the new five-story Mount Zion opened in 1914, it completely relieved the Federation of Jewish Charities of its responsibility to care for the indigent sick and also provided ongoing care for sick children in the Pacific Hebrew Orphan Asylum.[76] By 1919, Mount Zion Hospital was one of only thirteen Jewish hospitals nationwide to gain accreditation by the American College of Surgeons (fig. 4.4).[77]

It had become the medical equal of any modern hospital, private or public. Like the city's prominent synagogues, Mount Zion became a tangible symbol of the power, religious identification, and social and financial dominance of San Francisco's Jewish elite.

In Los Angeles, because of its rapid population growth, philanthropic practices and community leadership followed a different pattern. Attracted by the city's boosterism, particularly the claim that the warm dry climate could heal the sick, many

Jews, including those afflicted with tuberculosis and other illnesses, brought their families to Los Angeles. The *L. A. Times* newspaperman George Ward Burton, one of the loudest voices proclaiming the benefits of Los Angeles, came west suffering from T.B. and after his recovery wrote books and articles touting the city's healthful climate. These claims did not just induce the sick to come west; they were also good for the city's economy. Burton's good friend, and a leader of the regional Jewish community, I. W. Hellman, believed that Burton's articles "attracted more population, capital, enterprise and industry to Southern California than those of any other newspaper writer."[78] The city became the "Capital of the Sanitarium Belt." Many of the health seekers were native-born white Protestants, whose new dominance changed the political and cultural atmosphere of southern California.[79] The simultaneous Jewish influx transformed Jewish health care and social services.

Directed by its mercantile elite, the Jewish community of Los Angeles, like its counterpart in San Francisco, created new institutions based on traditional forms of charity. Benevolent societies changed their focus to support the newcomers.[80] As one resident remembered, "In those days people did not travel to [southern] California unless they had T.B. or other illnesses that they hoped the climate would cure."[81] Soon, requests almost exceeded the society's funds, so merchandise and advice were substituted for money. Eventually the society joined with the nondenominational Associated Charities of Los Angeles to "coordinate and systematize the charitable work of the city."[82] This 1893 partnership between public and private charities, led by the Hellman and Newmark families, mirrored the relationship these pioneer families maintained with gentile leaders to solve other community problems.[83] This system, which sometimes sent Jews to public charities, differed from that in most communities, where Jews always took care of their own. With set limits "benevolent societies gradually moved from a position of assuming complete responsibility for the needs of Jewish families to one of sharing the responsibility for welfare with other private and public agencies."[84]

After 1900, when the Los Angeles Ladies' Hebrew Benevolent Society evaluated cases, it began to use the principles of "scientific" charity. The society assessed the applicant's ability to work, applying a similar standard for relief to men and women. For example in 1903, it denied a return applicant because it determined that she "could secure employment if she would exert herself."[85] The societies usually granted religious requests; both the Los Angeles men's and women's Hebrew Benevolent Societies frequently provided matzoth during Passover.[86] And in 1918, when the two societies merged to become the Jewish Aid Society (a precursor to Jewish Family Service of Los Angeles), they also reflected changing views on gender. Their choice of Dora Berris of the Ladies' Hebrew Benevolent Society as executive director allowed them to join Seattle in affirming that a woman with ability could manage welfare services as well as a man could.[87]

To support this new professional infrastructure in meeting health needs, fund-raising methods had to be reimagined as well.[88] Rabbi Edgar Magnin of Congregation B'nai B'rith, with the support of other community leaders, shifted philanthropic efforts from elite membership organizations with infrequent fund-raising events to continual community fund-raising. Magnin, from a San Francisco pioneer family and one of the first rabbis to be born in and serve in the West, had a cult-like following. A dynamic speaker, he guided the community's philanthropic concerns by harnessing the resources both of founding families like the Hellmans and the Newmarks and of powerful newcomers, especially the movie moguls. With Magnin at the helm, Congregation B'nai B'rith members included leaders of the movie studios with names such as Mayer, Fox, and Warner. According to the Hollywood writer Budd Schulberg, "Moguls were happy to contribute large sums for front-row pews, and Rabbi Magnin rewarded them with flattery that poured like honey, and with a sanctimonious air that played up to their image of a man of God. Magnin was the right rabbi in the right temple in the right city at the right moment in time. If he had not presided over our B'nai B'rith, God and Louie B. Mayer—whose overpowering presences tended to overlap—would have had to create him."[89] In 1926, Louis B. Mayer became city chairman of the United Jewish Campaign. According to the city's Jewish newspaper, "Whenever Jews of the motion picture industry have been called on to help the Jewish community financially, they have done so."[90] These prominent gifts, alongside the small, but numerous, donations from the growing number of new immigrants, changed the face of western Jewish health care, especially in Los Angeles. Philanthropy and community control soon moved from the founding families to the newcomers, including movie moguls.

Early-twentieth-century hospitals reflected these changes in philanthropic leadership, medical policies, and local governance. As was common in other cities, Jews in Los Angeles established separate, sometimes duplicate, hospitals for the contagious sick, those with injuries or other illnesses, and the presumed incurable.[91] The 1902 Kaspare Cohn Hospital (later Cedars of Lebanon) resembled San Francisco's Mount Zion. Founded and supported by the Reform descendants of the pioneer community, it sought to treat the poor of

the community as well as the other Jews needing hospitalization. It was joined in 1918 by the predecessor to Mount Sinai, which drew its support from Eastern European immigrants who wanted to take care of their own.[92] In addition, the nationally known and supported City of Hope was established at Duarte as a sanitarium for long-term care of T.B. patients.

The impetus for these endeavors was the arrival of many tuberculosis sufferers. Jacob Schlesinger, president of the Los Angeles Hebrew Benevolent Society, responded to daily requests for medical care by proposing that the society sponsor a hospital.[93] Eventually, he persuaded other members of the Hebrew Benevolent Society, including Harris Newmark and Kaspare Cohn, to join him.[94] Cohn donated a large Victorian house in an upscale neighborhood for an eight-bed hospital. Converted home-hospitals were common at the turn of the century, but in this instance the city council, at the instigation of neighbors who feared the presence of contagious patients, barred consumptive patients from private hospitals in the city.[95] With that, the hospital became a general service facility.

Like Rabbi Voorsanger at Mount Zion, Rabbi Sigmund Hecht of Congregation B'nai B'rith served on the board of the hospital and encouraged women of the temple to involve themselves with hospital work. They sought donations of food, clothing, and English and Yiddish newspapers and sewed for needy patients and newborn babies. But the real work of the hospital became the responsibility of a professionally trained woman, the administrator physician Sarah Vasen, who lived at the hospital.[96] By 1914, the hospital, like its San Francisco counterpart, sought to expand beyond charity cases to attract paying patients. One of its volunteer doctors instructed the public: "Talk this institution up to those who need hospital care and have the means to pay for good service, so that the small amount of profit made from them may help care of some other sick fellow who hasn't a cent."[97] Thus even the ill could be philanthropists. The hospital by 1930 had moved to Hollywood, renaming itself Cedars of Lebanon Hospital.[98]

The management and the funding of Cedars remained in the hands of Reform Jews and never gained the support of the Eastern European community, which founded its own facility. As Boris Bogen, who lectured at Hebrew Union College, taught his students, "at the turn of the century condescending attitudes and superiority feeling on the part of the givers of service aroused wide resentment and led to immigrant self-organizations."[99] The new hospital grew out of a traditional Bikur Cholim Society (Visiting the Sick), whose members founded a hospice for victims of the influenza epidemic of 1918, and later the Bikur Cholim Hospital, a two-room bungalow in the immigrant neighborhood of Boyle Heights. As opposed to Kaspare Cohn, rather than funding from wealthy backers, they attracted numerous small donations from supporters and women's auxiliaries, as did many new immigrant institutions, such as Denver's Jewish Consumptives' Relief Society.[100] Jewish doctors donated their time to the hospital, and soon they acquired a nine-room house paid for in part from the "sale of bricks for the foundation at $5.00 a piece."[101] Described as a "people's hospital," Sinai accepted all patients regardless of "color, race or creed." This was important to the founders, who wished to show their American civic responsibility, but also to meet the needs of Orthodox Jews who might require a synagogue and kosher food.[102] Furthermore, Mount Sinai did not require its patients to be residents of Los Angeles, nor did it limit a patient's stay. These conditions differentiated it from some facilities that discouraged newcomers

and did not treat so-called incurables.[103] Its founders believed strongly in creating a comfortable atmosphere for Los Angeles's newest—and sometimes sickest—migrants.

With this in mind, community activist Peter M. Kahn, a newcomer himself, accepted the presidency of the hospital. The hospital merged with the Beth Israel Hospital and Clinic Association and, changing its name again, finally became the Mount Sinai Hospital and Clinic. The free clinic became an important facility in Boyle Heights and an important symbol of immigrant leadership in Los Angeles.[104]

Eastern Europeans in Los Angeles made a significant contribution to the West's Jewish health care system when in 1914 they established the City of Hope, whose lay leadership overlapped with Mount Sinai's.[105] During the pioneer generation, San Francisco provided the logical location for the regional institutions such as the orphan asylum. But as the Jewish population center shifted farther south, Los Angeles with its beneficial climate had become the logical sight for a regional tuberculosis hospital. The founders of the City of Hope believed that as healthy Angelenos, some of whom had overcome T.B. themselves, they had an obligation to help others. As one supporter emphasized, "Because I regained my health, I felt I had a debt to repay, and I wanted to help those unfortunate people so they would have the same chance."[106] The City of Hope gave western T.B. sufferers another western destination. Denver had established two sanitariums, one in 1899 by elite German Jews and a second in 1904 by Eastern Europeans.[107] Denver's Eastern European sanitarium founders welcomed the City of Hope; they believed that to take care of T.B. patients, "we need more Sanatoria. We need more workers."[108]

City of Hope founders undertook their work

with considerable zeal. Like the B'nai B'rith founders of the Orphan Asylum, they wanted to build a regional institution, that "add[s] to the fame and honor of not only Southern California, but the entire Pacific Coast."[109] However, this was not just an act of charity. They believed that public health was at risk, because with all of the sick in the community there was a "need of self-preservation."[110] Therefore much like the Denver Jewish Consumptives' Relief Society they planned to treat T.B. sufferers without questions of payment or citizenship in a gesture of kindness as well as an attempt to prevent the spread of the disease.[111] This gesture included relieving immigrants of the fear of deportation. Immigrant T.B. sufferers who did not hold U.S. citizenship were hesitant to risk deportation by entering a public institution. Likewise, the founders, most of whom had lived in other parts of the United States before settling in Los Angeles, had witnessed patronizing tensions between the assimilated and new immigrants and stated explicitly that they dedicated the City of Hope to the "Spirit of Duarte," an attitude without condescension, where donors, doctors, and patients shared languages and ethnic and religious backgrounds, where patients became involved in the daily workings of the hospital (fig. 4.5). They wanted the patient to feel completely comfortable, so "that he has finally come home to live and if it is so ordained, to die among his own people."[112] This atmosphere further extended to food and housing. The City of Hope served Eastern European Jewish foods from a kosher kitchen, and all rooms were private or semiprivate. These policies contrasted sharply with the National Jewish Hospital in Denver, whose German Jewish founders expected to treat only those they deemed curable and only for a six-month stay.[113]

The founders of the City of Hope, of course, had more in common with those of Denver's Jewish Consumptives' Relief Society. Many, like the society's founder, Dr. Charles Spivak, supported socialism and were members of the Workmen's Circle. Indeed, one of the first discussions of a West Coast sanitarium took place in New York at a Workmen's Circle conference, when the Los Angeles delegate complained of the large numbers of T.B. sufferers who had become ill while working in eastern sweatshops and who arrived in southern California needing support.[114]

Predictably, the Los Angeles Jewish community was not united in how to respond to the tubercular migrants. Los Angeles's founding philanthropic leadership had been insular; now newcomers outnumbered them. A struggle ensued between the Eastern European migrants and the founding families over the scope of their new institution. Representing the pioneer community, Isaac Norton, who served as president of both the Hebrew Benevolent Society and the Hebrew Consumptive Relief Association, believed that only Los Angeles residents should be cared for. In 1906, Jewish T.B. sufferers began to be placed at established sanitariums.[115] This was not satisfactory for newer migrants, who believed that Jews needed their own facility. In January 1914, Dr. Kate Levy, a City of Hope supporter, tried to clear the air:

> There is involved not only the question of caring for the sick and the helpless among us, but there is involved and unsolved another very serious question. Can all classes of our people assimilate and work harmoniously for one great cause? Is there a spirit of tolerance among the rich and the poor, the educated and uneducated, the agnostic and the believing Jew? In other words, is there a Melting Pot of reverence and respect for each other's various views and aims?[116]

FIG. 4.5 *Fresh air was part of the treatment at the City of Hope in Duarte, Calif., ca. 1920. Courtesy of City of Hope Archives.*

Despite philosophical differences between the two groups, respect and cooperation did come. Unlike the wealthy pioneers, the founders of the City of Hope, like their counterparts in Denver, started a "people's movement" by seeking small donations from support groups and fraternal organizations.[117] At one meeting a group of women who had come west because their husbands had T.B. discussed working for the sanitarium. A participant remembered, "It was from little groups such as this . . . our vision of a home for those afflicted with the white plague became a goal for us . . . the great humanitarian ideal of caring for the sick and sending them back to their families and society."[118]

In 1912, the Jewish Consumptive Relief Association was established by forty men and women, mostly Eastern Europeans, with a constitution and bylaws calling for a nationally supported, free sanitarium, for anyone who ventured west. In 1913, the association acquired land and the following year pitched two tents on the property.[119] Although most initial funding was raised locally, delegates from around the country determined the hospital's policies and future at biennial conventions.[120] The City of Hope, like Denver's Jewish Consumptives' Relief Society, opened "it doors to persons of every race and creed" and did not charge for services.[121] Its slogan became "Build first and worry afterwards."[122] Because of this, it was in constant need of funds and only stayed afloat through the work of a national network of auxiliaries, especially many women's auxiliaries. Growing from a virtual subculture of women's organizations, the City of Hope's women's auxiliaries became a significant fund-raising arm for the hospital.[123] These women, many also Eastern Europeans like the patients, volunteered at the sanitarium and supported it with small donations. Fanny Sharlip, an early worker for the sanitarium, described trying to cheer up patients, visiting and bringing groceries, glasses, gifts, and necessities, including an "ear phone" for a man who was hard of hearing. She explained, "My heart went out to those seeking help. They came with high hopes in the power of the California climate. They found discouragement and death." Sharlip noted that when letters telling of a recovery reached the East it "brought more people out here for their health than the most successful campaign of the Chamber of Commerce could have put on."[124]

Larger donations came from the movie industry. Families of moguls as well as stars joined the effort. The Warner family donated a projection room and the Warner Memorial Clinic, and Al Jolson contributed funds for gardens.[125] West Coast auxiliaries were especially numerous, with groups in Portland, San Francisco, Long Beach, the East Bay, and even the small San Jose community all supporting the work of the sanitarium.[126] As the City of Hope grew, it gained a national reputation

that attracted funds from elsewhere and further established Los Angeles as a major center of American Jewish life. In 1921, members of the San Francisco auxiliary erected the first stucco building.[127] The Portland Builders of Health, originally established to raise funds for a sanitarium in Denver, transferred its allegiance to the new Duarte center after a Portland woman was treated by the City of Hope.[128] Oakland and other East Bay communities and individuals contributed thousands of dollars to the City of Hope between 1918 and 1933.[129]

Away from the large population centers, both Portland and Seattle were too small to support their own Jewish hospitals. The Council of Jewish Women in Portland instead decided to provide hospital beds at St. Vincent and Emanuel hospitals for women who could not afford a hospital stay.[130] In Seattle, when the women of the National Council of Jewish Women built the Educational Center in 1916, they included two emergency bedrooms and a medical clinic.[131]

These health care institutions demonstrate the various ways in which western communities evolved. Migration trends influenced the type of institution a community required, who funded it, and who would require its services. Some facilities were possible only in San Francisco and Los Angeles, where large Jewish populations and great wealth brought grand projects to fruition.

BENEVOLENCE BEYOND THE FOLD: JEWISH WOMEN AND GENERAL PHILANTHROPY

In this city [San Francisco] . . . the Jewess . . . keeps pace with the world's advancement equally with her sisters of other creeds. Of course in the charities of their own people, they are here, as elsewhere,

deeply interested . . . but with broad-minded liberality, they are active in the most important societies
that bring relief to the needy of all classes.

Western Jewish women supported secular and even
Christian institutions that built the region's educational and child-care infrastructure.[132] Catholic
nursing and teaching orders provided the model for
women's responsibility by establishing standards of
health care and education to meet pressing western needs. As early as the 1850s in San Francisco,
the Sisters of Charity and the Sisters of Presentation opened schools, which at first received public
funds. Similarly, the Sisters of Charity were invited
to Los Angeles in 1856, where they quickly built a
school, an institute, and an orphanage.[133]

Jewish women joined societies and organized
fund-raising fairs for some of these institutions
and were recognized for their activities, considered eminently respectable for elite women in the
mid-nineteenth century.[134] In Los Angeles, Jewish
women were active in the German Ladies Benevolent Society, the Ladies Benevolent Society, and
the Los Angeles Orphans Home Society (associated with the Catholic Sisters of Charity). Sarah
Newmark, the wife of community leader Joseph
Newmark and the mother of a large and prosperous family, was a member of eighteen non-Jewish
associations.[135] Her daughter, Rosa, followed in her
footsteps, organizing an 1865 fund-raising fair to
help establish a Roman Catholic college, St. Vincent's, later renamed Loyola College.[136]

Further contact with non-Jews showed Jewish
women the necessity of cooperating with public
and private organizations to achieve their goals.
According to the Los Angeles historian Karen S.
Wilson, women were sometimes more involved
in raising funds for secular needs than were men:
"The same separation of gender spheres of influ-

ence that allowed women to be active in charity
work also apparently enabled Jewish women to
cross religious and ethnic boundaries with ease
in the name of benevolence." Wilson concludes,
"The extensive Jewish involvement in non-Jewish
charitable causes and organizations appears related
to the greater diversity and lesser development of
nineteenth-century Western cities." Western Jews,
women as well as men, interacted daily with the
community-at-large and could "integrate into the
larger community, while maintaining [their Jewish]
distinction."[137]

Jewish women not only contributed to Christian
philanthropies but also borrowed their strategies
and initiatives as models for their own activities.
When Protestant women in Portland in the 1870s
campaigned for public schools and opened missions
along the waterfront or homes for unwed mothers,
they dealt with public health and law enforcement
officials. Jewish women in the early twentieth
century in Portland, Seattle, and San Francisco
were mindful of these precedents when they moved
beyond their mothers' benevolent societies to create
settlement houses. They, too, negotiated with officials of public schools, city councils, and the new
juvenile courts.

In San Francisco, before the Jewish women
created settlement houses they joined with gentile
women in emulating the Women's Educational and
Industrial Union, which had been founded in Boston in 1877.[138] The San Francisco union in 1888
sought to "increase fellowship among women,
in order to promote the best practical means for
securing their educational, industrial, and social
advancement."[139] The union sponsored lectures,
classes, vocational assistance, entertainment, and
a lunchroom; helped with protection and legal
claims; and built a gym. In her president's statement of 1891, Hannah Solomons delineated the

organization's principles, avowing "the democratic principles which underlie our American institutions. Not a patronizing of poor women by rich ones; not a handing down of benefits from women on one plane of life to women on another, but a true union of women for mutual help and sympathy—for united progress and advancement—each helping each other."[140]

The presidency of the Women's Educational and Industrial Union was the culmination of Solomons's achievements. After arriving in San Francisco in 1853, she had taught in a public school and at the Pacific Hebrew Orphan Asylum, married a prominent pioneer, and, in 1868, served as president of the first Jewish fund-raising fair, which benefited the Orphan Asylum.[141] Solomons bemoaned the treatment of working women in an editorial in the *Fair Journal*. She questioned why elite women's volunteering during the fair was seen as respectable, while orphan girls who needed to work for pay to support themselves were often denigrated. With the Women's Educational and Industrial Union, Solomons could act on her principles, because the union offered working girls and women a place where they could socialize, recreate, and receive job training.

For Solomons and other Jewish women, the union proved to be a mixed experience because some gentile members feared a Jewish takeover of "their" organization. When Solomons became president some gentile members resigned, and when she left the union the non-Jewish founders returned to leadership.[142] The benefits of the union's training for its volunteers, however, became evident in the generation of Jewish women that followed. For example, Jessica Peixotto, who received her first social service training at the union teaching English while her mother taught chorale singing, would become a leader in the San Francisco chapter of

the NCJW, the first female full professor at the University of California, and an authority on social work.[143] Hannah Solomons's daughter, Selina, also active in the union, became a leader of the California suffrage movement.[144]

SETTLEMENT HOUSES AND JEWISH COMMUNITIES

In the late 1880s, when Rabbi Kaufman Kohler and others transformed Reform Judaism's "Mission of Israel" into a pursuit of social justice, rabbis encouraged the wives and adult daughters of their members to provide assistance to the growing number of poor immigrant Jewish families.[145] Jewish women soon became involved in building organizations and institutions that would reshape secular models to address the needs of the Jewish community. From southern California to Seattle, Jewish women created settlement houses in immigrant neighborhoods, while in the two largest communities, San Francisco and Los Angeles, they also built residence homes for Jewish girls and young working women. Eventually, all of these communities conformed to standards of modern social work, employing professionally trained workers who provided guidance and day-to-day contact with their immigrant "clients." Such professionalization, however, at times worked against the goal of creating tighter bonds between native and immigrant, because the settlement house staff stood between volunteer patrons and their immigrant clients. Portland's stalwart Blanche Blumauer complained that her section members would not visit the settlement house and see the results of their hard work.[146]

As with most nineteenth-century western endeavors, San Francisco was the first city to adopt new forms of women's volunteerism. In

1889, Temple Emanu-El's Rabbi Jacob Voorsanger encouraged "the Helpers," a women's organization, to perform "friendly visiting" under the auspices of the Eureka Benevolent Society. Working with the Associated Charities, the women at first visited homes of needy cases to dispense provisions and medicine. As patrons of their city, they in the beginning visited as many gentile as Jewish cases. As Naomi W. Cohen suggests, "Jewish philanthropy appeared especially praiseworthy when it benefited non-Jews."[147] However, by the mid-1890s, when the number of Jews increased and the local economy declined, a larger proportion of their services focused on Jewish families.[148]

With the financial support of Lewis Gerstle, the Helpers reorganized in 1894 to form the Emanu-El Sisterhood for Personal Service to provide relief and to find work for the Jewish unemployed. Not only was this organization the first of its kind undertaken in the Pacific West, but also it was one of the first Jewish settlement houses in the country.[149] The women felt responsible for poor Jews, whom they feared would be ignored by other, largely church-based, charitable agencies and who might even resort to public begging. The Emanu-El ladies believed that this last recourse would sully the name of the Jewish community. Like caring for the sick, caring for the poor had previously been the function of benevolent societies. The sisterhood offered temporary monetary relief as well as medical services to families, established an employment bureau for men, and organized classes to teach sewing skills to girls and women who could then supplement family income.[150]

The women then adopted new tactics for assisting the poor and new moral criteria to determine who should receive aid. Reflecting the concept of "personal service" defined by eastern settlement workers like Robert Wood, the sisterhood women became "friendly visitors" to the families receiving their support.[151] Members of the sisterhood took specific needy families as their personal charges and provided them with information intended to *prevent* poverty. The families receiving their support had the responsibility of utilizing the information about job training or employment to end their own impoverishment.

The sisterhood edged closer to modern settlement work when it rented a building in the immigrant district south of Market Street and instituted more formal social services, including classes and a mothers club for child-care relief.[152] By 1895, the sisterhood initiated separate clubs for boys and girls, which met in their building. Sidney Peixotto, brother of Jessica, returned from heading the East Side Boys Club in New York to start the Columbia Park Boys Club.[153] He mixed instruction in chair caning and carpentry with outdoor games, military drills, and, by 1902, hikes in the Sierras, a format that foreshadowed the Boy Scouts. As Sidney's brother, Eustace, explained, "The club's mission is to offer to ambitious boys opportunities beyond those afforded by public schools."[154] Peixotto raised an endowment, built his own clubhouse, and separated from the sisterhood.

A Working Girls Friendly Club reflected the view of "girl workers," women like Jane Addams who specialized in working with adolescent girls whom they believed needed the friendship and leadership of women if they were to proceed from the dangers of puberty to the self-assurance and skills needed for adult domesticity.[155] The club combined instruction to upgrade marketable needlecraft skills with social activities like reading, reciting, and dancing, where expressive individuals might identify and support one another. Both sewing and dancing were widely acclaimed as appropriate outlets for developing feminine "instincts."[156]

The propriety of any instruction, when such instruction should be given, and the number of persons allowed to attend dances sponsored by the sisterhood continued to vex settlement workers into the 1920s.[157] They believed they had to maintain a balance between promoting adult ideas of decorum and allowing the young women to develop social skills and meet possible marriage partners.

For the majority of western Jewish women outside San Francisco and Los Angeles, local sections of the NCJW provided the impetus for moving from charity to settlement work. The national organization developed out of the frustrating experiences of Jewish women who participated in the religious forums at the Chicago Columbian Exposition in 1893. Well-educated women such as Hannah Solomons, Sadie America, and California's lay "rabbi" Ray Frank rejected the subordinate role in which men had cast them and started a society intended initially to further instruction in Jewish culture and history among their colleagues. The first local sections consisted of study groups under the direction of local Reform rabbis. As the depression of the 1890s deposited growing numbers of impoverished Jewish immigrants in major cities across the country, the women enlarged their commitment to social services. With Jane Addams in Chicago and Lillian Wald in New York modeling new forms of women's social activism, the younger, often unmarried, women in NCJW sections adapted the ideas of friendly visiting and personal service to fit their local needs. For some western Jewish women, settlement work served "as an outlet for the growing restlessness—pent-up energies of those among us who for their leisure hours needed a new field of activity."[158] However, in contrast to Addams, most Jewish volunteers did not live in immigrant communities, nor did they see themselves as political activists. Many saw

their role as part of a relief effort, a continuation of their mothers' charity and fund-raising activities. The foundation for Jewish settlement work in the Pacific West was benevolent, but beyond material relief they sought to educate clients to become a part of successful American Jewish community life.[159]

Whether it was under the direction of a Personal Service Sisterhood, Jewish Aid Society or the NCJW, the women's activities in western cities were similar: forming study circles; teaching English, citizenship, Judaism, and domestic skills to adults and children, especially immigrants; providing recreational activities; helping with employment; protecting young women and working girls; and working with the juvenile justice system. They emphasized prevention of poverty over relief and believed that they could be a moral force in the lives of young people and families. Their goals were to influence immigrants to become good citizens, which would make them better Jews, and good representatives of the American Jewish community.

For an example, western Jewish women could look to the work of Ray Frank. Although Frank believed that the most important role for Jewish women was as a mother and wife, her career as a public speaker and a leader of synagogue services gave a contradictory impression. In San Francisco, she spoke at congregation Emanu-El and at the homes of the elite, forcefully arguing for respect for the new immigrants, many Orthodox Jews. In 1895, she worked for the establishment of a NCJW section in her adopted hometown of Oakland "to further the best and highest interest of humanity in religious, philanthropic and educational fields."[160] Frank's lectures in Portland certainly motivated Jewish women to support the national council.

NCJW sections in Portland and Seattle developed in tandem. Their formation was similar to the nationwide movement. In contrast to San Francisco, where the sisterhood's activities already existed, settlement work had not yet reached the Northwest. The members of the new sections built on the long-established mutual aid practices of benevolent societies, but they introduced Progressive ideology that reinforced a gender-based interpretation of American womanhood.[161] Where their mothers had focused inward, the NCJW daughters sought to help the "larger community" by building centers for social services.[162]

Founded in 1896, just three years after the Chicago founding of the national organization, the Portland section played a significant role in educating and integrating Jewish and other immigrants into the broader community. Its membership grew quickly from 84 in 1897 to 298 in 1907. Most members came from elite German Jewish households, with little religious training but strong traditions of community service. The women reflected the changing demographics of the Jewish community. Many were unmarried, and 70 percent were born after the 1860s, too young to have been community founders. While internal tensions between elite women volunteers and immigrants arose in Portland, councilwomen did try to assuage them. Most followed the precepts of noted professor of Jewish social work Boris Bogen, who taught that "the lesson of absolute tolerance, as far as ideas and beliefs are concerned, is one of the most important functions of a true settlement."[163]

Under the direction of the newly arrived Rabbi Stephen Wise and his wife, Louise, the council in 1901 rented two small buildings on the northern edge of the immigrant district to initiate a sewing school, a Sunday school, and gymnastics and manual arts classes for boys.[164] Council members believed that sewing classes were a way to pass on American values to immigrants, and they opened

their classes to all the neighborhood children. Tillie Selling, the wife of Ben Selling and the section's first president, who taught sewing for more than thirty years, lamented that there were more gentiles than Jews in the sewing classes.[165] The first girl to graduate from the sewing school was African American, not Jewish.[166] However, the NCJW's success with immigrants was noted in other parts of the region.

Encouraged by their Portland peers, Jewish women in Seattle organized a section of the NCJW in 1900, four years after the founding of Portland's section and the same year as San Francisco's. One of the thirty-four charter members, Babette Schwabacher Gatzert, widow of the former mayor, called for the organizational meeting.[167] Blanche Blumauer of Portland helped the Seattle women organize and became an advisor. As per national recommendations, the section established religious, social, and philanthropic committees and study circles.[168] At first, the section followed traditional concepts of service, visiting the sick, helping the Ladies' Hebrew Benevolent Society care for the graves of indigent Jews, and renting rooms for a sewing class and a Sunday school for children of poor families. Not until Mrs. Blumauer "chastised" the women in 1906 for lack of initiative did they rent a flat to start a settlement house, first referred to as a "mission school."[169] Separate from the section's leadership, the settlement house was overseen by its own set of officers. The Seattle council soon enjoyed further encouragement from newly arrived rabbi Samuel Koch of the Reform Temple De Hirsch. The women valued his "cooperation and able assistance" and his strong support of the section's religious school.[170] Influenced by Portlanders, the house came to be called the Educational Center, rather than "settlement house," because the founders believed that education "typified the spirit of the work the Seattle Section was desirous of accomplishing."[171] Although many of its activities mirrored those of other settlement houses, Seattle's Educational Center hoped to create opportunities for immigrants and locals alike.

In Los Angeles, without a dynamic Reform rabbi such as San Francisco's Voorsanger, Portland's Stephen Wise, or Seattle's Koch, Jewish women delayed in modernizing their benevolence work. Congregation B'nai B'rith's rabbi at the time, Sigmund Hecht, believed that the way to enhance the city's ability to handle the increased demand for social services was through the federation of existing organizations such as the Jewish Aid Society. Perhaps as a result, Los Angeles was the last of the major communities to begin settlement work. It was not until 1907 that three women, including Rabbi Hecht's daughter, founded a residence, the Mendelssohn Settlement Home, to shelter girls who were in need.[172] The women could not sustain the project, but it became the precursor of the Hamburger Home for Working Girls. Finally, in 1911, the same three women established the Educational Alliance in central Los Angeles to promote the "moral education and social welfare of the Jewish immigrant." But because Los Angeles generally attracted Jews who had lived elsewhere in the United States, Americanization was not as great a priority there as it was elsewhere.[173]

Almost a decade after the other western cities, Los Angeles's Jewish women became affiliated with the NCJW in 1909 and initiated settlement work.[174] Despite its late start, Los Angeles's rapid growth and vast size led to the quick expansion and need for settlement houses in each of the three immigrant neighborhoods. The Jewish Aid Society joined the new NCJW section and the Educational Alliance in initiating this settlement work. The settlement work of the Los Angeles council, con-

sequently, grew by accretion as much as through its own initiative. For example, the Mendelssohn House Settlement was taken over by the council in 1910, when its founders joined the council. They rented a new building and offered classes in sewing, religion, and personal hygiene.[175] The council established the Ida Straus Nursery (later called the Julia Ann Singer Day Nursery), which provided for children of working mothers, and started a home for orphan girls who were too old to live at the Jewish Orphanage (another precursor to the Hamburger Home).[176]

When San Franciscans founded a section of the NCJW in 1900 (five years after nearby Oakland), they differentiated themselves from the Emanu-El Sisterhood, to which many of them also belonged.[177] The San Francisco section, like most others, started with committees on religion and philanthropy, but since the Emanu-El Sisterhood already operated a settlement house, the council felt no urgency to initiate similar work.[178] Instead, it drastically revised the study circle model emphasizing the problems of immigrant Jews. Indeed, it was the only section in the West to debate the question of appropriate topics for discussion. Prominent sociologist and council member Jessica Peixotto proposed that the women take a broad approach. Based on her studies of French socialism and her ability to turn a humane concern for relief into criteria for analyzing the causes of poverty, she understood how women could influence public policy. The members duly voted that any topic was permissible, so long as it involved some practical application to the Jewish community. And Peixotto demonstrated that, as Jewish children from immigrant families enrolled in larger numbers in the public schools, they would need professional support.[179]

Other western sections did not have members

with the education or dedication of Peixotto to lead them. All sections, however, initiated lectures and study circles, some led by stellar local rabbis. The council established some programs for their members alone as well as others that encouraged community participation. In 1905, the president of the Portland section proudly noted that its monthly programs succeeded "in bring[ing] together the reform Jewess and her orthodox sister, giving to both a common interest in Jewish thought, Jewish history and the Jewish woman's relation to the non-Jewish world."[180] Led by Rabbi Stephen Wise, the Portland section read *Children of the Ghetto* as well as apocryphal literature and the "historical, prophetical and poetical books of the Bible."[181] Section president Blanche Blumauer, expressed the opinion that Portland "has advantages second to none in this work. It is not remarkable, therefore, that our class in the study of the Bible should be the subject of inquiry from women of other clubs and other churches many of whom consider it a privilege to receive the benefits of this class."[182] Significantly, these Bible classes brought together not only Reform and Orthodox Jewish women but also Jews and gentiles.

Beyond educating themselves, the women of the NCJW sought to educate neighborhood children. A Jewish educator recommended that settlement houses should offer children both traditional Jewish education and modern (Reform) education, letting the success of the school decide which is better for the neighborhood.[183] In Portland, the Neighborhood House allowed Morris Ostrow, a Russian immigrant and proprietor of a South Portland furniture store, to start a Talmud Torah.[184] Eventually, it grew into the Portland Hebrew School. Some women saw as part of their mission personally teaching the children of Orthodox immigrants Reform Judaism; others wanted to expose children

who were receiving no Jewish education to religious practice. The classes concentrated on small children and stressed Bible stories introducing Orthodox Eastern European and Sephardic children to Reform practices. To teachers and students alike, these classes demonstrated what it meant to be an American Jew. According to Sara Efron of Seattle, "it amazes me that my parents being so orthodox would have permitted me to go there, but it was innocuous. The stories were [from the] Bible, and I believe they felt that they should in every way try to be become Americanized and take on American ways . . . this was one of the ways that we [were] given a glimpse of how things were being done in America in comparison to the way we lived in our own homes."[185]

Along with education, all of the settlement houses saw themselves as quite progressive because they stressed recreational activities and sports for girls and boys. Boys and girls clubs formed with interests ranging from Sephardic girls studying English and American customs in Seattle to music and literary clubs in Portland.[186] Gyms and swimming pools were built, sport teams formed, and coaches hired (fig. 4.6). As part of the settlement movement philosophy, recreational activities were deemed a wholesome way to keep youngsters off the dangerous and corrupting streets. Charity and philanthropic activities grew to encompass basketball, swimming lessons, and stage productions. In Portland, girls danced, played basketball, and engaged in "dumb bell drilling and jumping."[187]

Seattle's NCJW Educational Center and the women who volunteered there acquired a reputation with civil officials, local schools, and child welfare organizations as a positive American force in a community where some immigrants were viewed with suspicion. At the height of the post–World War I Red scare and Palmer raids,

FIG. 4.6 *Neighborhood House pool, Portland, 1925. Oregon Jewish Museum OJM3049.*

the women were visited by a representative of the juvenile court and the secret service, who requested them to "counteract and to crush by good influence and constructive work in the proper direction the effect of radical teaching carried on in this neighborhood." The representative believed that "the source of this insidious work is a school called the 'working man's circle' where children of five years and up are taught the principals of bolshevism from text books." In response, the women who had been considering selling their building to the Talmud Torah School decided that they must remain

FIG. 4.7 *Americanization class at Neighborhood House, Portland, 1914. Oregon Jewish Museum OJM217.*

in the community and maintain their influence.[188]

With this aim in mind, NCJW women redoubled their efforts in the neighborhood, joining with non-Jewish reformers in promoting themselves as "managers of other women's homes" and offering Americanization schools (fig. 4.7).[189] The historian Gayle Gullett points out that the power of the women's argument lay in their use of gender-specific language that called for a "home defense."[190] Many Progressives believed that American values would never gain a foothold in immigrant families unless wives and mothers instructed their children, so the settlement house offered classes in English

and citizenship. To further the transformation of foreigners into Americans as quickly as possible, American holidays, especially George Washington's and Abraham Lincoln's birthdays and Thanksgiving, became grand pageants.[191] Section members also emphasized the need for immigrant mothers to "read, write and talk the English language," so that their children would not be considered foreigners.[192] They stressed that in "learning the new language [the immigrant] also learns to love his country."[193] In patronizing terms, Portland's leadership underlined the importance of English for women who they believed would especially benefit from their instruction: "This is especially true of the women whose gratitude has no bounds, she is full of pride, because she learns how to read and write. Often she has no opportunity to learn to read and write even her native language, and she remain[s] forever an illiterate."[194]

Americanization was deemed so important to Seattle NCJW members that they babysat children of immigrants while their mothers attended citizenship classes. Many of these classes truly served the entire neighborhood, as they were open to all residents—Greek, Italian, and Jew alike.[195] In Portland, according to a 1923 report, at Neighborhood House "one not only gains the spirit of democracy, but finds friendships and also an optimistic spirit."[196] Council member Miriam Aiken explained, "We taught them to eat American style, you know . . . we had dances for them and they really enjoyed it very much."[197]

Despite the occasionally patronizing atmosphere, many immigrants found the help they received with English, citizenship, and American customs invaluable. The settlement houses' staff—volunteer and paid—walked a delicate line between teaching and patronizing their clients. Foreseeing that problems could develop, the NCJW advised: "Visit the girl in the same way [you] would visit someone recommended by a personal friend, without patronage and merely in the friendly spirit."[198] In settlement houses, patrons, headworkers, and clients forged complicated relationships that were substantially different from the "lady bountiful" and charity case paradigm.

Volunteers trained themselves to be teachers and eventually lay social workers. As their activities expanded, council sections hired women to manage the facilities. These women acted as "mothers" and role models, teaching immigrants American ways, helping them solve problems, joining in their cel-

ebrations, and often becoming an essential part of their lives. Relationships changed again as the field of social work matured in the early twentieth century, and settlement houses hired educated professionals to work with both their volunteer board of administrators and their neighborhood clientele. In each of these relationships, a new dynamic between native-born westerner and newcomer emerged.

For example, at Portland's Neighborhood House, Americanization was the aim of patrons and clients, though each group may have viewed the settlement house differently: "Patrons tended to see the House as a piece of their broad, civic involvement, [while] clients tended to view the institution as the lynchpin of their insular neighborhood."[199] Thus, while the volunteers strongly believed that Neighborhood House should be open to all "regardless of race, creed, color or ethnic background," their clients—the immigrant women and children who made use of the house's services—believed that it was "their" center, an institution uniquely serving the Jewish community. They perceived that "everyone" there was Jewish. Gertrude Feves called it her "second home."[200] In contrast, it was just one of several places (Jewish and secular) where women of German Reform background volunteered, and they usually did not see themselves as peers of the Eastern European women whose community they served and whose children they instructed in table manners.[201]

In San Francisco, because of the Jewish community's wealth, the gulf between the goals of patrons and the aspirations of clients was even greater. The founders of the Emanu-El Sisterhood, who considered themselves "ideal role models uniquely qualified to teach immigrant women to uplift themselves and their community," arrived for classes and meetings at the settlement house in chauffeured limousines.[202] Their purpose, they boasted, was "elevating the moral standard of the people, improving the condition of their homes, teaching them self-reliance and self-respect, promoting their moral and mental education, and developing technical skill."[203] Members of the Emanu-El Sisterhood believed that their relationship with immigrants would "broaden . . . [the immigrants'] characters and refine their manners."[204] As patronizing as some elite women were, they offered services that benefited most immigrants: free classes and an opportunity to learn English so that they could obtain American citizenship and more effectively become a part of their new country.

Although some volunteers kept in regular contact with their clients, once they built settlement houses, paid women, known as headworkers or matrons, had the most effect on both children and adults. In Seattle, for example, the Educational Center hired Hannah Pelz Schwartz, a widow from San Francisco, who came to the attention of a Seattle council member in 1908 through one of her friends in California.[205] Schwartz, described as a "very, very small but very, very pleasant woman" (fig. 4.8), although not a trained social worker, had previously worked with immigrants.[206] An early evaluation noted that "her understanding of her fellow man, her sweet sympathy and good common sense soon won for her the confidence and love of the entire Jewish community, Orthodox, and Reform, Sephardic and Eschkanzim [sic]."[207] Accepted by all segments of the Jewish community, Schwartz was hired for thirty-five dollars a month. According to reports, "Our resident worker, Mrs. Hannah Schwartz, has proven herself a rare treasure. Beloved by all who know her, she has become a factor in the neighborhood, Jew and Gentile coming alike to her for help and advice."[208] Schwartz not only instructed those who entered the settlement house, but she also went into homes

FIG. 4.8   Hannah Pelz Schwartz, Seattle, 1910. University of Washington Libraries, Special Collections, neg. UW27644z.

and taught cleanliness and housekeeping, worked with benevolent societies to find jobs for those in need, served as the banker for the young boys club, and "patch[ed] up differences in families [and gave] advice and encouragement."[209] Sara Efron, involved in settlement house activities as a youngster, remembered that Schwartz "gave us girls lessons in deportment, in how to properly sit and how to properly speak."[210] Respected widely in the local community, Schwartz was an honored guest at an Orthodox wedding and the trustee of a boy of fifteen.[211]

Although immigrants may have not been aware

of it, council members and staff in port towns also viewed it as their civic duty to supply immigration officials with knowledge about new arrivals. In one year, Schwartz sent information from the council to the Bureau of Immigration in New York about the welfare and location of more than twenty people. In a 1916–17 report, she noted, "Advice given to 59, visits to 70, miscellaneous cases 30, immigrant cases 2, city baby clinic cases 32, council sewing days 6, employment secured for 32, immigrant girls' houses [sic] 3, helpful aid 39, free baths taken 118, Menorah Society rehearsals 12, school report cases 14, different organizations using the hall 9, library contains 970 volumes, and pass through the house each week in activities other than the use of auditorium and library 692 children."[212] These numbers increased each year as more activities were added. When Schwartz retired and returned to California in 1922, she was replaced by a professional social worker. The era of the settlement house mother was over.

Accelerated by the maturation of graduate social work schools, the nationwide turn to certified professionals influenced secular, religious, and ethnic settlement houses alike. Western cities often recruited social workers from the East as women's national networks grew and "Jewish women replaced the pioneering ideal of communal self-reliance with a more cosmopolitan ideal that subordinated volunteers to professionals."[213] Sadie Bloch came from Baltimore to Portland in 1911 to serve as Neighborhood House's first headworker, but she stayed for only one year.[214] Ida Loewenberg, then a volunteer, replaced Bloch and through both "on-the-job" training and formal schooling became a professional, serving as the director for more than thirty-three years.

Loewenberg fully involved herself with all of Neighborhood House's numerous activities. After more than ten years' service in 1923, she wrote of her work: "Thruout [sic] the years we have stressed the spirit of Jewishness, hospitality and kindness, and have now the joy of knowing that the House is indeed the cherished center for all neighborhood activities and organizations, the social and recreational oasis, not alone for the young people but for the older men and women as well; in truth an institution promoting systematic Jewish and moral training besides departments in art, schience [sic], English, civics and athletics."[215] Not unlike her volunteer or untrained predecessors, Loewenberg formed personal relationships with her clients. Indeed, in one extraordinary case she arranged for an immigrant woman with many children and an unreliable husband to have tubal ligation surgery. According to Loewenberg's niece, the woman came to Loewenberg asking for a method of birth control, stating, "I don't know what to do. I just don't want any more children. I can't take care of the ones I have."[216] To help her, Loewenberg accompanied the woman to the hospital in the middle of the night for the surgery.

This example of Loewenberg's intervention not only demonstrates the intimate relationships that developed between social workers and their clients but also shows how the social work professional went beyond charity by seeking modern solutions to prevent families from needing additional aid. In the case of birth control, Loewenberg was engaging in a political act by defying the law. Beyond relationships with immigrants, arranging for a tubal ligation required Loewenberg to have a working relationship with neighborhood doctors and nurses who shared her concerns. Through well-baby clinics and dental clinics she initiated at Neighborhood House, she had developed such networks, which she utilized to aid her clients. Loewenberg had been mentored by social reformer Edward Thomas

Devine (1867–1948), who believed that the social worker should "seek out and strike effectively at those organized forces of evil, at those particular causes of dependence and intolerable living conditions which are beyond the control of individuals whom they injure and whom they too often destroy."[217]

WHAT TO DO ABOUT THE GIRLS

As social workers like Loewenberg developed programs to assist dependent individuals, they were particularly challenged by the issue of female adolescents. The question of what to do about teenage female orphans had been discussed in the San Francisco Jewish community for many years. Unlike boys, who served apprenticeships, adolescent orphan girls could not find employment that middle-class women deemed suitable. In 1878, well before the beginning of the settlement movement, the president of the Pacific Orphan Asylum, Samuel Wolf Levy, reported to his membership and patrons that a difficult question for the board was what to do about girls "after they have reached the age when their future life has to be molded, and when they have to be prepared to earn a livelihood?"[218] Since its founding, the aim of the orphanage had been to "have the girls brought up as good housekeepers"; however, according to Levy, "the difficulty is to find suitable places . . . where the employers take more interest in the physical welfare and moral culture of our ward than is bestowed upon domestics generally."[219] Acknowledging that domestics did not receive respect and that families did not change their practices for Jewish domestics, Levy asked for the help of those present: "Whenever, ladies and gentlemen, an opportunity offers to place one of said wards in a good home, or to procure a situation for our boys, remember the same and communicate with the Board."[220]

Despite Levy's efforts to find appropriate placements, very little changed. As late as 1904 (a whole generation later), the Emanu-El Sisterhood concluded in its annual report that, "although our pupils are taught housework and our endeavor is to make neat little housekeepers of them, the desire is lacking altogether to take positions as such."[221] Placing girls as domestics would have solved two problems: it would have created a dependable source of home assistants, and it would have placed them in households under the watchful eyes of Jewish matrons.[222] However, as new clerical jobs were being created, most girls were not interested in working as domestics when they could make more money and have more freedom as office workers or salesgirls.[223] In the 1890s, however, elite women were only beginning to see this type of work as appropriate. In fact, as late as the 1930s the women of the Emanu-El Sisterhood joined with the Chinese Young Women's Christian Association (YWCA) to form the Institute of Practical Arts, which trained women in domestic work.[224]

In the early decades of the twentieth century, anticipating the Panama Canal's completion and San Francisco's rapid growth, publicity about the dangers of white slavery finally shifted the concern from "what are we going to do about the girls" to "how are we going to protect them." In San Francisco, according to Mary Ann Irwin, this shift coincided not only with increased immigration to the West but also with the Emanu-El Sisterhood's and NCJW's attending juvenile court sessions and learning of the potential temptations that awaited unattended girls.[225] The Emanu-El Sisterhood and the western sections of the NCJW agreed with the national organization that "the greatest single threat to female immigrants was the white slave trade."[226] The sisterhood feared that this was a threat both to the girls and to the Jewish community's reputation. The Emanu-El Sisterhood finally acted in 1909 when the Pacific Orphan Asylum, unable to continue to house them, announced that it was going to release orphans who had reached the legal age of sixteen. The sisterhood took in its first girl that year, and by the following year it had opened a residence for the young women that aimed to keep them pure and out of harm's way.[227]

By 1915, the Emanu-El Sisterhood had completed a new building modeled after a home erected in 1910 by the New York section of the NCJW. The sisterhood then brought Ethel R. Feineman, who had been trained in social work in Kansas City by Jacob Billikopf and then at Hull House in Chicago, to provide resident guidance in a Jewish atmosphere for the young women living there. Feineman reported to her board in 1921 that, while only thirty-three girls could reside there at one time, most of the seventy-one girls accommodated during the year were aged nineteen or under and had jobs. Usually, they left the home either to leave the city or to marry.[228] Through the 1920s the home never lacked applicants, and a building across the street had to be acquired to meet the growing demand. As part of the newly federated network of Jewish social agencies in San Francisco, the home by the early 1920s drew on the expanding network of health care and guidance professionals that the Jewish community attracted and which became a model for the smaller communities in the region.

In San Francisco, the social workers who directed residence homes became legendary. Feineman and Grace Weiner dedicated years of service to San Francisco's girls and working young women who lived at the sisterhood's residence (fig. 4.9).[229] Feineman was described as "a young woman of

efficient executive ability, keen intelligence, and warm sympathies, whose understanding has increased the great social work carried on there [the Emanu-El home] as a great up-building force for the womanhood of the community."[230] Even more than Loewenberg, Feineman had a twofold job; she worked as an employee of the ladies of the Emanu-El Sisterhood, and she established an intimate relationship with the girls and women of the residence. She had to be both a model professional capable of proper bookkeeping and casework and an educated matron who established a Jewish home for her young women.[231] She succeeded ably in both arenas. As one girl wrote, "The intense interest that you show in me is more than any human being can deserve."[232] The annual Passover Seder demonstrated both the organizational skills of Feineman and the cultural goals of the sisterhood (fig. 4.10). Along with the Sabbath meal, the seder emphasized the Jewishness of the home, and it was the one event where the girls could count on seeing their benefactors. With seders led by State Supreme Court judge M. C. Sloss, son of San Francisco pioneer Louis Sloss, this evening symbolized the founders' continuing Jewish commitment to future generations.

Similarly, Jewish women in Los Angeles established a home for older girls who had outgrown their orphanage.[233] The NCJW, along with the Jewish Alliance Club, "became aware of a wide gap between discharge from the Jewish Orphan's Home and the ability of a young person to be self-supporting." This small home eventually led to the founding of the Hamburger Home, which by 1934 housed forty-five women (one of whom came directly from the San Francisco orphanage) and also served as a settlement house.[234]

Joining other Progressive reformers, the women's interest in the welfare of young women and in the

FIG. 4.9 *Girls learning to cook with Ethel R. Feineman in San Francisco, ca. 1910–23. Western Jewish History Center, Judah L. Magnes Museum (1970).*

juvenile court system further extended their political activities. Their organizations continued to move away from direct charity and fund-raising to work in the public arena for social, legal, and governmental changes. In recounting the beginnings of the Los Angeles section of the NCJW, a member wrote, "These early members were no Lady Bountifuls. They were serious and realistic work-ers, paving the way for the sort of welfare program which was soon to win for the Section the respect and acclaim of the entire community."[235] Although many of the women valued the social dimension of philanthropy, their involvement with schools, city councils, juvenile courts, and the press, just as women were acquiring the suffrage, led them directly into the political arena. In the American

FIG. 4.10 *Seder service, Emanu-El Sisterhood, San Francisco, 1917. Photograph: Morton and Co. Western Jewish History Center, Judah L. Magnes Museum (1970).*

Jewish community of the early twentieth century, as Hasia Diner argues, the alleged dichotomy between "men doing politics, [and] women volunteering to do good—has little analytic substance behind it."[236] In Portland, for example, the NCJW as well as the B'nai B'rith took a public stance against offensive portrayals of Jews. The Portland

women, in 1907, passed two resolutions, the first condemning the juvenile court for calling Jewish children "unclean" and the second protesting the use by local newspapers of "Jew" or "Jewish" with the name of an arrested or convicted individual. The council asked the newspaper to stop the practice unless it was also willing to "adopt the same system against all others and designate them as Presbyterian, Episcopalians, Catholics, Unitarians or otherwise as the case may be."[237] After a meeting at the newspaper office, the editors agreed to end the practice.

WORLD WAR I AND THE NEW CHALLENGE OF IMMIGRATION

In addition to housing orphans and young women, local sections of the NCJW responded to "calls" by the national leadership. During World War I, New York–based organizations paid closer attention to the West, as warfare in the Atlantic led to increased Pacific immigration. Seattle, the closest U.S. port to Japan, became a prime point of entry for immigrants. Helen Winkler the chairman of the NCJW Department of Immigrant Aid warned, "Now it looks as though there might be a larger Jewish immigration through the Western ports than through those of the East, and we must be alert and thoroughly informed in order to be able to give the necessary friendly aid and protection both at the port and inland, whenever and wherever such service is warranted by the size of immigration."[238]

To prevent "white slavery," in 1905, at the request of the U.S. government, the national leadership had established an immigrant aid station at Ellis Island to interview Jewish women and ensure that they reached their destinations safely.[239] The national officers then sent letters to their sections in port cities asking them also to monitor female immigrants and inform the national headquarters if there were sufficient numbers of unaccompanied women to warrant establishing additional stations.[240] Seattle's NCJW added port monitoring to its settlement work by joining the city's Travelers'

Aid Society to make sure that "immigrant girls of our Faith were looked after on their arrival." The section also "pledged itself to care for many girls temporarily in need of advice and assistance in finding suitable quarters" and to "keep in touch of the new-comer until the stranger [was] comfortably and satisfactory placed."[241] A letter from Winkler also requested that the section check all docking steamer manifests for the notation "Hebrew" in the "Race or Nationality" column and then forward the specifics about the immigrant, including sex, age, and final destination, to the council's Department of Immigrant Aid. The Seattle section complied, incorporating port monitoring as part of its settlement work. Besides requesting information, Winkler was also concerned about the relationship between the male Hebrew Sheltering and Immigrant Aid Society (which had established a Seattle branch in 1915) and the council section in Seattle.[242]

As immigration through Pacific ports increased as a result of World War I, western sections were drawn into the national conflict between the two organizations. Winkler advised the Seattle section not to notify the Hebrew Sheltering and Immigration Aid Society that the council was contemplating placing a "port worker" in Seattle, which would be similar to the council's Ellis Island aid station. She intimated that potential trouble between the two national organizations could affect local conditions.[243] According to Diner, NCJW was seen by the men as competition. Male professionals in several key Jewish agencies deeply resented its activities and successes. The Hebrew Immigrant Aid Society, for instance, tried to convince the Baron de Hirsch Fund, which funded both bodies, to replace the "volunteer" women with professional men. The Eastern European men lost to the more elite women, thus scoring a political victory for the

NCJW based on its successful manipulation of the Jewish political system.[244] This battle was not only about gender but also about class, origins, and the right to "protect" new immigrants. The agendas of the national Jewish organizations, their tensions and their priorities, now became an aspect of western Jewish life.

World War I brought the West Coast into contact with international organizations as well. Similar to its liaison work with the council's national Department of Immigrant Aid, the Seattle section worked with the Joint Distribution Committee in New York to help locate immigrants for family reunification. These requests especially supported family reunification in Seattle. The Joint Distribution Committee often requested that councilwomen interview new immigrants to ascertain whether they planned to assist their friends or relatives.[245] While the NCJW interviewed immigrants in many cities, it now became especially important in the port cities of the West, where many immigrants were now arriving.

Attention to the immigration issue not only increased local service activities but also led Seattle NCJW women further into the political arena. Seeking to influence politics on an international issue that affected their community, the Seattle NCJW section appealed to President Warren Harding after World War I, "in the name of HUMANITY . . . to permit some 3,000 Turkish Jews, refugees from the War stricken zone, to remain in this country."[246] Their concern reflected the rapid growth of Seattle's immigrant Sephardic population, some of whom were attending classes at Seattle's Educational Center.

World War I had major long-term effects on western Jewish communities: it increased immigration to the West and forced the national Jewish leadership to increase the participation of western Jewish communities in their organizations. Jews, especially women, gained experience during the war in working with immigrants, governmental offices, the Red Cross, and sheltering organizations. This experience made it easier for them to obtain leadership roles in both Jewish and secular organizations and to move easily into civic roles.

CONTRIBUTIONS TO NATIONAL AND WORLD CHARITIES

Just as individuals from the eastern United States and even Europe contributed to the building of Mount Zion Hospital and the City of Hope, western Jews sent aid to the eastern United States and beyond in response to emergencies like the Chicago Fire and the Johnstown flood and to appeals by impoverished Jewish communities in places as far away as Gibraltar, Morocco, and Jerusalem.[247] However, a major change in overseas charity came with the founding of Hadassah chapters on the West Coast. In contrast to giving charity for disaster victims or attempting to alleviate poverty, Hadassah, the first women's Zionist organization, was founded as a membership organization with practical, obtainable goals that engaged women's interest in supporting Jewish settlement in Palestine.[248] These goals included building medical clinics and working with mothers and children, all projects familiar to American Jewish women. Previous Zionist and proto-Zionist organizations had been for men alone.

In Seattle, Hadassah members raised funds for Palestine through "card parties, raffles, the circulating library and rummage sales and donor luncheons."[249] They also formed sewing circles, making children's clothes in support of Youth Aliyah. These personal acts helped form a bond between the women of the West and children in Palestine. Sonia Myers Wachtin, who served as president of Hadassah in the early 1920s, exclaimed, "We're all young mothers with young children, we felt it was the most wonderful thing to do something for Israel. . . . Hadassah was helping children . . .[the women] made Layettes for babies." After sewing they were served a "real Jewish lunch with wonderful food and cakes. . . . The ladies loved it, it was a lot of fun, And at the same time we were doing something."[250] Religious women also held similar meetings in support of the vocational schools and centers of the Mizrachi Women's Organization of America (today known as AMIT, Americans for Israel and Torah). Sewing circles often took place in settlement houses, community centers, and the Young Men and Young Women's Hebrew Association buildings.

Involvement in organizations like Hadassah and the NCJW led western Jewish women to leadership roles beyond the region. Blanche Blumauer of Portland and Evelyn Aronson Margolis of San Francisco (granddaughter of Michel Goldwater) joined the board of the NCJW, while Josephine Hirsch of Portland and Hattie Sloss of San Francisco served as council honorary vice presidents. Activism led Jewish westerners to play an expanding role as part of a national and world Jewish community.

PHILANTHROPY: A WESTERN INSTITUTION

The mix of immigrants, ports that faced Asia, and the phenomenal growth of cities gave western Jewish communities a unique environment. Charity and philanthropy lay in overlapping spaces, connecting American Jewish and western identi-ties. Families not only established institutions for communal welfare but also passed this work on as a civic responsibility to their children. The existence of numerous benevolent societies and associations in a given locale not only reflected the size of the supporting population but also suggested its diverse character. Before the turn of the twentieth century, San Francisco, the hub of western Jewish life, was home to a large number of institutions and charities, including the Pacific Hebrew Orphan Asylum and Home, the only institution of its type in the Pacific West. When the western Jewish center shifted to southern California, Los Angeles, with its host of new settlers, became home to diverse charities, hospitals, and the regional T.B. sanitarium, the City of Hope.

Community organizations throughout the region provided one another with support and advice. In 1917, on completion of its new settlement house, the Seattle section of the NCJW rejoiced that many contributions came from Portland and San Francisco. Its yearly report noted, "The most gratifying encouragement came to us spontaneously from out of town friends who forwarded substantial checks commemorating happy events in their respective families. San Francisco and Portland were well represented in these donations to our Settlement House."[251] For Portland and Seattle, the ties went beyond monetary support, as the two cities mirrored each other in their community services. Farther south, the Los Angeles Federation of Jewish Welfare in 1926 established an advisory committee that planned to include members in San Francisco, Portland, and Seattle. The *B'nai B'rith Messenger* reported, "I. Irving Lipsitch, executive director of Federation of Jewish Welfare organization in Los Angeles, . . . stopped in San Francisco to solicit members for Advisory Board of JCR [Jewish Consumptive Relief Association]," and added, "He wants to create similar Advisory Boards in Portland, Seattle, other leading cities."[252]

Western women and their organizations largely shaped the daily implementation of regional philanthropy, as they built organizational infrastructure and worked with all segments of the community. In Portland, "the women simply eclipsed the men in their understanding and organization of welfare, and thereby gained a far larger civic role."[253] From the first benevolent associations to the settlement homes, hospitals, and national membership organizations, gender was refracted though a western lens that allowed women autonomy and greater freedom, enabling them to gain exceptional knowledge of their growing cities.

In contrast to this marked evolution in women's roles, men's roles in most charitable and philanthropic endeavors remained remarkably stable over this sixty-year period, with men largely contributing funds through benevolent associations, through the B'nai B'rith, or as individuals. What changed were the multiplicity of concerns that needed attention and the inclusion of new immigrants and migrants in the process. As western communities grew in importance, local men gained positions in national and international organizations. Men like Lucius L. Solomons and David Lubin became known for their connections to national and international immigrant charities and resettlement plans, while Peter M. Kahn and other new

Angelenos became known nationally for their work in establishing the internationally recognized City of Hope. For men, this national and international philanthropic work was a natural extension of their business and fraternal networks.

The period from the 1870s to the 1930s saw great changes in the way western Jews defined their relationship to those in need. In the 1870s, benevolence and the giving of charity could help a family recover from an economic setback, recover from an illness, or bury the dead. By the 1920s, philanthropies and community organizations' concern changed to prevention.[254] Social welfare became a profession, not an avocation, and federations of charities, rather than elite men and women extending a personal helping hand, monitored communal needs.

In the years that followed, the western Jewish population continued to grow. As the children of the early-twentieth-century immigrants came of age and began to enter the professions, the gap between "founding families" and "newcomers" in most of the West's communities began to shrink. In Los Angeles, old divisions were eclipsed by the rapid population growth beginning in the 1920s. A period of consolidation in the decades preceding World War II would lead to new organizational and philanthropic strategies for the 1930s, the 1940s, and beyond.

5 CONSOLIDATION, INTEGRATION, AND DIVERGENCE DURING THE INTERWAR YEARS

There were many Orthodox young people
as well as Reform young people, who came
[to Congregation Herzl's Junior Guild] as
a common meeting ground.

In many metropolitan Jewish communities, one would not expect to
find Samuel Koch and Jacob Kaplan rubbing elbows (fig. 5.1). Koch,
the rabbi of Seattle's Temple De Hirsch for more than thirty-five
years, was a paragon of Reform Judaism. Born in America to German
Jewish parents and raised in Denver, Koch was ordained at Hebrew
Union College in Cincinnati just after the turn of the century. Soon
after his arrival in Seattle, he married Cora Dinkelspiel, daughter of a
prominent local German Jewish family. Koch exemplified the values of
his generation of Reform rabbis, embracing the Pittsburgh Platform,
which defined Judaism strictly as a religion, emphasized universal values,
and denounced any hint of Jewish nationalist tendencies. He occasionally exchanged pulpits with liberal Protestant ministers and enjoyed
personal friendships with President Henry Suzzallo and his successors
at the University of Washington.[1] Koch dedicated himself to a variety of
Jewish and secular causes through involvement in the Seattle Council of
Social Agencies, the YMHA, the Council of Jewish Women, Seattle's
Children's Hospital, and the Seattle Committee for Syrian and Armenian
Relief.

S.B. Asia

Herman Kessler

Dr. Samuel Koch

J.C. Lang

Aubrey Levy

Ben Levine

Irving C. Lewis

David Lipman

Myer Cohen

Elkan Morgenstern

SEATTLE LODGE No. 503, I. O. B. B.

PAST PRESIDENTS' HONOR CLASS MEMBERSHIP CAMPAIGN

April 22 to May 6, 1925

Dr. F. Faik

Lou Friedlander

Maurice Grunbaum

Otto Grunbaum

Max Hardman

Joseph Hurwitz

FOR THE CAMPAIGN	COLONELS	COLONELS	COLONELS
SOL ESFELD, Chairman	VICTOR CAPELOTO	JACOB KALINA	JULIUS SHAFER
S. B. ASIA, Vice Chairman	LOUIS CASSERD	JACOB KAPLAN	HERMAN SHAPIRO
I. C. LEWIS, Vice Chairman	JACOB S. FRIEDMAN	DAVID LIPMAN	ALFRED SHEMANSKI
	MAURICE GERBER	MANDEL NIEDER	SOL G. SPRING
	MAX HARDMAN	MORRIS ROBBINS	PHILIP TWOROGER
			LEO WEISFIELD

April 3, 1925

To the Members
Seattle Lodge No. 503.

Worthy Brethren:

It has long been the ambition of Seattle Lodge to boast a membership of 1,000. With your help this ambition can now be realized.

We have a total of 830 members; only 170 short of our goal. We shall endeavor to take in this number during our next membership drive to be held April 22 to May 6. We are particularly anxious to reach this goal, as it will help our delegates to obtain recognition from the Grand Lodge in choosing Seattle for the District Lodge Convention in 1926.

This drive is being held in honor of all past presidents of Seattle Lodge, which number about 30, and whose pictures are reproduced above. How much do you appreciate your president? Has he earned your support and cooperation, and are you willing to make a little effort to prove that he has?

The most important factor in the membership campaign is to obtain a good list of prospects. This is where you can help. All we ask you to do is to fill in the names of several of your friends or relatives who are not members of the lodge. This will take but a few minutes of your time and costs you nothing. The enclosed card is addressed and stamped, ready for mailing.

If each member will send in this card filled out, the success of our drive will be assured. Your past presidents and your lodge are entitled to this much support from you. Please fill in the card and mail it now, so that the committee can get started at once.

Cordially yours,

MEMBERSHIP COMMITTEE,

SOL ESFELD, Chairman.

SE:IL

"EVERY MEMBER GET A MEMBER"—"MAKE IT 1,000"

Mandel Nieder

Samuel Ostrow

Julius Rickles

Morris Robbins

Emanuel Rosenberg

Herbert Schoenfeld

Jacob Kaplan

G. Schwartz

Julius Shafer

E.J. Spear

Sol Spring

Leopold Stern

Leo Weisfield

Sam Schwabacher

Kaplan immigrated to the United States from Russia as a child and came to Seattle as a young man just after the turn of the century. Like the majority of Russian Jewish immigrants in the West, he and his father operated a small business. Their print shop would, by the 1910s, fill an important niche in the Jewish community, printing documents such as organizational bylaws, event programs, and campaign posters in English and occasionally in Yiddish. Like many Russian immigrants, Kaplan was staunchly Orthodox and a passionate Zionist. He was an early member of Congregation Bikur Cholim and, along with other Zionists, a leader in the breakaway group that founded the Zionist Orthodox congregation, Herzl.[2] Unlike Koch, who was involved in causes both within and outside the Jewish community, most of Kaplan's many volunteer hours were focused internally. Among the numerous organizations he served were his two congregations, Bikur Cholim and Herzl; the Talmud Torah; the Seattle Jewish Fund; and regional Jewish groups like the Jewish Consumptive Relief Association of California.

Koch and Kaplan clearly identified differently as Jews. While Koch saw Zionism as a threat to the identity of Jews as Americans and as an affront to his view of Judaism as a religious faith, Kaplan embraced it as essential to his Jewish identity. While Koch worked to create interfaith dialogue and saw himself as part of a Judeo-Christian tradition, Kaplan hoped to perpetuate Judaism as a culture—even with its own language, Yiddish—

that set Jews apart from their Christian neighbors. Koch's community at Temple De Hirsch was part of the merchant and professional elite of Seattle. His personal friends and acquaintances included wealthy and prominent gentiles as well as Jews. Kaplan, by comparison, associated primarily with the other small Jewish business owners in the Central District of Seattle.

Yet, for all of their differences, the two men, whose houses of worship were merely blocks from each other, shared much common ground. Both were prominent in the 1928 founding of the Seattle Jewish Fund, the city's first centralized Jewish philanthropic organization.[3] Although the fund failed a few years later in the midst of the Depression, they cooperated in other efforts to unify the community. For example, Koch and Kaplan were both members of Seattle B'nai B'rith Lodge No. 503—a consolidated lodge formed in 1921 by merging separate lodges that had been based largely on synagogue affiliation.[4] Even before the consolidation, men like Koch and Kaplan had the opportunity to meet and play together at various B'nai B'rith athletic tournaments and picnics.[5] And the ties between Koch and Kaplan went beyond the Jewish community: both men clearly valued their identity as Masons. They both saved among their papers letters of recognition from the Washington Lodge of Perfection of the Ancient and Accepted Scottish Rite of Freemasonry.[6]

The men's fraternal ties are suggestive of some of the ways in which the consolidation and integration of western Jews traced in chapter 2 were deepened and broadened during the decades leading up to World War II. With the exception of Los Angeles, a city whose enormous influx of newcomers pushed its Jewish community in a different direction, most western Jewish communities grew only slowly and faced the crises of depression and

FIG. 5.1 *(Facing page) Samuel Koch, top, third from left, and Jacob Kaplan, bottom left, appear among the former presidents of Seattle B'nai B'rith Lodge No. 503, ca. 1925. University of Washington Libraries, Special Collections, neg. UW27641z.*

world war with an increasingly unified front. Even San Francisco, with its history of snobbish class divisions, was able to unify in order to confront the challenges of the interwar years.

The relative unity evident in western Jewish communities during the 1930s and early 1940s distinguishes the region, as historians have characterized these decades as an era in which American Jewish communities were torn by conflict. Arthur Goren, for example, writes of this era: "Probably no other period in the communal life of American Jews was as contentious."[7] Although others, like Jonathan Sarna, note how diverse Jewish groups worked together through national organizations like the Joint Distribution Committee and the National Jewish Welfare Board, many historians of the interwar years emphasize that bitter internal conflicts severely compromised the Jewish community's response to national and international crises.[8] In the West, although individuals might differ sharply over issues like Zionism, men like Koch and Kaplan were able to cooperate as they faced the decade's challenges. Such unity was rooted in strong regional and intra-city networks, reinforced by the continued tradition of personal, business, and organizational ties; a strong western identity, based on a long history of acceptance and recognition as civil and political leaders; and relative demographic and occupational stability.

Exceptional in this regard was Los Angeles, where the unprecedented growth of both the city and its Jewish community created increasing fragmentation. As the city doubled in size and replaced San Francisco as the region's industrial and commercial hub, its Jewish community grew even faster, overtaking San Francisco as the region's largest as well as the most socially and culturally diverse.[9] Los Angeles became the new center for synagogue creation and fund-raising for philanthropy and a magnet for Jewish intellectual life, both religious and secular. Its Boyle Heights neighborhood became the West's primary Jewish ethnic enclave, while Hollywood and Beverly Hills became the new glamour capital, not only for American Jewry, but also for the nation as a whole. Perhaps equally important, the movie industry, with its adjunct in a new sportswear industry, provided an expanding base of employment—Jewish and otherwise—cushioning the local economy and society from the worst ravages of unemployment and fostering continued population growth even during the Great Depression.

While the Los Angeles Jewish community functioned as a part of the regional Jewish network, its extraordinary position in the city led it to experience a different political situation and to respond differently to the challenges of the interwar period. It grew so fast and drew so much new wealth to the city that its most prominent civic leaders, centered in the movie colony, became rivals to the old Protestant leadership in central Los Angeles. While Jews continued to be appointed to prominent judgeships and to statewide boards, the nouveau riche moguls also faced exclusion from elite housing in San Marino, from country clubs, and from access to the political circles around the *Los Angeles Times*. This shift meant that, more than in other cities in the Pacific West, Jewish Angelenos experienced anti-Semitism and developed the need to resist it. The Los Angeles Jewish elite continued to rely on traditional, behind-the-scenes work to counter threats. But the burgeoning second-generation Eastern European population was more oriented toward direct protest, which would turn into an assertive Jewish politics in the 1950s. Los Angeles Jewry, to some degree, was beginning to follow eastern patterns and to set a tone that other western communities would not emulate until after World War II.

REGIONAL CONSOLIDATION: BEYOND ELITES

During the interwar years, the issues capturing the attention of western Jews differed little from those exciting Jews elsewhere in the country. Community newspapers up and down the Pacific Coast focused much of their coverage on national and international issues, including the rise of domestic anti-Semitism, the plight of European Jews, the politics of Zionism, and the building of the Yishuv in Palestine. With stories on anti-Semites like Henry Ford and Father Charles E. Coughlin, national Jewish efforts to assist European Jews or settlers in Palestine, and, later, the impact of the war on their European brethren dominating their coverage, it is often difficult to discern anything "western" about the news pages of these publications.

Given the heavy focus on national and international issues during the 1920s and 1930s, the centralization occurring in American politics under the New Deal and during World War II, and improved communications and transportation that made the West less geographically remote, it might be expected that western Jewish communities would become less distinct during these years. Yet western Jews reinforced their own organizations and continued to claim distinctive identities that reflected regional conditions, including Los Angeles's new status as regional center. As the Koch and Kaplan profiles suggest, many western Jews, although fitting the stereotypes of "new" and "old" leadership groups and differing sharply on issues

like Zionism, adhered to a strong regional identity that muted differences and fostered cooperation.

As in earlier years, close personal connections among the region's rabbinical and lay leadership were a key component of this regional identity. Among Reform rabbis, as had been the case since early in the century, close relations among the leaders of congregations from Seattle to Los Angeles were built on a common commitment to civic involvement and interfaith dialogue, as well as on personal ties that often went back decades to shared experiences at Hebrew Union College. Their correspondence demonstrates the personal and professional ties both among them and with their regional communities. The papers of Seattle's Rabbi Koch, for example, include letters from West Coast colleagues such as Rabbi Edgar Magnin of Temple B'nai B'rith in Los Angeles. Newspaper reports, continuing a pattern dating back to the nineteenth century, provide evidence of exchange and community among western rabbis, with frequent notices of rabbis visiting one another to lecture or to attend an event such as a building dedication. In 1928–29, for example, the *Transcript* noted a visit to Seattle by Portland's Rabbi Henry J. Berkowitz (Temple Beth Israel) to address Temple De Hirsch's men's club, a visit by a Los Angeles rabbi to raise money for an orphanage in Palestine, and a visit by Rabbi Koch to San Francisco to address a B'nai B'rith lodge.[10] Similarly, Los Angeles's *B'nai B'rith Messenger* carried a front-page story by Rabbi Magnin reporting on the dedication ceremony for Temple Beth Israel's new building in Portland, in which he participated along with the rabbis of virtually every large Reform temple on the Pacific Coast. When his own Wilshire Boulevard Temple was dedicated two years later, his rabbinic colleagues paid him a return visit.[11]

Rabbis within the region frequently succeeded one another in synagogue pulpits, just as they had since the founding of the earliest western congregations. In just one four-month period in 1930, Rabbi Jack Levy, formerly of Temple Emanu-El in Victoria, British Columbia, was appointed to a post in Oakland; Rabbi Julius Liebert of Temple Emanu-El in Spokane moved to the congregation of the same name in Los Angeles; Rabbi B. Ostrynski who had served Seattle's Herzl Congregation for the previous year was called to serve a congregation in Los Angeles; and Rabbi Solomon Wohlgelernter, formerly of Vancouver, British Columbia, was elected rabbi of Bikur Cholim in Seattle. In Ostrynski's absence, Congregation Herzl called on Rabbi Spector of Tacoma to officiate during the high holidays.[12] As these examples make clear, the tight network among western rabbis was not limited to Hebrew Union College graduates. Rather, as the Ostrynski and Wohlgelernter cases suggest, Orthodox rabbis and congregations in the region were also in close communication.

While it might be expected that rabbinical colleagues would maintain close ties, laypeople also saw themselves as part of a regional Jewish network. As in earlier decades, regional ties were often based on personal relationships. Newspaper notices hint at that interconnectedness, as when the Seattle *Transcript* published a notice of the fiftieth wedding anniversary of Mr. and Mrs. Ben Selling of Portland, noting that Mrs. Selling was a native of San Francisco.[13] The Shemanskys and Sierotys, who owned the men's clothing firm, Eastern Outfitting, with stores in Portland, San Francisco, and Los Angeles, used their commercial ties up and down the coast to raise funds for Zionist causes. After a visit to Palestine in 1928, Mrs. Sieroty spoke at various Zionist rallies, which were covered in newspapers in Los Angeles, Portland, and

San Francisco. Working through the same regional network, Louis Lipsky spoke for United Jewish Appeal, Chaim Arlozoroff for Histadrut, Shmarya Levin for the Jewish National Fund, and Gedalia Bublick, the leading figure in Mizrachi, used Los Angeles as his base for speaking tours along the Pacific Coast. While Lipsky and Levin might speak at B'nai B'rith meetings or Reform temples, Orthodox laymen arranged Bublick's tour, during which he spoke at Orthodox synagogues like Bikur Cholim in Seattle and Shaarei Torah in Portland.[14]

Regional organizations—most notably the B'nai B'rith District Grand Lodge No. 4, which convened members from the Pacific West and as far east as Salt Lake City for its annual conferences—brought local lay and rabbinic leaders to regional prominence. The geographic boundaries defined by the B'nai B'rith district were also used by other organizations, bringing Jewish leaders, professionals, and laypeople together in regular meetings. In 1934, for example, eighty-five delegates from eleven cities in Washington, Oregon, and California attended the inaugural gathering in San Francisco of the Pacific Coast Conference of Jewish Religious Schools.[15] Groups ranging from Hadassah to communal agencies held annual regional conferences where lay leadership from the various western cities met and strengthened personal ties. The regional Jewish press covered these events extensively, often in detailed front-page stories with photographic spreads.

Interaction did not take place only at annual conferences. Members of some of these Jewish communities apparently traveled several hours for special events. For example, in 1930, events in Portland, including a lecture by San Francisco's Rabbi Louis Newman and a concert by the Jewish prodigy Yehudi Menuhin, also from San Francisco, were advertised in Seattle's *Transcript*.[16]

This was particularly pronounced in communities like Seattle and Portland, which were smaller and more likely to look to each other and to their larger counterparts for resources like speakers and newspaper columnists, as well as for broader social contacts. The Portland and Seattle B'nai B'rith lodges frequently sent delegations back and forth, including speakers and debate teams, and held very popular interstate athletic competitions for adults and youth.

By contrast, the sprawling Los Angeles community was far more self-sufficient. In that city's *B'nai B'rith Messenger* the events listed show a far larger proportion of lectures presented by local Jews.[17] In addition, while the Portland and Seattle newspapers noted the regional ties of visitors and newcomers, Los Angeles's *Messenger* did so less consistently. Thus Seattle's *Transcript* reported that Rabbi Liebert, newly appointed to Temple Emanuel in Los Angeles, had several years before served in Spokane (and had spoken frequently in Seattle), while the *Messenger* said only that Liebert was "formerly of Long Beach."[18] Throughout this period, Portland's *Scribe* regularly reported news from the Washington and California Jewish communities.

As is evident from such coverage, the western Jewish press, as it had since the days of the *Gleaner*, continued to play an important role in fostering a strong sense of regional identity. Columns by the West's leading rabbis served a similar function. For instance, Seattle's *Transcript* and Portland's *Scribe* both carried the column of Rabbi Newman of San Francisco's Emanu-El during the time he served there.[19] Both papers called his departure for a pulpit in New York in 1930 a loss for the region. Noting that western Jewry was "one community," which worked together while being somewhat separate from the rest of the nation, the

Transcript called Newman an "inspired leader of the region."[20] Rabbi Nieto of San Francisco recognized this sense of regionalism when he called in 1928 for a conference of rabbis in the region to discuss common issues.[21]

In addition to reading news items in their local papers about Jewish events throughout the region, individuals often subscribed to Jewish newspapers from elsewhere on the coast. Evidence of this practice can be found in correspondence, such as a 1919 letter from Solomon Prottas, a leader of Seattle's Orthodox Bikur Cholim, to Jonah Wise, rabbi of Portland's Reform Temple Beth Israel and editor of that city's *Scribe*, chastising him for his opposition to Zionism and threatening to cancel his subscription. Despite his dissatisfaction with Wise's stand, Prottas reconsidered: "On second thought, however, from careful consideration of the other good articles and editorial comments appearing in *The Scribe*, I believe it is worthy of being in the home of every Jewish person on the coast, and I therefore send my yearly subscription in advance."[22]

Just as active laypeople like Prottas, and his son Sam, were connected to a regional network, they were also closely tied to national organizations. Yet while regional contacts linked Jews across the religious and ideological spectrum, ties to national organizations tended to be more religiously or ideologically specific. The Prottas correspondence with national organizations, spanning a period from the 1910s to the 1940s, shows a strong affinity for Orthodox and religious Zionist organizations such as the Vaad Bitachon, Keren Hayesod, and Palestine Hebrew Culture Fund. Locally, however, they were involved with a broader spectrum of organizations, ranging from Zionist and Orthodox institutions to community-wide groups such as the B'nai B'rith, the Seattle Jewish Federation, various congregational building funds (other than those of their own congregation), and Jewish philanthropic causes.[23]

The consolidation of B'nai B'rith lodges and of community fund-raising in the 1910s and 1920s played a key role in providing spaces where Jews as different as Jacob Kaplan and Samuel Koch, and especially the children from different strata, could relate to one another as "brothers" and work together toward common goals.[24] The B'nai B'rith's role in the West as an organization uniting diverse groups of Jews anticipated a role it began to define nationally during World War II, when national B'nai B'rith president Henry Monsky argued that his organization's inclusive nature could "bridge the gap between the Zionist and non-Zionist camps in American Jewish life."[25] The western organizational unity among Jews of diverse backgrounds stands in contrast to the East, where, according to Henry Feingold, *Landsmanshaften* based on common roots in Eastern European hometowns were in the 1920s still the most extensive organizational network.[26] In Los Angeles, prior to the explosive growth that began in the 1920s and led to a proliferation of small religious, cultural, and social organizations, B'nai B'rith played a unifying role and emerged as "the representative Jewish organization." By 1924, the city's consolidated Lodge No. 487 was among the nation's largest, with two thousand enrolled, and had become the major "conduit for bringing new personages to the foreground of Jewish communal affairs."[27] Likewise, in Portland, the consolidated lodge claimed more than 35 percent of the community's adult male population and became a "unifying and democratizing force in the Jewish community."[28] In Seattle, the 1926 roster of the consolidated lodge listed nearly one thousand individuals, including elite Reform Jews, Orthodox Eastern European immigrants, and second-generation, upwardly mobile professionals. The lodge

counted both elite temple members and leaders of Orthodox Bikur Cholim and Herzl congregations as past presidents.[29]

Lodge consolidation and federated community fund-raising facilitated the construction of increasingly inclusive facilities, thus expanding opportunities for interaction among adults and youth from diverse backgrounds. In Portland, the unification of B'nai B'rith lodges led directly to the construction of the B'nai B'rith Building, a recreational, social, and cultural facility, serving mostly middle-class Jews who had moved out of the South Portland immigrant district. By the 1930s, the facility (renamed the B'nai B'rith Center in 1923) became a central institution, serving Jews throughout the city.[30] The increasing interaction among Portland Jews from varying backgrounds was also reflected in synagogue memberships, as growing numbers of second-generation Eastern Europeans joined Temple Beth Israel and sent their children to its Sunday school, often in addition to membership in the congregations to which they (or their parents) had long belonged.[31]

A similar process occurred in San Francisco, where, as the existing YMHA building grew inadequate in the 1920s, planners began to look beyond an institution that would serve just one neighborhood, to one that would in fact be modeled after Portland's B'nai B'rith Building:[32] "There was developing a growing conviction that recreational facilities were needed not for one but for all segments of the Jewish Community. This conviction had been strengthened by the spread of the Jewish Community Center Movement in the country, and by the fact that other communities had been constructing modern Jewish Center buildings. The Jewish Welfare Board had been stimulating communities to think in terms of community-wide Center services."[33] Despite the onset of the Great

Depression, the Building Fund Campaign was launched in the spring of 1930, the ground broken in the summer of 1932, and the building dedicated in November 1933.[34]

The cooperation and consolidation evident in such endeavors were fostered by the occupational profiles of the various communities. By the second quarter of the twentieth century, the gap between elite pioneer entrepreneurs and more recently arrived immigrant storekeepers was eroding as the latter built more prosperous businesses and, especially, as their sons rose in status. At the most elite levels, successful Eastern European businessmen, like the Schnitzers of Portland, and especially the immigrant Hollywood moguls, amassed fortunes that rivaled or surpassed those of their most illustrious predecessors. As second-generation Eastern Europeans came of age, many attended college, entered the professions, and rose to prominence within the community. The historic absence of class conflict within western Jewish communities, due to a long-standing concentration in trade and low rates of industrial employment, continued during the interwar years. In San Francisco, for example, in the 1930s, 83 percent of Jews were listed as professionals, "proprietors, managers and officials," or clerks and only about 15 percent as skilled, semiskilled, or unskilled laborers.[35] Even in Los Angeles, where factory work was more widespread among Jews, the occupational profile continued to be dominated, as it had been from the community's founding, by commerce and also by employees in the movie industry. Union activity among Jews was sporadic, and the International Ladies Garment Workers Union had only limited success. Indeed, the presence of Jewish union activists had led to exaggerated assumptions about Jews as factory workers. In actuality, the workers in the supposedly "Jewish" industries like garment work

were, by the 1930s, largely Mexican women.[36]

With the exception of Los Angeles, cooperative relations among different segments of these Jewish communities were also fostered by relative demographic stability. The Jewish population of San Francisco, which had reached 30,000 before the close of the first decade of the century, took until 1927 to reach 35,000, and eleven years later it was estimated at 40,910.[37] The Jewish population of Portland actually fell during the 1920s and 1930s, as members of younger generations left the state to seek opportunities elsewhere. In addition, those who remained in Portland began to disperse through the city, moving away from the concentrated immigrant district in South Portland.[38]

In Seattle, while growth continued, it was slow: in 1922, the Jewish population of the Central District numbered approximately 6,000–7,000; eighteen years later in 1940, the area's Jews numbered just under 9,000 (out of a total Seattle Jewish population of 10,300).[39] The residential concentration in the Central District continued until after World War II, making this neighborhood unusual in that it contained *all* of the major Jewish institutions—including the Reform temple—as late as 1940.[40] This meant that children of the "elite" and those of later arriving immigrants lived in the same general area and attended the same public schools. In addition, as had been the case in earlier decades, it was not uncommon for the children of Orthodox Sephardic and Eastern European immigrants to attend Temple De Hirsch's Sunday school or for their parents, like their counterparts in Portland, to take out memberships at the temple in addition to their "own" congregations.[41] Adult Jews of diverse backgrounds, while continuing separate religious identities as Reform, Conservative, or Orthodox Jews, tended to know one another and to work across religious and ethnic boundaries.

As elsewhere in the United States, the philanthropic and social service challenges brought by the Depression furthered community consolidation. Contraction in available funds led to a thinning of the number of separate organizations and increased coordination among various agencies, both within and beyond the Jewish community. As Shelly Tenenbaum's study of community responses to the Depression in San Francisco suggests, Jewish self-help and philanthropic organizations played a major role in supporting the Jewish needy, coordinating with secular charities and supplementing public relief.[42] Often, Jewish agencies used their funds to supplement aid provided by local, and later federal, relief agencies. This meant that members of the community were able to receive assistance beyond the meager funds provided by those agencies. In Los Angeles, for example, the Jewish Social Service Bureau proved more flexible about residency requirements and was willing to support clients at a level slightly higher than public agencies.[43] In San Francisco, where the community's occupational structure lessened the impact of the Depression, Tenenbaum shows that "poor and working class Jews were provided with cash assistance, student scholarships, subsidized hospital expenses, children's summer camps, vocational guidance, aid to prisoners and to the mentally ill in state institutions, interest-free loans, matzoth at Passover, and spectacles and medical appliances. Housing was provided for orphaned children, young single women and the elderly. Moreover, during the last years of the Depression, the San Francisco Jewish community gave financial assistance to refugees fleeing Nazi Germany."[44]

Likewise, in Seattle, where Hebrew benevolent associations had played active roles as early as the turn of the century in the citywide Charity Organization Society, and later in the city's community chest, the Jewish Welfare Society (JWS) "became part of the federal, state, and county welfare system during the Depression and used most of their funds and volunteer help to supplement government money."[45] As in San Francisco, Seattle's JWS supplemented public assistance, as May Goldsmith, director of the city's Hebrew Benevolent Society, reported in 1932: "Federal Aid gives food ($1.20 per person per week), fuel (wood), some clothing, and lodging. Are these all that our Jewish families need? Can you visualize a family of five, mother, father, and three children, living on five dollars and sixty cents a week? This includes bread, milk, meat, and all grocery supplies. Often a family needs some extras, [and] the JWS provides this when necessary."[46] In addition to providing supplemental allocations for families, the JWS played a central coordinating role:

> Throughout those turbulent times, one of the JWS's main strengths was its ability to collaborate with other Jewish organizations. For example, it administered the funds allocated to the Ladies' Montefiore Aid Society by Seattle's Community Chest; worked with the NCJW, Seattle Section's Americanization program to assist refugees trying to establish citizenship; collaborated with the NCJW, Seattle Section, to establish a scholarship to pay the cost of a second-year student studying social work at the University of Washington; and in 1941, in partnership with the Jewish Welfare Board, began assisting servicemen.[47]

Such cooperation, and the more general consolidation of organizations, did not signal complete harmony among Jews in these cities. Indeed, the Seattle Jewish Fund broke up after several years as a result of tensions between temple members and the Orthodox. A desire by Sephardic and Ashkenazic Orthodox leaders for independence from

Temple De Hirsch likely slowed the federation movement. When a new cooperative fund-raising organization—the Seattle Jewish Federated Fund—emerged in 1936 in response to the growing European crisis, a controversy erupted over the group's first-ever dinner meeting in 1941, held at a Jewish country club that did not have a kosher kitchen. By the following year, the dinner was advertised with the tagline "Kosher? Of Course!"[48] Although tensions sometimes flared over real differences such as levels of ritual observance or adherence to dietary laws, a spirit of unity is clearly visible in the files of individual community groups and congregations. It was, for example, common for the Orthodox Bikur Cholim to advertise Council of Jewish Women events in its newsletter.[49] Ideological divisions were certainly present in these communities, but the desire for unity tended to prevail.

Yet increasing organizational unity did not necessarily translate into uniform social amiability. While some breakdown in social divisions is evident in Seattle and Portland, this was far less true in San Francisco, where class distinctions had always been more pronounced, and in Los Angeles, where enormous growth in the community led to *greater* social distance between newcomers and elites. In Seattle, while oral histories reflect a continuing social gap between members of the elite temple and of the city's other congregations, they also provide evidence of increasingly porous boundaries, as second-generation Eastern European Jews began joining the temple in the 1920s and 1930s. In the 1930s, Congregation Herzl's Junior Guild provided opportunities for youth from various backgrounds to mix, according to one informant: "There were many Orthodox young people as well as Reform young people, who came there as a common meeting ground."[50] Although some Sephardic children also attended the temple

Sunday school, they remained socially segregated from both Orthodox and Reform Ashkenazi children. At the University of Washington, Sephardic students were not welcomed in the Jewish fraternities until after World War II.[51]

In Portland, although children of Eastern Europeans did attend the temple Sunday school, the social gap between the temple's elite and "other" Portland Jews continued into the 1930s and 1940s. As Felice Lauterstein Driesen recalled, Rabbi Henry J. Berkowitz, who led Beth Israel from 1928 to 1949, insisted that temple teens socialize *exclusively* with one another:

> Rabbi Berkowitz was very profoundly determined and proud of Reform Judaism and he said, "my children are Reform Jews, and I want them to be raised as Reform Jews. I want them to be proud and to understand and to live their lives as Reform Jews and I don't want it dissipated." He not only definitely discouraged, but often prohibited (social contact with others). . . . [So] that when we had an Octagonal Party, we members of Temple Beth Israel were we to say "Rabbi, I have a date with Johnny Shmul from Temple Neveh Zedek, can I bring him to the party?" "No," he said, "you date somebody from Temple Beth Israel. This is where you belong." You couldn't bring a Christian date, God forbid, to an Octagonal Party. By the same token you couldn't bring somebody from the Ahavai Sholom either.[52]

In San Francisco, the social gap based on ethnic origins and wealth remained fixed well into the twentieth century. The elitism and "introverted clannishness" of San Francisco's wealthy Jewish pioneers "persisted through three and four generations."[53] As Irena Narell writes in her chronicle of the pioneer families, even in the fourth generation there was still pressure to marry within a tightly

drawn circle. As a fourth-generation descendant recalled, "Nothing would have made them happier than if I had married someone on the family tree."[54] Beyond this most elite circle, German Jews of Emanu-El continued to be associated with money, prestige, and power and to view members of other congregations as second-class.

ZIONISM, ANTI-ZIONISM, AND COMMUNITY COHESION

Along with social tensions, the issue that posed the largest potential threat to the emerging unity of western Jewish communities was Zionism. Historians have characterized the West as a stronghold of anti-Zionism, arguing that the tolerance that made Jews feel at home as westerners fostered antipathy to a movement that many felt called into question their identity as Americans.[55] After the anti-Zionist rhetoric of Rabbi Voorsanger in the early twentieth century, and the pro-Zionist work of Rabbis Martin Meyer and Louis Newman, San Francisco's elite Temple Emanu-El under Rabbi Irving Reichert in the 1930s and early 1940s reemerged as a hub for anti-Zionism. Reichert was an active opponent of Zionism during the 1930s and became a prominent national leader in the anti-Zionist American Council for Judaism (ACJ) when it was founded in 1942 (fig. 5.2). Other anti-Zionist leaders came from Reform congregations from Seattle to Los Angeles.[56]

The reputation of the West as a stronghold for anti-Zionism is largely based on its San Fran-

FIG. 5.2 *American Council for Judaism anti-Zionist advertisement, 1949. Jewish Community Bulletin (San Francisco), October 7, 1949. Western Jewish History Center, Judah L. Magnes Museum.*

cisco spokesmen. Much of the ACJ's opposition to Zionism was grounded in a classical Reform understanding of Judaism as a religion only—not a national or ethnic group. San Francisco's anti-Zionists believed that conceiving of Judaism in terms of "peoplehood" would betray a Reform ideal and even expose them to accusations of dual loyalty. As Rabbi Reichert explained in a 1936 sermon, "Our political nationalism is American," and "[embracing Jewish nationalism] is fraught with grave danger to our position in the Western world."[57] Reichert's congregants, according to Fred Rosenbaum, "joined the Council almost to a man," and their chapter alone raised about a third of the national organization's budget.[58] Narell agrees that "old Western Jewry flocked" to the ACJ, noting that, when Rabbi Reichert spoke out against Zionism in his 1943 Kol Nidre sermon, "one hundred resignations were tendered to Hadassah the following morning."[59] It is also true that others—including Rose Rinder, the wife of Emanu-El's cantor and leader of the San Francisco Hadassah group—continued to support Zionism.[60] Indeed, Reichert's sermon resulted in heated exchanges, including one in which Mrs. Rinder, "in a most uncharacteristic fit of anger, compared the rabbi to Hitler within earshot of many worshipers."[61]

Although Zionists like the Rinders rejected Reichert's position, the rabbi made anti-Zionism "the highest priority of his career," arguing that Jewish nationalism was incompatible with Americanism and that Zionism would lead to suspicions that Jews were not fully loyal to America. Despite the tragedy befalling European Jews, Rosenbaum argues, "virtually unprecedented freedom, toleration, and prosperity in the San Francisco Bay Area had rendered the leaders of that Jewish community incapable of adequately assessing the needs and desires of the rest of world Jewry."[62] Across the

Bay, Oakland, too, was largely anti-Zionist until World War II: "Even as anti-Semitism became more visible in the inter-war years, Zionist voices remained in the minority since most Jews feared that with the creation of a Jewish state they might be accused of 'double loyalties.'"[63] Oakland Jewish Community Center scrapbooks indicate that debates over Zionism were held on several occasions and that both Rabbi Reichert and Elmer Berger, the national leader of the ACJ, spoke in Oakland on anti-Zionism as late as 1945.[64] Elite members of prominent Reform congregations echoed this anti-Zionism in other West Coast cities. In Seattle, several anti-Zionist activists served on the Temple De Hirsch board in the early 1940s, and Rabbi Koch, who stepped down because of illness in early 1942, had for decades opposed political Zionism.[65] In Portland, as in Los Angeles, members of the prominent Reform congregations joined the ACJ.

Yet a survey of community activities and the community press in this period provides clear evidence that anti-Zionism was not the dominant force in this period—even in San Francisco. The major Jewish newspaper in each of these cities had been supporting Zionist projects, Zionist speakers, and Zionist fund-raising since at least the early 1920s. Seattle's *Transcript*, Portland's *Scribe*, San Francisco's *Emanu-El*, and Los Angeles's *Messenger* all reported extensively on Palestine and the crisis of European Jewry and presented Zionism as a solution to that crisis. The *Messenger*, for example, included extensive coverage by the late 1920s of local Zionist organizations and activities, as well as featuring stories like one on Alfred Kauffman, a native Californian turned Palestinian citrus farmer.[66] Zionist groups used the *Messenger* to advertise programs and recruit members, and articles about these events encouraged participation and lauded program goals. An article about an upcoming Jewish National Fund banquet in 1937 indicated that the fund-raiser was a major contributor to "the redemption of the Land in Palestine."[67] Even in San Francisco, the weekly *Emanu-El* was clearly sympathetic to Zionism. While Temple Emanu-El's bulletin, the *Chronicle*, featured Reichert's anti-Zionist sermons and statements on a regular basis in the early 1940s, the citywide *Emanu-El* published articles favorably reporting on Zionist efforts in Palestine and on the activities of Zionist leaders like Chaim Weizman and generally painted Zionism as the solution to the Jewish problem in Europe.[68] Congregation Beth Sholom's rabbi, Saul White, wrote a regular column for *Emanu-El*, in which he ridiculed Reichert for his anti-Zionism and carefully constructed an argument in favor of Jewish nationalism.[69]

Beyond such written endorsements, there is evidence of extensive Zionist activity in western communities. Since Jews of Eastern European origin tended to be the most enthusiastic supporters of Zionism, it is not surprising that many of the Orthodox and Conservative congregations that served this group were outspokenly Zionist. In Seattle, where Zionism had been the motivating force behind the organization of Congregation Herzl in 1906, it continued to be enthusiastically embraced by that congregation and by Orthodox Bikur Cholim as well. The Bikur Cholim newsletter published one of many calls for support of the United Jewish Appeal in 1935: "Seattle Jewry will again be called upon to demonstrate its loyalty to the distressed and stricken Jewish communities in Germany and other European lands, and to manifest its interest in the rebuilding of the Jewish National Home in Palestine by generously contributing to the United Jewish Appeal."[70] Board minutes and the congregation's newsletter,

the *Synagogue Tribune*, are filled with support for Zionist causes, as when the *Tribune* called the Orthodox Zionist Mizrachi "the mouthpiece of the Jewish masses who wish to see our homeland rebuilt in the spirit of Torah and our religious and national traditions." In July 1942, the congregation officially joined Mizrachi.[71] During the war, the congregation's board wrote letters to Congress, urging a vote in support of the creation of a Jewish commonwealth in Palestine and actively supported the Seattle Emergency Committee for the Abrogation of the Palestine White Paper, a group chaired by Bikur Cholim's Rabbi Wohlgelernter.[72]

In Portland, the unified Hebrew school serving the South Portland neighborhood was an explicitly Zionist institution. This is readily evident in the school's curriculum, which emphasized Hebrew language as well as "the whole spectrum of subjects that emanate from the study of a language: culture, history, and <u>nation</u>."[73] The North Dakota colony veteran Israel Bromberg served as the first chairman of the board and was a major figure shaping its development as a modern, culturally oriented school.[74]

While such Zionist enthusiasm might be expected at schools and congregations serving Orthodox, Eastern European congregations, the Portland Hebrew School's Zionism is notable because its administration came not only from the Eastern European community but from all sectors of Jewish Portland. The Jewish Education Association, which provided financial support for the school and included "Reform and prosperous" elites, passed a resolution in 1924 declaring the following:

WHEREAS historical events made necessarily [*sic*] the emphasis on new values in Jewish life; and
WHEREAS one of these new values is to train the

rising generation to speak Hebrew and to be prepared to live in Palestine or to share in its living culture; BE IT RESOLVED: That the Portland Hebrew School . . . pledges itself to help Hebraize our cultural life in the Diaspora.[75]

The unusual level of support for Zionism among Portland's Reform community can be traced to the early influence of Stephen Wise, who served Temple Beth Israel as rabbi from 1900 to 1906. Although his tenure was short, his influence was lasting, and his presence in Portland did much to engender sympathy for Zionism among his congregants.[76] His name, along with those of several of his most prominent congregants—individuals like Julius Meier, Judge Otto Kraemer, Ben Neustadter, and Blanche Blumauer—appeared in an announcement of the founding of "Portland's first Zionist group" in the *American Israelite* in 1901.[77] Decades later, when the anti-Zionist ACJ was organized, it found a few supporters among Beth Israel's membership but failed to win the endorsement of any Portland rabbis or to generate a strong following in that city. Rather, community-wide organizations like the Jewish Welfare Fund strongly supported Zionist causes. In 1936, four of the eleven organizations supported by the fund were explicitly Zionist.[78]

Zionist activity among temple members was not unique to Portland. As early as 1930, Zionist meetings had been held at Seattle's Temple De Hirsch—despite the clear anti-Zionist position of Rabbi Koch.[79] Five years later, the temple men's club held a celebration of Hebrew University's tenth anniversary. The event, noted Bikur Cholim's newsletter, "marks a turning point in the attitude of certain sections of our community toward the problem of Eretz Yisroel which ought to be welcomed by everyone who hopes for the ultimate unity in Israel with regard to the upbringing of the Homeland."[80]

Although anti-Zionists in Seattle launched an alternative to the Zionist *Transcript* in 1932, the effort folded quickly in the interests of community unity.[81] After Rabbi Koch stepped down in 1942, his successor, Rabbi Raphael Levine, despite his personal rejection of Judaism as a *national* (rather than a religious) identity, served during the war with Congregation Bikur Cholim's Rabbi Wohlgelernter as cochair of the Seattle Emergency Committee for the Abrogation of the Palestine White Paper.[82]

Zionist activity was more extensive in Los Angeles and was evident even among Temple B'nai B'rith (Wilshire Boulevard) members. The Los Angeles *B'nai B'rith Messenger* reported in 1928 on a Zionist lecture at Temple B'nai B'rith and in 1930 on the first meeting of Zionists at Temple Sinai. In the same year, Temple B'nai B'rith announced that "all Zionist groups" were invited to participate in its Balfour Night and held a regional session in conjunction with local Zionist organizations. Rabbi Magnin was one of several Los Angeles–area B'nai B'rith leaders who supported coordination of the B'nai B'rith district meeting with the first western regional Zionist meeting in 1930.[83] The conciliatory attitude of Rabbis Levine and Magnin toward Zionism suggests that in western communities the desire for unity generally superseded ideological divisions. Despite Levine's personal opposition to Zionism, he studiously avoided taking a stand, and, when the issue threatened to split the temple at the end of the war, he delivered a sermon titled "A Plague on Both Your Houses."[84] Even Rabbi Reichert, while maintaining his opposition to Zionism, was willing to advocate opening Palestine to refugees. At the urging of Rabbi Abba Hillel Silver, Reichert and Emanu-El president Lloyd Dinkelspiel sent a telegram to President Franklin Roosevelt, asking him to urge the British to keep Palestine open to Jewish refugees. "I will assist in every way consistent with my opposition to political Zionism," Reichert wrote to Silver.[85]

Even in San Francisco, there is evidence of Zionist activity, albeit on a modest scale. In addition to the Hadassah chapter led by Rose Rinder, Hashomer Hatzair, a Zionist youth group, had an active chapter supported by Congregation Beth Sholom's rabbi, Saul White. The group "held dances and songfests, studied Hebrew, set up summer camp in the Santa Cruz Mountains—and never ceased to talk world politics."[86] Rabbi Elliot Burstein of Beth Israel, an Eastern European immigrant congregation, served as president of the small San Francisco Zionist Organization of America chapter in the early 1940s.[87]

Social, religious, and political differences, then, were present in these communities, but, as the consolidation of community organizations and philanthropy suggests, community members tended to emphasize the commonalities over the differences. Unity in most western Jewish communities was fostered by the stabilization in population. In Los Angeles, however, where a healthful climate, economic expansion, and a rapidly budding Yiddish culture led to an explosion of growth beginning in the 1920s, community harmony was more elusive.

LOS ANGELES: CREATING ITS OWN PATTERN

The staggering growth in Los Angeles was the critical factor distinguishing it from other western Jewish communities, as a flood of new migrants continued to arrive, even during the Depression. The Jewish population increased from 30,000 in 1920 to 70,000 in 1930 and 130,000 by 1941.[88]

Among the newcomers were many Yiddish-speaking immigrants seeking to live in identifiably Jewish neighborhoods, contributing to a residential concentration that reached its zenith in these years and made the Jews the plurality in that area. The Boyle Heights neighborhood, with about 2,000 Jewish households in 1920, had approximately 10,000 by 1930 and 14,000—possibly as many as 50,000 Jews—by the end of that decade.[89] While the Jewish migration to Los Angeles was part of a larger population influx, the Jewish rate of growth far exceeded that of the city as a whole.[90]

The size of the Jewish community led to the development of several Jewish sections, delineated partially by income and partially by social orientation. City Terrace, adjacent to Boyle Heights but just beyond the city limits and with lower property taxes, saw its population of Jewish home owners double in just a few years during the Depression. It developed a distinctive identity as a haven for Yiddish secularists. The Jewish population in Hollywood and the Wilshire-Pico District, home to a more secular middle class, also increased in this period.[91] So, just as the other western Jewish communities were becoming more cohesive, the distance between the large numbers of newcomers in Los Angeles and the established community was growing. A proliferation of Yiddish cultural institutions, a diverse array of political clubs, and mushrooming small shuls were evidence that forces in Los Angeles were centrifugal.

Los Angeles's most distinctively Jewish neighborhood was a product of the westward migration of immigrants who had sojourned for years or even decades in the East or Midwest. While descriptions of the Boyle Heights neighborhood suggest a cultural life similar to that in eastern and midwestern Jewish immigrant neighborhoods at the turn

FIG. 5.3 *Interior view of Talmud Torah Synagogue in Boyle Heights, known as the Breed Street Shul, at 247 North Breed Street, 1976. Security Pacific Collection, Los Angeles Public Library.*

of the century, very few of the residents seeking a secure ethnic neighborhood were truly greenhorns. Many were Orthodox, as evidenced by the growth of the Breed Street shul and Talmud Torah (fig. 5.3), the support for Mizrachi, and the columns of Dr. George Sayles, an Orthodox, Zionist activist, in the *B'nai B'rith Messenger*. But as the historians Vorspan and Gartner emphasize, the Jewish orientation of the community was as much cultural as religious, with considerable activity in Yiddish language clubs and a vital community of Yiddish writers.[92]

Oral histories capture the neighborhood's richness and diversity, often in conflicting accounts—

one informant recalls that there were eight major synagogues, almost all of them "orthodox," [93] while another claims that

> eighty, eighty five percent of the population were secular Jews. I hear there were so many synagogues here, so many synagogues there. I remember three. That's all. Three is all I remember. You never saw anybody with yarmulkes. You just didn't see it, except maybe the very, very old people. So it was a secular community. And of this eighty or eighty five percent who were secular Jews, I would say ten or twenty percent of them were apolitical. Liberal, but apolitical. The balance of them, let's say sixty, seventy percent of the Jewish population were pretty evenly divided between communists and socialists. So there were discussions going on all the time.[94]

Similarly, while some former residents remember the neighborhood as intensely Jewish in character, describing it as like a shtetl, others emphasize the diversity of the area, recalling, "at school we were all very social. I had Mexican friends, Armenian, Japanese . . . Roosevelt [High School] was truly a Melting Pot."[95] Both perceptions were accurate: the Jewish presence dominated, as the community was at least double the size of the Mexican American community, yet there were substantial concentrations of Mexicans and Japanese, as well as smaller enclaves of Italians, African Americans, Armenians, and Russian Molokans.[96] Although adults tended to socialize with and patronize the stores of those sharing their ethnic background, children mixed in classes, sports, and clubs, particularly in the junior high and high schools.

The atmosphere of Jewish Boyle Heights is captured in Gershon Einbinder's Yiddish novel *Zalmen the Cobbler*. Zalmen is able to partake in a variety of Yiddish cultural activities, ranging from lectures to hiking clubs. Explaining the attractions of Los Angeles, Einbinder's Zalmen says,

> My *landsman* Noah, the former baker, found joy in California not only because, in his later years, he became a father and not only because an orange tree was growing in his yard, but also because he could attend lectures in the evening. In Los Angeles he had become an enthusiastic attendant at lectures. There was no lecture in the city that he missed. This was his way of making up for the time in New York when, because he worked nights, he could not go to lectures much as he wanted to. I myself also thirsted for a lecture in Yiddish.[97]

Zalmen was attracted to Yiddish lectures despite the fact that he had resided in the United States since the mid-1890s, lived in the American hinterland, and was perfectly capable of speaking English. For the fictional Zalmen, as for many who reveled in Los Angeles's Jewish culture, Yiddish was a cultural choice rather than a linguistic necessity forced by an ignorance of English. This choice suggests how the community of newcomers resisted the consolidation with the established community that characterized other western communities in this period.

A working-class, pro-unionist identity was an important part of Yiddish cultural life in Boyle Heights. Oral histories suggest that, for many, politics were fundamental to Jewish identity and culture. Fred Okrand, who received his Jewish education at the Workmen's Circle, described his family as both secular and "very Jewish." He explained, "The Workmen's Circle, which is a Jewish organization, was socialist. . . . That was their main [Jewish] contact." When asked what aspects of Jewishness were celebrated at the Workmen's Circle, he responded, "Well, first they would study socialism. They would read Marx and learn about his views."[98] The casting of studying of Marx as a Jewish activity reflects the reality of leftist politics in Los Angeles, where, for example, the Communist Party was overwhelmingly Jewish.[99]

While strongly supportive of working-class causes, a substantial proportion of the Jewish population ran small businesses. Boyle Heights, although having a greater proportion of Jewish blue-collar workers than was typical in the Far West, did not contain large contingents of Jewish workers. Because the garment industry provided an accessible path to ownership for many Jews in Los Angeles, as firms became established, the owners moved their residences out of Boyle Heights and into more upscale—and less ethnically concentrated—neighborhoods to the west.[100] Rabbi Jacob Alkow, former principal of the Modern Talmud Torah in Boyle Heights, noted when he returned from a brief sojourn in Palestine in 1929 that many Jewish families had already moved to the west side.[101] And when Jewish labor activist Rose Pesotta came to Los Angeles to organize the garment industry in 1933, she found that most of the workers were Mexicans.[102]

The affluence of the 1920s allowed clothing designed and manufactured in Los Angeles to gain unique exposure through the region's glamorous new industry, the motion pictures. The movie industry has been analyzed as a revolutionary cultural tool that transformed popular consciousness. Its immigrant entrepreneurs were quite aware of its ability to shape tastes, but they saw it primarily as an entertainment business. Between 1915 and 1926 they built five major corporations and several smaller ones into a "studio system" that integrated the exhibition, distribution, and production of films.[103] By 1920 the movie industry was already the nation's fifth largest. Jewish moguls such as Carl Laemmle, Louis B. Mayer, and William Fox and their gentile colleagues such as Cecile B. DeMille and Daryl Zanuck catered to but also cultivated their audience. The moguls had often begun as storefront film exhibitors and felt they knew what their immigrant, working-class audiences wished to see.[104] But in the 1920s, as America grew more affluent, the moguls hired writers, women and men in almost equal numbers, who were American-born, usually college graduates, and who understood the tastes of a younger generation. They placed a cosmopolitan view of culture at the center of American popular consciousness. Through public relations they even conveyed a glamorous image of Los Angeles, especially Hollywood and Beverly Hills, where Jews mingled with gentiles in a liberated, affluent, casually attired, and perpetually warm and sunny locale.[105] As Lary May claims, "Jewish producers' status as marginal businessmen and cultural brokers made it possible for them to cater to the moral revolution associated with the rise of mass art."[106] Put somewhat differently, Henry Ford, as early as 1920, saw the movie industry as yet another way in which "the Jews" used their insidious genius to subvert a pristine American democracy.

But quite apart from the cultural wars to which the motion pictures gave rise, the existence of this new industry whose key producers were Jews created extraordinary support and visibility for the local Jewish community and helped shift the focus of regional Jewry to Los Angeles. Studios like MGM, Laemmle's Universal, Warner Brothers, and Twentieth Century Fox acquired large tracts of real estate to produce movies and became major, long-term players in the local real estate business. Their immediate impact on local employment was even greater. In 1926, an estimated seventy-five thousand people worked in some aspect of film

FIG. 5.4 *Grauman's Chinese Theater on the premier night of* Morocco, *starring Marlene Dietrich, ca. 1930. Security Pacific Collection, Los Angeles Public Library.*

production, distribution, and exhibition in the Los Angeles area.[107] The most ostentatious theater, Sid Grauman's "Chinese," was a major part of promoting feature films (fig. 5.4). While the number of Jews working in Hollywood is not known, in addition to the many studio heads, directors,

production managers, and writers who were Jewish, columns in the *B'nai B'rith Messenger* for the 1920s sketched the biographies of casting directors, cameramen, film editors, and others with technical expertise. While there may not have been a Jewish proletariat in the Los Angeles garment industry, there were thousands of middle-income Jewish employees in the movie industry.

The arrival of the moguls and their families added a new layer of affluence, visibility, and cosmopolitanism to the region's Jewish life. Jewish community newspapers chronicled their achievements, and the awards presented to Mayer, his appearances at community fund-raising events, and the amassing of theater chains by Fox were all the subject of feature stories in newspapers as far away as Portland. Though the German Jewish elite at the Hillcrest Country Club may have blackballed the moguls in the 1920s, they were carefully courted for philanthropic causes.[108] Mayer and Jack Warner were the largest fund-raisers for the new Cedars of Lebanon Hospital in 1928, and when the City of Hope sanitarium at Duarte needed funds, the Warner brothers hosted a "mid-night gala" highlighted by Fanny Brice and Al Jolson.[109] The new Wilshire Boulevard Temple building (fig. 5.5), dedicated in June 1929, featured murals of Bible scenes and Jewish history, commissioned by Jack, Harry, and Abe Warner in memory of their deceased brothers, Milton and Samuel.[110]

Relatives of the moguls and the studios' salaried workers supported a variety of Judaisms in the neighborhoods of West Los Angeles. Mayer's father-in-law, Hyman Shenberg, came from Boston to become rabbi of Congregation Knesseth Israel, while B. P. Schulberg's father-in-law and the parents of other studio heads rented a Hollywood bungalow, which studio carpenters transformed into an Orthodox shul. The officers and board of directors of Temple Israel of Hollywood in 1928 consisted of executives of Fox and Universal Studios.[111] Rabbis cultivated movie people to raise funds to create the largest and most diversified set of religious institutions west of Chicago, and city directories indicate that during the 1920s more new synagogues and community centers were built in Los Angeles than in the rest of the Pacific region combined.

In the 1930s, as the Depression slowed economic growth and depleted community budgets throughout the country, the movie industry faced deficits. But the studios became profitable again by mid-decade by shifting the themes of feature films toward the depiction of hardships facing Americans and the crime that created a Los Angeles underworld and by producing lavish musicals and costume adventures that distracted audiences from their problems.[112] In addition, as the Nazi government in Germany blamed the economic collapse on a Jewish conspiracy and persecuted Jews, Warner Brothers became a focal point for combating anti-Semitism. Not only did Warner Brothers, unlike the other studios, cease its business in Germany by 1934, but its movies like *The Confessions of a Nazi Spy* and *The Black Legion* constituted a vanguard of Jewish self-defense in the mass media.[113] While Jack and Harry Warner did not see themselves as spokesmen for American Jewry, their films are one indication of the way in which Los Angeles Jewry came to house a unique vehicle of national Jewish self-expression, self-defense, and fund-raising. They also foreshadowed how influential West Coast communities would become within American Jewry.[114]

WESTERN JEWS AND THE CHALLENGES OF THE INTERWAR YEARS

While Jews in the Pacific West focused on many of the same challenges as their counterparts elsewhere, the regional stature and historic acceptance of Jewish communities created a different context for their responses. Western Jews usually received news stories by wire services, so readers

in San Francisco encountered in their hometown Jewish paper many of the same stories that they would have read had they lived in New York. Regional papers and organizational records focused intensely on anti-Semitism, reporting in detail on the rise of Nazism abroad and national and local manifestations in America. Even as they worried about these trends, however, western Jews' responses were shaped by their continued view of their home region as exceptionally hospitable. While faced with many of the same forms of social and employment discrimination as their counterparts elsewhere in the country, their belief in their acceptance—and the many examples of Jewish business and political prominence—worked as a counterweight.

Nationally, domestic and international anti-Semitism emerged as the foremost challenge facing American Jewish communities during the interwar years.[115] Anti-Semitism manifested itself in the post–World War I years in anti-immigrant and antilabor rhetoric, circulation of anti-Semitic tracts (most notably by Henry Ford), the emergence of quotas restricting Jewish enrollment in elite private universities, and exclusions from elite neighborhoods, social clubs, and professional opportunities. Unease increased in the 1930s as anti-Semitic figures like Father Coughlin (whose radio broadcasts reached as many as thirty million listeners) became national personalities, and slurs and insinuations about Jewish influence in the Roosevelt administration became common. Abroad, the anti-Jewish measures in Germany after the rise of

Hitler topped the agenda of many Jewish organizations and spawned the creation of new groups to deal with these challenges. Columns predicting a dire future for German Jews, and later for other European Jews, became commonplace. The various forms of anti-Semitism shook the American Jewish community and revealed deep divisions about how best to respond.

Nationally, this challenge came just as the American Jewish community experienced a distinctive shift in leadership, as a result of the mass migration from Eastern Europe. Many historians of American Jewry mark the ascendancy of second-generation Eastern Europeans and their challenge to established leadership as the critical development shaping American Jewry in this period.[116] The different outlooks and approaches of these two major groups and the organizations they created led to sharp disagreements about how to confront domestic and international challenges. The established leadership group, the product of classical Reform Judaism, saw itself as fundamentally American and distinctive only in religion. They were reluctant to engage in public or political campaigns for "Jewish" causes, denying "that there was, or should be, a separate Jewish interest expressed through the ballot."[117] Their efforts to work against domestic and international anti-Semitism through organizations like the American Jewish Committee usually included behind-the-scenes meetings with officials. In contrast, many who were second-generation Eastern European immigrants, as well as some of the more outspoken Reform leaders like Stephen Wise, saw ethnic, cultural, and national expressions like Zionism as fundamental to their Jewish identity and to the ethnic pluralism of American life.[118] They challenged established patterns and participated in ethnic politics through the Democratic Party and new organizations like the Ameri-

FIG. 5.5 *Wilshire Boulevard Temple (Congregation B'nai B'rith) as viewed from Wilshire Boulevard. The temple is listed on the U.S. Register of Historical places. Security Pacific Collection, Los Angeles Public Library.*

can Jewish Congress, which did not hesitate to call public attention to "Jewish" issues through boycotts, and rallies.[119] An attempt to form a unified national body for European rescue and relief dissolved after one year.[120]

The dynamics of response differed in the West, in part because the primary evidence of anti-Semitism in the region before the 1930s was social discrimination against a burgeoning and affluent Jewish community in Los Angeles. Western Jews had long trumpeted their high level of acceptance and had remained relatively unscathed even by the Ruef affair in San Francisco and by the ascendancy of the Klan in Oregon politics in the early 1920s. In the 1930s, however, despite the historic acceptance of Jews as founders, pioneers, and citizens, local anti-Semitism was increasingly noted in the Jewish press up and down the Pacific coast. Most local incidents were expressions of social or professional exclusion. For example, most Jewish students in the region attended public universities, which did not have quotas, but exclusion from fraternities led to the extension of a national pattern of separate Jewish fraternities at campuses from Seattle through Eugene, Berkeley, and Los Angeles.[121] Complaints in the files of the Jewish Welfare Federation in San Francisco include allegations of firms refusing to hire Jews or firing them for taking off Jewish holidays; accounts of insurance company discrimination against Jews; and reports of protests alleging that Jews were overrepresented on some city boards or commissions. Such concerns were vented publicly in *Emanu-El*, as in a March 1936 editorial discussing anti-Semitism in the job market.[122] In 1938, San Francisco's Anti-Defamation League (ADL) organized a meeting to discuss local and international anti-Semitism and to strategize about responses. Options considered included boycotts of discriminating firms, lawsuits, and plans to divert

Jews from "overcrowded" professions.[123] While such meetings suggest that San Francisco Jews shared many of the concerns of their brethren back East, what is remarkable about that city's Jewish Welfare Federation's "anti-Semitism" file is that it contains only one folder for the entire period and that the first entry is dated 1933. Although there were residential restrictions that excluded Jews in some Santa Barbara and Los Angeles neighborhoods and in well-to-do areas like Pasadena and San Marino, Jews lived in other nearby cities like Santa Monica and Alhambra, and there is no evidence of such restrictions in San Francisco.

In the 1930s, concerns about international and political anti-Semitism begin appearing regularly in the files of the Oakland Jewish Community Center, particularly in response to the formation of local Silver Shirt and German-American Bund organizations. In the fall of 1941, an antiwar rally in Oakland featured rhetoric blaming the push for war on the Jews. Temple Sinai's Reform rabbi, William Stern, became alarmed about anti-Semitism, both locally and internationally. As Rosenbaum notes, "When put in sequence, his Rosh Hashanah sermons of the late 'thirties and early 'forties—surveys of the state of world Jewry at year's end—read almost like a Greek tragedy."[124] An Oakland Jewish Community Center scrapbook from the 1930s demonstrates considerable concern about anti-Semitism, such as lectures with titles like "How Can Jews Help Christians Fight Anti-Semitism" and "Jews and Other Minorities in the American Melting Pot," both offered in 1935. More common, however, were lectures focusing on Jews worldwide, with titles like "The Arab-Jewish Situation in Palestine Today" (1937), "Jews under Fascism" (1937), "Jews in the Soviet Union" (1938), "The Jews in Poland and Russia" (1939), and "The World War on Jewry" (1939).[125] And unlike in

Newark, New York, and elsewhere, Jewish under-world figures did not feel compelled to lead attacks on mass rallies of the German-American Bund.

In Portland and Seattle, too, concerns about both local and international anti-Semitism began to increase in the 1930s. Exclusion from social clubs, including high school and college fraternities, and from major corporations and law firms captured the attention of local branches of the Council of Jewish Women and the ADL during the interwar years.[126] Harry Ash, an ADL leader in Seattle, noted, "Discrimination in employment that was very evident. There were other forms of discrimination that existed in the 1930's, in clubs, such as the Rainier Club, the Washington Athletic Club, the College Club, the Women's University Club, and various other organizations. We had incidents with the Elks Clubs, especially in the outlying areas, from Tacoma, Puyallup, Bellingham. There were Jews accepted by the Elks here in Seattle. There was discrimination in housing, such as the Broadmoor area, the Windemere area."[127] A survey of dozens of racial covenants in Seattle housing deeds shows that, while the overwhelming majority targeted Asians and African Americans, three neighborhoods specifically excluded "Hebrews" in the late 1920s and early 1930s.[128] Rabbi Raphael Levine considered anti-Semitism in the form of social exclusions to be the "number one" problem when he moved to Seattle in 1942.[129]

Despite the increased attention to anti-Semitism, westerners continued to view their region as socially tolerant. While the Jewish press expanded coverage of anti-Semitism, it continued to remind its readers of their region's unique hospitality. This was the explicit message of *Emanu-El*'s 1936 editorial, "Our Splendid Isolation," which contrasted the welcome that Jews found in the West with increasing levels of anti-Semitism in the East.[130]

Seattleites could point with pride to the emphasis on cultural pluralism in the schools attended by Jewish children in the Central District. The school district's Progressive curriculum, introduced in the mid-1930s, embraced tolerance and intercultural education as key principles and encouraged schools to hold assemblies that conveyed "the artistic achievements of ethnic groups; [and] provided a forum for visiting ethnic group leaders," communicating the value of immigrant cultures to their students.[131] Accommodations were made for the religious ritual that did not fit the school calendar, as when the Congregation Bikur Cholim newsletter in 1935 informed students attending Garfield High School that they would be excused from exams given on Shavuot.[132] Oral histories consistently characterize the Central District as diverse ("a melting pot") with little discrimination ("we all got along wonderfully").[133] This testimony, contemporary community documents, and community histories consistently emphasize inclusion over exclusion.

Again, Los Angeles stands out as the exception, with concern about anti-Semitism coming earlier and rising to higher levels than elsewhere in the West. Beginning just before the turn of the century and continuing until the Great Depression, a huge influx of native-born, midwestern Protestants, "drawn to the promise of an exotic landscape and determined to transform it into a white refuge," overwhelmed "native Latino, Chinese, and Jewish Angelinos."[134] The newcomer's desire for a "homogeneous utopia" was at odds with the city's traditional inclusiveness and led, over the course of the first three decades of the twentieth century, to increasing discrimination and exclusionary practices. Early in the century, Jewish Angelenos still prided themselves on their city's tolerance. As the *B'nai B'rith Messenger* claimed in 1905, "Never has Los Angeles contained stubborn hotel proprietors who would distinguish the Jews and Gentiles, as in some cities. Los Angeles is too up-to-date for such miserable folly."[135] Over the next several decades, however, elite Jews found themselves facing exclusion from "the corporate directorships, law firms, philanthropies and clubs that in many cases they had helped to establish."[136]

By the 1930s, while elite Jewish families remained influential in the city, social and professional exclusionary practices had become common.[137] The chamber of commerce, a body that counted Jews among its founders, began an "unspoken but recognized policy" of excluding Jews, as did prominent social and business clubs that had earlier accepted them.[138] Elite Jews, who had earlier associated with non-Jews through business partnerships, civic organizations, and social clubs, increasingly began to rely on exclusively Jewish networks.[139] During that decade, Los Angeles Jews, in contrast to their counterparts to the north and in the state as a whole, "remained partly outside municipal politics. Groups or individuals not belonging to white Protestantdom were little recognized in the city's political life."[140] While Jews held a number of appointed offices, including several judicial positions, running for office in Los Angeles was considered "unrealistic" until the 1950s.[141] The fall of Jews from positions of influence within the Los Angeles power structure was part of a larger shift toward what the journalist Mike Davis calls "WASP [white Anglo-Saxon Protestant] dominance." As he explains, in Los Angeles the typical pattern of "WASP dominance followed by Catholic and Jewish bids at power" was reversed: "Here the early preeminence of non-Protestant elites was superseded by a long era of WASP exclusionism as once cosmopolitan Los Angeles became, culturally and demographically, the most nativist

and fundamentalist of big cities. The social and political purge of elite Jews in particular precipitated a bifurcated ruling class, perhaps unique in the United States."[142]

Even more ominous, in the mid-1930s southern California became a stronghold for the anti-Semitic Silver Shirt movement. The Silver Shirt Pacific Coast Division was based in San Diego and claimed the strongest concentration of members in the country—although estimates of San Diego–area members range wildly—from seventeen to two thousand.[143] Whatever their numbers, they were taken seriously by federal authorities, and in 1935 a special committee of the House Un-American Activities Committee held hearings in Los Angeles to look into their activities.[144] The Los Angeles Jewish Community Committee was formed in 1934 to monitor these groups. Using undercover agents to infiltrate them and report on their activities, the committee eagerly shared its reports with government agents and the special committee, warning that their combination of pro-fascist and anti-Semitic beliefs was dangerously un-American.[145] Similarly, Jews in San Diego, concerned by the activities of the Silver Shirts, who had important contacts with local business and government leaders, formed an organization to monitor their activities and succeeded in infiltrating the group.[146] Even after Pearl Harbor, southern California attracted attention as a center for pro-fascist activities. "Home Fascists! Los Angeles Proves Breeding Center for Subversive Groups" proclaimed a front-page *Emanu-El* headline in the spring of 1942.[147]

Despite the evidence of such activities, historians differ on the extent and significance of anti-Semitism in Los Angeles and southern California. While some, like Davis, focus on the increasing exclusion of Jews at elite levels, Vorspan and Gartner argue that the increasing Jewish residential concentration

PLATE I
Stained-glass window, Congregation Sherith Israel, California Street, San Francisco, ca. 1905.
Courtesy of Congregation Sherith Israel, San Francisco. Photograph: Ben Ailes.

PLATE 2
Yosemite Valley, California. British, Day and Son (active ca. 1850).
Lithograph attributed to Robins and Snow (active ca. 1864).
Bancroft Library, University of California, Berkeley, BANC PIC 1963.002:1416.

PLATE 3
Brandeis-Bardin Institute, Simi Valley, California, 1990s.
Photograph: Hannah R. Kuhn.

PLATE 4
Francis Samuel Marryat (British, 1826–55). Crossing the Isthmus, 1855.
Lithographer: M. and N. Hanhart (active ca. 1851–57).
Bancroft Library, University of California, Berkeley, BANC PIC 1963.002:1440:8.

PLATE 5
Interior view of Sutro baths showing large pool, smaller pools, and platforms.
Chromolithograph mounted on canvas.
Bancroft Library, University of California, Berkeley, 1974.014-FR.

HE ABOVE ILLUSTRATION WAS MADE FROM A PHOTOGRAPH OF SAN FRANCISCO TAKEN SHORTLY AFTER THE EARTHQUAKE AND IN THE EARLY STAGES OF THE FIRE WHICH FOLLOWED INCIDNTAL THERETO THAT LAID IN ASHES NEARLY FTHS OF THE BEAUTIFUL CITY. THE SCENE ESPECIALLY SHOWS THE VERY CENTER OF THE CLOSELY BUILT BUSINESS SECTION, WHERE MAY BE OBSERVED THE TOWERING TEMPLE OF THE PRESS; THE EIGHTEEN STORY CALL BUILDING FTEEN STORY CHRONICLE BUILDING AND THE NEW SHREVE OFFICE STRUCTURE, JUST OCCUPIED APRIL FIRST; THE MAGNIFICENT ST. FRANCIS HOTEL, RECENTLY CONSTRUCTED AT A COST OF ABOUT TWO AND ONE-HALF MILLION DO ND MANY OTHER MORE OR LESS PROMINENT EDIFICES. THIS PORTION WAS REACHED BY FLAMES WEDNESDAY NIGHT AND WAS TOTALLY DSTROYED BEFORE THE CLOSE OF THE FOLLOWING DAY.

PLATE 6
San Francisco in the early stages of the April 1906 fire. From a photograph by Rieder Cardinell Co.
Bancroft Library, University of California, Berkeley; 1906 San Francisco Earthquake
and Fire Digital Collection, Crocker Pano, F869.S3.93.R35.

PLATE 7
This bold 2007 logo of the Federation of Jewish Men's Clubs, Western region,
highlights the new Jewish prominence on the Pacific Slope.
Federation of Jewish Men's Clubs, Western Region.

PLATE 8
*Visitors enjoy the Liberty Gallery in the Skirball Cultural Center's
permanent exhibition "Visions and Values: Jewish Life from Antiquity to America."
Skirball Cultural Center, Los Angeles, 2006. Photograph: John Elder.*

that occurred as the population grew was linked to international events and "a sense of external menace" rather than to overt, local anti-Semitism: "At no time during the harsh years of depression, reform, and slow recovery were Jews attacked in any reputable quarter. No significant public figure or major party spoke against Jews."[148]

Coverage by the local Jewish press supports the view that, despite the limited appearance of Jewish Angelenos in civic and political leadership in this period, for many, anti-Semitism was not a critical *local* issue, even in the 1930s. The *Messenger*, for example, featured stories on European anti-Semitism throughout the decade, but mentions of local incidents were few and not always blatant. In May 1930, the *Messenger* published an editorial objecting to a form sent to lawyers by the Los Angeles Bar Association asking them to designate whether they were Protestant or Catholic. While suggesting the possible anti-Semitic motives behind such a query, the column asked readers whether it should be considered an example of prejudice at all.[149] Throughout the period, local press coverage in Los Angeles, like that elsewhere in the West, contained evidence of anti-Semitism as far more of an international and national concern than as a local one. A September 1937 issue of the *Messenger*, for example, featured three front-page stories on anti-Semitism abroad (focusing on Italy, Romania, and Japan) and two on domestic anti-Semitism—neither with a local angle.[150] The Jewish Labor Committee, which formed in Los Angeles in 1934, focused on anti-Semitism—but exclusively in Germany (fig. 5.6).[151]

Up and down the Pacific coast, Jewish communities' responses to emerging anti-Semitism were shaped by their history of acceptance and prominence in politics and civic affairs. Western Jewish leaders—like their counterparts in New York who

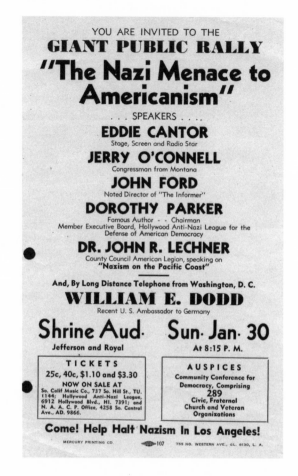

FIG. 5.6 *"Nazi Menace to Americanism," 1937. As concerns about anti-Semitism mounted in southern California, groups like the Hollywood Anti-Nazi League organized rallies. Urban Archives Center, Delmar T. Oviatt Library, California State University, Northridge, CRCms137.*

endorsed the quiet diplomacy of the American Jewish Committee—had long used their political connections and influence to intervene in response to local anti-Semitic incidents. Elite western Jews continued to use this "behind-the-scenes" approach well into the twentieth century. In the 1920s, rabbis like Edgar Magnin used their connections with Hollywood producers to try to thwart pejorative images of Jews in film. Rabbi Magnin's attempt to steer Cecil B. DeMille away from anti-Semitic themes in his 1927 film *The King of Kings*, while unsuccessful, was a classic use of this approach. Magnin first tried to convince DeMille to forgo making the film. Failing that, he tried to reduce the negative images of Jews. Although Magnin claimed that he had persuaded DeMille to remove a line from the Gospel of Matthew that "condemned future generations of Jews for the crime of deicide," he had little time to devote to the project and soon passed it on to three "lesser-known rabbis and Jewish educators," among them Rabbi Jacob Alkow. Despite their efforts to work with DeMille, the final version of the film was replete with anti-Semitic images. While Rabbi Alkow felt the Jewish actors playing major roles did their best to depict Jews in a favorable light, most of his suggestions ended on the cutting-room floor.[152] The release of *The King of Kings* led to widespread outcry against the film—and against the ADL and Magnin for being unable to prevent it. The most persistent critic was Rabbi Louis Newman of San Francisco's Temple Emanu-El. Arriving from New York in 1924, Newman brought the confrontational style of his mentor, Stephen Wise, and on this issue rallied a contingent of Bay Area colleagues including Jacob Nieto and Rudolph Coffee.[153] Writing in his regular column in Portland's *Scribe*, Newman called for a boycott, lambasted Jews who worked for DeMille or who distributed or exhibited the film, and condemned the apparent indifference of Magnin and the Pacific Coast branch of the ADL, then headed by the San Francisco lawyer and his own congregant Isadore M. Golden.[154] Reporting to his readers that at least one San Francisco theater owner had decided not to show the film, Newman praised him, using language suggesting the need for ethnically based public action: "We need this type of fine Jewish consciousness among our Jewish theater owners."[155] To deflect Newman's dramatic accusations, Golden published a lengthy and point-by-point denial that the ADL knew about the film prior to its release and then noted how the B'nai B'rith national president, Alfred Cohen, had gone through appropriate channels by working with the president of the Motion Pictures Producers of America to accept a system of consultation and prescreening of films that might defame Jews.[156]

The quiet diplomacy advocated by national groups like the ADL and the American Jewish Committee to mitigate anti-Semitism in *The King of Kings* remained popular among Jewish leaders in Los Angeles. By the 1930s, the Los Angeles Jewish Community Committee was working actively—and secretly—to avoid anti-Semitism in films. Interestingly, it also tried to discourage overtly philo-Semitic or anti-Nazi themes, which it feared might reinforce the notion that "the Jews controlled Hollywood" and were using films as a vehicle for Jewish propaganda. These efforts supplemented the group's primary focus on monitoring pro-Nazi groups in the region.[157]

The Los Angeles Jewish Community Committee strategy of working behind the scenes provides evidence of the embrace by some western Jewish leaders of what has been termed an "accommodationist" response to anti-Semitism, associated with the elite German Jews of the American Jewish Committee. The strategy of quiet persuasion rested on access to the civic networks that pioneer Jewish families enjoyed and was reinforced by the view that reason, tolerance, and Jewish interests always coincided. Marc Dollinger has characterized this approach as one that emphasized consensus, "rejected activist political strategies that distinguished Jews from other citizens, and funded programs intent on homogenizing their more traditional co-religionists."[158] As Portland's *Scribe* declared in its first edition in 1919, "We are convinced that the Jewish population forms an integral and *politically indistinguishable* part of our American commonwealth" (emphasis added).[159]

In more perilous times, Oakland's Rabbi William Stern gave this emphasis on the Jew as disinterested citizen a conservative gloss when he encouraged patriotism and denounced radicalism within the Jewish community. Believing that Jewish participation in radical politics would inflame anti-Semitism, Oakland's Jewish leadership monitored radical groups like the leftist League to Prevent Violence and the Organization for Jewish Colonization in Russia, or ICOR, a group dedicated to support for Birobidzhan, the Soviet-created Jewish autonomous area in the Russian Far East. In 1934, the Oakland Jewish Community Center instituted a rule barring "any communistic or fascistic or anti-democratic or anti-American organization" from using the facility. In addition, the Oakland Commission on Americanism tried to ensure that the community avoided the impression that there was a Jewish vote.[160] The commission, which "[held] itself responsible for the public relations program of our Jewish community," indicated in a 1940 letter its concern about "the frequent appearance in local newspapers of items concerning Jews and Jewish organizations." Interestingly, the concern was not that these items were in any way anti-Semitic but simply that "almost daily, harrowing accounts of the suffering of our people" were drawing too much attention to Jews as a group.[161]

Ethnic politics along the lines practiced in the East were untenable in most western cities for several reasons. As a practical matter, Jewish politicians in the West rarely could count on an ethnic constituency large enough to dominate a district, and during the Progressive Era cities like Portland,

San Francisco, and Los Angeles amended their charters to elect council members on an "at-large" basis. Thus, while representing civic causes that appealed to many coreligionists, Jewish politicians avoided specific ethnic appeals. Oregon governor Julius Meier, for example, focused his efforts on populist issues such as curtailing corporate power, conservation, old age pensions, and public economic development.[162]

Many western Jewish leaders also had an ideological aversion to ethnic politics. The emergence in San Francisco of the ACJ chapter suggests their distaste for the very idea of Judaism as an *ethnic* identity. In 1928, David Cohen, editor and publisher of Portland's pro-Zionist *Scribe*, condemned the idea of a Jewish vote in American politics when he criticized New York Republicans for nominating a Jewish gubernatorial candidate whom they expected would mobilize Jewish voters for Herbert Hoover in the presidential race.[163] Such a perspective exemplifies accommodationist determination to emphasize patriotism and avoid the perception that Jews held interests different from other patriotic Americans.

In addition, although second-generation Eastern Europeans became part of the leadership group in these cities during the interwar years, they did not displace the established elite. The rabbis of the four premier Reform congregations on the West Coast, in Los Angeles, San Francisco, Portland, and Seattle, continued to serve, like their predecessors, as spokesmen for the local Jewish community. Rabbi Newman, for example, estimated in 1930 that five thousand people were affiliated with Temple Emanu-El either as full members or as "associates"; in 1925, eight thousand people, roughly a quarter of the city's Jewish population, attended his Kol Nidre service—joined by others who listened to the live radio broadcast.[164] Among these was a younger generation of Reform congregants, who followed their parents' tradition of service, stepping into roles as both Jewish community leaders and members of the civic elite, even as second-generation Eastern Europeans began to join them. Not surprisingly given these patterns, western Jewish communities continued their established practice of political engagement as individual Jews, rather than engage in the ethnic politics that by the 1920s enabled Democrats to build a strong following among immigrant and second-generation Jews in the East.

Despite the use of quiet diplomacy by western Jewish leaders and the aversion to ethnic politics, it would be inaccurate to suggest that this translated into a full embrace of the so-called accommodationist response to anti-Semitism typical of the ADL and the American Jewish Committee. While ethnic politics did not develop in western cities, neither did Jewish leaders restrict themselves to a behind-the-scenes strategy or to universal issues. Rather, they publicly addressed anti-Semitism, called attention to the plight of European Jews, and became proactive in promoting interreligious understandings and intercultural work. Despite notable exceptions such as the controversy that followed the release of *The King of Kings*, there was little polarization between advocates of the two approaches in the West. Indeed, many western Jewish leaders combined the two.

Thus many western rabbis who at times used quiet diplomacy also engaged in direct, public activity as well. Rabbis of the leading Reform temples in all four of the major West Coast cities drew on their close relationships with Christian clergy as well as their ties to secular fraternal organizations and humanitarian groups to publicly counter anti-Semitism. In Seattle, both longtime rabbi Samuel Koch and his successor, Raphael Levine,

made interfaith work a centerpiece of their tenures. Events like a brotherhood dinner, held at the temple in May 1930 and attended by four hundred Protestant, Catholic, and Jewish men, suggested that ecumenical work would help to counter intolerance.[165] In Los Angeles, Rabbi Magnin, while a spokesman for the ADL, was never more at home than when addressing brotherhood banquets with Protestant ministers and bishops of the Catholic Church.

In San Francisco, Temple Emanu-El's Louis Newman, through his weekly column in Portland's *Scribe*, vehemently criticized what he saw as the accommodationist approach of organizations like the ADL. As a protégé of leading Zionist and American Jewish Congress leader Rabbi Stephen Wise, such an "antipathy for the elite and decorous organizations like the ADL" might be expected.[166] Yet Newman's assertiveness was shared by his successor, the anti-Zionist Irving Reichert. A longtime American Civil Liberties Union (ACLU) activist, Reichert had supported the Scottsboro boys and the rights of migrant farm workers. In 1942, he would break the silence among liberals and Jews in the face of racist wartime policy and become one of a very small number of civil rights advocates to publicly defend Japanese Americans against incarceration, explicitly linking their civil liberties to those of other minorities, including Jews.[167]

While Reichert was active in supporting universal civil rights causes, he did not hesitate to speak out publicly on more parochial, Jewish issues. In contrast to those who feared calling attention to Jewish issues, Reichert was just as aggressive in calling attention to anti-Semitism as to discrimination against African Americans and Japanese Americans. In 1933, he was an early and outspoken critic of American Jewish inaction against the Nazis. In his Rosh Hashanah sermon in 1933, titled "The New Year and Nazi Terror," Reichert condemned the inaction of American Jews as "incomprehensible," characterized the German Jewish situation as "hopeless," and warned, "this much seems fairly certain: the more fortunate will emigrate and the more miserable hundreds of thousands will be killed, or shunted off into social if not actual ghettos, condemned to degradation by a constant stigma of inferiority." Reichert not only voiced strong support for a boycott of German goods—a boycott strongly opposed by both the American Jewish Committee and the B'nai B'rith—but he also warned of "the sinister implications which Hitlerism holds for American Jewry," because of its desire to incite anti-Semitism in America.[168]

While his West Coast rabbinical colleagues did not subscribe to all of Reichert's positions, they did share his practice of speaking out publicly and using interfaith alliances to address issues like anti-Semitism. From Seattle to Los Angeles, West Coast rabbis not only spoke from their pulpits but also addressed fraternal organizations (such as the Masons, to which a number of them belonged), church groups, and radio audiences. In Seattle, Rabbi Koch was a central figure in secular humanitarian and civil rights causes throughout his long tenure at Temple De Hirsch. He served "on the board of virtually every social service organization in Seattle" as well as serving the state as an arbiter in contentious labor disputes like the Centralia Affair.[169] The ties he developed through organizations like the Masons provided him opportunities to share his views and embody intercultural ties through fraternal activities.

In an era when American Jews generally compartmentalized their Jewish defense activities from their more general civil libertarian causes, many of these western leaders explicitly merged the two.

Stuart Svonkin argues that "before World War II American Jews pursued a bifurcated program of social action, working to protect the rights and liberties of others through nonsectarian organizations while restricting their own communal agencies to more narrowly Jewish objectives."[170] Certainly, prominent western Jews, like their counterparts elsewhere, joined progressive civil rights groups like the National Association for the Advancement of Colored People (NAACP) and the ACLU, but they also advocated for universal causes within specifically Jewish groups and used their alliances with nonsectarian groups to support Jewish causes.

It was not uncommon, for example, for Jewish weeklies to publish editorials urging Jewish condemnation of prejudice directed at other groups. In 1922, Portland's *Scribe* published several such editorials, urging readers to vote against a referendum that would mandate public school attendance. The referendum, sponsored by the Masons and strongly backed by the Oregon Ku Klux Klan, was aimed primarily at outlawing Catholic schools. The *Scribe* explained to its readers that, despite the fact that "we Jews are opposed in principal to parochial schools [and] have none of our own," the bill was a "critical" matter of "freedom of conscience and belief." In the same edition, among a number of paid ads on both sides of the issue, was an advertisement opposing the bill and signed by several of Portland's most prominent Jews. They denounced the bill as "a weapon of religious intolerance which may someday be directed against Jews."[171]

Such connections between the fate of other minorities and that of Jews were not uncommon. Rabbi Elliot Burstein of Temple Beth Israel in San Francisco made this explicit when he explained in a speech titled "What Is Americanism," presented at Odd Fellows Hall in 1941: "There is still plenty of prejudice against the Negro, the Jew, the Catholic. As long as this exists, our democracy will be sick and needs a good dose of tolerance. But even tolerance is not enough. Tolerance is arrogance. Our Americanism should include definite efforts made to unite all Americans on their common tasks and to urge groups not to capitalize on their differences."[172]

Rabbis like Burstein, Newman, and Koch reached broad audiences in their cities and beyond when their addresses were broadcast on the radio. Rabbi Magnin's sermon, "Labels That Are Libels," broadcast on his weekly radio show and published on the front page of the *Messenger* in late February 1942, appeared to question the widely popular policy of mass internment that was taking shape at the time. Although he never specifically mentioned Japanese Americans, he criticized efforts to "condemn a whole group of people by reason of the faults or sins of some of them." He directly referenced the Jewish experience in Nazi Germany when he argued that "prejudice against any group of people is harmful not only to that group, but to the majority of the citizens of any country."[173] Rabbi Reichert's sermons were regularly featured on the *Message of Israel* radio program, and in 1937 he began a five-year run of weekly radio broadcasts, carried by eighty-three western radio stations, as distant as St. Louis.[174] The civic prominence of these rabbis, as well as their strong relationships with Christian clergymen and secular civic groups, enabled them to call on Christians to help them counter anti-Semitism.

Western Jewish involvement in civil rights coalitions extended well beyond the rabbinical leadership. In Los Angeles, the Jewish Community Committee became a leader in civil rights activity. During the summer of 1942, with the burden of monitoring pro-Nazi groups fully assumed by the federal government, the committee shifted its focus toward intergroup relations. Believing that fighting prejudice in all of its forms was central to the fight against anti-Semitism, the committee's executive secretary Leon Lewis began a campaign focusing on "building bridges" with other minority groups, particularly Mexican Americans and African Americans. The group changed its name to the Los Angeles Community Relations Council and became "one of the most active catalysts for civil rights coalition building in Los Angeles during the World War II and postwar decade."[175] Likewise, in San Francisco, Jews helped to build a municipal civil rights coalition in the late 1930s that was based on "the assumption that no one can be safe unless everyone is free." Jewish leaders, working with Catholic liberals and others, created an "interracial council that revitalized the civil rights movement in the Bay Area."[176]

While ethnically based candidacies were untenable in West Coast cities, the long history of Jewish prominence in municipal affairs gave them a seat at the table. Beginning with the very lengthy administration of James Rolph (1911–30), San Francisco mayors provided the city's various ethnic/religious groups representation through appointments to city commissions and boards. Prominent Jews, who were strongly involved in both political and civic fund-raisers, were rewarded for their largess. Thus, ironically, in a city where leading Jews had long eschewed "ethnic politics," they increasingly filled commission and board positions known as "Jewish seats."

As David Dalin demonstrates, Jewish representation on ten major municipal boards and commissions between 1935 and 1965 ranged from 21.8 percent to just over 30 percent, a high reached during the war years. The board of education during this period had two semiofficial Jewish seats, one of which was held from 1922 to 1935 by

Mary Goldsmith Prag, mother of Congresswoman Florence Prag Kahn. Similarly, the police commission had a Jewish seat, and the art and library commissions, according to Dalin, were "quasi Jewish domains."[177] The individuals holding these positions also served prominently on the boards of Jewish institutions such as the Jewish Welfare Federation, the Jewish Community Center, Temple Emanu-El, and various Jewish philanthropic organizations. Indeed, being active in Jewish organizations seemed a prerequisite for being appointed to a city board. While this practice was not as formalized in other cities, Jewish participation in city commissions and agencies was common. For example, David Robinson, the first director of the ADL in Oregon, had been Portland's first public defender in 1915 and later served as a lawyer for the U.S. Public Health Service. As a leader, along with Portland lawyer Roscoe Nelson, in social justice movements, B'nai B'rith work, and civil rights advocacy, Robinson was later appointed to chair Portland's Mayor's Commission on Human Rights.[178] After World War II he served as president of the Urban League, the reformist City Club of Portland, and Temple Beth Israel and as chair of the Civil Rights Division of the Oregon Labor Bureau.[179]

Extensive participation of prominent Jews on human rights commissions, interfaith organizations, and civil rights groups, of course, is not uniquely western. Historians have noted the emergence of intercultural work in Jewish communities nationwide, although there is some disagreement as to whether this took place before or during World War II.[180] In most western Jewish communities, leaders explicitly embraced a "universalist perspective" and championed mutual "understanding" between Catholics and Jews in the 1920s.[181] They also sponsored public presentations by Protestant ministers calling on churches to desist from stigmatizing Jews and generally enrolled in the fight against discrimination well before the war.

In addition to intergroup work, public protests and rallies—tactics that contrasted sharply with behind-the-scenes diplomacy—were common in the West. Since the Mortara mass meeting of 1859, Jews and Protestants in the region had united to protest injustice.[182] In Los Angeles, the Jewish Labor Committee in October 1934 emerged from a mass meeting of sixty-five hundred workers "to learn about developments in Europe."[183] The group remained active in the 1930s, publicizing a boycott of German goods, raising funds to help Polish Jews, and, in the wake of Kristallnacht, organizing a monthlong series of anti-Nazi activities, including neighborhood protests, leading up to a mass meeting in early January 1939. By the late 1930s and early 1940s, the connection between the fight against anti-Semitism and the embrace of tolerance and acceptance as fundamental American values was clearly articulated in community documents and the press. For example, the B'nai B'rith District Grand Lodge No. 4 in its Americanization program from 1940 linked the promotion of Americanism to the campaign against anti-Semitism: "The Grand Lodge Americanism Committee is the aggressive force that supplements the defensive work of the Anti-Defamation Committee. Its job is to foster the spirit of Americanism in our members, in the Jewish community and in the general public and by so doing, overcome the savage attacks of those who would tear down our democratic institutions." The program included a list of suggestions, emphasizing the need to stress patriotism in order to counter anti-Semitism through activities such as flag ceremonies, the encouragement of naturalization, the celebration of and "proper attention" to national holidays in religious schools, and the initiation of public schools programs emphasizing American values like "tolerance," a "sense of fair play," "respect for the rights of others," and "acquiescence to the will of the majority with respect for the rights of the minority."[184]

The fight against discrimination at home and abroad not only led to alliances between Jewish and non-Jewish civil rights groups but also reinforced the consolidation of Jewish communities of the West. Thus, despite the acrimonious relationship between the national American Jewish Committee and the American Jewish Congress, the San Francisco branch of the American Jewish Committee's Survey Committee, established in 1937, cooperated with both the ADL and the local American Jewish Congress to monitor "local Nazi Bund and other anti-Semitic organizations."[185] While the General Jewish Council—the national organization that brought together the American Jewish Committee, the B'nai B'rith, the American Jewish Congress, and the Jewish Labor Committee in 1938—lasted for only one year, the cooperation in San Francisco lasted through the war years, despite bitter divisions locally between Zionists and anti-Zionists.[186] Rabbi Reichert, one of the nation's most outspoken anti-Zionists, supported the American Jewish Congress's boycott of German goods.[187]

This cooperation on critical issues facing the Jewish community, unfortunately, was not characteristic of the American Jewish community in general during the 1930s and 1940s. In the West, particularly among those communities that saw growth slow during the interwar years, the cooperative attitude can be traced to a number of factors. The recruitment of successful businessmen and young lawyers of Eastern European descent into positions of communal leadership through the huge B'nai B'rith lodges created a sense of communal continuity rather than discord. Rabbinical comradeship, through men like Samuel Koch and Jonah Wise and, then, Henry Berkowitz and Edgar Magnin holding pulpits for long terms and men like Elliott Burstein moving from smaller to larger cities, created cohesive religious leadership. The appointment of rabbis like Rudolph Coffee and Edgar Magnin and social workers like Irving Lipsitch to statewide social service boards created a sense of Jewish civic prominence. And the sponsorship of regionwide fund-raising visits by Zionists created a mutual sense of philanthropic purpose. A strong sense of regional identity fostered pride and unity among Jews from varied backgrounds, and a more balanced ethnic composition within the Jewish community meant that, unlike Jewish communities elsewhere, there were no extreme shifts in the composition of the leadership group during this period. In most cities, the sense of continuity would remain after the war, but in Los Angeles unprecedented population growth would create a drastically different future for regional Jewry.

6 JEWS OF THE WESTERN SUN BELT, 1945–1980

In a few years there will be two major centers
of Jewish creative effort in this land, New York
and Los Angeles. —1927

As part of the large migration of Americans after World War II to what publicists called the Sun Belt, Jews moved in unprecedented numbers to the Pacific West, especially to Los Angeles.[1] Although their numbers overwhelmed the older Jewish communities, the newcomers built their institutions on the familiar notion that the West should be a cultural as well as an economic frontier, where Jews might join non-Jews in breaching barriers. The most notorious portend of new economic and moral influence might have been the day in 1941 when Benjamin "Bugsy" Siegel, who ran illegal gambling in Los Angeles for criminal syndicates, took Meyer Lansky, his boyhood friend from New York's Lower East Side, to examine a barren tract south of the city limits of Las Vegas, where Siegel also owned a small casino.[2] Ten years earlier gambling had been legalized in Nevada in conjunction with the construction of the Boulder (later Hoover) Dam, and the source of abundant water and electricity nearby led Siegel to envision an extraordinary new casino, the *Flamingo*. In this desolate Nevada terrain only a few hours drive from Los Angeles he hoped to combine Hollywood's nightclub scene with high-stakes gambling in order to launder the profits of organized crime. A tropical bird whose name already adorned a Miami hotel would create legitimate jobs for a network of Jewish and Italian compatriots.[3]

When World War II ended, Lansky found backers, and the *Flamingo* took flight. But with costs mounting, receipts lagging, and Siegel skimming funds, another of Lansky's boyhood friends, Lucky Luciano, in June 1947 had Siegel murdered in his girlfriend's Beverly Hills apartment.[4] With the temporarily more reliable Gus Greenbaum installed to make the *Flamingo* profitable, new money ultimately appeared from sources like Mormon bankers and Jimmy Hoffa's Teamster's Central States Pension Fund (administered by Hoffa's Jewish friends from Chicago, Paul and Allen Dorfman), to create still more casinos.[5] In the 1950s, a construction style derived from the Jewish architect of Miami Beach hotels, Morris Lapidus, shaped new Las Vegas icons like the *Sands*, the *Desert Inn*, and the *Stardust*.[6] The historian Hal K. Rothman, himself an active member of the Las Vegas Jewish community, concluded, "Postwar Las Vegas was really a Jewish mob town."[7]

A Jewish "network noire" spread the casino "skim" throughout southern California. Moe Dalitz, who controlled the *Stardust* and the *Desert Inn*, and his Beverly Hills partner, the real estate tycoon (and future founder of Lorimar Pictures) Mervyn Adelson, recycled millions of casino dollars three hundred miles to the south in San Diego County.[8] Here they cooperated with savings and loan mogul Irvin Kahn to build an opulent golf resort and gated community at La Costa and to develop residential and commercial property at Rancho de Los Penquitos, near La Jolla.[9] Federal defense contracts more than any other source funded the vast expansion of the southern California cities, as well as Phoenix and Tucson, from World War II through 1990.[10] But the network of Jewish casino owners, movie moguls, and savings and loan executives blended the shady into

the legitimate to shape "discretionary" consumer spending. And, like their thoroughly upright nineteenth-century predecessors Bailey Gatzert, I. W. Hellman, and Kaspare Cohn, they gave generously to Jewish and general philanthropic causes. Dalitz, the most conspicuous of the casino operators, contributed to the construction of the Sunset Hospital and Temple Beth Shalom in Las Vegas, was honored by the American Cancer Society, and received awards from the state of Israel and the Anti-Defamation League of the B'nai B'rith.[11]

A far more respectable moment in the cultural maturation of Pacific Coast Jewry occurred in 1947, when Shlomo Bardin arrived in Los Angeles to start a camp that would imbue the Jewish search for identity with a western emphasis on self-discovery. What came to be called after Bardin's death the Brandeis-Bardin Institute ceased telling laymen what they as Jews *should* know and explored what an audience hungry for Jewish knowledge *was willing to learn*. Bardin had many programs to attract an eclectic group, but in effect he shifted educational emphasis in Jewish communities throughout the Pacific region from children to college students and adults. In postwar Los Angeles, "he found people willing to take chances, to build, to dream, to plant their own unique roots."[12] Like the shady Jewish moguls of Las Vegas, the entrepreneurial and charismatic Bardin also saw his followers as an audience he could cultivate with what one scholar has termed "a pastiche of traditions."[13]

A native of Zhitomir, Russia, Bardin in 1919, two years after the Russian Revolution, left with a group of Zionist friends for a kibbutz in Palestine. After university training in Europe, he earned a doctorate at Columbia University's Teachers College, where he met Justice Louis Brandeis. Brandeis taught him that young American Jews faced a dilemma: they often lacked knowledge of their her-itage and consequently lacked pride in themselves. Bardin, preoccupied with the ongoing problems of the Yishuv, returned to Palestine in the mid-1930s. By 1943, however, he had returned to the United States, where he established a summer camp in the Pocono Mountains of eastern Pennsylvania to bring Jewish culture, and especially the Zionist culture of the Yishuv, to young Americans.

By 1947, he had attracted a following among Jewish Angelenos, who acquired a twenty-two hundred–acre property in the Simi Valley for a permanent Brandeis Camp Institute.[14] Here the ter-rain and climate allowed him, as it had the movie moguls thirty years before, to pursue his dream throughout the year. While still residing part-time in New York, he initiated weekend camp experi-ences for adults and summer sessions for college students that reattached Jews with limited religious instruction to a revitalized Jewish people. He also subtly changed his focus from an overtly Zionist message to accommodate the spiritual needs of his audience. As Deborah Dash Moore has noted, he "developed a form of spiritual recreation specifi-cally tailored to address the needs of the uprooted Jews of Los Angeles."[15] His use of scholar-in-residence programs, Israeli dance, drama, and music would soon percolate up to Hillel Houses, synagogues, and folk dance clubs throughout the region. And he appealed specifically to young women, whose homes would make their children feel good about retaining a Jewish identity. Partici-pants in adult weekends and college programs stud-ied with prominent artists, writers, and scholars, including Abraham Joshua Heschel, Horace M. Kallen, and Elie Wiesel. Over the next forty years, in Los Angeles, Jewish secular leaders—real estate developers, movie producers, and fund-raisers,

often inspired by their wives—would integrate their Jewish learning acquired "at leisure" at Brandeis into their daily pursuits.[16] In effect, Bardin trans-muted Judaism from a ritualized religion into a culture suitable to the outdoor world of southern California, which, like Israel itself, had become home to a new Jewish society.

Just as Bardin helped define a culturally expres-sive western Jewish identity, twenty-two-year-old Rosalind Weiner in 1953 helped redefine an asser-tive western Jewish politics by bringing community issues into the political arena. Elected to the Los Angeles city council from a newly drawn Fifth District in heavily Jewish Beverly-Fairfax, she was the youngest person and the first Jewish woman ever elected to the council and the first Jew to serve in fifty years (fig. 6.1). Her prominence followed a decade of efforts by Jewish activists, in reaction to the spread of Nazi propaganda in Los Angeles and a war during which racial tensions had been played out on the city's streets, to build coalitions with other minority groups. The internment of the Japanese American community, attacks by soldiers and sailors on zoot-suit-wearing Mexican youths, and the Nazi racial war against Jews had led defense organizations for each of these groups, as well as the NAACP, to mobilize. Racial tensions had also led officials like Mayor Fletcher Bow-ron to recognize the political legitimacy of their public activities and the need by the city to respond positively.[17] Despite the objections of Rabbi Edgar Magnin, whose anxieties about a conspicuously Jewish agenda went back to the 1920s, Weiner made issues like a state Fair Employment Practices Commission, an end to restrictive covenants in housing deeds, and the defense of Israel the key goals of her program. She argued that the Los Angeles Jewish community, as it grew in size,

FIG. 6.1 *Sandy Koufax was presented with a symbolic gift by Councilwoman Rosalind (Weiner) Wyman. Its inscription reads, "This box contains baseballs used by Sandy Koufax, No hit game, June 30, 1962 (The way the Mets saw them)." Koufax was also presented with a resolution by the city council honoring his no-hit game. Los Angeles Herald Examiner Collection, Los Angeles Public Library.*

wealth, and confidence, should no longer position itself as a junior partner to a gentile Republican elite, as it had been under Rabbi Magnin's stewardship. Instead, it should become a major component of a racially diverse Democratic coalition.[18] She used support for civil rights and for Israel and opposition to communism to win election, and she joined Edward Roybal, elected from Boyle Heights in 1949 as the first Mexican American councilman

since 1887, to challenge the power of the WASP elite.[19]

The post–World War II migration of hundreds of thousands of Jews made the election of Weiner possible and was a significant part of a population movement that shifted the demographic, economic, cultural, and political balance of the nation.[20] After 1945, pent-up savings and delayed plans sent Americans on the move. For Jews, as for other Americans, these migrations had clear generational patterns, whose only parallel—at least for Jews— was the movement of their Eastern European ancestors to America between 1881 and World War I. Although most successful middle-aged children of Jewish immigrants just after World War II moved short distances to the suburbs of eastern and midwestern cities, a growing minority of this generation undertook lengthier and more momentous migrations.[21]

In the 1950s, many Jews were among the retirees who relocated to warm climates especially in South Florida. New union pensions and private savings, the federal programs of Social Security (and in 1965, Medicare), and technological innovations like home air-conditioning and the commercial jet airplane made this migration possible. In a reversal of the emigration from Eastern Europe, for the first time in history hundreds of thousands of older Jews left their children behind to seek a more comfortable life. As the historian Gary Mormino noted, "The notion that grandparents should move away from their families and hometowns cut across the ethical and ethnic grain of history."[22] Florida was the major benefactor, attracting three times as many elderly migrants as its nearest competitor, California.[23] The Pacific West, whose postwar economy rested on defense contracts far more than did Florida's, attracted a different generation.[24]

Young adults, including both a disproportionately high number of Jews with varying levels of formal schooling and those willing to take greater risks, left their parents behind for new lives in the open spaces of Los Angeles.[25]

LOS ANGELES: FROM PROVINCIAL CENTER TO SECOND CITY

Though the Jewish West added major population centers in the years between 1945 and 1980, Los Angeles remained the focal point. With its federally funded defense industries, it became the primary magnet for migratory Americans, including young Jews, looking for work. Though in 1950 Chicago was still the second largest city in the United States and would remain so until the early 1980s, Los Angeles by 1960 would hold the second largest Jewish population, as San Francisco had ninety years before. And Los Angeles Jewry would aspire to become culturally as well as demographically American Jewry's "second city."[26] The demographer Bruce Phillips explains that "the dramatic growth of the Los Angeles Jewish community occurred as part of the growth of Los Angeles itself and can only be understood within that context."[27] But because of their early rate of growth and their occupational profile, Jews were at the region's "leading edge." Between 1940 and 1950, about 170,000 Jews came to Los Angeles, more than had come in any previous decade and more than would come in any succeeding one. In ten years, twice as many Jews came to Los Angeles as then lived in San Francisco, Oakland, Seattle, Portland, Phoenix, and Tucson combined. To suggest the dramatic expansion of Los Angeles Jewry, in 1951 only 16 percent of Jewish households had been living in the city for more than fifteen years.[28]

Jews settled into districts of the city according to income. The large manufacturers in the garment industry, the medical and legal professionals, and the entertainment industry executives moved into West Los Angeles. Many lower-income residents of City Terrace and Boyle Heights, which in 1940 had held the largest Jewish population in the city, moved to the Fairfax District. By 1950, Boyle Heights was 43 percent Latino, and its passing as the center of traditional Jewish culture was marked as institutions like Solomon's Judaica and Book Shop and Leader Beauty Shop relocated to Fairfax Avenue.[29] According to one neighborhood historian, the signal of the ascension of Fairfax came in 1948, when Canter's Deli opened a branch there, to be joined by restaurants, bakeries, fish markets, produce stands, and butcher shops. Even those Jewish proprietors who kept their stores in Boyle Heights to serve a diverse clientele had themselves moved elsewhere.[30]

The majority of Jewish newcomers to Los Angeles had modest incomes and found attractive new housing to meet their budgets on the wide streets of the city's unsettled northwestern region, the San Fernando Valley. The Jewish war veterans and their families arriving from Brooklyn or Chicago, like their gentile counterparts, were attracted by the opportunity to find work, the warm climate, the inexpensive housing, and the size of the lots.[31] While the San Fernando Valley's population grew by almost 60 percent during the war, the construction of new aircraft and automobile factories after 1945 led to an even more rapid growth of more than 75 percent between 1946 and 1950. Young Jewish families clustered in the less expensive areas like Reseda or Panorama City, a community of prefabricated housing constructed by Kaiser Community Homes, the housing arm of Henry J. Kaiser's gigantic industrial corporations. Jews with more money and a desire to live in hilly, open spaces settled into Encino on the southern edge of the Valley against the Santa Monica Mountains. By 1955, retail sales in the Valley exceeded those in downtown stores, and the Broadway, Robinsons, and other department stores built branches in Panorama City to serve the sprawling middle-class communities.[32] By 1965, a survey found, the Jewish population of the San Fernando Valley exceeded that of the Beverly-Fairfax and Hollywood areas combined and held the largest single segment of Los Angeles Jewry.[33] At the same time, wealthier Jews continued to move into west-side neighborhoods, further separating the community by income, length of residence in the city, and, to some degree, political interests, which would be expressed dramatically in the 1980s.

The core of employment, and the largest source of contributions to Jewish philanthropy, remained real estate financing and construction and the entertainment and garment industries. One of the two more prominent owners of savings and loans companies, Mark Taper, financed the largest home-buying market in the country. The largest builder of homes, especially for first-time buyers, was Eli Broad, who had relocated the headquarters of his home construction business, Kaufman and Broad, from Detroit. Joseph Eichler came from New York in the 1940s to design and build architecturally distinctive, moderately priced homes. Most of Eichler's homes were built in the San Francisco area, but more than a thousand were erected in the San Fernando Valley, where to this day they retain their cachet. By 1950, Tishman Construction, a Jewish family firm founded in New York City, had completed the first high-rise office towers on Wilshire Boulevard and would build many other large structures on the west side.[34] By 1960, Jews comprised 20 percent of homebuilders, construct-

ing 40 percent of the homes in Los Angeles and contributing more than 20 percent of the budget of the United Jewish Welfare Fund of Los Angeles.[35] The Jewish garment industry also grew dramatically in downtown Los Angeles, though it became increasingly complex, marked by an ethnic division of labor. At the core of marketing clothing was the CaliforniaMart, built in stages between the mid-1950s and mid-1960s as a center for wholesale business by two Jewish brothers who had come from New York. The manufacturers, the most successful of whom were Jewish, rented space in the building to display their lines to buyers from department stores and clothing chains. As the chain of production developed over the next several decades, the Jewish manufacturers contracted with Korean and other Asian owners of sewing facilities to assemble the garments.[36] With its far lower rents and easier access to low-wage labor from Southeast Asia, Mexico, and Central America, Los Angeles by 1993 actually had more jobs in both men's and women's clothing than did New York.[37]

The movie studios after the war faced two crises, the more permanent based on the Supreme Court's interpretation of the industry's structure as well as on unrelated changes in communications technology, and the more dramatic and temporary provoked by the politics of the Cold War. In 1949, the Court found the studios in violation of federal antitrust laws and required them to sell their theater chains. Shortly thereafter, movie audiences declined precipitously because of the rise of network television, which by the 1970s used 80 percent of the production facilities in the Los Angeles area. The Jewish studio owners adjusted only slowly.[38] Employment for actors, writers, and cameramen and other technical people increased, because the television networks built studios in Hollywood and Burbank to film their own programs and to transmit live broadcasts. The movie studios then turned to television and to the universities to find new talent that could reach a youthful audience and replenish their revenues. A vignette from the 1970s suggests how a media built mostly by Jews, but open to all talents, transformed itself by using old social networks to tap its rivals. In 1979, Michael Eisner, the chief operating officer at Paramount Pictures, signed a unique distribution deal with Steven Spielberg and non-Jew George Lucas, two of the most successful young filmmakers in Hollywood, to make and market an adventure film, *Raiders of the Lost Ark*. The high production costs of $25 million were paid by Eisner's studio, which then shared the extraordinary domestic profits of $250 million with Spielberg and Lucas.

The routes to this meeting illustrate how outsiders were recruited through persisting Jewish networks to revitalize the industry and with it neighborhoods and communities. Eisner, the son of a wealthy Jewish family in New York, had started after college in 1966 at the ABC television network and progressed under the tutelage of other Jewish executives like his friend Barry Diller by producing soap operas and children's programs. He had come to Los Angeles in 1973 to develop evening television programming for ABC. When Diller became chairman of the board of Paramount Pictures in 1977, Eisner came along to be his chief operating officer. By 1984, Eisner would be recruited to be chief executive officer at Walt Disney Studios, which until then had been Hollywood's most renowned non-Jewish studio.[39] Though a newcomer from New York, Eisner was quickly absorbed in the network of West Los Angeles filmmakers. "The entertainment business so dominates West Los Angeles," Eisner noted, "that almost everybody you know is somehow involved in making movies and television. . . . I am referring to friends . . . who have kids in the same school as yours, and also have film and television projects at the network or studio where you happen to work."[40]

Spielberg followed a more maverick route to prominence in the more idiosyncratic "creative" side of the movie industry. His career illustrates the new production and distribution system that came to dominate the industry. As the studios lost touch with young audiences in the 1960s, new graduates of film schools at the University of California, Los Angeles (UCLA), and the University of Southern California, such as Francis Ford Coppola and Lucas, developed new ideas for films that appealed to wider audiences. Spielberg, whose poor high school grades disqualified him from admission to film schools, in the mid-1960s wheedled internships at Universal Studios. A short film he made in 1968 earned him a directing contract, not for films, however, but for television specials. Freeing himself financially in the late 1970s, he tapped family memories to make films with decidedly Jewish themes, especially *Schindler's List*.[41] In the 1990s, Spielberg emerged as one of the wealthiest philanthropists in Los Angeles, creating the Shoah oral history project to document the lives of survivors of the Holocaust and the Righteous Persons Foundation to distribute grants primarily to Jewish projects.[42]

The easy national acceptance of Eisner and Spielberg as leaders in a new era for the motion picture industry, as well as the movies with Jewish content that they chose to make, suggests to some degree how Jewish Hollywood survived its second crisis by coming through the Cold War to overcome a long-standing suspicion of their use of the industry to subvert American values. In 1944, Ben Hecht in great frustration observed that the producers kept movies free of Jewish roles or interests, "to convince the world that their Americanism is untainted by any special considerations for Jews."[43] In all fairness, by the end of the 1930s Warner Brothers did produce dramatic films warning the country of Hitler's murderous intentions. But Harry Warner's cry for the defense of Jewish lives, unlike Hecht's, was not tinged as well with a concern for left-wing causes. During the 1930s, many screenwriters, actors, and others who hated fascism were employed in the studios, but many of them, like Hecht, had also joined organizations with Communist Party affiliations. When the war ended, the House Un-American Activities Committee launched a highly publicized investigation of Communist Party influence in Hollywood, whose Jewish leadership was eager to cooperate.[44] Public hearings in Hollywood, at which personalities like Edward G. Robinson, Robert Taylor, and Humphrey Bogart were coerced into "naming names" of suspected Communist Party members or "fellow travelers," led to a horrendous sense of betrayal within the Hollywood community. When a group of ten prominent writers including Dalton Trumbo refused to answer questions about Communist Party membership, Harry Warner convinced the major producers to issue a statement declaring that the studios would never hire known Communists. Thus was born in 1947 the Hollywood "blacklist."[45]

In the 1950s, studios made biblical epics, mysteries, and science fiction and continued to avoid controversial political subjects, while the state of California imposed a loyalty oath on all public employees.[46] The prohibition at the Hollywood studios against hiring alleged Communists lasted until 1958, when Otto Preminger, in bringing to the screen Leon Uris's novel *Exodus*—the heroic story of Labor Zionism's struggle to build a Jewish

state—allowed Trumbo to receive credit for writing the screenplay.[47] The production of *Exodus*, in addition to glossing over an internal trauma of the movie colony, also used film to transform the Jews of Hollywood from subversive individuals to publicists for a modern national struggle to regain a homeland. *Exodus* depicted contemporary Jews as descendants of biblical heroes and survivors of the Holocaust who were struggling for freedom from British military control. The freeing of a land from its colonial occupier and the demeaning of its indigenous occupants as murderous "primitives" were themes with which an American public could identify.[48] The Jews of Hollywood were here dramatizing and transposing America's founding narrative and key political values rather than importing subversive ones.

SUBMERGING RADICAL POLITICS

As Jewish community organizations in Los Angeles pursued civil rights work after the war, they too evoked American values to shield themselves from accusations of communist sympathies. The rise of pro-Nazi propaganda in Los Angeles before the war and of violence against Japanese Americans, Mexican American youths, and blacks during the war led the Jewish Community Relations Council (CRC) to reconsider the need to "build bridges" to other minority groups, while also disavowing Jews with communist affiliations.[49] The effort to disentangle accusations of subversion from antiracist struggles was played out most dramatically in Boyle Heights, where it became embedded in the urban themes of ethnic succession and political coalition building. Most young Jewish couples, like William Phillips and his wife, Hannah (Catch), were leaving the area. Phillips and the music store he operated for fifty years on Brooklyn Avenue, however, became a venerated neighborhood institution and a symbol of interethnic cooperation because generations of aspiring African American, Mexican American, and other young people used it to make professional contacts.[50] Broader interethnic contacts occurred at the Soto-Michigan Center, which was funded by the Jewish Welfare Federation and through which the CRC had influence. Many older Jews who remained in the neighborhood were affiliated with the center because socialist groups like the Workmen's Circle and a communist fraternal order, the Jewish People's Fraternal Organization, met there. As Mexicans became the largest group in Boyle Heights, the Soto-Michigan Center also welcomed them, with the Hollenbeck Youth Council enabling African American, Mexican American, Japanese American, and Jewish youths to discuss their differences and to plan athletic and cultural events.[51] In addition, the neighborhood became the scene of debates between various brands of radicals and students organizing against racism. In late 1945, Jewish students at Roosevelt High School led several marches to protest a permit that the school board had issued to allow the anti-Semitic and racist Gerald L. K. Smith to speak at Los Angeles Polytechnic High School. The student protest reinforced a broader set of rallies against Smith that were endorsed by mainstream Jewish leaders including Judge Isaac Pacht, Judge Harry Holzer, and Rabbi Magnin, all of whom had led local Jewish self-defense organizations for decades.

The CRC found itself in the midst of the city's Cold War racial politics, in part because opposition to Smith's array of public speeches around Los Angeles was coordinated by the communist-led Civil Rights Congress, a group that had the same abbreviation as the Community Relations Council and which had a similar goal of gaining the allegiance of the city's racial minorities. Coordinating opposition to Smith required the Jewish CRC to follow a strategy of deflecting attention from itself by reinforcing its coalition with moderate African American organizations like the NAACP and a new Mexican American group with a strong presence in Boyle Heights, the Community Service Organization, led by army veteran Edward Roybal.[52]

Jewish adults in Boyle Heights followed the lead of the CRC by supporting Roybal when, as a thirty-year-old insurgent in 1947, he ran for a seat on the city council.[53] When he lost, Saul Alinsky, the community organizer from Chicago with Jewish roots in the neighborhood and a strong opposition to Communists, returned to help Roybal raise funds for his Community Service Organization. Through it, Roybal would promote a political agenda that featured his own experiences combating tuberculosis among Mexican immigrants and his interest in initiating bilingual education, as well as Mexican American voter registration. The CRC pledged seventy-five hundred dollars for Roybal's successful 1949 campaign for city council, in part because it hoped that the Community Service Organization might moderate growing Mexican American resentment against the relative economic success of their departing Jewish neighbors.[54]

The CRC strongly supported interracial work, but within the Jewish community it moved to purge its image of any subversive tinge. In the 1920s, Communist Party and leftist activity in general in Los Angeles had been centered in Boyle Heights, brought there largely from New York by Jewish men and women seeking work in the local garment industry. By the 1930s, the most committed families sustaining Communist Party activities had moved several miles to the northwest, to the hills of Edendale (now called Silver Lake), where they created an even more intense "culture of participation" based on Communist Party organizing and the support of artists as well as writers and technicians in the movie industry, all of whom lived in the area.[55] The state legislature's Un-American Activities Committee, however, still believed that party activity was focused in Boyle Heights, and in the 1940s it was investigating Jewish institutions like the Soto-Michigan Center. The Jewish Welfare Federation then asked its constituent agencies like the Jewish Centers Association to deny access to its facilities to any group that seemed to have communist affiliations and to require all employees to sign loyalty oaths. Those who refused were to be eased out, and many social workers and doctors lost their jobs.[56]

The fear of subversives spread through the neighborhood to include public employees associated with the Soto-Michigan Center. Nettie Peltzman, who had been born in Boyle Heights and educated in its schools, served on the center's board. She had worked since 1945 as a very popular children's librarian at the local Benjamin Franklin branch of the public library. In 1953, despite testimonials from teachers, principals, parents, the center's board, and councilman Roybal, she was unceremoniously transferred from her library position.[57] For the Jewish Welfare Federation, the Soto-Michigan Center had attracted excessive notoriety; it was merged with a nearby center that emphasized Zionist rather than interracial activities, and federation funding was shifted to the construction of the new Westside Jewish Community Center, which opened in 1954.[58]

By then, the Jewish population of Los Angeles had expanded to an estimated 315,000, and the left-wing conflicts of the past seemed to be forgotten. A survey of the Jewish community in 1953

boasted of Boyle Heights and City Terrace as areas of high synagogue attendance and low intermarriage rates, with no reference to its "left-wing" politics or its demographic decline. In the late 1950s, many elderly Jews relocated from Boyle Heights to the beach at Venice, which, since the 1920s, had had a small Jewish contingent of storekeepers and an Orthodox shul, Mishkan Tephilo. By 1964, the Israel Levin Senior Adult Center had opened there to serve perhaps as many as ten thousand Jews. Sitting on benches looking out toward the ocean, the Yiddish-speaking elderly, far removed from their socialist youth and the growing population center in the San Fernando Valley, faced the carnival atmosphere of Venice Beach. Death soon removed some, while the spiraling real estate market occasioned by new condominium towers in Santa Monica to the north and the construction of Marina del Rey to the south forced out the remainder. By the early 1970s, the Jewish population of Venice had shrunk to about four thousand.[59]

In other areas of Jewish Los Angeles just after the war, rabbis promoted progressive changes in forms of worship, cultural undertakings, and even political activism to try to rejuvenate Jewish cultural identity. Between 1947 and 1953, the Los Angeles Jewish Community Council, the San Fernando Valley Jewish Community Center, and Rabbi Magnin moved to transform Jewish identity from narrowly religious to more inclusive and cultural. In 1947, in conjunction with its promotion of Zionism, the Jewish Community Council brought Samuel Dinin from the Teachers Institute of the Jewish Theological Seminary in New York to Los Angeles to head its Bureau of Jewish Education. Dinin wished to supplement public school instruction with a Hebrew high school that would meet daily in the late afternoon. Hebrew language, Bible, and Jewish culture would provide the core of the curriculum. By 1950, two such schools were started, though their enrollment remained small. As a cultural Zionist and, like Bardin, a disciple of Justice Brandeis, Dinin believed that in America a Jewish education must provide the Jewish child with knowledge of Judaism, not only as a set of moral beliefs or religious rituals, but as a cultural identity with a language, history, and homeland, so that he or she might take pride in what must inevitably be in America the status of a minority. As Americans, Jews must democratize all features of their communal life, but their institution building in America must also be affected by their Jewish "nationality," including knowledge of Israeli culture.[60]

In the same year that Dinin arrived, the San Fernando Valley Jewish Community Center hired Rabbi Aaron Wise, who soon encouraged the creation of a "University of Judaism," which was then intended to be a teacher-training and adult education institute. Though hardly conceived of as a rival to Brandeis University, which was soon to open in Waltham, Massachusetts, the University of Judaism would demonstrate that Los Angeles Jewry could initiate Jewishly focused higher education to complement the renaissance in secondary schooling and informal adult cultural awareness. In 1948, Rabbi Mordecai Kaplan, the founder of the Reconstructionist movement in American Judaism, came to Los Angeles to preside over the opening of the university (now the American Jewish University). With Dore Schary as its first board chairman, the University of Judaism, like the Brandeis Camp Institute, raised money in Hollywood to build a campus, which was eventually located between the old Jewish population center of West Los Angeles and the young families moving into the San Fernando Valley.[61]

Rabbi Magnin, seeing the founding of the University of Judaism under the sponsorship of the Conservative movement, planned a competing Reform college, and in 1953 brought young Rabbi Isaiah Zeldin to start such a venture. When the president of Hebrew Union College stopped the project to avoid potential competition with Brandeis, Zeldin resigned to organize the new Stephen S. Wise Temple. For Rabbi Zeldin, Judaism meant not a denominational affiliation and worship service but an adaptation to a Los Angeles philosophy of identity based on lifelong cultural consumption. Learning from the successful local evangelical churches, Zeldin located his campus near the new population centers and adjacent to the University of Judaism. The temple hired buses to bring older people to services and especially to adult education classes and also sponsored preschools for the very young.[62] In the 1980s, a jaundiced observer from the East Coast, appalled by what he saw as the transience and superficiality of Jewish life in the San Fernando Valley, wrote dismissively that "Stephen Weiss [sic] Temple is responsible for enough social functions to stagger a cruise director."[63] Nevertheless, its ten thousand members—by 1980 into their second generation as congregants—seemed quite pleased with their new open lives as Jews. By 1990, the temple had a separate Milken Community High School, "committed to religious pluralism within the Jewish community," which enrolled more than eight hundred students in the seventh through twelfth grades.[64]

In 1953, newly ordained Reform rabbi Leonard Beerman also arrived at newly founded Leo Baeck Temple in West Los Angeles near Stephen S. Wise Temple. Beerman envisioned a synagogue that would, in the spirit of the martyred German rabbi after whom it was named, revitalize prayer for personal fulfillment but also develop social activism. Growing up during the Depression in a small Michigan town, Beerman saw the effects of unemployment and of anti-Semitism. If the Stephen S. Wise Temple prepared Judaism for mass consumption, Rabbi Beerman made Leo Baeck Temple a center for political dissent, by opposing nuclear proliferation, the death penalty, and then the Vietnam War. He also promoted local issues of social justice like labor activism and civil rights, which were supported by political figures such as Rosalind (Weiner) Wyman. Under the influence of rabbis like Beerman, the board of directors of the Los Angeles CRC reiterated its commitment to civil rights and civil liberties and to Zionism, which became the ideological core of the community's public agenda. While never growing very large, Rabbi Beerman's Leo Baeck Temple influenced many young members to join the rabbinate, including his successor, UCLA graduate Sanford Ragins. As one reporter for the *Jewish Journal of Greater Los Angeles* noted, "Leo Baeck . . . had a strong impact on liberal Los Angeles politics and leftist activism."[65]

Beerman, Bardin, and Zeldin had transformed ideas about "Jewish knowledge" from ritual observance to cultural inquiry and social activism, so that Jews might more easily create their own niche in an open secular society. In 1962, a survey by Fred Massarik of the estimated fourteen thousand Jews of Long Beach, south of Los Angeles, suggested the effects of their efforts. The great majority of "heads of households" had ceased their Jewish education at age thirteen. Only 10 percent attended religious services more than once a month, while only 13 percent felt that bar mitzvah should be the most important Jewish educational goal. Less than 11 percent felt that knowledge of either Hebrew or Yiddish was important, while the great majority chose as most important some knowledge of Jewish history and culture. Most of these respondents felt comfortable where they were, because almost 80 percent said that being Jewish had had no impact on their ability to find work.[66]

Not all institutions started in Los Angeles represented a local cultural orientation. Orthodox rabbi Marvin Hier migrated from Vancouver, British Columbia, in 1976 to open a yeshiva, which subsequently became affiliated with Yeshiva University. Two years later he rode the crest of a renewed national interest in the Holocaust to found a center named after Nazi-hunter Simon Wiesenthal (fig. 6.2).[67] Learning from other Los Angeles institutions like the Brandeis Institute and the University of Judaism, however, the Wiesenthal Center soon presented itself as a venue for teaching. Hier understood the need to attract a broad audience in a multiracial city facing perpetual interethnic tensions, and in 1993 he opened the Museum of Tolerance, whose permanent exhibit depicts the struggles against racism around the world. Indeed, the technology of the exhibits, as well as the financing, landed Rabbi Hier directly in the culture of Hollywood. The center also successfully pursued grants from the state of California to offer seminars taught by non-Jews as well as Jews to law enforcement and other public officials on topics like prejudice and interethnic relations.[68] To expand the Wiesenthal Center Rabbi Hier raised $50 million, primarily among the new movie moguls, to add a library of documents illustrating examples of genocide and to plan an expansion of the tolerance displays. Raising additional funds from politically conservative American Jews like Gary Winnick and Mervyn Adelson, Hier in 2005 opened a New York Tolerance Center and broke ground for a $120 million Museum of Tolerance in Jerusalem, the latter designed by one of the most illustrious Jews in Los Angeles, the world-renowned architect Frank Gehry.[69]

Grandchildren of Holocaust survivors stand in front of memorial flame at the Simon Wiesenthal Center, September 1986. Los Angeles Herald Examiner Collection, Los Angeles Public Library. Photograph: Dean Musgrove.

According to some critics, however, the Wiesenthal Center, to suggest the continuing tension between Jewish integration in a multiracial city and the need to remember how Jews have been the quintessential victims of European racism, depicts the Holocaust as a Nazi rampage uniquely against Jews.[70] Liberal critics of Rabbi Hier also believe that the Holocaust section of the museum is designed to prey on a sense of guilt among American Jews in order to raise funds for right-wing Israeli causes. But recent scholars suggest instead that the museum, particularly in its plans for expansion, as a whole reflects the ambivalence that persists in the broader identity of American Jews—especially the publicly active Orthodox—as the Holocaust fades from direct memory but as the need for tolerance of differences persists.[71]

A CIVIC PRESENCE IN THE SECOND CITY

In the 1950s, Jewish institutions appealing to the broader Jewish community started to dot the Los Angeles landscape, while in the 1960s the Jewish presence was officially recognized as a central pillar in the city's hierarchy. Dorothy Chandler, the wife of the publisher of the *Los Angeles Times*, invited the savings and loan mogul Mark Taper and his gentile colleague Howard Ahmanson to endow two buildings that would flank her own Dorothy Chandler Pavilion in a downtown center for elite entertainment. She proposed to rejuvenate the central business district by making it also a center of culture, surpassing the Civic Center in San Francisco. When the project was completed in the mid-1960s, the city's Jewish secular elite finally had a public monument, the Mark Taper Forum, to rival civic landmarks like Fleischacker Zoo, Steinhart Aquarium, and Stern Grove that had long honored the Jewish stewardship of San Francisco.[72]

As Jewish philanthropy in Los Angeles grew, it became directed increasingly to secular causes, especially its support of education and the arts and an expansion of its emphasis on medical research. By the early twenty-first century, Eli Broad, listed by *Forbes* as the second wealthiest person in Los Angeles, remarked candidly: "If I had only a little to give away, my emphasis would be on Jewish and Israeli causes. Once you get beyond several hundred thousand dollars, you become a better and more respected citizen if you also give to the Music Center and the universities."[73] In Los Angeles many of these institutions, like the Los Angeles County Art Museum and especially UCLA, were located close to the center of the Jewish population, on the west side. In the years just after the war, Jews faced discrimination trying to gain admittance to local medical schools and obtaining internships and residencies at private hospitals. The Jewish hospitals (the primary beneficiaries of Jewish philanthropy)—Cedars of Lebanon and Mount Sinai—felt compelled to provide facilities that would allow Jewish medical school graduates to acquire the

necessary advanced clinical experience.[74] But as the UCLA Medical Center expanded to its current mammoth size, doctors from the now-merged Cedars-Sinai Medical Center were added to its staff. By the early 1990s, Cedars-Sinai was identified as "the largest nonprofit healthcare facility west of New York," with research facilities supported by different sectors of the Jewish business community.[75]

The prominence of Jews in the city's philanthropic life was matched by the gradual emergence of the most powerful Jewish political organization in the country. Within twenty years of Rosalind Wyman's first election to city council, UCLA friends Henry Waxman (Hollywood) and Howard Berman (Van Nuys, Panorama City) were elected to Congress from adjoining districts on the city's west side. In 1976, Anthony C. Beilenson, a fourteen-year veteran of the California legislature, was elected to represent the western portion of the San Fernando Valley in the House of Representatives. He held this seat for ten consecutive terms.[76] The ability of Jewish political activists to generate funds and votes led African American and later Latino politicians to see that support of Jewish issues—especially the defense of Israel—provided for successful coalition politics.[77]

At the local level, Jewish politicians followed Wyman's lead and gradually developed mutual interests with rising black politicians, who also resented the power of downtown white Protestant businessmen and even more so the brutality of the overwhelmingly white police department. The fulfillment of Wyman's vision of the place of Jews in city politics unfolded in the wake of the infamous Watts riots, which broke out in August 1965 in South-Central Los Angeles. It was the most severe social upheaval in a western city in the twentieth century, at least until that time.[78] Just as in the wake of the San Francisco catastrophe in 1906, when Jews played major roles in rebuilding the commercial core and the philanthropic life of what was then the region's key city, so in the wake of the Watts riots, Jews played a crucial role in reknitting the political structure of what was now the region's key city. Jews had lived in South-Central Los Angeles since the 1920s and still owned many of the businesses that were burned during the riots.[79] While Jews generally did not reopen their stores, Jewish politicians saw a need to turn a struggle for influence into a symbiotic coalition. Over an eight-year period black supporters of city councilman Thomas Bradley and his Jewish campaign strategist, Maurice Weiner, engineered an insurgency against white Protestant control of city government. The coalition achieved its goal in 1973, when, with Jewish backing, Bradley was finally elected.[80] Bradley used affirmative action to provide blacks access to public employment, while a modus vivendi was worked out so that Jewish incumbents would usually not find their district boundaries realigned or their seats endangered.[81] The city also encouraged Jewish commercial development of the west side as well as hotels, sports complexes, and other business and entertainment structures in the city center.

By the 1980s, the continuing Jewish migration to Los Angeles had created not only the second largest and most politically cohesive Jewish community in the nation but also an educational infrastructure that embodied what its leaders perceived to be an inclusive approach to Jewish life. Its distinctive buildings marked off regions of the city as Jewish cultural spheres, while its greatest philanthropists played key roles in endowing the city's major medical and cultural institutions and its major research universities. Their very success, in fact, had become so obvious that they would pose a challenge to

national spokespersons for Jewish self-defense organizations and religious institutions and to the fund-raising arm of the national Democratic Party.

THE BAY AREA: RADICAL ORIGINS OF OUTREACH

In contrast to the dramatic transformations experienced in Los Angeles during the postwar decades, change came more slowly to other Jewish communities in the Pacific West, including the San Francisco area. Earl Raab, in an article on the Jewish community of San Francisco in a 1950 issue of *Commentary*, noted that "the Jewish population has increased, along with the general population, not by spectacular leaps, but by normal accretion."[82] The surge in population that had occurred in San Francisco, as in all other Pacific Coast cities during the war, quickly subsided. The city—confined to its peninsula—seemed to settle back into quiet gentility. As a consequence, among the city's fifty thousand Jews, representatives of "old families" retained control of communal institutions, which seemed well tended. San Francisco had been a center of elite Jewish opposition to Zionism and especially to the establishment of a Jewish state in Palestine. But by 1948, the decision by the Zellerbachs (who, according to Fred Rosenbaum, exercised dominant influence) to bring former army chaplain, labor Zionist, and civil rights activist Alvin Fine to be rabbi at Temple Emanu-El was well accepted.[83] Some observers, like Raab, attributed this new pro-Zionist consensus in part to the many children of Eastern European Jews and to the many German émigrés who had by then joined the congregation. As Raab concluded, "The most remarkable fact of San Francisco is not the vanishing (or shrinking) Jew, but on the contrary, the insistent Jew—the Jew who insists on being a San Francisco Jew despite the historical distance (and geographical distance) from his ethnic origins . . . and the relative isolation and absence of pressures."[84]

Rabbi Fine, however, injected an activism that differed significantly from the quiet political influence exercised by many of his wealthy, conservative Republican congregants. In 1948, he supported the free speech rights of a prominent English clergyman who defended communist causes. In May 1949, he urged a convention of the International Longshore and Warehouse Union, headed by the radical Harry Bridges, not to be intimidated by demagogues, and, in 1952, he opposed the loyalty oath required by the state of all public employees. As the black freedom struggle in the South (led at that point largely by clergymen) gained national publicity, Fine organized a reception for Martin Luther King, Jr., at Temple Emanu-El. By 1963, when Fine was forced by failing health to resign his pulpit, he had encouraged many Jews in the Bay Area to see a defense of civil liberties and civil rights as a key component of a Jewish identity.[85]

Across the San Francisco Bay in Oakland, a portent of liberalization within the synagogues could also be found. In 1952, Harold M. Schulweis, with a new degree from the Conservative Jewish Theological Seminary in New York, accepted a pulpit at Temple Beth Abraham in Oakland. "I enjoyed the West," he recalled, "and I felt it would be more open to experimentation." Like Rabbi Aaron Wise in Los Angeles, Schulweis had been influenced by the innovative views of Mordecai Kaplan. Schulweis accepted women in the minyan and initiated bat mitzvah, and in the era of civil rights he, like Rabbi Fine, started dialogues with black ministers. Schulweis remained at Beth Abraham for eighteen

years, until called to Los Angeles's Valley Beth Shalom in wealthy suburban Encino.[86]

While Schulweis and Fine believed that the religious community should support movements for social justice (fig. 6.3), the local rabbinate would soon find itself facing more divisive Jewish student radicalism. In the early 1960s, Joseph Gumbiner, ordained at Hebrew Union College in the mid-1930s and serving as Hillel rabbi at the University of California, Berkeley, demonstrated his commitment to social justice by participating in the Freedom Rides through Alabama (fig. 6.4).[87] Back on the Berkeley campus he found Jewish students like Jack Weinberg and non-Jews like Mario Savio shifting their focus from support for integration in the South to demonstrations against local businesses whose employment practices were racially discriminatory. Student activists found a willing audience among a rapidly expanding student body that resented paternalistic surveillance and found living space in co-ops and apartments around campus.[88] When members of the university's board of regents pressured the administration to close a strip on the edge of campus that had previously been available to students to distribute political literature, Weinberg, Savio, Art Goldberg, Bettina Aptheker, Jackie Goldberg, and others claimed that their free speech rights were being violated. Large student demonstrations supported them, as did the great majority of the faculty, including many young Jewish professors, who were living in the shadow of the loyalty oath, which Rabbis Fine and Gumbiner had both opposed.[89]

Student demonstrations spread from demands for free speech in a designated area to demands for uncensored content of speech and then to even larger demonstrations against the American war in Vietnam. As the student movement persisted,

observers began to note that except for Savio, who came from a Catholic working-class family, most of the leaders were Jewish. The historian William Rorabaugh has argued that the Jewish participants had no interest in religion and little understanding of Jewish history but brought a passion that reflected "working class, immigrant roots that suggested success came only to those who struggled against power and authority."[90] While some of the Jewish students who picketed for civil rights and later marched to oppose the Vietnam War were from the East, the great majority were Californians, many from west-side Los Angeles neighborhoods that in the 1950s had supported the California Democratic Council. The council, an insurgency within the Democratic Party, drew its support from a well-educated, largely Jewish middle-class that supported civil rights, public housing, and other issues of importance to minorities.[91]

As a counselor to students, Rabbi Gumbiner joined several Protestant clergymen to support the Berkeley free speech movement and its link to the larger civil rights movement.[92] Throughout the 1960s, Rabbi Gumbiner supported civil dissent on campus, but not the personal excesses to which some students gave vent. In the years after 1966, the rise of a black power philosophy that condemned the state of Israel for its treatment of Palestinian Arabs estranged Jewish activists from black radicals.[93] At Berkeley, Jewish students who ardently supported civil rights were divided on how to deal with black power. Generally, they turned inward. Some joined the movement led by Bay Area activists and rabbis, including Gumbiner, to bring freedom to Jews in the Soviet Union, while others sought spiritual renewal in reinterpreted versions of Judaism.[94] In the early 1970s, the university initiated the Berkeley Citation, which celebrates "extraordinary achievement in the recipient's field coupled with outstanding service to the Berkeley campus."[95] In 1971, Rabbi Gumbiner was one of the first recipients.

Rabbi Gumbiner also supported the retrieval of regional Jewish history through the work of Seymour Fromer, who had been recruited to the Bay Area in 1958 to become the first director of the Jewish Education Council of the Jewish Welfare Federation of Alameda and Contra Costa counties. Fromer focused first on preserving the memory of Judah L. Magnes, Bay Area Jewry's most famous international figure, because he found that local Jews had little knowledge of Magnes or of Jews in the East Bay.[96] Fromer and his wife, Rebecca, sought to educate westerners, exhibiting rescued Jewish arts, objects, and manuscripts, and preserving Gold Rush–era Jewish cemeteries in California's mining country. The Fromers cultivated a group of supporters and founded the Judah L. Magnes Museum and the Western Jewish History Center in Berkeley, which has grown into the most important Jewish archive on the Pacific Coast (fig. 6.5).[97]

Attracted by the atmosphere of academic adventure in Berkeley in the 1970s, undergraduates from Los Angeles like David Biale and many friends who had attended Shlomo Bardin's Brandeis College Institute formed the Radical Jewish Union. Publishing a Jewish student newspaper, the *Jewish Radical*, they steered an ideological path that defended Zionism against the secular left while arguing in favor of a Palestinian state against the leadership of the local Jewish federation. Biale's subsequent academic training in modern Jewish history proceeded at UCLA under the direction of Amos Funkenstein, who emphasized "imagination and creativity" that "fit somehow into the California atmosphere of experimentation."[98] Biale's work highlighted the preparation of young scholars who would after 1980 staff new programs in Judaic

FIG. 6.5
Ground breaking for the Reutlinger Gallery addition to the Judah L. Magnes Museum, March 1981. Seymour Fromer, the museum's founder/director, is fourth from left. Western Jewish History Center, Judah L. Magnes Museum (1967). Photograph: Andrew Partos.

studies at private universities like Stanford and at the large public universities along the Pacific Coast.

Berkeley in the 1960s, of course, conjures up not only an image of activist political dissent but also a youth culture perusing Asian religions, mysticism, psychedelic drugs, and percussive music for escape or inspiration. Young Jews joined this search, and men like Allen Ginsberg in the 1950s came to San Francisco, still America's gateway to East Asia, to popularize the cross-fertilization of religious pursuits.[99] A more explicitly Jewish religious expression of this search for spiritual innovation came in 1967, when Shlomo Carlebach and Zalman Schachter, two men who had honed their outreach

skills in the Lubavitch movement in the 1950s, arrived to participate in a folk music festival. They found a welcoming concentration of young people eager for a version of their emotional outreach shorn somewhat of its theological trappings.[100]

The charismatic Carlebach provided the musical aura, inspired by the Hasidic tradition, to introduce innovative ritual, to promote a philosophy of spiritual healing, and to emphasize a communal inclusiveness intended to attract young people to Judaism. He attracted hundreds of followers with his emphasis on the Hasidic idea of *tikkun olam*, "healing the world"; his reliance on music to transform Sabbath and other prayer services;

his use of public spaces like Golden Gate Park for religious rituals; and his tolerance for drugs. While Bardin in the Simi Valley brought cultural innovation, often through dance, music, and arts, in a controlled camp setting to stable teenagers and adults, Carlebach in his House of Love and Prayer in Haight-Ashbury reinvented religious ritual, also using music, to bind individuals in emotional flux to a joyful and permissive version of Judaism.[101]

Although neither Carlebach nor Schachter resided there, the House of Love and Prayer was organized as a commune and functioned as a hostel until 1977, when many of its members moved to a moshav sponsored by Carlebach in Israel. Residents were mostly Jewish young people in a district of San Francisco that also housed the Hare Krishna, a Sufi group headed by Sufi Sam, followers of Meher Baba, Zen Buddhists, and Christian evangelicals like the Jews for Jesus.[102] Assuming a comfortable ecumenical focus, the leaders of the House of Love and Prayer encouraged the study of other religions while combining "the practices of the counterculture with those of Hasidic Judaism."[103] Jewish participation in a regional spiritual realm made distinctive because it was fertilized by Eastern religions was expressed in this experimental bastion of youth culture.[104] In 1974, Schachter held a month-long kabbalah workshop in the Bay Area, and his followers then founded the Aquarian Minyan (fig. 6.6). Over the next few years, hundreds of young people searching for a spiritualized Judaism elevated the Aquarian Minyan into a Renewal congregation, including a number of rabbis, many ordained by Schachter. The Renewal congregations, today often called P'nai Or (Face of Light), meet in rented quarters from Phoenix to Eugene to Seattle, where rabbis like Aryeh Hirschfield and Yitzhak Husbands-Hankin in Oregon constantly modify their own liturgy and add to the religious

music that Carlebach composed.[105] The atmosphere of cultural experimentation and outreach would in the 1980s reverberate through Reform and Conservative synagogues throughout the region and throughout the Jewish world.

Carlebach, like Bardin, hoped to bring individuals to Judaism through a personal encounter, but Michael Lerner, who came to Berkeley from New York in 1964 as a graduate student in philosophy, appropriated the idea of *tikkun olam* for broader political goals. Caught up in the revolt against authority on the Berkeley campus, Lerner believed that the Jewish Theological Seminary in New York, where he had been a student, had, except for Rabbi Abraham Joshua Heschel, ignored social problems. He began a quest to understand how Jewish values might be used to resolve political dilemmas, especially those embroiling the Jewish community. After the Israeli occupation of the West Bank during the 1967 war, for example, many American Labor Zionists like Rabbi Joachim Prinz called for a "two state solution" to what was being redefined as an "Israeli-Palestinian conflict." Lerner founded the Committee for a Progressive Middle East, which as much as any unique proposals for resolving conflicts between Jews and Arabs asserted the autonomy of youth.[106] Turning his search inward in the 1970s, Lerner pursued studies in clinical psychology, founded an East Bay *havurah*, and inspired by the Hasidic tradition initiated study toward ordination with Orthodox rabbis.[107]

In 1986, Lerner and his then wife, Nan Fink, founded *Tikkun* magazine to offset the conservative orientation of *Commentary*, funded by the American Jewish Committee in New York. For Lerner, the Hasidic idea of *tikkun olam* required that Jews abandon moral chauvinism and recognize that each person has the capacity to do good by embodying God's presence.[108] As a practi-

FIG. 6.6
Aquarian Minyan, 1976.
Aquarian Minyan Festschrift.
Photograph: Jeffrey (Gabe)
Dooley. Courtesy of Yehudit
and Reuven Goldfarb.

cal matter, Jews were obliged to hold the Israeli government to high moral standards and to sustain dialogues with Palestinians, something that the Jewish organizational leadership in New York and especially the neoconservatives around *Commentary* refused to do. Within the Jewish community, it meant an embrace of the intermarried, efforts

to convert non-Jewish spouses, and especially efforts to teach their children the Jewish basis for a philosophy of social justice.[109] Lerner remained outside the major Jewish denominations, but his popularization of the idea of *tikkun olam* through *Tikkun* magazine and more recently through online communications has become a mantra for

Reform, Renewal, and many Conservative rabbis on the Pacific Coast and beyond.[110]

QUIESCENT COMMUNITIES: THE PACIFIC NORTHWEST

The extraordinary growth of Los Angeles and the intellectual and political ferment there and in the Bay Area were not reflected in the 1950s and 1960s in the Pacific Northwest. The Jewish communities in Portland and Seattle grew very little in the twenty-five years after World War II and were not invigorated by contingents of activist Jewish students on their periphery.[111] But minimal patterns of growth masked substantial neighborhood change, some institution building, and the beginnings of intergenerational tensions that were being expressed more articulately in California. Between 1950 and 1970, the Jewish population of Seattle increased by 38 percent to reach thirteen thousand, largely by in-migration, while Portland grew far more slowly, increasing by 12 percent, to eight thousand. A report in the *Oregonian* in 1972 on fund-raising for Israel noted that the "Man of the Year," Morris Rosencrantz, belonged to "all three local synagogues."[112] While the reporter overlooked the Sephardic synagogue, Ahavath Achim, whose congregation met only occasionally, Portland apparently had fewer synagogues for the peripatetic Rosencrantz to join than it had had thirty years earlier.

The arrival in Portland of three young rabbis, Joshua Stampfer in 1953 at Conservative Ahavai Shalom, Emanuel Rose in the same year at Reform Temple Beth Israel, and Yonah Geller at Orthodox Shaarei Torah in 1960, brought new vitality. None retired until the first decade of the twenty-first century, thus providing extraordinary continuity in leadership and, in effect, demarking an era in the community's history.[113] In the wake of urban renewal and a decline in membership at the old Conservative synagogue Neveh Zedek, Rabbi Stampfer, whose congregation was attracting young families and doubling in size, suggested a consolidation with his own synagogue. By 1964, the merged congregations, now called Neveh Shalom, constructed a new building in the southwest suburbs, to which many young Jewish families were moving.[114] The Jewish Welfare Federation soon built a new community center nearby. Orthodox Shaarei Torah survived both urban renewal, which forced it to move in 1960 to Portland's Park Blocks, and federal highway construction, which forced a second move in 1964 to northwest Portland, where the congregation constructed a synagogue and a religious school.

Although Beth Israel did not move in this period, the doubling of its congregation, largely through the affiliation of newly arrived families, led it to construct a new school building and greatly expand its staff. Rabbi Rose, when interviewed in 1981, was particularly proud of the professional training of an assistant rabbi, a female cantor, and a female educational director who had emigrated from Israel. But despite the marked growth of the congregation in the 1960s, he was concerned by the early 1980s with the inability of the community to grow, which he correctly attributed to the stagnation of the local economy and, equally important, to his own reticence in addressing the issue creating the most anxiety among his congregants, the intermarriage of their children. Rabbi Rose initially refused to officiate at mixed marriages and watched young people leave the congregation. After wrestling with the issue for several years, he established criteria that would enable him to preside at such ceremonies, which

TABLE 3. Jewish population of selected western and other cities

City	1950	1960	1970	1980	1999
New York City	2,000,000	1,936,000	1,836,000	1,998,000	1,048,900
Greater NYC	xxx	2,401,000	2,381,000	xxx	1,450,000
Miami	40,000	80,000	140,000	225,000	134,000
Hollywood, FL	1,500	49,000	15,000	55,000	213,000
Fort Lauderdale	xxx	1,925	4,000	75,000	xxx
Palm Beach					74,000
Boca Raton					93,000
Los Angeles	225,000	400,000	535,000	503,000	519,000
Long Beach	4,500	9,500	15,000	13,500	15,000
Orange Co. cities	xxx	655†	15,000	40,000	60,000
San Diego	6,000	8,500	11,000	32,500	70,000
San Francisco	50,000	66,000	73,000	75,000	49,500
Oakland	7,500	21,000*	18,000	28,000	32,500
San Jose	1,200	3,800	7,000	15,000	33,000
Portland	7,128	7,900	8,000	8,735	25,000
Seattle	9,500	10,500	13,000	16,000	29,300
Spokane	xxx	750	620	800	1,500
Phoenix	3,500	8,750	13,500	29,000	60,000
Tucson	3,500	6,000	6,500	12,000	20,000
Las Vegas		2,000	2,000	16,000	55,600

SOURCES: *American Jewish Year Book, 1950,* 51:71–73; *American Jewish Year Book, 1961,* 62:57–61; *American Jewish Year Book, 1970,* 71:348–53; *American Jewish Year Book, 1981,* 82: 175–81; *American Jewish Year Book, 2000,* 249–58.

NOTES: Where no data were collected is indicated by xxx. Community surveys or estimates place the 2002 populations of Phoenix at 80,000, San Diego at 89,000, Las Vegas at 80,000, and the San Francisco Bay Area (including San Jose, Oakland, and Berkeley and Marin County) between 400,000 and 450,000. See United Jewish Federation of San Diego County, "The Jewish Community's Strategic Plan," http://sandiego.ujcfedweb.org/content_display.html (accessed July 25, 2008); "Wages of Sin City: Vegas Grows but Lags in Basic Jewish Services," *Forward,* May 3, 2002; Joe Eskenazi, "Bay Area's Growing Jewish Scene," *Ynetnews,* June 3, 2005, http://joi.org/bloglinks/Ynetnews%20-%20Bay%20Area%20growing%20Jewish%20scene.

* Includes Berkeley, Oakland area in Alameda, and Contra Costa counties.

† Data for Santa Ana only.

included the promise by the couple to raise their children as Jews. He noted with much pleasure, "The result has been that I now see the kids. . . . They are members of the Temple and they are here.

I don't accept a burden of responsibility for having said 'no' before, so again it is not a matter of right, wrong; it's just a matter of taking situations and trying to perpetuate Jewish life."[115]

Similarly, Rabbi Stampfer indicated that most of his counseling focused on "potential converts who are exploring Judaism and one simply has to spend a lot of time explaining to them what Judaism is."[116] To respond to the growing need, the three rabbis cooperated to create a course in elementary Judaism for converts.[117] Indeed, as national surveys indicated that intermarriage rates, starting in San Francisco in the 1950s, were higher in western cities than the national average, rabbis and lay counselors along the Pacific Coast would reframe the issue as part of a larger multigenerational pattern of assimilation. Following initiatives in the Bay Area, they would develop innovative strategies of outreach and conversion.[118]

Both Rabbis Stampfer and Rose also raised the perennial issue that had exercised rabbis in Portland and Seattle since the early 1920s and which has become a touchstone to community change, that is, the need for better instruction in Hebrew. During the first three decades of the twentieth century, Portland had had an impressive, centralized Hebrew school, established by men with strong cultural Zionist commitments and supported at first by Neighborhood House and then by the Jewish Welfare Federation. In the 1970s, Portland still had a truncated Hebrew school, called Hillel Academy, which was supported by the federation and temporarily located at Orthodox Shaarei Torah. But the rabbis now saw it, not as an institution promoted by an innovative vanguard, but an underutilized facility supported by an archaic minority. Hillel Academy educated relatively few students and was clearly a victim of shifting residential patterns and cultural values.[119] The rabbis, despite their support of Zionism, criticized the school because they had come to believe that knowledge of Hebrew should be primarily for religious purposes. Rabbi Stampfer, for example, hoped that "there would be

a much better coordination between the Hebrew education they receive and the religious education that they receive."[120] As an antidote to issues of "entrenched power," the rabbis hoped that their own synagogue-sponsored religious schools would resolve the problem.[121]

The rabbis' ideas about the goals of Jewish education and the parents' views of educational priorities in an increasingly assimilated social context framed the ongoing debate over Jewish education. The rabbis suggested that because Portland's Jews were more scattered than previously and because the Reform and Conservative synagogues offered a wider array of services than ever before, members saw the synagogue as the new basis for their institutional loyalty rather than identification with a more abstract idea of community sustained by an immigrant neighborhood. Indeed, the same transfer of loyalty occurred in Seattle as families migrated from the Central District. In both cities, the small synagogues of the 1920s and 1930s had not been able to support their own graded Hebrew schools, but the much wealthier congregations of the 1970s could. In the 1980s, Hillel Academy, as a day school, was renamed the Portland Jewish Academy and relocated to the Jewish Community Center near Beaverton, where it currently educates about 250 youngsters in grades one through eight. But far from being a supplement to public schooling like the old Portland Hebrew School, the new academy provides a culturally Jewish alternative in emulation of a local Episcopal private school.[122]

Even though Portland's Jewish community barely increased in population through the 1970s, it did produce several young men who came to exercise political leadership for the city as a whole. In the years just after the war, lawyers like David Robinson had joined with the African American leader of the local Urban League, William Berry, to press for an end to de facto segregation of down-town businesses and for a state fair employment practice law, which finally was enacted by the state legislature in the mid-1950s. But unlike Los Angeles, whose black and Jewish populations were growing rapidly and whose leaders were struggling to keep abreast of community needs, in Portland only a handful of Jewish lawyers and businessmen, as well as a federal district judge, Gus Solomon, advocated for labor unions, civil liberties, and civil rights.[123] Indeed, in Seattle, leaders of Jewish defense organizations, who were recruited from outside, had to struggle to convince local Jewish businessmen to protest at all against anti-Semitic discrimination in social clubs.[124]

In Portland, Jews who were elected to local office succeeded not because, like Rosalind Wyman, they promoted issues that arose within the Jewish community but because they articulated generalized local needs. A prominent figure was Richard Neuberger, whose parents had owned a popular restaurant in northwest Portland, a district that since the 1920s had held a substantial Jewish population. With a national reputation as a jour-nalist who celebrated the natural beauty of Oregon but who also called for the economic moderniza-tion of Portland, Neuberger was elected to the state senate in 1950. His wife, Maureen, a non-Jew, was elected simultaneously to the state assembly. By 1954, Neuberger was elected to the United States Senate, but with his undemonstrative nature he lived in the shadow of Oregon's senior senator, Wayne Morse. When Neuberger died prematurely of cancer, he was succeeded in office by his wife.

Neuberger's career perhaps inspired younger Jewish men to aspire to political office, because in 1963 Senator Maureen Neuberger hired young Neil Goldschmidt, a Eugene native, as a temporary aide. After graduating from the University of California,

Berkeley, law school, Goldschmidt took a job in Portland as a public defender. Like Richard Neu-berger he joined Jewish organizations, and also like Neuberger he saw himself politically not as a spokesman for Jewish interests but as a catalyst for citizen participation. He quickly came to appreciate the underlying resentments that activists in Port-land's various lower-income neighborhoods held against the city bureaucracy. Through a rousing campaign in 1971 that encouraged neighborhood groups to resist urban renewal, Goldschmidt was elected to the five-person city commission, and two years later, at age thirty-two, he was elected mayor. He quickly enhanced his popularity by creating an agency in city government to formally recognize and consult with neighborhood groups. Goldschmidt gained a national reputation by sup-porting Oregon governor Tom McCall's empha-sis on land-use planning, augmented by his own support of zoning to reroute inner-city traffic and requiring new buildings to have multiple uses. The capstone of his vision for the city was a high-speed rail line to the suburbs, built with federal subsi-dies, to diminish inner-city traffic and attract new businesses downtown.[125] For his charisma and his political skill in turning innovative ideas into pub-lic policy, he was selected to be secretary of trans-portation late in the administration of President Jimmy Carter.[126]

In Seattle, by 1968 the Ashkenazic and Sep-hardic synagogues had left the Central District for neighborhoods farther to the east, and a Jewish Community Center was being built in stages on Mercer Island, which, along with Bellevue, now held the largest contingents of Jews.[127] But the most important sign of population change in the com-munity came with the founding of Reform Beth Am in 1956 in the area north of the University of Washington. New Jewish faculty members often joined, and, in 1962, Rabbi Norman Hirsh arrived to provide youthful and socially conscious leadership that a university community—which, by 1977, included approximately eleven hundred Jewish students—found valuable.[128] Rabbi Hirsh, like the three rabbis in Portland, provided stability by remaining for thirty-three years. The era of suburban synagogue construction commensurate with a new surge of population growth would not occur until the 1980s.

A 1979 Seattle community survey by James McCann reflected demographic changes in the Jewish population, some of which were quite different from Los Angeles, and prompted anxieties similar to those around the country. Community leaders, trying to plan future institutional growth, were alarmed by the apparently loose sense of commitment to the organized community by Jewish residents, especially compared to what had been the case before World War II. The local Jewish population, for example, had become quite elderly compared to the general American population and was even somewhat more elderly than the national Jewish population. More important, those of childbearing age were either less prone to marry or more prone to divorce and had fewer children, and 44 percent of the intact marriages involving a Jewish partner included a non-Jew. In addition, a rather large proportion of the population was unaffiliated with a synagogue or other Jewish organization, which the investigators attributed both to the transience of the local Jewish population and to the low religious affiliation rates for the general population in the region. Commensurate with the aging of the population and the relatively small number of children, most community members responding to the survey felt that the community should care for the elderly and for those facing crises, but they placed

a low priority on Jewish day schools or recreation for youth.[129] Indeed, the migration of both older residents and newcomers to the western suburbs of Bellevue and Mercer Island reflected most of all an extraordinary new affluence rather than communal vitality. The new Mercer Island Jewish Community Center was a response to the migration that the affluence allowed, while the expansions in the 1980s to some extent represented an effort to attract the unaffiliated. As the local Jewish population continued to grow, the community center was substantially expanded. Its program combined recreational facilities for young people with adult education and various clubs and summer camps. When an economic downturn in 1982 left the board unable to meet mortgage payments, the philanthropist Samuel Stroum developed a plan for generating funds and enabled the Jewish Community Center to retain its building.

But Seattle, unlike Portland, contained a unique asset that might be utilized for the Jewish community's long-term nurture, the University of Washington. To accommodate the growing number of Jews settling near the university, in 1984 a branch of the Jewish Community Center was established nearby. Stroum and his wife, Althea, were instrumental in developing a Jewish academic presence at the university, where Stroum served on the board of regents from 1985 to 1998. The Strooms endowed an internationally renowned lecture series, fellowships, and a chair in Jewish studies, which has provided the focus for an expanding and prestigious program.[130] One consequence of the increased affluence of both Seattle and Portland Jewry, augmented by a growing Jewish studies program at the University of Washington and later at Portland State University as well as at Reed College, has been a diminished need to turn to Jewish communities in California for stimulation and leadership.

ON THE CUSP OF NATIONAL ASSERTIVENESS

After 1980, a new pattern of Jewish growth emerged within the Pacific region. Despite a temporarily stalled economy, in the early 1980s Bruce Phillips concluded that "Los Angeles represents the emergence of a new Jewish America in the Sunbelt, particularly in the West."[131] While the continuing growth of Los Angeles Jewry suggested a community shaped by patterns different from the cities of the East, by various demographic and other measures it constituted the most stable community in the region. It did have a smaller proportion of Jews over age sixty and a larger proportion between ages twenty and forty than did large cities with declining Jewish populations like Chicago, Philadelphia, and New York. It also had lower rates of Jewish institutional affiliation and more Jews aged twenty to forty either unmarried or married with no children than did the large eastern population centers. But compared to smaller western cities like Las Vegas, Phoenix, and San Diego, it had a far lower rate of population growth, a lower rate of intermarriage, and an array of well-established centers for religious and cultural education.[132] In 1980, it seemed the cornerstone of a region still growing and developing an unprecedented level of cultural sophistication.

Between 1950 and 1980, several thousand Jews were attracted to the San Francisco area, with the Oakland/Berkeley area almost tripling its Jewish population to twenty-eight thousand. San Jose, which had only twelve hundred Jews in 1950,

by 1980 held more than fifteen thousand, many employed in the electronics industry in "Silicon Valley."[133] At first, cities in Nevada and Arizona hardly seemed touched by a sense of expansion. Tucson, although the home of dozens of Jewish business families in 1950, hardly seemed to have a cohesive Jewish community at all. Benjamin N. Brook, a World War II veteran with a new master's degree in social work from New York University, was recruited in 1949 to become the first executive director of Tucson's new Jewish Community Council. When he arrived from the intense Jewish world of New York, he noted the lack of a Jewish residential area or of any tension between Jewish social classes. "I also sensed," he wrote, "that what held the Jewish people in Tucson was the feeling of freedom and equality. . . . On the whole it was a free, open community."[134]

But when the cities of the Southwest did start to grow dramatically in the 1980s, their Jewish communities grew even faster. The explanation lies largely with the economic trajectories of the specific cities, which depended on defense contracts, the growth of research universities for computer software design, electrical engineering and biotechnology, and the reinvention of gambling and conventions as lavish entertainment. As young Jews in the East and Midwest acquired the engineering, accounting, medical, or research skills to make them mobile, they located to cities that needed their services. As James McCann concluded, "High levels of education and professional training qualify incumbents for a national labor market and thus increase the likelihood they will settle outside the community in which they were raised." The extension of a growth rate formerly unique to Los Angeles and to Jewish communities in nearby cities was confirmed by a survey done in 1983 in

Phoenix. In the early 1980s, the Phoenix area was growing at a rate faster than any city of comparable size in the nation, as electronics firms like Motorola and Intel expanded into the adjoining cities of Chandler and Mesa.[135] By 1983, Phoenix was estimated to have more than forty-three thousand year-round Jewish residents (more than twice as many as Seattle), 58 percent of whom had arrived in the previous decade. In addition, while Phoenix had already attracted thousands of retirees from the Midwest, compared to Seattle it had a larger proportion of children, a larger proportion of young adults between ages twenty-five and thirty-four, and a smaller proportion of persons over age sixty-five.[136]

As with Los Angeles after the war, Phoenix was attracting young families, but the newcomers were also far better educated than those arriving in Los Angeles twenty years earlier had been. In Phoenix, 71 percent of Jewish men between ages eighteen and thirty-nine—most of whom were newcomers—had earned at least undergraduate degrees. Not surprisingly, 60 percent of Jewish men in Phoenix with full-time employment were either managers or professionals.[137] Even though in Seattle half of employed Jewish men under age forty-five were professionals and another 26 percent were man-

agers,[138] the economic expansion was far greater in Los Angeles and Phoenix than in the Pacific Northwest, so most young Jews coming West in the early 1980s were settling there. The religious infrastructure—the synagogues and community centers—remained as yet largely unaffected.

The Pacific West in the mid-1980s was about to undergo yet another growth spurt, again propelled by industries in which Jews would heavily participate. In the West of the late twentieth century, in Jewish communities dominated by business and professional men and women, visionaries like Bardin and Carlebach would see affirmed their mission to reorient Jewish identity away from denominational affiliation and toward individual inquiry and ritual innovations. Rabbis and secular leaders would seek to "heal" the rifts within Jewish communities and assuage the tensions between Jews and their neighbors. As individuals with a need for Jewish religious leadership formed new congregations and sought professional guidance, they would hire young rabbis, often born in the West, with a more inclusive view of Judaism. The network of Jewish institutions and philanthropies would gain unprecedented visibility, and Jewish influence in civic life would reach unprecedented proportions (plate 7).

EPILOGUE

Aspiring to National Leadership

The kosher section at Smith's—a $700,000 investment
for the Mormon-owned supermarket chain—is the latest
evidence of the explosion of Jewish life that has taken
place here [Las Vegas] in the past 15 years. —2004

The themes that have shaped the Jewish communities of the
Pacific West since the Gold Rush—selective migration to a
distant frontier, concentration in the largest cities as pioneering merchants and professionals, civic prominence and philanthropic
leadership, and cultural diversity and outreach—have persisted into
the twenty-first century. The regional center remains Los Angeles. Its
Jewry has grown larger, but more important its institutions are far better endowed, more sophisticated, and by design more fully integrated
into the life of the general community.[1] Newcomers from Israel, Latin
America, and especially Iran have also made Los Angeles Jewry more
distinctive than ever, a Jewish segment of the globalized economy in
which Los Angeles plays so large a part.[2] And the enormous growth of
Jewish communities in Las Vegas, Phoenix, San Diego, and the cities
south of San Francisco has created autonomous centers. Older Jews, like
older gentiles, who retired from work in Los Angeles, sought a slower
pace and less expensive property in or near these smaller cities. But far
from finding peace and quiet, they have found rapidly sprawling urban
complexes, where young Jews continue to seek professional employment

213

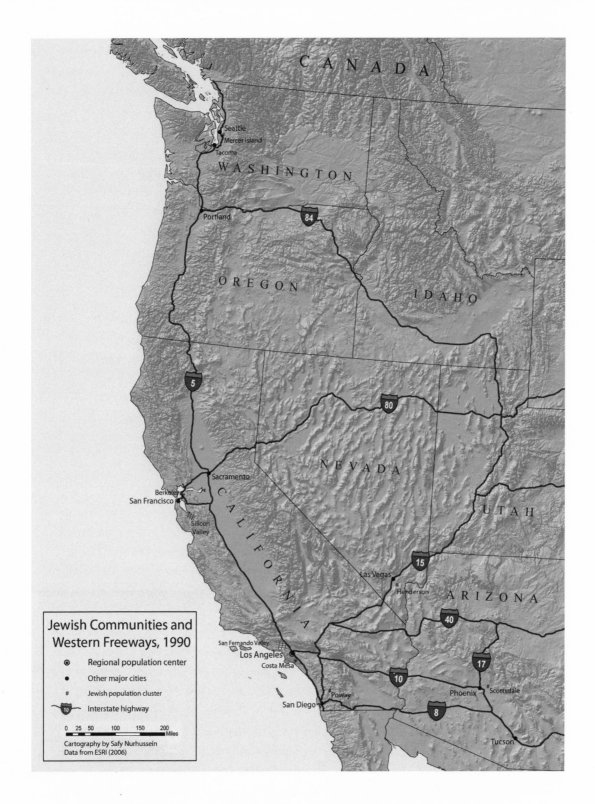

MAP 2. *Jewish Communities and Western Freeways, 1980. Map prepared by Safy Nurhussein.*

Within the image:

Jewish Communities and
Western Freeways, 1990

⊙   Regional population center

●   Other major cities

Jewish population cluster

🛣 10   Interstate highway

0 25 50   100   150   200
                                Miles

Cartography by Safy Nurhussein
Data from ESRI (2006)

and business opportunities among the millions of new immigrants from Mexico, Central America, and East Asia, whose presence has again transformed the urban West.[3]

The enormous expansion of the public universities and the subsidy of engineering research by the Department of Defense have drawn thousands of young professors and graduate students to the West, especially to California. From their ranks have come engineers, many of them Jewish, who have capitalized on their inventions to create companies that, like the department stores of one hundred years ago, have become some of the largest employers in their respective cities. Like the mercantile pioneers of the Gold Rush era, the engineer-entrepreneurs have encouraged thousands of others, again many of them Jews, to open smaller firms, which comprise a major segment of the region's new economic base.[4] One recent study shows that in the Los Angeles area Jews have made a rapid transition from an exceptional concentration in small businesses to an even greater concentration in a few professions like law, medicine, psychology, and the movies that require high levels of education, result in high incomes, and constitute virtually a "post industrial ethnic niche."[5] From this base has come the financial support for the religious and cultural infrastructure observed in the community centers and synagogues in "edge cities" like Scottsdale, Henderson, San Mateo, and Poway that have become the new instant cities of the western Jewish landscape.[6] Within the universities, public as well as private, Jewish philanthropy has since the 1980s endowed Jewish studies centers, which enable students to see the Jewish heritage afforded equal status in the liberal arts curriculum. Universities like Stanford or UCLA have attracted distinguished scholars, while directors of Jewish studies programs at "commuter"

universities like Portland State, San Diego State, or California State, Northridge, often see their audience as the general public as well as students and view their mission as "programming" to spread Jewish knowledge.[7]

Also as in the era of the Gold Rush, Jewish entrepreneurial achievement created the base for pervasive political leadership. Reflecting the sea change in gender relations, however, Jewish women especially emerged as mayors in San Francisco, Portland, and San Diego; as congresswomen in Las Vegas and San Diego; and, of course, as California's two senators, former congresswoman Barbara Boxer and former San Francisco mayor Dianne Feinstein. The immense expansion of the Hispanic population has led to the election of many women and men of Mexican descent to pubic office in southern California. In the sprawling area between the Ventura county line and the Mexican border, only seven "white" Democrats still represent districts in the House of Representatives. All are Jewish. And as a consequence of their "survival," Jewish leaders in California now feel that their expertise in creating interethnic bridges should play a vanguard role in helping Jewish America in general adjust to the nation's new ethnic politics.[8]

The political prominence of West Coast Jewish politicians, however, highlights a growing tension within American Jewry. The increased proportion of Jews now living in the Pacific West has led local officers of major Jewish organizations in Los Angeles especially to believe that their political priorities should have greater weight in national Jewish affairs. They believe that the philosophies of Jewish life that first achieved currency on the Pacific Coast and that emphasize inclusion, outreach, and loose denominational loyalties—philosophies that mark western religious life in general—should have a greater impact on national Jewish life.[9] A brief sketch of how the population boom stretched the boundaries and enriched the institutional life of a cohesive region should also suggest why local leaders have reassessed the national significance of their constituency.

LOS ANGELES: AN ENHANCED CENTER

Within Los Angeles, much of the new commercial construction has been directed along the Wilshire Boulevard corridor to Century City, a complex of office towers situated on the old Twentieth Century Fox lot. Working in this area are many Jewish professionals, especially in financial services, which, along with motion pictures and thousands of small electronics and manufacturing firms, have replaced heavy industry as the region's primary source of economic growth and key points of contact with the global economy of the Pacific Rim.[10] Residentially, Jews with higher incomes, rather than scatter randomly, remain clustered in a small subset of expensive neighborhoods, many quite close to Century City.[11] Jews have chosen to live in these neighborhoods in part because of the prior existence of Jewish residents, the relative cost of housing, or the attractiveness of specific locales. The migration to the San Fernando Valley has continued, while smaller contingents moved farther west to Agoura Hills and Ventura, and still others moved south to Orange County. In 1986, two hundred thousand Jews (an addition of about eighty thousand since the early 1960s) lived in the San Fernando Valley, and the areas of highest "Anglo" concentration like Calabasas, Encino, Sherman Oaks, and Studio City remain the areas of heaviest Jewish settlement.[12] Since the move toward Ventura was often of lower-income people, some of Orthodox background,

Chabad has established a headquarters in Agoura Hills, and its emissaries have opened more than half a dozen small houses for worship and pre-schools in smaller cities throughout the area.[13]

As Jews have moved they have become caught in the political struggles of the area. The continuing growth of the San Fernando Valley, for example, has led many residents to resent what they feel is an inadequate response of city government to their need for services. Jews, since the 1950s accustomed to political assertiveness in Los Angeles, have been among the leaders of a political reaction against the control of city government by Democratic liberals.[14] In the late 1970s, less affluent areas of the Valley like Northridge resisted a plan to desegregate public schools by busing their children to minority neighborhoods near the center of the city. Two Jewish parents, Bobbie Fiedler and Roberta Weintraub, were elected to the Los Angeles school board to oppose busing. In the fall of 1980, Fiedler, running as a Republican, defeated incumbent Democrat James Corman for a seat in the House of Representatives, which she held for three terms.[15]

At the other end of the political spectrum, liberal Jewish leaders in 1992, in response to the riots in the wake of the acquittal of police officers who had beaten the African American motorist Rodney King, encouraged interracial coalitions to rebuild Los Angeles. Rabbis like John Rosove of Temple Israel in Hollywood, Harvey Fields of Wilshire Boulevard Temple, and Laura Geller, then executive director of the local office of the American Jewish Congress, encouraged cleanup activities, diversity training sponsored by David Lehrer of the local office of the ADL, and the passage of a Los Angeles Charter Amendment giving the police commission greater authority over the police department. Rabbi Geller, who in 1994 became senior rabbi at Temple Emanuel in Beverly

Hills, came to play perhaps the longest-lasting role by sponsoring a social justice committee at her synagogue.[16] A new dimension of social justice also received institutional expression in 1992, when Reform Congregation Kol Ami was organized in West Hollywood to promote feminist Jewish theology and to reach out to gays and lesbians. Its spiritual leader, Rabbi Denise Eger, has received many awards from local gay and lesbian organizations, much as Rabbi Nieto was honored by San Francisco's labor unions almost one hundred years ago.[17]

Jews still largely vote for Democrats, and their persistence and cohesiveness have led to the ascent of Zev Yaroslavsky from advocate for Soviet Jewry to city councilman from Beverly-Fairfax to Los Angeles county commissioner, where he represents more than two million constituents. Yaroslavsky gained citywide attention in 1986 when he and fellow west-side Jewish councilman Marvin Braude sponsored a ballot initiative that limited future high-rise development in the city, except in the downtown area and along the Wilshire corridor in his own district.[18] Yaroslavsky has subsequently combined the national Jewish emphasis on the defense of Israel with the local Jewish concern for pollution control and for building coalitions with the city's Latino majority to constitute a regional Jewish agenda.[19]

As ethnic tensions persisted, the Jewish community of Los Angeles looked to institutions like the Museum of Tolerance, and especially the new Skirball Cultural Center, which opened its first building in 1996, for educational enrichment and outreach to the general public. In keeping with the postwar idea that Jewish institutions in Los Angeles should explore the relationship between Jews and the cultures in which they are embedded, the Skirball Center—unlike the Wiesenthal Cen-ter—uses its exhibits to situate Jews triumphantly in the American experience (plate 8).[20] Echoing the local consensus on Jewish commitment to a multicultural city, Uri Herscher, the founder and chief executive officer of the Skirball, told the *New York Times* that the center "is designed to tell the story of how Jewish tradition, Jewish values, and Jewish vision intersect with the fabric of American life."[21]

The columnist Gene Lichtenstein, writing in the *Jewish Journal of Greater Los Angeles*, noted that the educational focus of the Skirball and the Wiesenthal centers has brought non-Jews into the Jewish experience and brought Jews into the center of the city's civic life. Jewish philanthropy has also provided the bulk of the funding for a variety of museums, including the Los Angeles County Museum of Art, the Museum of Contemporary Art, the Pasadena Museum of California Art, the Norton Simon Museum in Pasadena, the Armand Hammer Museum (run by UCLA), and even the J. Paul Getty Museum. Lichtenstein noted that "one result is that it blurs the line of living apart, or being an outsider in gentile America."[22] As Jews remain virtually the only white population group within the city whose numbers have not declined, their commitment to public art symbolizes their exceptional prominence and their commitment to civic inclusiveness.[23]

STABILITY THROUGH DIVERSITY: THE ISRAELI AND IRANIAN PRESENCE

Since the 1920s, Los Angeles, perhaps originally because of its climate, has attracted Jewish migrants directly from the Middle East, and the visibility of Middle Eastern Jews has been among the community's distinguishing features. As George Sanchez recently noted, the emigration of Jews from Israel and Iran, as well as from Latin America and Russia, "now play[s] a fundamental role in shaping whatever Jewish identity is that can be considered western in Los Angeles."[24] In the 1970s, émigrés from Israel came to Los Angeles because their level of skills, resources, and social ties connected them to networks in both countries.[25] The Israelis, however, brought intense ideological baggage, because their government and country-men through the early 1990s disparaged emigra-tion and often derided them as *yordim*, that is, those descending from Zion and traitors to Zionist ideals.[26] But from their arrival, Israelis reinforced the influence of Shlomo Bardin by staffing Hebrew schools and introducing Israeli cuisine and culture to the region. According to one successful business-man, Israelis felt far less alienated in California than in the Northeast. "In California we have the Latino population and many other populations, and many recent immigrants. You hardly notice that actually anything changes when they [Ameri-cans] talk to you. So I would say, in California we didn't feel as a minority, or an outsider. In New England, which is more homogeneous—from time to time—yes, we did feel it."[27]

A survey in 1983 placing the number of Israelis in Los Angeles at up to one hundred thousand was greatly exaggerated. The federal census of 2000 found that about fourteen thousand Angelenos had been born in Israel, but a sociological study found that more than twenty-six thousand claimed to be of Israeli nationality.[28] As Steven J. Gold notes, the sense of collective loyalty has been stronger among Israeli émigrés in Los Angeles, and their social net-works link them to both countries, so many Israelis may have returned to their homeland. But when some émigrés proposed a separate Israeli federa-tion, other prominent spokesmen—in contrast to

the leaders of the Persian community—opposed the idea.[29]

A far more conspicuous source of diversity has been the relocation since 1980 of perhaps as many as thirty thousand Jewish émigrés from Iran. Ayatollah Ruholla Khomeini's revolution in 1979 sent hundreds of thousands of Iranians, dispro-portionately minorities like the Baha'i, Armenians, and Jews, into exile.[30] While émigrés from Rus-sia and Israel were more likely to settle in New York, Persians, perhaps because of the climate or their greater affluence, disproportionately came to Los Angeles.[31] Each of the Iranian religious com-munities organized its own resettlement, with a conspicuous contingent of Jews settling into what was already a largely Jewish—and very affluent—area in Beverly Hills. A recent survey suggests that perhaps eight thousand of Beverly Hill's thirty-five thousand residents are Iranian.[32]

Iranian Jews are known for their concentration in the jewelry, textile, and imported rug businesses, all located downtown, to form what Joel Kotkin calls a Middle Eastern "Casbah trading culture."[33] They have located in the same lofts that Eastern European Jews had used to create the garment industry in the 1920s and 1930s. Expanding on the regional emphasis on lower-cost sportswear, both American and Iranian Jews have found a better environment for start-up firms in Los Angeles than in New York. And Persian Jewish émigrés seem more comfortable doing business with one another or with émigré Israelis who also have Persian roots.[34]

Because Iranian Jews, like the Sephardim in the early twentieth century, initially hoped to return to their homeland, were accustomed to commu-nal self-support, and felt uncomfortable among American Jews, they started their own welfare organizations and their own federation.³⁵ For religious worship many Iranians have founded their own synagogues, but a large number have joined the Conservative Sinai Temple in West Los Angeles. After two decades they have assumed leading roles on the board of directors, the men's club, and the sisterhood. Jimmy Delshad, the temple's president from 1999 to 2001, was elected mayor of Beverly Hills in 2007.³⁶ Rabbi David Wolpe, a national leader of the Conservative movement who has held the Sinai pulpit since 1997, noted diplomatically that the antagonism between Iranian and American congregants has "evaporated out of respect for each other's contributions."³⁷ The ability of Iranian congregants to use their Magbit Foundation to raise substantial amounts of money for philanthropic causes like college scholarships in Los Angeles and medical and educational projects in Israel has contributed to Rabbi Wolpe's sanguine view.³⁸

Unlike most immigrant groups, Iranian Jews have been driven into American politics, not by local concerns, but because they fear for the survival of Israel and the treatment of their relatives in Iran.³⁹ Lacking exposure to a liberal political culture, Iranian Jews, like most Iranian émigrés, have built their political views on anticommunism and conservative values rather than on issues that encourage ethnic coalitions.⁴⁰ By the late 1990s, they had created their own political action committees and responded with demonstrations in the streets of West Los Angeles when Jews in Iran were threatened. Perhaps because of their fear for Israel, their desire to dislodge the regime of the ayatollahs, or their opposition to government welfare programs, Iranian Jews have likened themselves to Cuban exiles rather than to American Jews and have supported Republicans. Indeed, local Jews

critical of Israel's treatment of the Palestinians consider Iranian Jews to be their primary local antagonists.⁴¹

URBAN CENTERS AS CULTURAL PERIPHERIES

While the Los Angeles Jewish community has responded to internal ethnic diversity and enjoyed its new national political prominence, communities in nearby cities have grown at rates very much like the growth of the San Fernando Valley in the 1950s. The opening and rapid expansion of a new University of California campus at Irvine in the late 1960s, for example, attracted a large number of Jewish professionals. Linda Beral, the founder in 1981 of the American Jewish Committee's Orange County branch, saw two even larger waves of Jewish migration to the area. In the late 1970s, the advent of busing in the Los Angeles public schools reputedly drove some Jews south to Santa Ana. In the mid-1990s, in the wake of the contraction of the aerospace industry in Los Angeles, new high-tech businesses relocated to Irvine, and thousands of Jews followed. Henry Samueli, who grew up in the Westwood neighborhood of Los Angeles and became a professor of electrical engineering at UCLA, typified the new academics who merged university research with entrepreneurial instincts to fund public, private, and Jewish philanthropic institutions. When Samueli's Defense Department research at UCLA declined in 1990, he founded the Broadcom Corporation to apply his engineering innovations to private uses. In 1995, he relocated the firm to Irvine. Samueli then endowed both universities, which would produce future high-tech employees, as well as a new synagogue and community center that reconnected him to his ethnic and religious origins.[42] The cities of Orange County also attracted Orthodox Jews from South Africa, which perhaps explains why Chabad has developed an impressive presence and why three Jewish day schools have a combined enrollment of more than one thousand pupils. By 2000, as Beth Krom, a Democrat and one of two Jews on the Irvine city council, noted while buying meat at a new kosher butcher shop in Tustin: "We're in the middle of a huge evolution."[43]

Farther south in San Diego, the Jewish community experienced equally large growth and a cultural renaissance that carried the community far beyond its nineteenth-century mercantile roots. A survey by the Jewish Welfare Federation in 2004, the first in San Diego's history, found eighty-nine thousand Jews and twenty-nine thousand non-Jews living in forty thousand households that identified themselves as Jewish. The community had grown as large as that of Phoenix and with an equivalent household composition. As in Phoenix and Las Vegas, less than half of the area's Jews had lived there for more than twenty years, about the same proportion as in Los Angeles twenty-five years before.[44]

The rapid expansion of local Jewry further illustrates the attachment of young Jews to new areas of scientific research and their willingness, like most highly educated Americans of their generation, to migrate in pursuit of new opportunities. The perception of San Diego as a center of biomedical research was pioneered in 1961, when Jonas Salk, then perhaps the most revered research scientist in America for his discovery of a vaccine against the polio virus, used a large grant from the March of Dimes and a gift of land from the city to start a research institute at La Jolla.[45] While Salk was not an active member of the local Jewish community,

the welcome he received from the city, as well as the subsequent growth of the University of California, San Diego, suggested that Jews could feel comfortable in what had been a navy town. Indeed, the creation of UC San Diego, adjacent to the Salk Institute in the late 1960s, like the creation of UC Irvine, ended restrictions against Jewish home ownership in the immediate area. One of the first young professors to come to the San Diego campus was Irwin Jacobs, who arrived from the Massachusetts Institute of Technology in 1966. Over the next two decades Jacobs developed communication theories and technical applications for use in cell phones. But, more important, he pioneered links between university research and entrepreneurship by starting several companies, including Linkabit (1969) and QUALCOM (1986). His colleagues were two other Jewish innovators in communications technology at UCLA, Leonard Kleinrock and Andrew Viterbi. With the decline of San Diego's aerospace industry after 1990, QUALCOM has become the city's largest industrial employer. Jacobs and his wife, Joan, have become the city's largest philanthropists by endowing the university's school of engineering and also the Jacobs Family Campus at the new La Jolla Jewish Community Center.[46]

The Jewish community has also shifted geographically in conjunction with its growth and new affluence. During the 1950s and 1960s, the small population of Jewish storekeepers had moved eastward from downtown to the area around San Diego State University. But by the 1990s, Jews redistributed themselves by income, age, and stage of life. Among the six areas of Jewish residential concentration, La Jolla, for example, held 17 percent of the Jewish population and relocated Reform Congregation Beth Israel. These were the most affluent and primarily older people.[47] Middle-income families with children were moving into an area called "North County Inland" around the city of Poway, while even larger numbers of Jews were moving up the coast to Encinitas.[48]

Surveys of other Jewish communities since 2000 amplify this picture of sprawling growth and new internal tensions. A study of Phoenix in 2002 recorded a 138 percent increase in the Jewish population since the last survey in 1983, a rate of increase almost double that of the city as a whole. In 2002, Jews numbered approximately eighty-three thousand, with twenty-four thousand additional non-Jews living in households headed by a Jewish person. By then the area had thirty-nine synagogues, two Jewish community centers, a welfare federation, and four Jewish day schools. It also supported a variety of services for college students at Arizona State University. With a rapid dispersal of Jews away from central Phoenix to Scottsdale in the northeast and to Chandler in the southeast, community leaders found that both newcomers and senior citizens felt a sense of disaffiliation.[49]

Even more than to Phoenix, the image of mushrooming Jewish growth in the 1990s was attached to Las Vegas, a city whose cultural veneer has extended excess to such proportions that it has defined a new aesthetic. Young entrepreneurs like Steve Wynn, who wished to reposition gambling as part of family entertainment and mass tourism, convinced the government of Nevada in the late 1970s to change the requirements for casino ownership so that national corporations and Wall Street banks could invest. By the early 1980s, hotel chains bought out individual crime figures and turned Las Vegas into the country's largest convention center.[50] In the 1990s, the old casinos with their aura of criminality were dramatically imploded, and Jewish impresarios like Wynn and Sheldon Adelson (the son of a Boston taxi driver),

as well as non-Jewish developers like Kirk Kerkorian, built billion-dollar entertainment/gambling extravaganzas that conjure a pastiche of images so garish and yet on such a vast scale that the world can only stare in disbelief at the extraordinary spectacle.[51]

Beneath the glitz, a new, professionalized managerial elite, many of whose members are Jewish, has asserted control. The corporations as well as Jewish and non-Jewish entrepreneurs who own the hotel-casinos have hired lawyers and business administrators with MBAs from Harvard and the Wharton School to provide the best-educated managers in the world.[52] A self-conscious, assertive Jewish community has outgrown the aspirations of the original casino managers, who gave their shady business life a respectable veneer by building auditoriums and school buildings at Reform Temple Beth Shalom.[53] By 2002, Jewish Las Vegas was estimated at eighty thousand, with nineteen synagogues, and three Chabad houses. As in San Diego, the Las Vegas Jewish community is also residentially segmented by age and income, with many retirees living in the northwest in Summerlin, while many younger families live to the southeast in Henderson. Without a Jewish community center, the various groups seemed to lack focus until one clever observer noted that a new freeway around the rim of the city joined the two suburbs. "In the American West, which is marked by vast spaces and stubborn individualism, and where the car is king, it seems only fitting that a six-lane stretch of blacktop is the road to community."[54]

Sudden growth has characterized not only the Jewish communities of the Sun Belt but the oldest western Jewish center, San Francisco, and even more so the educational centers on its edges like Berkeley and Palo Alto. A survey in 2004 of the San Francisco Bay Area Jewish population showed a doubling since the mid-1980s, a rate much more rapid than for the general population and remarkable for a region whose Jewish population had been stagnant for decades. With an estimated population of at least 450,000 Jews, the Bay Area now holds the fourth largest clustering of Jews in the country. As in Phoenix and Las Vegas, most Jews moved to suburban areas, particularly toward the center of the electronics industry south of San Francisco in the Silicon Valley. For the first time, the cities of the "South Peninsula" like San Mateo and Palo Alto, which have become a center for families with young children, held more Jews than did the metropolis.[55] Their congressional representative from 1980 to 2008 was Tom Lantos, the only Holocaust survivor elected to the House of Representatives, who developed an international reputation as a defender of human rights.[56]

In San Francisco, the Jewish Community Federation has responded to the political activism of a newly vocal group, gays and lesbians, who have settled there because the local political atmosphere encourages inclusion. Harvey Milk, the first openly gay man elected a city supervisor in San Francisco, attended services at Reform Congregation Sha'ar Zahav in the Mission District in the 1970s.[57] In the mid-1980s, according to Avi Rose, then in charge of the AIDS project for the Jewish Family and Children's Service in San Francisco, "we were really the first Jewish community to take this on full-time in terms of delivering direct services to Jews with AIDS, doing education and prevention work, and mobilizing the Jewish community."[58] Shortly thereafter the Reform movement formed an AIDS committee for the national coordination of congregational work that had begun at Sha'ar Zahav and was assumed quickly in most major population centers. In 1997, the San Francisco federation, pushed by an openly gay board member,

created a task force to study how the Jewish community should provide whatever unique outreach gay members might need. Yair Silverman, rabbi of Orthodox Congregation Beth Israel in Berkeley, echoes the mood of East Bay Jewry when he notes, "We want to be counter to the American mainstream . . . isn't religion a force of social change? It ought to be that everywhere, and it certainly is in Berkeley."[59]

ASSERTION OF REGIONAL AUTONOMY

The demographic growth and political success of western Jewish communities and the philosophy of inclusiveness their leaders espouse has led to some friction with national Jewish leaders, primarily in New York. An estimate of Jewish populations drawn from a very small sample by the veteran San Francisco demographer Gary Tobin suggested that the National Jewish Population Survey coordinated in New York in 2000–2001 provided an undercount of the national Jewish population by 28 percent and an undercount of western Jewry by 44 percent. "Something in the sampling methodology has missed significant portions of Jews in the West," Tobin said.[60] Adding up the populations of California and the growing communities of Las Vegas, Phoenix, Tucson, and Seattle, Tobin believed that the New York group had missed as many as a half million Jews in the West. Tobin argued, in effect, that the New York group counted Jews individually and defined a Jew in the traditional way by religious identification. Tobin took what he felt was a broader and more realistic view of what now constitutes a Jewish community, at least as he observed it in the Bay Area. He defined a Jewish community by its households, most of which, especially in the West, included a non-Jew, who became for Tobin a member of the "community."[61] Spokesmen for the New York group dismissed Tobin's loose definition of who should be included in a survey of Jews.[62] Their differences came to symbolize two contradictory views of both the proper content and purpose of a Jewish community, each identified with scholarly authorities on the East and West coasts.[63]

The surge in Jewish population growth in the West since the mid-1980s has led to some friction between western affiliates and national leaders who assert the historical dominance of their headquarters. In a 2002 article, the Jewish Telegraphic Agency reporter Tom Tugend noted a "widespread conviction by those in southern California that the top professionals who run national Jewish organizations are unwilling to grant meaningful decision-making latitude to their regional outpost in America's second largest Jewish community."[64] Such convictions have been inflamed by and have shaped the perception of conflicts between the Los Angeles branches of organizations like the ADL and the American Jewish Congress and the national leadership in New York. For example, in a major confrontation in December 2001, the longtime director of the Los Angeles branch of the ADL, David Lehrer, was "summoned to New York," according to Tugend, and fired by the national director, Abraham Foxman.[65] Lehrer, who was born in Los Angeles and holds a law degree from UCLA, had during his long tenure with the ADL beginning in 1973 promoted interracial dialogue, especially a new initiative with Latino leaders, on which he felt the influence of the Los Angeles Jewish community continued to rest.[66] Los Angeles Jewry provided 10 percent of the national ADL budget, more than any other section, and had seen its income triple under Lehrer's direction. Given these initiatives, many Jewish Angelenos were stunned by Lehrer's ouster. ADL officials in New York asserted that the firing was not an indication of regional ideological or policy disagreements, but Los Angeles coverage had cast the confrontation in exactly those terms.[67]

This sense of a divide between East and West was expressed by community leaders at a conference in November 2005 at the Autry National Center in Los Angeles. Congressman Henry Waxman, the journalist Joel Kotkin, Rabbis David Wolpe and Daniel Bouskila of Sephardic Temple Tifereth Israel, and the Iranian UCLA scholar Nahid Pirnazar agreed that their community had become the focal point for an entire region whose distinctive—they used the word "unique"—patterns of growth were redefining American Jewry. Los Angeles Jewry, they felt, stood apart because of the continuing cultural diversity of newcomers, the ability of spokespersons for newcomers quickly to become a part of communal leadership, and because the community's "outreach" stressed coalition building with other ethnic groups. As Congressman Waxman put it, "People here aren't pigeonholed as they are in the East. They can become part of the community right away." As a case in point, Professor Pirnazar explained how after only two decades Iranian Jews had entered the larger civic life.[68]

Though scholars have measured the demographic dimensions of the Jewish migration west, they are only slowly coming to appreciate its consequences for reallocating Jewish resources, identifying American Jewish leadership, and even redefining American culture. Politically, Jewish leadership is shifting away from New York, across the country in general and certainly with a key component along the Pacific Coast. Psychologically, the moral evaluation of Jewish behavior has accommodated to shifts that began in the West but have now moved across the country. This prong of the postwar Jewish migration has integrated Jews into the most dynamic patterns of American economic, political, and cultural innovation at a crucial node of the Pacific Rim. It has created new centers of power, a new emphasis on outreach in community building, and new icons of Jewish culture. As Rabbi Wolpe has concluded, a new paradigm affording parity to western patterns of Jewish community development is needed if a balanced understanding of American Jewish history is to be achieved. A projection of these themes into the future suggests that American Jewry will have multiple centers, competing ideologies, and contending leadership elites.

INTRODUCTION: WESTERN LANDSCAPES, WESTERN JEWS

Epigraph. Daily Evening Herald (Marysville, Calif.), October 3, 1853, 3, quoted in Ava F. Kahn, *Jewish Voices of the California Gold Rush: A Documentary History, 1849–1880* (Detroit: Wayne State University Press, 2002), 390.

1. For example, the 2006 Biennial Scholars' Conference on American Jewish History featured several panels including an opening plenary session on regionalism. The subject was also featured in "A Sense of Place," ed. Deborah Dash Moore and Dale Rosengarten, special issue, *American Jewish History* 93, no. 2 (2007).

2. For a discussion of how westerners, including Native Americans, transformed the space of the West into a landscape embodying different sacred dimensions, see Richard V. Francaviglia, *Believing in Place: A Spiritual Geography of the Great Basin* (Reno: University of Nevada Press, 2003), 1–19. For a criticism of the historiography of the American West for failing to consider the importance of cities and ethnic groups, see Richard W. Etulain, "Visions and Revisions: Recent interpretations of the American West," in *Writing Western History: Essays on Major Western Historians*, ed. Richard W. Etulain (Albuquerque: University of New Mexico Press, 1991), 339–43, 346–50.

3. Bauman concludes that "the issues raised here point to the existence of patterns across regional boundaries. They assume that the factors in American and Jewish history affecting acculturation and tradition bred greater similarities both qualitatively and quantitatively than differences." Mark K. Bauman, *The Southerner as American: Jewish Style* (Cincinnati: American Jewish Archives, 1996), 30. See also Bauman, "Southern Jewish Women and Their Social Service Organizations," *Journal of American Ethnic History* 22, no. 3 (2003): 34; Mark K. Bauman and Bobbi Malone, eds., introduction to "Directions in Southern Jewish History," special issue, *American Jewish History* 85, nos. 3–4 (1997): 191–93.

4. Gary Zola, "Why Study Southern Jewish History?" *Southern Jewish History* 1 (1998), quoted in Marcie Cohen Ferris and Mark I. Greenberg, eds., introduction to *Jewish Roots in Southern Soil: A New History* (Hanover, N.H.: University Press of New England / Brandeis University Press, 2006), 2.

5. Ferris and Greenberg, *Jewish Roots in Southern Soil*, 2.

6. Laurie F. Maffly-Kipp, "'Eastward Ho!' American Religion from the Perspective of the Pacific Rim," in *Retelling U.S. Religious History*, ed. Thomas Tweed (Berkeley: University of California Press, 1997), 132.

7. John Higham, *Send These to Me* (Baltimore: Johns Hopkins University Press, 1984), 142–44; see also Jonathan D. Sarna, "The Jews of Boston in Historical Perspective," in *The Jews of Boston*, ed. Jonathan D.

Sarna and Ellen Smith (Boston: Jewish Philanthropies of Greater Boston, 1995), 4.

8. Jacob Nieto, editorial in the *Jewish Times (San Diego)*, November 17, 1911, clipping in Jacob Nieto Papers, American Jewish Archives, Cincinnati. While evidence abounds on Jewish attitudes toward being westerners, Bauman notes that "more needs to be done on attitudes of Jews in the South toward the South." Bauman, *Southerner as American*, 38.

9. Lee Shai Weissbach, *Jewish Life in Small-Town America: A History* (New Haven, Conn.: Yale University Press, 2005), chap. 3; Weissbach, "The Jewish Communities of the United States on the Eve of Mass Migration," *American Jewish History* 78, no. 1 (1988): 231–62.

10. Richard White, *"It's Your Misfortune and None of My Own": A New History of the American West* (Norman: University of Oklahoma Press, 1991), 391.

11. Patricia Limerick, *The Legacy of Conquest* (New York: Norton, 1987), 27.

12. Leonard Rogoff, "Is the Jew White? The Racial Place of the Southern Jew," in "Directions in Southern Jewish History," special issue, *American Jewish History* 85, no. 3 (1997): 195–230.

13. For discussions of whiteness, see Matthew Frye Jacobson, *Whiteness of a Different Color* (Cambridge, Mass.: Harvard University Press, 1998); and Eric Goldstein, *The Price of Whiteness: Jews, Race, and American Identity* (Princeton, N.J.: Princeton University Press, 2006).

14. William Toll, "A Regional Context for Pacific Jewry, 1880 to 1930," in *The Columbia History of Jews and Judaism in America*, ed. Marc Lee Raphael (New York: Columbia University Press, 2007), 220–24, 233–36; Ellen Eisenberg, "Fellow Whites or Fellow Minorities? Ethnic Identity and Responses to Prejudice among Jewish Oregonians" (paper presented at the conference "Through the Prism of Race and Ethnicity: Reimagining the Religious History of the American West," Arizona State University, Tempe, March 2006).

15. Linda Gordon documents this transformation particularly vividly in *The Great Arizona Orphan Abduction* (Cambridge, Mass.: Harvard University Press, 1999).

16. Maffly-Kipp, "Eastward Ho," 134. On western,

and particularly Californian, religious diversity, see also Eldon G. Ernst, "The Emergence of California in American Religions Historiography," *Religion and American Culture: A Journal of Interpretation* 11, no. 1 (2001): 31–52.

17. D. Michael Quinn, "Religion in the American West," in *Under an Open Sky: Rethinking America's Western Past*, ed. William Cronon, George Miles, and Jay Gitlin (New York: Norton, 1992), 158.

18. Ferenc Morton Szasz, *Religion in the Modern American West* (Tucson: University of Arizona Press, 2000), 4–5. See also Sandra Sizer Frankiel, *California's Spiritual Frontiers: Religious Alternatives in Anglo-Protestantism, 1850–1910* (Berkeley: University of California Press, 1988), x–xi.

19. Dale E. Soden, "Contesting the Soul of an Unlikely Land: Mainline Protestants, Catholics, and Reform and Conservative Jews in the Pacific Northwest," in *Religion and Public Life in the Pacific Northwest: The None Zone*, ed. Patricia O'Connell Killen and Mark Silk (Walnut Creek, Calif.: AltaMira Press, 2004), 57–62.

20. Szasz, *Religion in the Modern American West*, 7. Jews usually used the term *social justice*.

21. "First Woman Rabbi," *San Francisco Chronicle*, October 19, 1893, Jewish Women's Archive, http://jwa.org/exhibits/jsp/general.jsp?&imgfile=exhibits%2Fimages%2Fexhban10.gif&media_id=arffrab1; "A Famous Jewess," *Cincinnati Times-Star*, ca. January 1893, Jewish Women's Archive, http://jwa.org/exhibits/jsp/general.jsp?&imgfile=exhibits%2Fimages%2Fexhban10.gif&media_id=arffamo1.

22. Jonathan D. Sarna, *American Judaism: A History* (New Haven, Conn.: Yale University Press, 2004), 140–42. Simon Litman, *Ray Frank Litman: A Memoir* (New York: American Jewish Historical Association, 1957), 79–80. For information about Frank beyond this memoir by her husband, see Reva Clar and William M. Kramer, "The Girl Rabbi of the Golden West," *Western States Jewish History* 18, no. 2 (1986): 99–111; 18, no. 3 (1986): 223–36; 18, no. 4 (1986): 336–51; and documents and articles at the Jewish Women's Archive, jwa.org. At this time, the Jewish population of Oregon was somewhere between one thousand and five thousand, although probably closer to the lower figure. Jacob

Rader Marcus, *To Count a People: American Jewish Population Data, 1585–1984* (Lanham, Md.: University Press of America, 1990), 181.

23. Sarna, *American Judaism*, 142.

24. Molly Cone, Howard Droker, and Jacqueline Williams, *Family of Strangers: Building a Jewish Community in Washington State* (Seattle: University of Washington Press, 2003), 15–17, 92. Babette continued her activity as a community leader even after Bailey's death and played a critical role in founding the Seattle section of the National Council of Jewish Women after the turn of the century.

25. Eugene Nudelman, "The Family of Joseph Nudelman" (unpublished manuscript, Oregon Jewish Museum, Portland, 1969). The manuscript details the various ventures in the West and also tracks extensive and complicated lists of family members.

26. Mormons saw the trek of the Jews through Sinai as the archetype for their own adventure in the Great Basin. See Francaviglia, *Believing in Place*, 131–33. During the Civil War, the minister of San Francisco's First Unitarian Church, Thomas Starr King, in his most famous sermon, likened Lake Tahoe to the Sea of Galilee to suggest that healing powers could be found in both bodies of water because people had faith in God. King was the most revered minister of his day, and his statue is one of two representing California in the National Statuary Hall in Washington, D.C. See Frankiel, *California's Spiritual Frontiers*, 24.

27. Sherith Israel's architect was Albert Pissis. The brothers were born in Mexico and brought to San Francisco by their French father. Joan Libman, "Beneath Its Beautiful Dome, a Synagogue Finds That It Houses Rare Treasures," *SFGate*, March 12, 2005, http://www.sfgate.com/cgi-bin/article.cgi?f=/c/a/2005/03/12/DDGLSBNEB71.DTL. According to congregation records, "All these windows have been obtained through the efficient work and influence of our rabbi solely and he is also, practically the designer of them." "Fifty-Fifth Annual Meeting," October 29, 1905, Sherith Israel minute book, 1905:6.

28. Kate Nearpass Ogden, "California as Kingdom Come," in *Art of an American Icon: Yosemite*, ed. Amy Scott (Los Angeles: Autry National Center, 2006), 23.

29. *American Hebrew News*, September 28, 1894.

30. For an excellent discussion of demographic trends, see Bruce Phillips, "The Challenge of Family, Identity, and Affiliations," in *California Jews*, ed. Ava F. Kahn and Marc Dollinger (Hanover, N.H.: University Press of New England / Brandeis University Press, 2003), 17–28.

31. Quinn, "Religion in the American West," 152, 158. The Pacific Northwest, in particular, has been characterized as the "none zone," where more people check "none" when surveyed about their religion than in any other region of the country—a distinction that is not a new development. On the Pacific Northwest, see Killen and Silk, *Religion and Public Life*, 9. On California, see Ernst, "Emergence of California," 35; and Frankiel, *California's Spiritual Frontiers*, x–xi.

32. Bruce Powell, "Shlomo Bardin's 'Eretz' Brandeis," in Kahn and Dollinger, *California Jews*, 171.

33. Marc Dollinger, "The Counterculture," in Kahn and Dollinger, *California Jews*, 155.

34. Several scholars have recently argued that Jews have rejected the idea of diaspora, in part because it posits an authentic central place against which all others should be measured. The experience and the imagination of Jews in the American West have pointed in this direction since the Gold Rush. The growth since World War II of large Jewish communities that are comfortable and prominent in their new geographies suggests that the regional community needs no external referents to give it meaning. See, e.g., Caryn Aviv and David Shneer, *New Jews: The End of the Jewish Diaspora* (New York: New York University Press, 2005), 20–22.

1. HISTORIES COLLIDE: JEWS AND THE PACIFIC FRONTIER

Epigraph. Daniel Levy to the editor of the *Archives Israelites* (Paris), October 30, 1855, quoted in Kahn, *Jewish Voices*, 83. A copy of the letter in the original French is held by the Western Jewish History Center, Judah L. Magnes Museum, Berkeley, Calif.

1. On the profile of the "forty-niner" as a single male in his twenties, see Earl Pomeroy, *The Pacific Slope: A History of California, Oregon, Washington, Idaho,*

Utah, and Nevada (Seattle: University of Washington Press, 1965), 40–41.

2. Cohen's letter was published in the *Jewish Chronicle (London)*, July 18, 1851, 327; quoted in Kahn, *Jewish Voices*, 72.

3. O. P. Fitzgerald, *California Sketches* (Nashville: Southern Methodist Publishing House, 1881), 153.

4. Rabbi Joshua Stampfer, *Pioneer Rabbi of the West: The Life and Times of Julius Eckman* (Portland, Ore.: self-published, ca. 1988), 22.

5. Bernard Goldsmith, "Dictation," 1889, 2, 3, Bancroft Library, University of California, Berkeley.

6. Later, his son would move farther north, settling in Seattle, where he became a partner in a large wholesale grocery with connections to the region's metropolis, San Francisco. B. Goldsmith, "Dictation," 15.

7. Kahn, *Jewish Voices*, 52.

8. Frank Soule, John H. Gihon, and James Nisbet, *The Annals of San Francisco* (New York: Appleton, 1855), 362.

9. Peter R. Decker, *Fortunes and Failures: White-Collar Mobility in Nineteenth-Century San Francisco* (Cambridge, Mass.: Harvard University Press, 1978), 277.

10. Axel Friman, "Two Swedes in the California Goldfields: Allvar Kullgren and Carl August Modh, 1850–1856," *Swedish-American Historical Quarterly* 34, no. 2 (1983): 108.

11. William Issel and Robert W. Cherny, *San Francisco, 1865–1932: Politics, Power, and Urban Development* (Berkeley: University of California Press, 1986), 14.

12. Laurie F. Maffly-Kipp, *Religion and Society in Frontier California* (New Haven, Conn.: Yale University Press, 1994), 10.

13. Rabbi Max Lilienthal, "Our Brethren in the West and San Francisco," *American Israelite (Cincinnati)*, June 9, 1876.

14. "The Day of Atonement," *Daily Alta California (San Francisco)*, September 18, 1858.

15. *Daily Evening Herald (Marysville, Calif.)*, October 3, 1853.

16. "Day of Atonement," *Daily Alta California*.

17. Sarna, *American Judaism*, 63; Marcus, *To Count a People*, 20, 181, 227. All figures are approximate.

18. Marks lived at the kosher St. Nicholas Hotel; in 1862, almost ten years after her arrival, she married Jewish community leader Seixas Solomons. Kahn, *Jewish Voices*, 232.

19. Sarna, *American Judaism*, 64.

20. Hasia R. Diner, *A Time for Gathering: The Second Migration, 1820–1880* (Baltimore: Johns Hopkins University Press, 1992), 47.

21. In Sacramento, Einstein became secretary of both the Hebrew Benevolent Society and one of the city's two congregations. In 1855, as the secretary of a meeting of Sacramento Jews, he wrote a letter to protest anti-Semitic remarks by California's Speaker of the House. Stefan Rohrbacher, "From Württemberg to America: A Nineteenth-Century German-Jewish Village on Its Way to the New World," *American Jewish Archives* 41, no. 2 (1989): 163–67, 165, 159; Jacob Rader Marcus, "Anti-Jewish Sentiment in California 1855," *American Jewish Archives* 21, no. 1 (1960): 30; Morris Einstein to Rev. Isaac Leeser, March 15, 1854, Western Jewish History Center.

22. "Jugenderinnerungen" Henry Cohn, quoted in Kahn, *Jewish Voices*, 127–33. Also see various translations of the complete manuscript at the Western Jewish History Center.

23. Hasia R. Diner, *The Jews of the United States, 1654–2000* (Berkeley: University of California Press, 2004), 87.

24. Bertram Wallace Korn, "Jewish 'Forty-Eighter' in America," in *Eventful Years and Experiences: Studies in Nineteenth Century American Jewish History* (Cincinnati: American Jewish Archives, 1954), 6, 10, 18. Jacob Voorsanger, "Our Weekly Chat: August Helbing," *Emanu-El (San Francisco)*, August 21, 1896, 6.

25. Kahn, *Jewish Voices*, 59.

26. Daniel Levy, *Archives Israelites*, letter, October 30, 1855, quoted in Kahn, *Jewish Voices*, 83. The "functionary" may have been Herman Bien. Levy was also a teacher and reader for congregation Emanu-El.

27. *Jewish Messenger (New York)*, December 9, 1859, 173. San Francisco miscellaneous collection, American Jewish Archives, Cincinnati.

28. Eveline Brooks Auerbach, *Frontier Reminiscences of Eveline Brooks Auerbach*, ed. and with introduction by Annegret S. Ogden (Berkeley, Calif.: Friends of the Bancroft Library, 1994), 21–22.

29. Ibid., 22.

30. Eveline Auerbach Collection, 92/757, Bancroft Library.

31. Auerbach, *Frontier Reminiscences*, 33. The family moved with the rising and falling economy between Marysville, Timbuctoo, San Francisco, Portland, Boise, and then finally back to Salt Lake City. For more about Brooks, see Kahn, *Jewish Voices*, 111.

32. Frank V. McDonald, *A Biography of Richard Hayes McDonald* (Cambridge, Mass.: John Wilson and Son, 1881), 63, cited in Kahn, *Jewish Voices*, 106.

33. Statement from Louis Sloss, August 10, 1886, Bancroft Collection, MSS C-D 574, 1, Bancroft Library. See the similar tale of wagon train adventures and pioneer settlement in San Diego, in Donald H. Harrison, *Louis Rose: San Diego's First Jewish Settler and Entrepreneur* (San Diego, Calif.: Sunbelt Publications, 2005).

34. Matthew J. Eisenberg, "The Last Pioneers in Alaska," *Western States Jewish History* 24, no. 1 (1991): 51–73. For more information about the Alaska Commercial Company and Sloss, see Kahn, *Jewish Voices*, 278–81, 105–10; and Rudolf Glanz, *The Jews in American Alaska, 1867–1880* (New York: F. Maliniak, 1953), 4–44.

35. Statement from Louis Sloss, August 10, 1886, BANC MSS C-D 574, 2, Bancroft Library, University of California, Berkeley.

36. Kahn, *Jewish Voices*, 105.

37. Steven Lowenstein, *The Jews of Oregon, 1850–1950* (Portland: Jewish Historical Society of Oregon, 1987), 43–44; "Louis Fleischner," *Oregon Native Son* 1, no. 1 (1899): 346.

38. Myer Newmark, "Ship's Log around the Horn, 1852–53," Myer Newmark diary, MS 725, Southwest Museum, Los Angeles, quoted in Kahn, *Jewish Voices*, 124.

39. Mary Prag, "Early Days," n.d., Florence Prag Kahn Collection, Western Jewish History Center.

40. An 1852 survey demonstrated that one out of ten ship passengers died before reaching California. Louis J. Rasmussen, *San Francisco Ship Passengers Lists* (Colma, Calif.: San Francisco Historical Records, 1970), 4:vi.

41. *Allgemeine Zeitung des Judenthums* (*Leipzig*), March 10, 1856, 151–52. The passengers were cared for by Dr. Israel Moses, who was presumed to be Jewish.

42. Isaac Markens, *The Hebrews in America* (New York: self-published, 1888), 336. Population figures vary and are unreliable, as there was much mobility and few records were kept.

43. Moses Rischin and John Livingston, *Jews of the American West* (Detroit: Wayne State University Press, 1991), 34–35; Jonathan D. Sarna and Nancy H. Klein, *The Jews of Cincinnati* (Cincinnati: Center for the Study of the American Jewish Experience, Hebrew Union College–Jewish Institute of Religion, 1989), 181.

44. Fred Rosenbaum, *Visions of Reform: Congregation Emanu-El and the Jews of San Francisco, 1849–1999* (Berkeley, Calif.: Judah L. Magnes Museum, 2000), 48.

45. Salo W. Baron, and Jeannette M. Baron, "Palestinian Messengers in America, 1849–79: A Record of Four Journeys," *Jewish Social Studies* 5, no. 2 (1943): 145.

46. Isaac Mayer Wise, "Jewish Institutions in San Francisco," *American Israelite*, September 14, 1877, 5, quoted in Kahn, *Jewish Voices*, 499.

47. Earl Raab, "There's No City like San Francisco," *Commentary* 10, no. 4 (1950): 371.

48. Karla Goldman, "In Search of an American Judaism," in *An Inventory of Promises: Essays on American Jewish History; In Honor of Moses Rischin*, ed. Jeffrey S. Gurock and Marc Lee Raphael (Brooklyn, N.Y.: Carlson, 1995), 142.

49. *Weekly Gleaner (San Francisco)*, May 22, 1857. San Francisco provided plenty of work for *shochet* Goldsmith, who in 1857 was employed by butcher B. Adler. As a way to demonstrate his adherence to kashruth Adler proudly listed Goldsmith's name in his *Weekly Gleaner* advertisements.

50. *Weekly Gleaner*, April 10, 1857.

51. Kahn, *Jewish Voices*, 398.

52. William M. Kramer and Norton B. Stern, "A Search for the First Synagogue in the Golden West," *Western States Jewish Historical Quarterly* 7, no. 1 (1974): 4.

53. Morris Schloss to the Honorable Board of Trustees Congregation Sherith Israel, August 3, 1904, Sherith Israel Collection, Western Jewish History Center. Although most historians today believe that the first services were on Jackson Street, near Kearny,

a State of California landmark plaque at Montgomery and Washington streets proclaims it as the location of the "First Jewish Religious Services." Several accounts note the Jackson Street location, while one participant, Lewis Lewis, who latter settled in Victoria, B.C., wrote in a solicited reminiscence dated January 25, 1904, that the location was on Kearny Street. This discrepancy could be because the location was near the corner of Jackson and Kearny or because he is remembering the following year, when they met at the Masonic Hall on Kearny Street. He also wrote that services were held in a building that they built and paid one thousand dollars for. This version has not been corroborated. Sherith Israel Collection, Western Jewish History Center. The above-cited letter from Schloss states that the meeting was on Jackson Street, but that the "tent" was that of a Mr. Rosenbaum, not Franklin.

54. Kahn, *Jewish Voices*, 147.

55. Lewis A. Franklin, "Sermon, 1850," *Asmonean*, November 15, 1850, 30–31, quoted in Kahn, *Jewish Voices*, 152.

56. For a detailed discussion of the controversy, see Kramer and Stern, "Search for the First Synagogue."

57. David Kaufman, "Early Synagogue Architecture," in Kahn and Dollinger, *California Jews*, 42. With the addition of Jews who belonged to small congregations, and also the unaffiliated, the Jewish population in the city may have already reached into the thousands.

58. Abraham Labatt, a Sephardic Jew, was Emanu-El's first president. Originally from South Carolina, he was among the founders of Charleston's Reformed Society of Israelites. Sarna, *American Judaism*, 58.

59. Minutes of congregation Sherith Israel, February 1854, quoted in Kahn, *Jewish Voices*, 158.

60. Sarna, *American Judaism*, 95.

61. Constitution of Sherith Israel, 1851 Minute Book, Western Jewish History Center, cited in Kahn, *Jewish Voices*, 155–56.

62. Israel Finestein, *Jewish Society in Victorian England* (Portland, Ore.: Vallentine Mitchell, 1993), 53.

63. For further discussion of Sherith Israel, see Ava F. Kahn and Ellen Eisenberg, "Western Reality: Jewish Diversity During the 'German' Period," *American Jewish History* 92, no. 4 (2004): 455–79.

64. Eckman's career was typical of that of many rab-bis of the period in the United States, who either chose to move on after a short time of service to a congregation or had difficulty finding a congregation that was willing to submit to their authority. Sarna, *American Judaism*, 100.

65. L. Tichner to Isaac Mayer Wise, 1857, *American Israelite*, May 22, 1857, 366, quoted in Kahn, *Jewish Voices*, 177.

66. The adopted prayer book, by Leo Merzbacher, rabbi of Emanu-El in New York, was the first liturgy compiled by an American rabbi. See Sarna, *American Judaism*, 101. This choice was more radical than the other major American prayer book, Isaac Mayer Wise's *Minhag America*. Rosenbaum, *Visions of Reform*, 49.

67. Many of Ohabai Shalome's founders were, like Emanu-El's, Bavarian merchants.

68. Founding minutes, Congregation Ohabai Shalome, 1864, quoted in Kahn, *Jewish Voices*, 186.

69. Founding minutes, Congregation Ohabai Shalome, 1864, cited in Kahn, *Jewish Voices*, 185.

70. Congregation Ohabai Shalome, Minute Book, 1865, 48, 64.

71. Congregation Ohabai Shalome, Minute Book, 1865, 55. Eckman was paid two hundred dollars for his services. He conducted the first day's service in German and the second in English. On Yom Kippur he gave two sermons, one each in German and in English.

72. *Weekly Gleaner*, April 10, 1857; April 17, 1857.

73. *Weekly Gleaner*, July 26, 1861, 5, quoted in Kahn, *Jewish Voices*, 218. This approach was in accordance with the teaching of Eckman's friend, the renowned Isaac Leeser of Philadelphia, publisher of the *Occident*, who believed that Jewish children should be taught in a Jewish classroom. Sarna, *American Judaism*, 80.

74. *Weekly Gleaner*, July 26, 1861, 5, quoted in Kahn, *Jewish Voices*, 219.

75. "Autobiographical Notes, Mrs. Joseph H. Newmark" (1900), 5, Bancroft Library. Eckman saw his role as introducing "harmony and unity" into the school. Also see Helen Newmark, "A Nineteenth Century Memoir," *Western States Jewish Historical Quarterly* 6, no. 3 (1974): 204–18.

76. The only known copy of this prayer book is in the collection of Temple Emanu-El, San Francisco.

77. Jacob Voorsanger, *Chronicles of Emanu-El*, quoted in Kahn, *Jewish Voices*, 217.

78. *Weekly Gleaner*, April 10, 1857.

79. Cyril Edel Leonoff, "Pioneer Jewish Merchants of Vancouver Island and British Columbia," *Canadian Jewish Historical Society Journal* 8, no. 1 (1984): 13.

80. For San Diego Jewish history, see William M. Kramer, Stanley Schwartz, and Laurel Schwartz, eds., *Old Town, New Town* (Los Angeles: Western States Jewish History Association, 1994); and Harrison, *Louis Rose*.

81. California State census of 1852, California History Room, California State Library, Sacramento.

82. Kahn, *Jewish Voices*, 81

83. 1870 U.S. Census, Multnomah County, Oregon.

84. "Jugenderinnerungen" Henry Cohn, quoted in Kahn, *Jewish Voices*, 321.

85. Philip Schwartz advertisement, *Columbia Weekly Times*, August 8, 1861, quoted in Kahn, *Jewish Voices*, 275.

86. *American Israelite*, November 13, 1857, 145, quoted in Kahn, *Jewish Voices*, 334.

87. *Occident (Philadelphia)*, April 1856, quoted in Robert E. Levinson, *The Jews in the California Gold Rush* (New York: KTAV, 1978; reprint, Berkeley, Calif.: Commission for the Preservation of Pioneer Jewish Cemeteries and Landmarks of the Judah L. Magnes Museum, 1994), 100–101. Citations are to the 1994 edition.

88. Linoberg's prosperity is demonstrated by the fact that he lost thirty thousand dollars in a fire that swept Sonora in 1852. *A History of Tuolumne County California* (1882; repr., San Francisco: B. F. Alley, 1983), 88.

89. *American Israelite*, November 13, 1857, 145, quoted in Kahn, *Jewish Voices*, 334.

90. For a discussion of Reform Judaism in the mid-nineteenth century, see Sarna, *American Judaism*, 62–134.

91. Harriet Lane Levy, *920 O'Farrell Street: A Jewish Girlhood in Old San Francisco* (Berkeley, Calif.: Heyday Books, 1996), 112.

92. Kahn, *Jewish Voices*, 332.

93. B., "An Interesting Letter from San Francisco," *Asmonean*, February 6, 1852, 141. The names of Linoberg and Meyers are misspelled in the newspaper article.

94. Kahn, *Jewish Voices*, 354. The constitution required members' stores to be closed for Rosh Hashanah and Yom Kippur and prohibited intermarriage. Jewish cemeteries still exist in Jackson, Sonora, and other Gold Rush communities.

95. *Sonora Union Democrat*, April 11, 1868; September 28, 1872.

96. *Weekly Gleaner*, April 9, 1858, 5, cited in "Early Nevada City Jewry: A Picture Story," *Western States Jewish History* 16, no. 2 (1984): 160.

97. "Caroline Auerbach Selling," obituary, *Portland Evening Telegram*, October 29, 1914. Levinson, *Jews in the California Gold Rush*, 160.

98. William M. Kramer and Norton B. Stern, "Early California Associations of Michel Goldwater and His Family," *Western States Jewish Historical Quarterly* 4, no. 4 (1972): 175.

99. Jeanne E. Abrams, *Jewish Women Pioneering the Frontier Trail: A History in the American West* (New York: New York University Press, 2006), 118.

100. An announcement of the new officers of the Sonora society was printed in the *Occident* 14, no. 1 (1856).

101. Goldwater married in England, where his first two children were born. He was fluent in French, English, Spanish, Yiddish, Polish, and German. See Kramer and Stern, "Early California Associations of Michel Goldwater," 173–96.

102. Leonoff, "Pioneer Jewish Merchants," 14.

103. I. J. Benjamin, *Three Years in America, 1859–1862*, trans. Charles Reznikoff (Philadelphia: Jewish Publication Society of America, 1956), 2:143.

104. "The Emanu-El of Victoria, Vancouver Island: A Short History of the Beginnings of Congregation Emanu-El," comp. Allan Kenman (Victoria, B.C.: Congregation Emanu-El, n.d.), 3. Emanu-El as of 2007 is still in its original building. For the 1863 population figure, see Gerald Tulchinsky, *Taking Root: The Origins of the Canadian Jewish Community* (Hanover, N.H.: University Press of New England / Brandeis University Press, 1993), 87.

105. Tulchinsky, *Taking Root*, 89–91.

106. Scott Cline, "The Jews of Portland, Oregon: A Statistical Dimension, 1860–1880," *Oregon Historical Quarterly* 88, no. 1 (1987): 6–7.

107. Scott Cline, "The Creation of the Ethnic Com-

munity: Portland Jewry, 1851–1866," *Pacific Northwest Quarterly* 76, no. 2 (1985): 57.

108. Ibid., 53. Several of the congregation's early presidents were also former Californians.

109. *Nevada City Journal*, December 11, 1857, 2, cited in Kahn, *Jewish Voices*, 294.

110. Rabbi Julius J. Nodel, *The Ties Between: A Century of Judaism on America's Last Frontier* (Portland, Ore.: Temple Beth Israel, 1959), 13.

111. Reva Clar and William M. Kramer, "Julius Eckman and Herman Bien: The Battling Rabbis of San Francisco; Part 2," *Western States Jewish Historical Quarterly* 15, no. 3 (1983): 237. The *Gleaner* reported that a congregant had called Laski a "modern quack." Cline, "Creation of the Ethnic Community," 58. In the 1870s the mobile Laski served congregations in Ohio and Kentucky. See Amy Hill Shevitz, *Jewish Communities on the Ohio River: A History* (Lexington: University Press of Kentucky, 2007), 124. It is unclear who served the congregation in 1859 and 1860, as the sources disagree. See Nodel, *Ties Between*, 20; and Clar and Kramer, "Julius Eckman and Herman Bien," 252.

112. Rosenbaum, *Visions of Reform*, 27. Rosenbaum in detailing Bien's career does not mention Portland. Nodel, *Ties Between*, 20.

113. *Weekly Gleaner*, March 22, 1861, 5, cited in Robert E. Levinson, "Julius Eckman and the *Weekly Gleaner*: The Jewish Press in the Pioneer American West," in *A Bicentennial Festschrift for Jacob Rader Marcus* (Waltham: Mass.: American Jewish Historical Society, 1976), 339n28.

114. Nodel, *Ties Between*, 19.

115. Ibid., 35.

116. By the end of the 1860s, the South Germans numbered 116 (54 percent), the Prussians 48 (22.3 percent), and the Poles 20 (9.3 percent). Cline, "Jews of Portland," 8.

117. English was the official language of the congregation, though it held some lectures in German through the end of nineteenth century.

118. Diner, *Time for Gathering*, 30.

119. Kahn and Eisenberg, "Western Reality," 464.

120. Reva Clar and William M. Kramer, "Julius Eckman and Herman Bien: The Battling Rabbis of San Francisco; Part 3," *Western States Jewish Historical Quarterly* 15, no. 4 (1983): 353.

121. For a discussion of this practice, see Sarna, *American Judaism*, 90.

122. Nodel, *Ties Between*, 26.

123. Ibid., 27.

124. Ibid., 28.

125. Reports of the altercation were printed in newspapers in Portland (*Daily Standard*, October 2, 1880; *Daily Oregonian*, October 2, 1880) and in Cincinnati (*American Israelite*, October 22, 1880), cited in Nodel, *Ties Between*, 28–31.

126. Minutes, Temple Beth Israel, Portland, November 27, 1881, Oregon Jewish Museum, Portland.

127. Nodel, *Ties Between*, 25–31; minutes, Temple Beth Israel, Portland, January 26, 1879; April 13, 1879; February 15, 1880; March 14, 1880; June 13, 1880; September 24, 1880; November 27, 1881, Oregon Jewish Museum.

128. Marco R. Newmark, "Wilshire Boulevard Temple: Congregation B'Nai B'Rith," *Historical Society of Southern California Quarterly* 38, no. 2 (1956): 167.

129. Max Vorspan and Lloyd P. Gartner, *History of the Jews of Los Angeles* (Philadelphia: Jewish Publication Society, 1970), 10; Norton B. Stern, "Jews in the 1870 Census of Los Angeles," *Western States Jewish Historical Quarterly* 9, no. 1 (1976): 79.

130. Norton B. Stern, "Myer Joseph Newmark: Los Angeles Civic Leader," *Western States Jewish Historical Quarterly* 2, no. 3 (1970): 138.

131. On Newmark's earlier Jewish communal work, see ibid.

132. Sarna, *American Judaism*, 70.

133. In 1861, I. J. Benjamin visited Los Angeles and noted that the Jews had organized congregation Beth El, which met only for the High Holidays. Benjamin, *Three Years in America*, 2:101. This was a short-lived congregation whose members joined B'nai B'rith when it was established.

134. Reva Clar, "The Jews of Los Angeles: Urban Pioneers; Los Angeles Jewry—a Chronology," November 2002, http://home.earthlink.net/~nholdeneditor/jews_of_los_angeles.htm.

135. *Los Angeles Star*, October 1, 1859, 2.

136. Clar, "Jews of Los Angeles."

137. For more on Rabbi Edelman, see Norton B.

Stern and William M. Kramer, "Jewish Padre to the Pueblo: Pioneer Los Angeles Rabbi Abraham Wolf Edelman," *Western States Jewish Historical Quarterly* 3, no. 4 (1971): 193–226.

138. Martin A. Meyer, *Western Jewry* (San Francisco: Emanu-El, 1916), 88. The *Hebrew (San Francisco)* reported that Edelman, "although a foreigner, uses choice expressions, and elegant, perfect English." Quoted in Stern and Kramer, "Jewish Padre," 203.

139. Meyer, *Western Jewry*, 88.

140. Stern and Kramer, "Jewish Padre," 213. In a complementary article the *Los Angeles Daily Star* noted that Edelman selected and slaughtered meat every morning "in accordance with certain [kosher] rules" (February 25, 1877).

141. "A Jewish Presence in Los Angeles," Timeline, Roots-Key, Jewish Genealogical Society of Los Angeles, newsletter, Summer and Fall 2003, http://home.earthlink.net/~nholdeneditor/contents.htm.

142. The historian Moses Rischin calls Prussian-born Choynski "the first satirist of American Jews" for his insightful columns in the *American Israelite*, where, using the pen name Maftir, he "regularly twitted his fellow Jews unsparingly." Moses Rischin, "The Jewish Experience in America," in Rischin and Livingston, *Jews of the American West*, 36.

143. Stern and Kramer, "Jewish Padre," 210. Most of these reforms were never accepted by Edelman's mentor, Rabbi Henry.

144. *Hebrew*, October 10, 1873.

145. Norton B. Stern and William M. Kramer, "The Major Role of Polish Jews in the Pioneer West," *Western Jewish States Historical Quarterly* 8, no. 4 (1976): 342.

146. This assumption was also held about San Francisco. See Kahn and Eisenberg, "Western Reality," 455.

147. U.S. Census, 1870.

148. *Los Angeles Daily Star*, as cited in Stern and Kramer, "Jewish Padre," 208.

149. Meyer served as the French consul in southern California. Their son Eugene Meyer Jr. became publisher of the *Washington Post*.

150. Rosa Newmark to Sarah Newmark, November 21, 1867, Rosalee Meyers Stern Collection, Western Jewish History Center. Governor Downey and Hellman became banking partners.

151. Cone, Droker, and Williams, *Family of Strangers*, 15.

152. Wallula is in eastern Washington at the intersection of the Snake and Columbia rivers, a port that supplied miners in Idaho and Montana.

153. Bailey Gatzert, "Dictation," Bancroft Library, P-B 76.

154. William Toll, *The Making of an Ethnic Middle Class* (Albany: State University of New York Press, 1982), 30; Cone, Droker, and Williams, *Family of Strangers*, 5; Julia Niebuhr Eulenberg, "Jewish Enterprise in the American West: Washington, 1853–1909," 209, 278. By the time of Gatzert's death in 1893 Seattle Jews had purchased land for a cemetery.

155. Cone, Droker, and Williams, *Family of Strangers*, 78.

156. Ibid., 15.

157. Diner, *Jews of the United States*, 135.

158. Constitution of the First Hebrew Benevolent Society, 1862, Western Jewish History Center, quoted in Kahn, *Jewish Voices*, 201.

159. *Weekly Gleaner*, February 26, 1858.

160. August Helbing, "How the Eureka Was Founded: A Reminiscent Sketch," n.d., Eureka Benevolent Society Collection, Western Jewish History Center. I. J. Benjamin believed that the Eureka Benevolent Society was guilty of not supporting Polish Jews. Benjamin, *Three Years in America*, 1:212.

161. Helbing, "How the Eureka Was Founded."

162. Ibid. They also held entertainment including anniversary balls; see *Weekly Gleaner*, October 2, 1857.

163. "Constitution and By-Laws of Chebra Berith Shalom," adopted October 20, 1860, art. 20, sec. 5, 56, Bancroft Library.

164. Benjamin, *Three Years in America*, 1:228.

165. In addition to being a columnist for the *American Israelite*, Choynski was coeditor of Eckman's *Weekly Gleaner* and a man of many trades.

166. "Two Letters to Harriet Choynski," *Western States Jewish Historical Quarterly* 7, no. 1 (1974): 46, quoted in Kahn, *Jewish Voices*, 345. Choynski's letter dated May 17, 1863, suggests that he observed a kosher diet.

167. If Choynski had been ill at home, instead of in the foothills, he would have been required by the

society's constitution to see its German-trained doctor. "Constitution and By-Laws of Chebra Berith Shalom," art. 23, sec. 1, 60.

168. *Sonora Union Democrat*, March 20, 1869, 2, quoted in Kahn, *Jewish Voices*, 343–44.

169. William M. Kramer and Norton B. Stern, "Sephardic Founders of the Los Angeles Community: Samuel K. and Joseph I. Labatt," *Western States Jewish History* 28, no. 4 (1996): 338. Henry Labatt, an American-born Sephardic Jew, was welcome on both sides of San Francisco's ethnic divides. He served as secretary both of the "German" Emanu-El and of the Sherith Israel–affiliated First Hebrew Benevolent Society.

170. Samuel K. Labatt to Isaac Lesser, February 1, 1854, Museum of the American West, Autry National Center, Los Angeles.

171. Max Vorspan and Lloyd P. Gartner state that the society was founded at the home of Joseph Newmark, but Norton B. Stern suggests otherwise. See Vorspan and Gartner, *Jews of Los Angeles*, 19; and Stern, "Myer Joseph Newmark," 141n28.

172. William M. Kramer, "Solomon Nunes Carvalho Helped in Founding the Los Angeles Jewish Community," *Western States Jewish History* 28, no. 4 (1996): 331.

173. Carvalho resided in Los Angeles for a short time. For more about Carvalho, see Ava F. Kahn, introduction to *Incidents of Travel and Adventure in the Far West with Colonel Fremont's Last Expedition*, by Solomon Nunes Carvalho (Lincoln: University of Nebraska Press, 2004).

174. *Los Angeles Star*, June 2, 1855, quoted in Kramer and Stern, "Sephardic Founders," 340.

175. *San Joaquin Republican*, October 18, 1851.

176. Benjamin, *Three Years in America*, 1:229.

177. Toll, *Ethnic Middle Class*, 48.

178. Virginia Katz, "The Ladies' Hebrew Benevolent Society of Los Angeles in 1892," *Western States Jewish Historical Quarterly* 10, no. 2 (1978): 157.

179. B'nai Israel in Sacramento sent funds through the auspices of Sir Moses Montefiore. Moses Montefiore to Moses Hyman, Esq., October 4, 1859, Western Jewish History Center.

180. Kahn, *Jewish Voices*, 461–63, 470–77.

181. For example, Cincinnati's Phoenix Club, founded in 1856, was a German-Jewish men's social club. See Sarna and Klein, *Jews of Cincinnati*, 102.

182. David A. D'Ancona, *A California-Nevada Travel Diary of 1876*, ed. William M. Kramer (Santa Monica, Calif.: Norton B. Stern, 1975), 79.

183. Kahn, *Jewish Voices*, 406.

184. Seymour Fromer, ed., "B'nai B'rith Centennial Convention: District Grand Lodge Number Four" (1963), Western Jewish History Center; Toll, *Ethnic Middle Class*, 26–27; Vorspan and Gartner, *Jews of Los Angeles*, 58; Cone, Droker, and Williams, *Family of Strangers*, 80.

185. "Preliminary Proceeding of the Past Presidents of Ophir Lodge No. 21, Etham Lodge No. 37, Modin Lodge No. 42, and Garizam Lodge No. 43, of the I.O.B.B. [Independent Order of the B'nai B'rith], for the Formation of a District Grand Lodge for the Pacific Coast" (San Francisco, March 29, 1863), quoted in Fromer, "B'nai B'rith Centennial Convention."

186. Letter to the Constitution Grand Lodge, New York, from San Francisco, April 14, 1863, quoted in Fromer, "B'nai B'rith Centennial Convention."

187. *Weekly Gleaner*, April 10, 1857. Newmark, Kremer and Company was founded in Los Angeles in 1856 by J. P. Newmark, Harris Newmark, Joseph Newmark, and Maurice Kremer. See Leo Newmark, *California Family Newmark: An Intimate History* (Santa Monica, Calif.: Norton B. Stern, 1970), 31.

188. These periodicals included the *Voice of Israel* (1856–57), the *Weekly Gleaner* (ca. 1857–65), the *Hebrew Observer* (ca. 1856–88), the *Hebrew* (1863–87), the *Progress* (1877–96), and the *Voice of Israel* (1870–74). See Rischin and Livingston, *Jews of the American West*, 36.

189. Eckman was able to set the type in both English and Hebrew characters. Levinson, "Eckman and the *Weekly Gleaner*," 333.

190. Bertram Wallace Korn, *American Jewry and the Civil War* (Marietta, Ga.: R. Bemis, 1995), 299.

191. *Weekly Gleaner*, January 16, 1857, 2, quoted in Kahn, *Jewish Voices*, 214.

192. Levinson, "Eckman and the *Weekly Gleaner*," 339n28. Eckman answered Linoberg that a Jew is always a Jew no matter what he did in his life and was entitled to a Jewish burial but that there was precedent

for Jews to be buried outside of Jewish cemeteries. Rabbi Julius Eckman "Communications," *Weekly Gleaner*, October 23, 1857, 324.

193. Levinson, "Eckman and the *Weekly Gleaner*," 339n28.

194. Rabbi Julius Eckman, "Communications," *Weekly Gleaner*, July 15, 1859, 2.

195. For more about this case, see David I. Kertzer, *The Kidnapping of Edgardo Mortara* (New York: Vintage Books, 1997).

196. *Proceeding in Relation to the Mortara Abduction Mass Meeting at Musical Hall* (San Francisco: Towne and Bacon, 1859), 8.

197. A Democrat, President Buchanan did not want to intervene in the international issue and risk losing his Catholic constituency. He also did not want to open up the United States to the scrutiny of foreign governments over American slavery, which separated parents from their children. For further discussion, see Sarna, *American Judaism*, 110–11.

198. After January 1865, no further copies of the *Gleaner* are known to exist. See Levinson, "Eckman and the *Weekly Gleaner*," 335.

199. Ibid.

200. D'Ancona, *California-Nevada Travel Diary*, 12.

201. Rosenbaum, *Visions of Reform*, 44.

202. Ibid., 55.

203. Kaufman, "Early Synagogue Architecture," 44–45.

204. Rosenbaum, *Visions of Reform*, 53.

205. Rischin, "Jewish Experience in America," 36.

206. Kaufman, "Early Synagogue Architecture," 44.

2. A BIRTHRIGHT OF ELITE STATUS

Epigraph. B'nai B'rith Messenger (Los Angeles), January 29, 1926.

1. *Emanu-El (San Francisco)*, March 28, 1930.

2. Gustav A. Danziger, "The Jew in San Francisco: The Last Half Century," *Overland Monthly*, April 1895, 395.

3. Sheffield Hebrew Congregation, December 9, 1889, special meeting to install Jacob Nieto as minister, teacher, secretary; card announcing installation of Jacob Nieto at Sherith Israel, June 14, 1893, microfilm, Nieto Papers.

4. Editorial, *Jewish Times (San Diego)*, March 1, 1907, clipping in Nieto Papers.

5. On the city's religious population, see U.S. Census Bureau, *Census of Religious Bodies: 1926* (Washington, D.C.: Government Printing Office, 1930), vol. 1, table 31. The statistics for San Francisco for 1926 identify 154,385 Roman Catholics; 35,000 Jews; 6,808 Protestant Episcopal; 5,025 Presbyterians; and 3,983 Methodist Episcopal.

6. San Francisco Labor Council, "Resolution," December 29, 1922; Meeting of the Board of Supervisors of the City and County of San Francisco, Monday, March 31, 1930, Nieto Papers.

7. Philip Selling to J. E. Andrews, January 30, 1883; Ben Selling to B. Scheeline, April 4, 1883, Ben Selling Papers, Oregon Historical Society, Portland.

8. Ben Selling to Benny, March 23, 1886, Selling Papers.

9. "Ben Selling Dies, City in Mourning," *Oregonian*, January 16, 1931, front page.

10. See Ben Selling to Stephen Wise, July 22 and September 17, 1899, Stephen Wise Papers, American Jewish Historical Society, New York City. See also the Portland file in the Industrial Removal Office Papers, American Jewish Historical Society.

11. The administration at the University of Oregon was aware of his support in the legislature and courted his goodwill. Prince Lucien Campbell to Rabbi Jonah Wise, December 9, 1915; George Rebec to Campbell, March 3, 1919, President's Office Correspondence, University of Oregon Archives, Eugene.

12. *B'nai B'rith Messenger*, February 22, 1924.

13. *Oregonian*, January 19, 1931, front page.

14. The importance of Jews as stabilizing elements is noted in Rudolf Glanz, *The Jews of California: From the Discovery of Gold until 1880* (New York: Southern California Jewish Historical Society, 1960), 41. For a rogues' gallery of Jewish mayors, see Harriet Rochlin and Fred Rochlin, *Pioneer Jews: A New Life in the Far West* (Boston: Houghton Mifflin, 1984), 158–59.

15. Frankiel, *California's Spiritual Frontiers*, 56. A challenge to a California Sabbath observance law (1857) by a Sacramento Jewish merchant was upheld by

the California Supreme Court. New legislation in 1861 was repealed by the legislature in 1882. See Frankiel, *California's Spiritual Frontiers*, 48, 53–54. For the text of the court case, and contemporaneous commentary related to the Sunday Laws, see Kahn, *Jewish Voices*, 408–16.

16. *Emanu-El*, August 7, 1896, 7. *Emanu-El* notes that Protestant ministers in Portland who were also members of the American Protective Association opposed the election of David Solis-Cohen to an unnamed office, probably the police commission. See also Ben Selling to Friend Leo, May 21, 1886; Selling to Uncle, May 21, 1886; Selling to A. Levy, May 29, 1886, Selling Papers.

17. Vorspan and Gartner, *Jews of Los Angeles*, 104; Toll, *Ethnic Middle Class*, 80–84; Issel and Cherny, *San Francisco*, 123; Gray Brechin, *Imperial San Francisco: Urban Power, Earthly Ruin* (Berkeley: University of California Press, 1999), 178. Brechin, while noting the relative absence of anti-Semitism, refers to San Francisco's "parallel aristocracies," one predominantly Protestant and the other exclusively Jewish. Harris Newmark, *Sixty Years in Southern California, 1853–1913*, ed. Maurice H. Newmark and Marco R. Newmark (New York: Knickerbocker Press, 1916), 383. Author Newmark notes that Jews were admitted to early clubs in Los Angeles, but by the mid-1890s the sons faced exclusion. The historian Karen Wilson, based on her study of membership lists, believes that the exclusion took place later, circa 1920. Personal correspondence with Ava F. Kahn, September 16, 2007.

18. Hiram Johnson, Governor of California, to Simon Lubin, August 20, 1912, Simon Lubin Papers, Bancroft Library. The letterhead of the Social Hygiene Society of Portland in 1912 lists Rabbi Jonah Wise as second vice president. See letterhead in Social Hygiene File, 1912, Prince Lucien Campbell, President's Office Correspondence, University of Oregon Archives.

19. *Scribe (Portland)*, September 28, 1928.

20. "Temporary Relief Committee," in *Third Annual Report of the Emanu-El Sisterhood for Fiscal Year 1896–97* (San Francisco, 1897), 11, 17, Western Jewish History Center.

21. William Toll, "Voluntarism and Modernization in Portland Jewry: The B'nai B'rith in the 1920s," *Western*

Historical Quarterly 10, no. 1 (1979): 21–38. The *Scribe* (June 22, 1928) describes the process of recruitment and notes that the lodges in Portland and San Francisco each numbered more than twenty-five hundred.

22. Issel and Cherny, *San Francisco*, 23–24.

23. Rebekah Kohut, *My Portion (An Autobiography)* (New York: Thomas Seltzer, 1925), 40. Rebekah married New York's Rabbi Alexander Kohut and later became a leader of the National Council of Jewish Women. See entry on Kohut in *Jewish Women in America: An Historical Encyclopedia*, ed. Paula Hyman and Deborah Dash Moore (New York: Routledge, 1997), 749–51.

24. Kohut, *My Portion*, 41–42, 55–56.

25. Also of mention were the cigar and tobacco warehouse of A. S. Rosenbaum, the clothing manufacturer of S. Reinstein, and the printer J. Levi, as noted in "Destruction of Property in Various Parts of the City," *San Francisco Call*, October 22, 1868, http://www.sfmuseum.org/hist1/1886eq.html. See also Michael Zarchin, *Glimpses of Jewish Life in San Francisco*, 2nd ed. (Berkeley, Calif.: Judah L. Magnes Museum, 1964), 52–59; and William Issel, "'Citizens outside the Government': Business and Urban Policy in San Francisco and Los Angeles, 1890–1932," *Pacific Historical Review* 57, no. 2 (1988): 126.

26. See Lynn Downey, "Levi Strauss Invented Western Work Clothes for Miners, Cowboys, and Engineers," in *The American Frontier: Opposing Viewpoints*, ed. Mary Ellen Jones (San Diego, Calif.: Greenhaven Press, 1994), 272–76.

27. Issel and Cherny, *San Francisco*, 33, 37.

28. See Gunther Barth, *Instant Cities: Urbanization and the Rise of San Francisco and Denver* (New York: Oxford University Press, 1975), 173. On the Fleishackers in San Francisco banking, see Zarchin, *Glimpses of Jewish Life*, 59; and Issel and Cherny, *San Francisco*, 41–42. On the Fleishackers' interest in power companies, real estate, and banks in Portland, see E. Kimbark MacColl, *The Growth of a City: Power and Politics in Portland, Oregon, 1915 to 1950* (Portland, Ore.: Georgian Press, 1979), 119, 186, 373, 382–83, 388–89.

29. Robert Glass Cleland and Frank B. Putnam, *Isaias W. Hellman and the Farmers and Merchants Bank* (San Marino, Calif.: Huntington Library, 1965), 88.

30. Ibid., 87. On the importance of the electric street railways for the unique development of Los Angeles, see Robert Fogelson, *The Fragmented Metropolis: Los Angeles, 1850–1930* (Cambridge, Mass.: Harvard University Press, 1967), 87–92.

31. Cleland and Putnam, *Isaias W. Hellman*, 15, 18–19, 57, 78–79. On Hellman and Giannini, see Neal Gabler, *An Empire of Their Own: How the Jews Invented Hollywood* (New York: Crown, 1988), 133. On movie moguls and the Giannini brothers, see Felice A. Bonadio, *A. P. Giannini: Banker of America* (Berkeley: University of California Press, 1994), 111–13; and Attilio H. Giannini, "Financial Aspects," in *The Story of the Films*, ed. Joseph P. Kennedy (Chicago: A. W. Shaw, 1927), 78–85.

32. "Los Angeles' Little Cutters," *Fortune* 31 (May 1945): 134.

33. For residential patterns of the Hass, Lilienthal, and Levison families, see Issel and Cherny, *San Francisco*, 31, 41. On Sutro's San Francisco life, see Irena Narell, *Our City: The Jews of San Francisco* (San Diego, Calif.: Howell-North Books, 1981), 253–61.

34. Issel and Cherny, *San Francisco*, 23–24; K. M. Nesfield, "The Jew from a Gentile Stand-Point," *Overland Monthly*, April, 1895, 418; Philip J. Ethington, *The Public City: The Political Construction of Urban Life in San Francisco, 1850–1900* (Cambridge: Cambridge University Press, 1994), 370–77.

35. Danziger, "Jew in San Francisco," 406, 409.

36. On "Julius Kahn Day," see *Emanu-El*, May 17, 1918. Mrs. Kahn held office until a Democratic landslide in 1936. See Kurt F. Stone, "Kahn, Julius," in *The Congressional Minyan: The Jews of Capitol Hill* (Hoboken, N.J.: KTAV, 2000), 237–38.

37. Ava F. Kahn and Glenna Matthews, "One Hundred Twenty Years of Women's Activism," in Kahn and Dollinger, *California Jews*, 144–45; Rochlin and Rochlin, *Pioneer Jews*, 137; "Resolution of Eulogy . . . on . . . Doctor Jacob Nieto," Nieto Papers; David G. Dalin, "Jewish and Non-Partisan Republicanism in San Francisco, 1911–1963," in Moses Rischin, *The Jews of the West: The Metropolitan Years* (Berkeley, Calif.: American Jewish Historical Society / Western Jewish History Center, 1979), 108–33.

38. Fred Rosenbaum, *Architects of Reform: Congregational and Community Leadership, Emanu-El of San Francisco, 1849–1980* (Berkeley, Calif.: Western Jewish History Center, 1980), 92–98.

39. Ava F. Kahn, "Looking at America from the West to the East, 1850–1920s," in *Jewish Life in the American West*, ed. Ava F. Kahn (Los Angeles: Autry Museum of Western Heritage / University of Washington Press, 2002), 25; *San Francisco City Directory, 1910*, 41.

40. *San Francisco City Directory, 1879*, 1072–73, 1051.

41. Danziger, "Jew in San Francisco," 395.

42. The minutes of San Jose's Bichor Cholim in the 1870s show it to have been traditional, but with a Sunday school, over which Rabbi Levy presided. Fred Rosenbaum, *Free to Choose: The Making of a Jewish Community in the American West; The Jews of Oakland, California, from the Gold Rush to the Present Day* (Berkeley, Calif.: Judah L. Magnes Museum, 1976), 8. Rosenbaum notes that the First Hebrew Congregation of Oakland in 1880 was Orthodox, but by the 1920s it was presided over by Levy's protégé, Rudolph Coffee, the social activist and Oakland native who was Reform. The movement of Levy's career around the Bay had precedents in the careers of Protestant ministers. See Frankiel, *California's Spiritual Frontiers*, 35.

43. Isaac Mayer Wise to Jacob Voorsanger, May 26, 1876; Goldstein to Jacob Voorsanger, August 22, 1876; Myer Noat to Jacob Voorsanger, August 21 and 25, 1877; John Richman to Jacob Voorsanger, August 5, 1878; Jacob Voorsanger to Elkan Cohn, June 30, 1886, Jacob Voorsanger Papers, American Jewish Archives. Rosenbaum, *Visions of Reform*, 80.

44. Voorsanger "never claimed rabbinical ordination." His bachelor and doctorate degrees from Hebrew Union College were honorary. Rosenbaum, *Visions of Reform*, 80, 79.

45. Danziger, "Jew in San Francisco," 395.

46. See Felicia Herman, "Sisterhoods of Personal Service," in Hyman and Moore, *Jewish Women in America*, 1264–65. For more on the Sisterhood for Personal Service, see chapter 4.

47. Samuel Shortridge to Rabbi Jacob Voorsanger, December 31, 1897, Voorsanger Papers; Marc Lee Raphael, "Rabbi Jacob Voorsanger of San Francisco on Jews and Judaism: The Implications of the Pittsburgh

Platform," *American Jewish Historical Quarterly*, 63, no. 2 (1973): 185–87; Rosenbaum, *Architects of Reform*, 45–65.

48. Danziger, "Jew in San Francisco," 382.

49. Norman Angell, *After All: The Autobiography of Norman Angell* (London: Hamish Hamilton, 1951), 51–52.

50. The apprenticeships of Julius and his brothers are noted in the manuscript census for Multnomah County in 1870 and 1880, when all were then living in their father's household.

51. Sylvan Durkheimer, interview, Portland, March 1975, Oregon Jewish Museum.

52. W. Turrentine Jackson, "Portland: Wells Fargo's Hub for the Pacific Northwest," *Oregon Historical Quarterly* 86, no. 3 (1985): 234, 237.

53. Robert E. Levinson, "The Jews of Eugene, Oregon," *Western States Jewish History*, 30, no. 1 (1997): 53. Levinson notes that the exact family connection between Charles Friendly of Portland and S. H. Friendly of Eugene is not known. Mannie Lauer gives the full given name of his uncle as Sampson H. Freundlich, who subsequently changed his name to Friendly. For the other details of Friendly's early life, see Mannie [Lauer] to Therese [Friendly] March 30, 1940 (copy in possession of Ava F. Kahn).

54. The memorial service held for S. H. Friendly on November 3, 1915, is noted in Prince Lucien Campbell to Board of Regents, University of Oregon, October 29, 1915, University of Oregon Archives.

55. Jeff W. Hayes, *Looking Backward at Portland: Tales of the Early 80's* (Portland, Ore.: 1911), 42, pamphlet in New York Public Library.

56. Blaine Lamb, "Jews in Early Phoenix, 1870–1920," *Journal of Arizona History* 18, no. 3 (1977): 301. The Korrick brothers also owned department stores in Arizona.

57. Ibid., 303; Robert Goldberg, *Barry Goldwater* (New Haven, Conn.: Yale University Press, 1995), 14–15, 18.

58. Lamb, "Jews in Early Phoenix," 306.

59. Leonard Dinnerstein, "From Desert Oasis to the Desert Caucus," in Rischin and Livingston, *Jews of the American West*, 140–41.

60. Lena Kleinberg Holzman, oral history, August 23, 1981, Jewish Community Oral History Project, University of Washington Archives, Seattle.

61. On the "Oregon System" and Joseph Simon's support, see William S. U'Ren, "The Initiative and Referendum in Oregon," *Arena* 29 (March 1903): 270–77; E. Kimbark MacColl, with Harry Stein, *Merchants, Money, and Power: The Portland Establishment, 1843–1913* (Portland, Ore.: Georgian Press, 1988), 322.

62. MacColl, *Merchants, Money, and Power*, 428.

63. The Santa Fe Railroad's deliberate isolation of San Diego from the intercontinental rail network is described in Fogelson, *Fragmented Metropolis*, 60–62.

64. See Robert A. Burlison, "Samuel Fox: Merchant and Civic Leader in San Diego, 1886–1939," *Journal of San Diego History* 26, no. 1 (1980), http://www.sandiegohistory.org/journal/80winter/fox.htm.

65. Data on the business and residential distribution of Spokane's Jews have been gathered from a membership list for Temple Emanu-El and from Spokane city directories and plotted on a street map of Spokane. Map in possession of William Toll.

66. Minutes and miscellaneous correspondence of the First Hebrew Congregation of Albany, Oregon, 1878–1924, microfilm, Bancroft Library.

67. Minutes, Temple Emanu-El Spokane, September 28,1890; August 4, 1891; June 12, 1892; February 12, 1893; June 7, 1897; June 12, 1897; June 29, 1897; July 7, 1897; July 12, 1897; October 24, 1897; American Jewish Archives.

68. Rabbi Cohen was recalled to Temple Beth Israel in Tacoma in 1924, after an absence of almost twenty years. See *B'nai B'rith Messenger*, April 9, 1926. Cohen had been a chaplain in the Officers Reserve Corp of the U.S. Army and an editorial writer for *B'nai B'rith Messenger* for more than twenty years.

69. *B'nai B'rith Messenger*, March 25, 1910; June 24, 1910.

70. Frankiel, *California's Spiritual Frontiers*, 95.

71. Ben Selling to Stephen Wise, July 22, 1899; Wise to Special Committee on Notification of Temple Beth Israel, August 2, 1899; Selling to Wise, September 17, 1899; Wise to President and Board of Trustees, B'nai Jeshurun, New York City, October 3, 1899; Wise to President and Board of Trustees, Congregation Beth

Israel, Portland, Ore., October 6, 1899; Solomon Hirsch, November 3, 1899, Wise Papers.

72. Abigail Scott Duniway to Stephen Wise, January 29, 1901, Wise Papers.

73. Stephen Wise to Louise Wise, September 1902 (Sunday afternoon), October 17, 1902; Annual Report of President Adolph Wolfe, Temple Beth Israel, October 29, 1903; Ben Selling to Stephen Wise, May 25, 1904, Wise Papers. For more on Neighborhood House, see chapter 4.

74. Stephen Wise to Louise Wise, April 14, 1902, Wise Papers; Justine Wise Polier and James Waterman Wise, *The Personal Letters of Stephen Wise* (Boston: Beacon, 1956), 73.

75. Stephen Wise helped arrange for Jonah Wise to replace him. See Leo Wise to Stephen Wise, September 7, 1906; Adolph Wolfe to Stephen Wise, November 11, 1906, Wise Papers.

76. The relationship between Rabbi Wise and President Campbell was cordial and substantive. See Jonah Wise to Prince Lucien Campbell, December 8, 1915; Campbell to Wise, October 9, 1917; George Rebec to Campbell, March 3, 1919; Wise to Campbell, May 5, 1919 [regarding the Oregon Society of Mental Hygiene]; Campbell to Wise, February 2, 1920; Wise to Karl Onthank, April 21, 1920; Wise to Campbell, September 23, 1920, President's Office Correspondence, University of Oregon Archives.

77. David Buerge and Junius Rochester, *Roots and Branches: The Religious Heritage of Washington State* (Seattle: Church Council of Greater Seattle, 1988).

78. Cone, Droker, and Williams, *Family of Strangers*, 226–27.

79. *Jewish Transcript (Seattle)*, April 15, 1924.

80. Documents verifying Rabbi Koch's many civic activities are found in Rabbi Samuel Koch Papers, accession no. 1759, University of Washington Archives.

81. The literature on the origins of social work is voluminous, but see Graham Taylor, *Pioneering on Social Frontiers* (Chicago: University of Chicago Press, 1930); Roy Lubove, *The Professional Altruist: The Emergence of Social Work as a Career, 1880–1930* (New York: Atheneum, 1969); and Mina Carson, *Settlement Folk, Social Thought, and the American Settle-*

ment Movement, 1885–1930 (Chicago: University of Chicago Press, 1990).

82. Philip L. Fradkin, *The Great Earthquake and Firestorms of 1906* (Berkeley: University of California Press, 2005), 190–91. Fradkin explains the discrepancy in estimates of the dead and why the current estimates are far greater than the numbers reported at the time.

83. James Hopper, "Our San Francisco," *Everybody's Magazine* 14, no. 6 (1906): 760a–760h.

84. The promotional bias in the magazines is noted in Fradkin, *Great Earthquake*, 263.

85. Arthur Inkersley, "What San Francisco Has to Start With," *Overland Monthly* 47, no. 6 (1906): 469; Cleland and Putnam, *Isaias W. Hellman*, 78.

86. Fradkin, *Great Earthquake*, 203.

87. On the place of Jewish families in this unique district, see Alvin Averbach, "San Francisco's South of Market District, 1850–1950: The Emergence of a Skid Row," *California Historical Quarterly* 52 (Fall 1973): 202–4.

88. On the devastation of Temple Emanu-El, see Dan Kurzman, *Disaster: The Great San Francisco Earthquake and Fire of 1906* (New York: William Morrow, 2001), photographic section, following p. 168. The temple was restored without the onion domes. On Voorsanger's role in the reconstruction, see Rosenbaum, *Architects of Reform*, 55–57. The structure had also been damaged in a previous earthquake on October 22, 1868. See "Destruction of Property in Various Parts of the City," *San Francisco Call*, October 22, 1868, http://www.sfmuseum.org/hist1/1886eq.html. For Jewish residential patterns, see Issel and Cherny, *San Francisco*, 67.

89. Fradkin, *Great Earthquake*, 209.

90. Kurzman, *Disaster*, 231.

91. Brechin, *Imperial San Francisco*, 184.

92. For details on Nieto's emergency services, see Jacob Nieto, "History Committee," manuscript, April 28, 1906, Nieto Papers.

93. Gerstle Mack, *1906: Surviving San Francisco's Great Earthquake and Fire* (San Francisco: Chronicle Books, 1981), 106.

94. Congregation Beth Israel (Portland), Minute Books, May 3, 1906, Oregon Jewish Museum.

95. The new Mount Zion building was completed in 1913. See Issel and Cherny, *San Francisco*, 67.

96. Jacob Nieto, editorial, *Jewish Times*, March 1907, clipping in Nieto Papers. Nieto noted, in what seems a peevish comment, that while Protestant and Catholic churches were being rebuilt, Jews from elsewhere had not volunteered funds to help the synagogues rebuild. See also Rosenbaum, *Architects of Reform*, 58–61.

97. Jessica Peixotto, "Relief Work of the Associated Charities from June, 1907 to June, 1909," 287, 295, table 106, Peixotto Family Papers, Bancroft Library, University of California, Berkeley.

98. On Ruef's place as an "ethnically conscious" politician in opposition to the elite reformers led by Phelan, see Judd Kahn, *Imperial San Francisco: Politics and Planning in an American City, 1897–1906* (Lincoln: University of Nebraska Press, 1979), 38–58; and James P. Walsh, "Abe Ruef Was No Boss: Machine Politics, Reform, and San Francisco," *California Historical Society Quarterly* 51 (Spring 1972): 3–16.

99. On how the rabbis became involved in the Ruef prosecution, see Walton Bean, *Boss Ruef's San Francisco: The Story of the Union Labor Party, Big Business, and the Graft Prosecution* (Berkeley: University of California Press, 1952), 198–213. See also "Rabbi Nieto's Statement" (undated clipping) and untitled memo on the Ruef Case, Nieto Papers.

100. George Kennan, "The Fight for Reform in San Francisco," *McClure's Magazine* 29, no. 5 (1907): 548.

101. Q, "Ruef—a Jew under Torture," *Overland Monthly* 50 (November 1907): 517–18. The use of racial stereotypes and of anti-Semitic prejudices to stigmatize Ruef is summarized in Fradkin, *Great Earthquake*, 29–31. Fradkin concludes, "There is little doubt that Ruef, like Phelan, was both perpetrator of questionable actions and victim of his ambitions during this troubled time" (30). On Phelan's commitment to the Burnham Plan, see James D. Phelan, "Rise of the New San Francisco," *Cosmopolitan Magazine* 41, no. 6 (1906): 576–78.

102. Fradkin, *Great Earthquake*, 228.

103. Ruth Barnes Moynihan, *Rebel for Rights: Abigail Scott Duniway* (New Haven, Conn.: Yale University Press, 1983), 212–14; Abrams, *Jewish Women Pioneering*, 164–83. For a nuanced view of women as lobbyists and then initially as voters, see Nancy F. Cott, *The Grounding of Modern Feminism* (New Haven, Conn.: Yale University Press, 1987), 99–114.

104. Julia Swett, "Good Results," *Oregon Voter (Portland)*, September 16, 1916, 215.

105. William Toll, "Gender, Ethnicity, and Settlement Work in the Urban West," in Gurock and Raphael, *Inventory of Promises*, 299–306.

106. *B'nai B'rith Messenger*, January 18, 1924.

107. For an analysis of this modernization of Jewish philanthropy at the national level, see Daniel J. Elazar, *Community and Polity: The Organizational Dynamics of American Jewry* (Philadelphia: Jewish Publication Society, 1980), 159–66.

108. On the regional leadership of Lubin and Coffee, see Hiram Johnson to Simon Lubin, August 20, 1912, September 13, 1913; Mary Antin to Lubin, May 27, 1925; and Rudolph Coffee to Lubin, October 16, 1923, Lubin Papers. Governor Richardson appointed Rabbi Coffee to replace Professor Peixotto on the state board of charities to oversee prisons. See *B'nai B'rith Messenger*, January 18, 1924. On Peixotto's role in training professional social workers, see Henry R. Hatfield, "Jessica Blanche Peixotto," in *Essays in Social Economics in Honor of Jessica Blanche Peixotto* (Berkeley: University of California Press, 1935), 11–13.

109. "Superintendent Blumenthal's Report," *B'nai B'rith Messenger*, February 15 and 22, 1924; both stories appeared on the front page.

110. For a discussion of the origins of the B'nai B'rith among young immigrant Jews in New York, see Deborah Dash Moore, *B'nai B'rith and the Challenge of Ethnic Leadership* (Albany: State University of New York Press, 1981), 8–34.

111. *B'nai B'rith Messenger*, September 16, 1910; January 29, 1911.

112. Harry Kenin, "The B'nai B'rith Center and the Center Movement," *Scribe*, September 23, 1927.

113. *Scribe*, January 9, 1920.

114. Louis Newman, "Telling It in Gath," *Scribe*, June 22, 1928.

115. *B'nai B'rith Messenger*, January 31, 1910; March 25, 1910; July 8, 1910.

116. *B'nai B'rith Messenger*, April 17, 1911.

117. In Oakland the annual budgets in the 1920s were about thirty-five thousand dollars and were

obtained from the community chest. See Rosenbaum, *Free to Choose*, 77.

118. On Swett's interest in unemployment, see the pamphlet "The Sixth Annual Commonwealth Conference," University of Oregon, May 27–29, 1914, President's Office files, University of Oregon Archives; and *Scribe*, October 10, 1919; December 5, 1919; January 9, 1920.

119. Philip Tworoger, "Weekly Brainstorms," *Jewish Transcript*, December 25, 1925. The dates when federations were achieved are listed in Elazar, *Community and Polity*, 163, table 17. Those for major West Coast cities, however, do not always correspond exactly with the various meetings announcing federation in local community newspapers.

120. Ethel R. Feineman to Samuel C. Kohs, September 15, 1923, Samuel C. Kohs Papers, Western Jewish History Center.

121. Rosenbaum, *Free to Choose*, 91.

122. *Emanu-El*, January 15, 1926; *B'nai B'rith Messenger*, January 29, 1926.

123. Kohs to M. J. Karpf, Training School for Jewish Social Work, New York City, July 16, 1927, Kohs Papers.

124. Rosenbaum, *Free to Choose*, 91.

125. *B'nai B'rith Messenger*, May 23, 1924.

126. *B'nai B'rith Messenger*, March 26, 1926.

127. Isaac Swett, "Report of Federated Jewish Societies [Portland]," *Scribe*, January 21, 1921, 5; Mrs. Isaac Swett, "Federated Jewish Societies Annual Report [1928]," *Scribe*, February 24, 1928; Jewish Service Association [Los Angeles], "Annual Federation Report, 1930," *B'nai B'rith Messenger*, December 19,1930, 1; "Federation of Jewish Charities Completes Nineteen Years of Service," *Emanu-El*, April 11, 1930.

128. Louis Newman, "Telling It in Gath," *Scribe*, February 1, 1929.

129. Carl Abbott, "Regional City and Network: Portland and Seattle in the Twentieth Century," *Western Historical Quarterly* 23, no. 3 (1992): 300–304.

130. U.S. Census Bureau, *Fifteenth Census of the United States: 1930*, vol. 2, *Population* (Washington, D.C.: Government Printing Office, 1933), 67–72, table 23. For a summary of the economic basis for the emergence of Los Angeles as regional metropolis, see

Steven P. Erie, *Globalizing L.A.: Trade, Infrastructure, and Regional Development* (Stanford, Calif.: Stanford University Press, 2004), 61–63.

131. On the origins of the movie moguls, see Gabler, *Empire of Their Own*; and "Los Angeles' Little Cutters," 138, 185.

3. EASTERN EUROPEANS, SEPHARDIM, AND THE BELATED CREATION OF JEWISH SPACE

Epigraph. Lucius L. Solomon's letter, "To Whom It May Concern," August 27, 1901, box 31, folder 12, Industrial Removal Office Records, I-91, American Jewish Historical Society, Newton Centre, Mass., and New York.

1. Information on Kayla Nudelman Lauterstein Bromberg comes from "The Story of Joseph Nudelman" (unpublished manuscript, Oregon Jewish Museum); and Felice Lauterstein Driesen, interview by Ellen Eisenberg, Portland, November 11, 1997. See also Ellen Eisenberg, "From Cooperative Farming to Urban Leadership," in Kahn, *Jewish Life in the American West*, 113–32. Israel Bromberg's communal leadership is noted many times in the *Scribe (Portland)* in the 1920s.

2. Cone, Droker, and Williams, *Family of Strangers*, 66. Albert Franco, oral history, 1978, transcript, 5, Jewish Community Oral History Project, University of Washington Archives. Sephardic immigrants to Los Angeles in the 1920s followed a similar pattern, often establishing flower shops.

3. Franco, oral history, 15.

4. Gershon Einbinder [Chaver Paver], *Clinton Street and Other Stories*, trans. Henry Goodman (New York: YKUF, 1974), 129. Einbinder died in 1964. For biographical information on Einbinder, see I. Goldberg's introduction, "Chaver Paver," in Einbinder, *Clinton Street*, vi–xii.

5. The unique ethnic diversity of the West is a central theme in the work of the "new western historians." See, e.g., Limerick, *Legacy of Conquest*, 260–69.

6. *Jewish Transcript (Seattle)*, January 29, 1926.

7. Arthur Goren, *New York Jews and the Quest for Community: The Kehillah Experiment, 1908–1922* (New York: Columbia University Press, 1970), 17.

8. 1878 census figures are from Weissbach, "Eve of

Mass Migration," 84–85; and Vorspan and Gartner, *Jews of Los Angeles*, 109.

9. Total immigration figures are from Gerald Sorin, *A Time for Building: The Third Migration, 1880–1920* (Baltimore: Johns Hopkins University Press, 1995), 58; San Francisco figures are from Ruth Kelson Rafael, *Continuum—a Selective History of San Francisco Eastern European Jewish Life, 1880–1940* (Berkeley, Calif.: Western Jewish History Center, Judah L. Magnes Memorial Museum, 1977), 7.

10. Hebrew Sheltering and Immigrant Aid Society of America, "Sixth Annual Report," *Jewish Immigration Bulletin (New York)* 5, no. 3 (1915): 49.

11. Weissbach, "Eve of Mass Migration," 84. San Francisco's Jewish population reached thirty thousand in 1907. As late as 1927, only thirty-five thousand Jews resided in that city.

12. Portland and Oakland figures are from Weissbach, "Eve of Mass Migration," 84–86. The Seattle figure is from Lori Etta Cohn, "Residential Patterns of the Jewish Community of the Seattle Area, 1910–1980" (master's thesis, University of Washington, 1982), 29. See also "Increase of Jewish Immigration in the Pacific Rim—Seattle, 1916," *Western States Jewish History* 26, no. 2 (1994): 158; reprinted from *Jewish Chronicle*, May 16, 1913, 3.

13. Goren, *New York Jews*, 17; Rosenbaum, *Visions of Reform*, 90.

14. The California towns appear in Weissbach's statistics, in "Eve of Mass Migration," table 2, 84–87. For Oregon, see Lowenstein, *Jews of Oregon*, chap. 3.

15. Lee Shai Weissbach, "East European Immigrants and the Image of Jews in the Small-Town South," *American Jewish History* 85, no. 3 (1997): 231–62. For example, of the seven Texas Jewish communities with populations greater than one hundred in 1878, four numbered one thousand or more by 1907, and six numbered more than one thousand by 1927. In contrast, of the eight California Jewish communities of one hundred or more in 1878, only three numbered more than one thousand in 1907, and four in 1927. See Weissbach, "Eve of Mass Migration," 84–85.

16. Cone, Droker, and Williams, *Family of Strangers*, 119, 129.

17. Rafael, "Continuum," 3. On Portland, see Low-enstein, *Jews of Oregon*. On Oakland, see Rosenbaum, *Free to Choose*, 48.

18. Cone, Droker, and Williams, *Family of Strangers*, 109–10; *Jewish Transcript*, January 29, 1926.

19. Jewish Genealogical Society of Los Angeles, "A Jewish Presence in Los Angeles" (timeline), *Roots–Key: Newsletter of the Jewish Genealogical Society of Los Angeles* 23, nos. 2–3 (2003), http://home.earthlink.net/~nholdeneditor/timelinea.htm.

20. Ibid.

21. Vorspan and Gartner, *Jews of Los Angeles*, 109.

22. Wendy Elliott, "The Jews of Boyle Heights, 1900–1950: The Melting Pot of Los Angeles," *Southern California Quarterly* 78, no. 1 (1996): 2.

23. U.S. Naturalization Records, 1907–14, Seattle. Of those arriving in the East, sixty-eight landed in New York City, six in Boston, five in Philadelphia, and two in Baltimore. Of those who entered the United States from Canada, twelve entered through midwestern states, one through Vermont, and eleven by crossing from British Columbia into Washington at Blaine.

24. Hebrew Sheltering and Immigrant Aid Society of America, "Seventh Annual Report," *Jewish Immigration Bulletin*, March 1916, 9–10. On the activities of such immigrant aid groups, see chapter 4.

25. Ellen Eisenberg, "Transplanted to the Rose City: The Creation of East European Jewish Community in Portland, Oregon," *Journal of American Ethnic History* 19, no. 3 (2000): 86. It is important to note that this represents a minimum number, since sojourns are detectable in these records only when a child was born in another state.

26. U.S. Naturalization Records, 1907–14, Seattle.

27. Eisenberg, "Transplanted to the Rose City," 86.

28. Amy Hill Shevitz, "Jewish Space and Place in Venice," in Kahn and Dollinger, *California Jews*, 68.

29. Rosenbaum, *Free to Choose*, 57.

30. Vorspan and Gartner, *Jews of Los Angeles*, 109.

31. Cone, Droker, and Williams, *Family of Strangers*, 54.

32. Rachel Silverstone, oral history, June 13, 1985, Jewish Community Oral History Project, University of Washington Archives.

33. Nathan Krems, oral history, July 12, 1973, Jewish Community Oral History Project.

34. Bailey Nieder, oral history, February 28 and March 8, 1987, Jewish Community Oral History Project.

35. Fannie Heppner, oral history, 1974, 10, San Francisco Jews of Eastern European Origin, 1880–1940: A Community Oral History Project, American Jewish Congress and Judah L. Magnes Museum, Western Jewish History Center.

36. New Odessa community, Articles of Incorporation, December 31, 1883, Records of Land Purchases and Incorporation, Douglas County, Oregon.

37. Ellen Eisenberg, *Jewish Agricultural Colonies in New Jersey* (Syracuse, N.Y.: Syracuse University Press, 1990), 45–52.

38. Weissbach, "Eve of Mass Migration," 83.

39. Cone, Droker, and Williams, *Family of Strangers*, 55–56.

40. White, *It's Your Misfortune*, 391.

41. Petaluma is discussed in more detail later in this chapter.

42. Vorspan and Gartner, *Jews of Los Angeles*, 109.

43. Mitchell Brian Gelfand, "Chutzpah in El Dorado: Social Mobility of Jews in Los Angeles" (Ph.D. diss., Carnegie Mellon, 1981), 38. The influx of T.B. sufferers and other health seekers prompted the establishment of Jewish hospitals to serve them. These institutions are discussed in chapter 4.

44. Abrams, *Jewish Women Pioneering*, 60.

45. Vorspan and Gartner, *Jews of Los Angeles*, 115.

46. Gelfand, "Chutzpah in El Dorado," 36.

47. Esther Midler, "Neighborhood Survey for the Educational Center of the Council of Jewish Women" (Seattle, 1922), manuscript, accession no. 2116-7, 4, Joseph Cohen Papers, University of Washington Archives.

48. Eisenberg, "Transplanted to the Rose City," 87; Eisenberg, "From Cooperative Farming to Urban Leadership," 119.

49. William Toll, "Jewish Families and the Intergenerational Transition in the American Hinterland," *Journal of American Ethnic History* 12, no. 2 (1993): 3–35; on Seattle, see Cone, Droker, and Williams, *Family of Strangers*, 59.

50. Sarna, *American Judaism*, 156.

51. Ibid., 157.

52. Reva Clar, "Jewish Acculturation in California's San Joaquin Valley: A Memoir," *Western States Jewish History* 19, no. 1 (1986): 55.

53. Phillips, "Challenge of Family," 24–25. See also Quinn, "Religion in the American West," 152, 158.

54. The council's network of settlement houses is discussed in chapter 4.

55. Eisenberg, *Jewish Agricultural Colonies*, chap. 2.

56. Jack Glazier, *Dispersing the Ghetto: The Relocation of Jewish Immigrants across America* (Ithaca, N.Y.: Cornell University Press, 1998), 202.

57. On the magnet effect, see ibid., 20. Toll's study of the IRO in Portland demonstrates that the organization often supported the travel of children joining relatives in the West. See William Toll, "They Built a New Home," in *Historical Scribe* (Jewish Historical Society of Oregon), Spring 1980, 1–2. Figures for Washington and Oregon can be found in Samuel Joseph, *Jewish Immigration to the United States* (New York: Columbia University Press, 1914), app. H; and in Glazier, *Dispersing the Ghetto*, 196, table 1.

58. Vorspan and Gartner, *Jews of Los Angeles*, 111–12.

59. Cone, Droker, and Williams, *Family of Strangers*, 42.

60. Edward Glazer, oral history, 1981, Jewish Community Oral History Project.

61. Eisenberg, "Transplanted to the Rose City," 85–86.

62. Solomons, "To Whom It May Concern." The Solomons had a strong history of volunteerism—Lucius's mother, Hannah, worked with both orphans and immigrants. See chapters 1 and 4.

63. Toll, "They Built a New Home," 1–2.

64. Eisenberg, "Transplanted to the Rose City," 82, 90.

65. Albert A. Ruskin, "Looking Backward," *Scribe*, March 20, 1936, 2.

66. Vorspan and Gartner, *Jews of Los Angeles*, 164.

67. Ibid., 101–2. B'nai B'rith formally affiliated with the Reform movement after Solomon's departure.

68. William M. Kramer and Reva Clar, "Michael G. Solomon (1868–1927): Rabbi and Lawyer of Los Angeles," *Western States Jewish Historical Quarterly* 14, no. 1 (1981): 3–4, 18–19.

69. L. G. Reynolds, "Historic Recollections of Congregation Sinai," in *The Burning of a Mortgage: An*

Historic Record of Congregation Sinai (Los Angeles: Congregation Sinai, 1945), 15.

70. Vorspan and Gartner, *Jews of Los Angeles*, 163.

71. Ibid., 162.

72. Ibid., 162–63.

73. Ibid., 164.

74. Congregation Bikur Cholim, 1921 Constitution, accession no. 2450-5, box 1, folder 3, Congregation Bikur Cholim Machzikay Hadath Collection, University of Washington Archives.

75. The individuals listed on a 1910 document titled "Membership of Congregation Bikur Cholum" were located in the 1910 U.S. census manuscript. "Membership of Congregation Bikur Cholum," accession no. 1960-2,3,4, folder 14, Jacob Kaplan Papers, University of Washington Archives; U.S. manuscript census, King County, Seattle, 1910, Ancestry.com. Category totals differ because information on the census is sometimes incomplete or illegible.

76. Krems, oral history.

77. Congregation Bikur Cholim, Minutes, 1912, accession no. 2450-001, box 2, folder 1, Congregation Bikur Cholim Machzikay Hadath Collection. Contract with Solomon Tovbin, accession no. 2450-5, box 3, folder 15, Congregation Bikur Cholim Machzikay Hadath Collection.

78. Souvenir program, Congregation Bikur Cholum, March 11, 1917, accession no. 1960-2,3,4, box 1, folder 14, Kaplan Papers. The day's program appears on page 17.

79. "A Short Historical Sketch of the Chevrah Bikur Cholum," souvenir program, Congregation Bikur Cholum.

80. Rabbi Faivusovitch migrated through China to Seattle. Lowenstein, *Jews of Oregon*, 105.

81. Ibid., 108.

82. Ibid., 109.

83. Vorspan and Gartner, *Jews of Los Angeles*, 160–61.

84. Rosenbaum, *Free to Choose*, 59, 48, 64–65.

85. Ibid., 65–69.

86. Sorin, *Time for Building*, chap. 5. New York's Lower East Side peaked in Jewish population in 1910. See Goren, *New York Jews*, 18.

87. Vorspan and Gartner, *Jews of Los Angeles*, 119.

88. Elliott, "Jews of Boyle Heights," 2. By 1920, the migration from Boyle Heights to West Los Angeles had begun; see chapter 5.

89. Elliott, "Jews of Boyle Heights," 4.

90. Cohn, "Residential Patterns," 34. Cone, Droker, and Williams, *Family of Strangers*, 138. While Jews were only 15 percent of the Central District as a whole, their percentage in individual census tracts was as high as 41 percent. Cohn, "Residential Patterns," 34.

91. Cohn, "Residential Patterns," 43, 55. Cohn shows that the dissimilarity index, "the degree to which the Jews are segregated residentially from non-Jews" (with 0 indicating even distribution and 100 indicating total segregation), rose from 40.1 percent in 1910 to 59.2 percent in 1940. This increase is at odds with the experience of eastern cities, where the highest dissimilarity scores came early in the century.

92. Jacqueline B. Williams, "Was It Strictly Kosher? Washington State, 1889–1937," *Western States Jewish History* 36, no. 3 (2004): 230–31.

93. Cone, Droker, and Williams, *Family of Strangers*, 146.

94. Campaign poster for W. K. Sickels, box 3, Kaplan Papers.

95. Congregation Bikur Cholim's documents, from its founding on, are nearly entirely in English. Newsletters, constitutions and bylaws, and minutes that have been preserved are all in English, although at least one copy of the constitution was also printed in Yiddish, and congregational newsletters occasionally included a page or two in Yiddish. The congregation's records are held at the University of Washington Archives.

96. Averbach, "South of Market District," 202–3; Toll, "Gender, Ethnicity, and Jewish Settlement Work," 294–95.

97. Lilian Gertrude Cherney, oral history, 1978, box 1, 51, San Francisco Jews of Eastern European Origin Project.

98. Rose Hartman Ets-Hokin, oral history, box 4, transcript, 5, San Francisco Jews of Eastern European Origin Project.

99. Steven Leibo, "Out the Road: The San Bruno Avenue Jewish Community of San Francisco, 1901–1968," *Western States Jewish Historical Quarterly* 11, no. 2 (1979): 99.

100. Jerry Flamm, *Good Life in Hard Times: San Francisco in the '20s and '30s* (San Francisco: Chronicle Books, 1999), 72.

101. Raye Rich, oral history with Ava F. Kahn, San Francisco, September 12, 2000, pt. 1, 4, Western Jewish History Center.

102. Flamm, *Good Life*, 72; Rich, oral history, pt. 1, 5, 9.

103. David Soren, interview by Zelda Bronstein and Kenneth Kann, 1974, Petaluma Jewish Community Oral History Project, Western Jewish History Center, 18.

104. Kenneth Kann, *Comrades and Chicken Ranchers: The Story of a California Jewish Community* (Ithaca, N.Y.: Cornell University Press, 1993), 3.

105. Ibid., 83. Later, a bitter dispute over communism split the community. See Kann, chap. 11.

106. Ibid., 97.

107. Ibid., 4. In 1975, Petaluma's Jewish population was triple what it had been fifty years earlier.

108. Oral histories, Sonia Myers Wachtin, March 18, 1975, and Laura Berch, February 7, 1973, and October 16, 1979, transcript, 1–2, Jewish Community Oral History Project.

109. Congregation Herzl, Articles of Incorporation, 1906, University of Washington Archives.

110. Cone, Droker, and Williams, *Family of Strangers*, 225.

111. The anti-Zionist movement peaked in San Francisco and Seattle during the World War II years. See chapter 5.

112. Aaron Riche, "Zionism in Los Angeles on Its Twenty-fifth Anniversary," *Western States Jewish Historical Quarterly* 23, no. 1 (1990): 33 (originally published in Jewish National Fund of Los Angeles, *Jubilee Number 1902–1927*, ed. George Saylin [1927]).

113. Eisenberg, "Transplanted to the Rose City"; Deborah Goldberg, "Jewish Spirit on the Urban Frontier: Zionism in Portland, 1901–1941" (B.A. thesis, Reed College, 1982).

114. Vorspan and Gartner, *Jews of Los Angeles*, 114.

115. 1891 articles of incorporation of Chevra Bikur Cholum, accession no. 1960, box 1, folder 11, Kaplan Papers.

116. Vorspan and Gartner, *Jews of Los Angeles*, 114.

117. Cone, Droker, and Williams, *Family of Strangers*, 71.

118. Vorspan and Gartner, *Jews of Los Angeles*, 115.

119. Eisenberg, "Transplanted to the Rose City," 89.

120. Free Loan Society records, Oregon Jewish Museum. Records for the 1910–13 period show prominent, established leaders such as Ben Selling and David Solis-Cohen serving as officers alongside Russian immigrant leaders like Israel Bromberg, Isaac Swett, and David Nemerovsky.

121. Toll, *Ethnic Middle Class*, 108, 126–30. See also discussion in chapter 2.

122. Ellen Eisenberg, "Immigrants, Ethnics, and Natives: Jewish Women in Portland, 1910–1940" (paper presented at the Western Jewish Studies Association conference, Seattle, March 1999).

123. For discussion of Poseners in the West, see Stern, "Jews in the 1870 Census of Los Angeles"; and Kahn and Eisenberg, "Western Reality."

124. Kahn and Eisenberg, "Western Reality," 478. The two congregations merged permanently more than half a century later, in 1961.

125. Kramer and Clar, "Michael G. Solomons," 18–19.

126. Marcus Rosenthal, "The Jewish Immigration Problem," *Western States Jewish Historical Quarterly* 6, no. 4 (1974): 279, 278–89 (originally published in *Emanu-El*, February 24, 1905).

127. William M. Kramer, *Sephardic Jews in the West Coast States*, vol. 2, *Los Angeles* (Los Angeles: Western States Jewish History Association, 1996), 313.

128. Cone, Droker, and Williams, *Family of Strangers*, chap. 3. See also Albert Adatto, "Sephardim and the Seattle Sephardic Community" (master's thesis, University of Washington, 1939).

129. Cone, Droker, and Williams, *Family of Strangers*, 60.

130. Adatto, "Sephardim," 64–74.

131. Elazar Behar, oral history, February–March 1990, transcript, 134, Jewish Community Oral History Project.

132. Midler, "Neighborhood Survey," 4. The survey lists for the total population of Washington Elementary School—the school with the largest Jewish immigrant population—the numbers of children speaking various languages at home and the languages spoken by

their mother and father. The two most commonly cited non-English languages are Yiddish (listed as "Jew") and "Spanish." Given the school's substantial population of Sephardic children and the fact that no other Spanish-speaking group is indicated, it can be assumed that "Spanish" referred to the Sephardics' Ladino, sometimes called Judeo Spanish.

133. Ibid., 17.

134. Tillie de Leon, oral history, May 5, 1986, transcript, 14, Jewish Community Oral History Project.

135. Franco, oral history, 15.

136. Behar, oral history, 125–26.

137. Mary Capeloto, oral history, 1982, transcript, 2, Jewish Community Oral History Project.

138. The practice of blackballing Sephardim from the Jewish fraternities at the University of Washington is mentioned in several oral histories, including those of Franco, Capeloto, and Benjamin "Bud" Asia, Jewish Community Oral History Project, University of Washington Archives.

139. Adatto, "Sephardim," 113.

140. Ibid., 85.

141. Lowenstein, *Jews of Oregon*, 110–11; Toll, *Ethnic Middle Class*, 129, 58.

142. Aron Hasson, "The Sephardic Jews of Rhodes in Los Angeles," *Western States Jewish Historical Quarterly* 6, no. 4 (1974): 245–47.

143. Aron Hasson, "A Rhodesli Register of Los Angeles Pioneers and a Sourcebook for Rhodesli Scholarship," *Western States Jewish History* 28, no. 4 (1996): 412. The Peace and Progress Society (Sociedad Pas y Progreso), which formed in 1917, kept its records in Ladino through the 1930s.

144. Hasson, "Sephardic Jews of Rhodes," 247–48.

145. Ibid., 251–52.

146. Aron Hasson, "The Los Angeles Rhodesli Sephardic Community," *Western States Jewish History* 28, no. 4 (1996): 386.

147. Rising levels of anti-Semitism in the late-nineteenth- and early-twentieth-century urban Northeast and South have been well documented by historians. Notable outbreaks of anti-Semitism occurred in the South, especially during the economic crises of the 1870s and 1890s. Some argue that Jews were not fully accepted as whites until the 1930s and 1940s. See Jacobson,

Whiteness of a Different Color; and Diner, *Jews of the United States*, 171.

148. An extensive literature on the application of racial thinking to Southern and Eastern European immigrants in the late nineteenth and early twentieth centuries has developed over the past decade. See, e.g., Jacobson, *Whiteness of a Different Color*; and Goldstein, *Price of Whiteness*. For a particularly vivid example of Jewish whiteness in the West, see Gordon, *Great Arizona Orphan Abduction*. Gordon demonstrates that Jewish men and women (as well as other "Euro-Latins" whose whiteness would have been questioned in the East) functioned as part of an Anglo group that seized white Irish orphans from their would-be adoptive Mexican families. For a discussion of Jewish whiteness in the West, see Ellen Eisenberg, *The First to Cry Down Injustice? Western Jews and Japanese Removal during WWII* (Lanham, Md.: Rowman and Littlefield, 2008).

149. On the role of the Native Sons organizations in defining "white space," see David Glassberg, "Making Places in California," in *Sense of History: The Place of the Past in American Life* (Amherst: University of Massachusetts Press, 2001), 167–202. The California Native Sons and Daughters organizations were notoriously anti-Asian and played a major role in the campaign to prohibit Asian immigration.

150. *Oregon Native Son* 1 (May 1899): 3; 1 (July 1899): 138, 175.

151. Laurence Stuppy, "Henry H. Lissner, M.D., Los Angeles Physician," *Western States Jewish Historical Quarterly* 8, no. 3 (1976): 212.

152. In *Oregon Native Son*, frequent stories on Native Americans present a range of stereotypes, from romanticized versions of supposed Indian lore to depictions of "savages," in both cases clearly situating them as the other, in contrast to white pioneers. On the rare occasion that African Americans were mentioned—even as "Negro pioneers"—they are often described in negative terms ("the sons of Ham") and their shortcomings highlighted ("truth was never a conscious ingredient of his character"). None of those mentioned as "Negro pioneers" were included as members of the all-white organization. Asian immigrants are notable in *Oregon Native Son* for their absence. The one mention of the possibility of "the Chinaman a pioneer" discusses an

effort by the British to trick a group of Chinese men into settling in the area and helping to secure the British claim. The story explains that the group of Chinese men never landed and suggests that they have no place in pioneer history, for "what ultimately became of them has not been made a matter of history." See *Oregon Native Son*, vol. 1. For examples of stories on Native Americans, see "Indian War Recollections," August 1899, 210–11; October 1899, 305. One story recalls the first "neck tie party" (lynching) in the region in celebratory tones, recalling a white trader who acted as "judge, jury, and executioner" and "Mr. Indian dangled to the music of the breeze" (October 1899, 337). On African Americans, see "Negro Pioneers: Their Page in History," October 1899, 432–433; on the Chinese, see "Chinamen a Pioneer," October 1899, 530.

153. Lowenstein, *Jews of Oregon*, 171.

154. The Portland Jewish *Scribe* editorialized strongly against the school bill. In addition, prominent Portland Jews including Rabbi Jonah Wise, Mrs. Solomon Hirsch, and Ben Selling campaigned against it. Selling served on the speakers bureau for the Protestant and Non-Sectarian Schools Committee, formed to combat the bill. *Scribe*, November 3, 1922. Lawrence J. Saalfeld, *Forces of Prejudice in Oregon, 1920–1925* (Portland, Ore.: Archdiocesan Historical Commission, 1984), 78.

155. Lowenstein, *Jews of Oregon*, 171.

156. Frank Van Nuys, *Americanizing the West: Race, Immigrants, and Citizenship, 1890–1930* (Lawrence: University Press of Kansas, 2002), 39–42, 67. The contrast between the progressive CCIH and California's Alien Land Law, which both emerged from the legislative session of 1913, is the subject of Spencer C. Olin, Jr., "European Immigrant and Oriental Alien: Acceptance and Rejection by the California Legislature of 1913," *Pacific Historical Review* 35 (1966): 303–15.

157. Van Nuys, *Americanizing the West*, 19.

158. For Voorsanger's comments, see Rosenbaum, *Visions of Reform*, 89. Kahn appears repeatedly in the league's proceedings and is listed as a member of its Lecture Bureau. *Proceedings of the Asiatic Exclusion League, 1907–1913* (New York, 1977); see September 1908, 13. Decades later, his wife, Congresswoman Florence Prag Kahn, worked closely with the Chinese American community and received its electoral support.

"Mrs. Kahn Invites Chinese Friends to Banquet to Show Thanks" (translated from the Chinese) *Zhong Xi Ri Bao*, October 28, 1936.

159. A brief summary of patterns of anti-Japanese discrimination is found in Ronald Takaki, *Strangers from a Different Shore: A History of Asian Americans* (Boston: Little, Brown, 1989), 203–29.

160. Rosenbaum, *Visions of Reform*, 108.

161. Rosenbaum, *Free to Choose*, 89.

162. Rosenbaum maintains that the incident "certainly had the potential for stirring a wave of anti-Jewish sentiment throughout the Bay Area . . . [but] it did nothing of the kind," whereas Fradkin sees anti-Semitism as playing a more important role. See Rosenbaum, *Visions of Reform*, 106–8; and Fradkin, *Great Earthquake*. See also the discussion of the Ruef incident in chapter 2.

163. A December 3, 1920, *Scribe* editorial praises Rabbi Jack for his courage in speaking out against anti-Asian measures, but, characteristically, the *Scribe* refused to take a position on the substance of the issue. For a detailed discussion of western Jewish responses to Asian immigrants, see Eisenberg, *Cry Down Injustice*, chap. 1.

164. Van Nuys, *Americanizing the West*, 24, 15.

165. For an assessment of the idea of a regional economy and why the economic base of the post–Civil War South remained stagnant, see Gavin Wright, *Old South, New South: Revolutions in the Southern Economy since the Civil War* (New York: Basic Books, 1986), 4–16. On the South as a "colonized" economy with low wages, heavy out-migration, and an undemocratic political culture for the black and white working class, see Jacqueline Jones, *The Dispossessed: America's Underclass from the Civil War to the Present* (New York: Basic Books, 1992), 130–66.

166. Clara Gordon Rubin, interview, 1982, Clara Gordon Rubin Papers, University of Washington Archives.

167. Midler, "Neighborhood Survey," 42.

168. Rubin, interview.

169. The individuals listed on a 1910 document titled "Membership of Congregation Bikur Cholum" were located in the 1910 U.S. manuscript census using the electronic census images on Ancestry.com. "Membership of Congregation Bikur Cholum," Kaplan Papers; U.S.

manuscript census, King County, Seattle, 1910, Ancestry.com.

170. Rosenbaum, *Free to Choose*, 61–63.

171. A brief overview of the growth of Los Angeles between 1900 and 1930 is provided in Greg Hise, "Industry and Imaginative Geographies," in *Metropolis in the Making: Los Angeles in the 1920s*, ed. Tom Sitton and William Deverell (Berkeley: University of California Press, 2001), 13–37.

172. In 1900, 45 percent of Eastern European Jews in Los Angeles were proprietors, another 10.6 percent did sales or clerical work, and less than a quarter worked in blue-collar clothing and textile positions. Gelfand, "Chutzpah in El Dorado," 63, 80.

173. Ibid., 122.

174. Vorspan and Gartner, *Jews of Los Angeles*, 127.

175. Ibid., 125.

176. Ibid., 212–15.

177. Rose Pesotta, *Bread upon the Waters*, ed. John Nicholas Beffel (Ithaca, N.Y.: ILR Press, 1987), 27, 32, 40.

178. William Toll, "Acclimatizing Fashion: Jewish Inventiveness on the Other (Pacific) Coast, 1850 to 1940," in *A Perfect Fit: The Garment Industry and American Jewry* (Lubbock: Texas Tech University Press, forthcoming).

179. Vorspan and Gartner, *Jews of Los Angeles*, 110.

180. Rosenbaum, *Visions of Reform*, 93–94, 89. See also Jane Schweitzer, "The Russian Jewish Immigration and Rabbi Jacob Voorsanger," *Western States Jewish History* 17, no. 2 (1985): 138–39.

181. Rosenbaum, *Visions of Reform*, 91.

182. Norton B. Stern and William M. Kramer, introduction to Rosenthal, "Jewish Immigration Problem," 278.

183. Rosenthal, "Jewish Immigration Problem," 278–89.

184. *B'nai B'rith Messenger (Los Angeles)*, January 31, 1910.

185. Rosenbaum, *Visions of Reform*, 119.

186. Simon Lubin correspondence with Judeans of Oakland, May 1914, Lubin Papers.

187. Hebrew Sheltering and Immigrant Aid Society of America, "Report of the Sixth Annual Meeting," *Jewish Immigration Bulletin* 5, no. 3 (1915): 50. His correspondence included, for example, inquiries to the New York Public Library regarding services for immigrants.

188. Simon Lubin and Christina Krysto, "The Strength of America III: The Significance of Modern Migration," *Survey* 43 (January 24, 1920): 461.

189. Leslie W. Koepplin, *A Relationship of Reform: Immigrants and Progressives in the Far West* (New York: Garland, 1990), 36–37. Kahn was the sponsor of several bills to restrict Asian immigration. See Reva Clar and William M. Kramer, "Chinese-Jewish Relations in the Far West: 1850–1950; Part 2," *Western States Jewish History* 21, no. 2 (1989): 148–49. In an earlier vote on a similar bill in 1915, Congressman Kahn was one of only two members of the House of Representatives who refused to vote and simply answered, "Present," when their names were called. Hebrew Sheltering and Immigrant Aid Society of America, "Sixth Annual Report," *Jewish Immigration Bulletin* 5, no. 3 (1915): x–xv.

190. Ben Schloss, presidential address, B'nai B'rith District Grand Lodge No. 4, Forty-third annual meeting, February 1906, 7, Western Jewish History Center.

191. Toll, "They Built a New Home," 1–2.

192. Jean Braverman La Pove, oral history, 1978, Western Jewish History Center.

193. Toll, *Ethnic Middle Class*, 62–63.

194. Midler, "Neighborhood Survey," 33.

195. William Toll, "The Feminization of the Heroic: Ethel Feineman and Professional Nurture," in *Crisis and Reaction: The Hero in Jewish History*, ed. Menachem Mor (Omaha, Neb.: Creighton University Press, 1995), 204–5, 208.

196. Vivian Dudune Solomon, oral history, 1977, San Francisco Jews of Eastern European Origin project.

197. Van Nuys, *Americanizing the West*, 68, 113, 117.

198. Simon Lubin and Christina Krysto, "The Strength of America, II: The Conception of Nationality," *Survey*, January 3, 1920, 353; Horace M. Kallen to Lubin, October 23, 1915, Lubin Papers; Van Nuys, *Americanizing the West*, 163–65.

199. Van Nuys, *Americanizing the West*, 180.

200. *Scribe*, June 8, 1928; November 23, 1928; January 11, 1929. Toll, *Ethnic Middle Class*, 104.

201. Cone, Droker, and Williams, *Family of Strangers*, 181–83.

202. Midler, "Neighborhood Survey," 25, 29–30.

203. Ibid., 13–14.

204. Moshe Menuhin, "Jewish Communal Education in San Francisco in 1926," *Western States Jewish History* 21, no. 2 (1989): 99–102 (originally published in *Jewish Education News*, March 1926). Menuhin was the father of the violin prodigy.

205. Federation of Jewish Charities, Executive Committee, Minutes, 1910–20, vol. 1, 79B, April 21, 1915, 132, Western Jewish History Center.

206. Menuhin, "Jewish Communal Education," 100.

207. Solomon, oral history.

208. Vorspan and Gartner, *Jews of Los Angeles*, 168.

209. Ibid., 170.

210. Menuhin, "Jewish Communal Education," 101.

211. Sarna, *American Judaism*, 225.

212. Rosenbaum, *Visions of Reform*, 95.

213. Zarchin, *Glimpses of Jewish Life*, 221–22; Rosenbaum, *Visions of Reform*, 123–24. An oral history in which Mrs. Reuben (Rose) Rinder discusses her role in Hadassah is available at the Western Jewish History Center in Berkeley.

214. Zarchin, *Glimpses of Jewish Life*, 201. It is notable that this support came despite the fact there were several Jewish National Welfare Fund board members and campaign organizers who later became anti-Zionist activists, including fund board member and American Council for Judaism activist Grover Magnin (cousin of Rabbi Edgar Magnin) and Lloyd Dinkelspiel and Rabbi Irving Reichert, both of whom chaired campaigns. See Zarchin, *Glimpses of Jewish Life*, 195–97.

215. Wachtin, oral history; *Jewish Transcript*, February 26, 1926.

216. National Council of Jewish Women (NCJW), "History of the Seattle Section, National Council of Jewish Women," accession no. 2089-29, box 1, folder 1, 48–49, NCJW, Seattle Section records, University of Washington Archives (hereafter cited as NCJW, Seattle Section, "History").

217. Felix Frankfurter to Solomon Prottas, December 14, 1917, accession no. 2216-3, box 1, folder 2, Sam Prottas Papers, University of Washington Archives.

218. Lowenstein, *Jews of Oregon*, 86.

219. Ellen Eisenberg, "Beyond San Francisco: The Failure of Anti-Zionism in Portland, Oregon, *American Jewish History* 86, no. 3 (1998): 318–19.

220. Thomas Kolsky, *Jews against Zionism: The American Council for Judaism, 1942–1948* (Philadelphia: Temple University Press, 1990), 206.

221. William M. Kramer and Norton B. Stern, "The Study of Los Angeles Jewish History: An Analytical Consideration of a Major Work," *Western States Jewish Historical Quarterly* 3, no. 1 (1970): 46. Some claim that Magnin had been a Zionist from his earliest days in Los Angeles. See William M. Kramer and Reva Clar, "Rabbi Edgar F. Magnin and the Modernization of Los Angeles Jewry," *Western States Jewish History* 19, no. 3 (1987): 240–41.

222. See, e.g., *B'nai B'rith Messenger*, April 6, 1928; June 22, 1928; January 3, 1930; January 10, 1930.

223. Vorspan and Gartner, *Jews of Los Angeles*, 186–88; Kramer and Stern, "Study of Los Angeles Jewish History," 46.

224. Riche, "Zionism in Los Angeles," 31–32.

225. *B'nai B'rith Messenger*, January 3 and 10, 1930. *Jewish Transcript*, January 3, 1930.

4. FROM CHARITY TO PHILANTHROPY: A REGIONAL MODEL, 1870s–1930s

Epigraph. This Eastern European expression was said to characterize Jewish immigration to California, especially southern California. Cited in Karen S. Wilson, "Citizens of Los Angeles: Jewish Families and the Naissance of the Metropolis" (master's thesis, Hebrew Union College–Jewish Institute of Religion, 2003), 65.

1. "Lewis Gerstle," in *Western Jewry: An Account of the Achievements of the Jews and Judaism in California*, ed. A. W. Voorsanger (San Francisco: Emanu-El, 1916), 92–94. It is unclear whether Gerstle gave all of the money himself or solicited his friends on behalf of the organization. Or the amount could have been less. A treasurer's report lists a gift from Lewis Gerstle of $2,160. *First Annual Report of the Emanu-El Sisterhood for Personal Service of San Francisco, California, for the Fiscal Year 1894–95* (San Francisco, 1895), Western Jewish History Center.

2. Lowenstein, Jews of Oregon, 83. It cannot be verified where Loewenberg trained in social work. According to Loewenberg's niece, she studied in New

York City. Gladys Trachtenberg, oral history, August 29, 1977, transcript, 3, Oregon Jewish Museum. However, the *News-Telegram (Portland)*, on July 19, 1937, reported that Loewenberg "studied social work at the University of Oregon under the noted authority Dr. Edward C. Divine and others, and after starting her career at Neighborhood House in 1912, continued those studies in New York and Chicago."

3. Toll, *Ethnic Middle Class*, 102. Loewenberg led Neighborhood House from 1912 to 1945.

4. Jeanne E. Abrams, *Blazing the Tuberculosis Trail: The Religio-ethnic Role of Four Sanatoria in Early Denver* (Denver: Colorado Historical Society, 1991), 19.

5. Erik Greenberg, "Peter 'Pete' Kahn: Los Angeles Jewish Leader, 1878–1952," *Western States Jewish History* 38, no. 1 (2005): 18.

6. Bonnie Rogers, "The Founders: The Story of the City of Hope," *Roots–Key: Newsletter of the Jewish Genealogical Society of Los Angeles*, April 2003, http://home.earthlink.net/~nholdeneditor/City%20of%20Hope.htm.

7. Greenberg, "Peter 'Pete' Kahn," 19–20.

8. Ibid., 39.

9. See Eldon G. Ernst, "American Religious History from a Pacific Coast Perspective," in *Religion and Society in the American West*, ed. Carl Guarneri and David Alvarez (Lanham, Md.: University Press of America, 1987), 21–28.

10. For a discussion of the western health rush, see John E. Baur, *The Health Seekers of Southern California, 1870–1900* (San Marino, Calif.: Huntington Library, 1959).

11. Protestant and Catholic women also formed relief societies. See Anne Firor Scott, *Natural Allies: Women's Associations in American History* (Urbana: University of Illinois Press, 1991).

12. Virginia Katz, "The Ladies' Hebrew Benevolent Society of Los Angeles in 1892," *Western States Jewish Historical Quarterly* 10, no. 2 (1978): 158 (originally published in Mrs. M. Burton Williamson, *Ladies' Clubs and Societies in Los Angeles in 1892*).

13. Kahn, *Jewish Voices*, 234; Wilson, "Citizens of Los Angeles," 61; Toll, *Ethnic Middle Class*, 48–49.

14. Katz, "Ladies' Hebrew Benevolent Society," 158.

15. NCJW, Seattle Section, "History," 18; Minutes of Board Meeting, Temple Beth Israel, May 3, 1906, Temple Beth Israel Collection, Oregon Jewish Museum.

16. See chapter 1 for more information about the society.

17. *Appeal, Jewish Orphan Asylum and Home, District 4, Independent Order of B'nai B'rith* (San Francisco: M. Weiss Oriental Printing House, 1870), quoted in Kahn, *Jewish Voices*, 226.

18. The female teacher was Hannah Marks Solomons (see chapter 1).

19. Annual Report to the Board of Directors, Pacific Hebrew Orphan Asylum and Home Society, 1878, Bancroft Library.

20. Minutes of the Ladies' Hebrew Benevolent Society show that children were sent to San Francisco in 1902, 1903, and 1905. As quoted in Benjamin Louis Cohen, "Constancy and Change in the Jewish Family Agency of Los Angeles, 1854–1979" (diss., University of Southern California, 1972), 19. Founded by the B'nai B'rith with the help of elite families, the Jewish Orphans' Home of Southern California grew into a premiere institution for children. The need for an orphan home grew after Los Angeles began attracting tuberculosis patients who then died and left children needing care. With the support of the Newmarks and other founding families the orphanage became the renowned Vista Del Mar Child Care agency. Vorspan and Gartner, *Jews of Los Angeles*, 177. Gertrude L. Shopera, President, Hebrew Benevolent Society, letter, October 5, 1925, Jewish Family and Children's Service reports, 2003, box 6, folder 18, Seattle Hebrew Benevolent Society Collection, University of Washington Archives.

21. As quoted in Abrams, *Jewish Women Pioneering*, 12.

22. Ibid., 84. For a discussion of southern Jewish women and their similarities to Jewish women in other regions, see Bauman, "Southern Jewish Women."

23. Gerald Gamm and Robert D. Putnam, "The Growth of Voluntary Associations in America, 1840–1940," *Journal of Interdisciplinary History* 29 (March 1999): 511–15, quoted in Abrams, *Jewish Women Pioneering*, 44. Gamm and Putnam's 1999 study indicated that in the later half of the nineteenth century voluntary associations were more active and prevalent in the small cities and towns of the West than in the East.

24. Abrams, *Jewish Women Pioneering*, 46.

25. William Toll, "From Domestic Judaism to Public Ritual," in *Women and American Judaism*, ed. Pamela S. Nadell and Jonathan D. Sarna (Hanover, N.H.: University Press of New England / Brandeis University Press, 2001), 139. For examples of women's activities in the West, see Peggy Pascoe, *Relations of Rescue: The Search for Female Moral Authority in the American West, 1874–1939* (New York: Oxford University Press, 1990); and Abrams, *Jewish Women Pioneering*. For a more general history of American Jewish women, see Hasia R. Diner and Beryl Lieff Benderly, *Her Works Praise Her* (New York: Basic Books, 2002).

26. Toll, *Ethnic Middle Class*, 57.

27. For an excellent discussion of framing women's volunteering and organization work as political action, see Hasia R. Diner, "A Political Tradition? American Jewish Women and Political History," in *Jews and Gender: The Challenge to Hierarchy*, ed. Jonathan Frankel (Oxford: Oxford University Press, 2000), 54–69.

28. See Rebecca J. Mead, *How the Vote Was Won: Suffrage in the United States, 1868–1914* (New York: New York University Press, 2004).

29. For background on Progressivism, see Robert H. Wiebe, *The Search for Order, 1877–1920* (Westport, Conn.: Greenwood Press, 1980); and Richard Hofstadter, *The Age of Reform: From Bryan to F.D.R.* (New York: Knopf, 1955). On tensions between reformers and immigrants, see Rivka S. Lissak, *Pluralism and Progressivism: Hull House and the New Immigrants, 1890–1919* (Chicago: University of Chicago Press, 1989).

30. See the discussion of "domestic feminism" and gender roles in Faith Rogow, *Gone to Another Meeting* (Tuscaloosa: University of Alabama Press, 1993), and Toll, "Gender, Ethnicity, and Jewish Settlement Work," 291–306.

31. See Van Nuys, *Americanizing the West*, 36–55.

32. Pascoe, *Relations of Rescue*, 209.

33. Abrams, *Jewish Women Pioneering*, 13.

34. Cohn, Droker, and Williams, *Family of Strangers*, 91; Toll, "Gender, Ethnicity, and Jewish Settlement Work," 293.

35. The name is sometimes spelled as May. Mae Goldsmith, who never married, served the Seattle community for eleven years until she was superseded by a professionally trained social worker.

36. The Sisters of Charity provided care in several western cities beginning in the 1850s. In San Francisco, the German Hospital, the French Hospital, the Catholic Hospital, and St. Mary's were organized by 1860.

37. See Sarna, *American Judaism*, 222.

38. Charles Rosenberg, quoted in Abrams, *Blazing the Tuberculosis Trail*, 4.

39. Diner, *Jews of the United States*, 177; Alan M. Kraut and Deborah A. Kraut, *Covenant of Care: Newark Beth Israel and the Jewish Hospital in America* (New Brunswick, N.J.: Rutgers University Press, 2007), 3.

40. Kraut and Kraut, *Covenant of Care*, 5.

41. Barbara S. Rogers and Stephen M. Dobbs, *The First Century: Mount Zion Hospital and Medical Center, 1887–1987* (San Francisco: Mount Zion Hospital and Medical Center, 1987), 5.

42. Jacob Voorsanger, "The Beginning of the First Jewish Hospital in the West," *Western States Jewish Historical Quarterly* 8, no. 2 (1976): 100 (originally published in *Emanu-El*, January 1, 1897).

43. Mount Zion Hospital Minute Book, 1887–1906, insert before page 99 and December 14, 1897, 101, Western Jewish History Center.

44. Kraut and Kraut, *Covenant of Care*, 24.

45. The opposition was led by Rabbi Marcus Friedlander of the First Hebrew Congregation of Oakland, who believed that the hospital should be supported by and for Jews alone. Rabbi Nieto, however, argued that the hospital should benefit "all suffering humanity, regardless of age or sex or sect or creed." *San Francisco Examiner*, January 23, 1897, quoted in Barbara S. Rogers, "To Be or Not to Be a Jewish Hospital?" *Western States Jewish Historical Quarterly* 10, no. 3 (1978): 197.

46. Rogers and Dobbs, *First Century*, 6. This made the hospital different from most, but not all, Jewish benevolent associations, but it was not unique among American Jewish hospitals. See Boris Bogen, *Jewish Philanthropy: An Exposition of Principles and Methods of Jewish Social Service in the United States* (New York: Macmillan, 1917), 146.

47. Kraut and Kraut, *Covenant of Care*, 16.

48. Joseph Levitin, "Mount Zion of San Francisco: The History of a Hospital" (manuscript, ca. 1965), 26, Western Jewish History Center.

49. Ibid., 32.

50. The hospital treated 755 individuals; 32 percent were Russian, 30 percent American, 20 percent German, and the rest were "from Mexico, Jamaica and Arabia." Many were treated in the clinic. Ibid., 30.

51. Annual Report, 1903, Mount Zion Hospital Minute Book, January 31, 1904, 324.

52. Mount Zion Hospital Board of Directors Minute Book, 1906–16, 174; http://history.library.ucsf.edu/building_hospitals.html.

53. Mount Zion Hospital Board of Directors, open letter to the Jewish community, December 15, 1896, San Francisco, quoted in Rogers and Dobbs, addenda to *First Century*, 198.

54. Levitin, "Mount Zion," 12.

55. Donations are registered in the hospital association's board minutes and annual reports pasted in their minute books. Mount Zion Hospital Minute Book; Levitin, "Mount Zion," 12.

56. Rogers and Dobbs, *First Century*, 21. Born in Cassel, Germany, in 1826, Brandenstein wholesaled tobacco and cigars. Voorsanger, *Western Jewry*, 80.

57. Rogers and Dobbs, *First Century*, 66.

58. Levitin, "Mount Zion," 23; Rogers and Dobbs, *First Century*, 53.

59. Kraut and Kraut, *Covenant of Care*, 22.

60. Rogers and Dobbs, "Donations," in addenda to *First Century*, 199; Kraut and Kraut, *Covenant of Care*, 227.

61. Frances Dinkelspiel, e-mail to authors, July 17, 2006. Frances Hellman was the wife of I. W. Hellman Jr., who served on the board of directors (1897–1915).

62. Levitin, "Mount Zion," 172. Such chores were common at other Jewish hospitals. Kraut and Kraut, *Covenant of Care*, 23.

63. Letter from the Executive Committee of the Mount Zion Hospital Association, May 8, 1900, Minute Book, 1887–1906, insert page 184.

64. Rogers and Dobbs, *First Century*, 16–17.

65. Annual Report, 1902, Mount Zion Hospital Association Minute Book, 1887–1906.

66. Minutes, October 9, 1907, Mount Zion Hospital Board of Directors Minute Book, 1906–16, 19.

67. Mount Zion Hospital Board of Directors Minute Book, 1906–16, 22–25. At Newark's Beth Israel, there was an attempt to limit the board to men because a leading rabbi believed that women could not handle finances. Kraut and Kraut, *Covenant of Care*, 32.

68. Rogers and Dobbs, *First Century*, 17.

69. At other Jewish hospitals women served as board members. Kraut and Kraut, *Covenant of Care*, 31. A possible difference is that Newark's Beth Israel was Eastern European run, rather than German dominated.

70. Mount Zion's first superintendent was Bertha Cohen (1897–1915); however, after her tenure this position was most often titled administrator and occupied by a man.

71. Bogen, *Jewish Philanthropy*, 146; Abrams, *Blazing the Tuberculosis Trail*, 39.

72. Rogers and Dobbs, *First Century*, 66.

73. Edward A. Levin, *Memoirs of Mount Zion Hospital, 1915–1986* (San Francisco: self-published, 1987), 7–9.

74. The board would accept only doctors who were among the elite of San Francisco's medical community. All had European training; locally trained doctors were not accepted. Levitin, "Mount Zion," 21.

75. Hellman contributed one hundred thousand dollars in memory of his wife, Esther, and the building was named for her.

76. Rogers and Dobbs, *First Century*, 14. In 1909, patients were referred by the Hebrew Board of Relief, by the Orphan Asylum, and from Hebrew Home for Aged. Mount Zion Hospital Board of Directors Minute Book, 1906–16, 174.

77. Kraut and Kraut, *Covenant of Care*, 64. This list included hospitals with one hundred or more beds.

78. Baur, *Health Seekers*, 130.

79. Ibid., 33, 177.

80. Wilson, "Citizens of Los Angeles," 62–63.

81. Fanny Sharlip, "My Memoirs," 101, Fanny Sharlip Collection, Western Jewish History Center.

82. Cohen, "Constancy and Change," 10.

83. Wilson, "Citizens of Los Angeles," 62–63.

84. Cohen, "Constancy and Change," 24.

85. Minutes of the Ladies' Hebrew Benevolent Society, June 8, 1903, quoted in Cohen, "Constancy

and Change," 16. In succeeding years, the society had predominantly female directors.

86. Cohen, "Constancy and Change," 17.

87. Minutes of the Meeting of the Board of the Jewish Aid Society, January 8, 1919, quoted in Cohen, "Constancy and Change," 22. In Portland in the early 1920s, Julia Swett succeeded her late husband, Isaac, as director of the Jewish Federation. See Toll, *Ethnic Middle Class*, 185.

88. These appeals were influenced by new Eastern European and Sephardic immigrants, who often "raised their funds by rather clamorous appeals instead of genteel private solicitation." Vorspan and Gartner, *Jews of Los Angeles*, 24.

89. Budd Schulberg, *Moving Pictures: Memories of a Hollywood Prince* (New York: Stein and Day, 1981), 232.

90. *B'nai B'rith Messenger (Los Angeles)*, March 26, 1926. An editorial noted that Jews in the motion picture industry raised in a half hour thirty thousand or forty thousand dollars for the United Jewish Appeal. *B'nai B'rith Messenger*, April 9, 1926.

91. Kraut and Kraut, *Covenant of Care*, 20.

92. Cedars of Lebanon and Mount Sinai merged in 1961 to form the Cedars-Sinai Medical Center.

93. Victor Harris, "The Beginning of Los Angeles' First Jewish Hospital," *Western States Jewish Historical Quarterly* 8, no. 2 (1976): 136.

94. "Schlesinger's wife was a Newmark, as was Kaspare Cohn's mother." Editor's note, in ibid., 137.

95. Kraut and Kraut, *Covenant of Care*, 23. Reva Clar, "First Jewish Woman Physician of Los Angeles," *Western States Jewish Historical Quarterly* 14, no. 1 (1981): 69. T.B. patients were allowed only in the county hospital and the Barlow Sanatorium. Baur, *Health Seekers*, 170.

96. Born to Central European parents, Vasen first served the Jewish Maternity Home of Philadelphia as resident physician and superintendent before settling in Los Angeles. Julie Beardsley, "Dr. Sarah Vasen: First Jewish Woman Doctor in Los Angeles, First Superintendent of Cedars-Sinai Hospital," *Roots–Key: Newsletter of the Jewish Genealogical Society of Los Angeles*, April 2003, http://home.earthlink.net/~nholdeneditor/City%20of%20Hope.htm; Clar, "First Jewish Woman

Physician," 68. In 1910, the hospital moved outside the city limits and opened an additional small T.B. cottage.

97. Vorspan and Gartner, *Jews of Los Angeles*, 178–79.

98. The renaming was per the wishes of Kaspare Cohn's family. Harris Newmark, *Sixty Years in Southern California, 1853–1913*, 4th ed., ed. Maurice H. Newmark and Marco R. Newmark (Los Angeles: Zeitlin and Ver Brugge, 1970), 683.

99. As quoted in Abrams, *Blazing the Tuberculosis Trail*, 28. Bogen became superintendent of the Federated Charities of Los Angeles in 1924. He had served as the superintendent of United Jewish Charities in Cincinnati (1904–10).

100. Abrams, *Blazing the Tuberculosis Trail*, 6.

101. Peter M. Kahn, Louis L. Silverberg, and Ben Tyre, eds., *Who Is Who in Sponsoring Mount Sinai Hospital and Clinic: Annual Directory* (Los Angeles: Associated Organizations of Los Angeles, 1945), 8.

102. Joseph L. Malamut, "The Mount Sinai Hospital Story," in *Southwest Jewry: An Account of Jewish Progress and Achievement in the Southland*, ed. Joseph L. Malamut (Los Angeles: Los Angeles Jewish Institutions and Their Leaders, 1957), 3:89; Kahn, Silverberg, and Tyre, *Who Is Who*, 10. Other hospitals followed this policy. See Kraut and Kraut, *Covenant of Care*, 34; and Abrams, *Blazing the Tuberculosis Trail*, 19.

103. Abrams, *Blazing the Tuberculosis Trail*, 21.

104. Accredited by the Public Welfare commission of Los Angeles in 1925, the hospital's capacity became sixteen patients. The following year, deciding that its mission was too broad, it limited its care and changed its name to Home for Incurables; however, a few years later it changed its name and mission again. Kahn, Silverberg, and Tyre, *Who Is Who*, 8, 10.

105. According to Susan Douglass Yates, City of Hope archivist, the name change to the City of Hope—A Jewish National Medical Center occurred in 1949. Before that there were several variations.

106. Sharlip, "My Memoirs."

107. For more about the Denver sanatoriums, see Jeanne E. Abrams, "Chasing the Cure in Colorado," in Rischin and Livingston, *Jews of the American West*, 93–115; and Abrams, *Blazing the Tuberculosis Trail*, 3.

108. Editorial, "The California Jewish Consump-

tives' Relief Association," *Sanatorium: Official Organ of the Jewish Consumptives' Relief Society (Denver)* 7, no. 2 (1913).

109. Leon Shulman, "The California Consumptives' Relief Association: A Historical Sketch," *Sanatorium: Official Organ of the Jewish Consumptives' Relief Society (Denver)* 7, no. 2 (1913): 38.

110. Manning Ostroff, "The Story behind the Story: Our Auxiliaries," in *Golden Book: Los Angeles Sanatorium, 1913–1933; Twentieth Anniversary Edition* (Los Angeles: Los Angeles Sanatorium and Expatients Home, 1934), 15.

111. See Abrams, *Blazing the Tuberculosis Trail*, 34–36.

112. Karl Fischel, "The Spirit of Duarte," in *Golden Book: Los Angeles Sanatorium*, 27, 28.

113. Abrams, *Blazing the Tuberculosis Trail*, 21.

114. Shulman, "California Consumptives' Relief Association," 38. The members of the Los Angeles's Workmen's Circle contributed the hospital's first wood cottage. Rogers, "Story of the City of Hope."

115. "Beginnings of the Jewish Consumptive Relief Association (City of Hope)," *Western States Jewish History* 20, no. 2 (1988): 122.

116. Ibid., 124; printed in the *B'nai B'rith Messenger*, January 23, 1914.

117. On Denver, see Abrams, *Blazing the Tuberculosis Trail*, 35.

118. Sharlip, "My Memoirs," 125.

119. In 1919, volunteers organized the free Ex-patient Home Society to house discharged patients and teach marketable skills. Eventually, the home joined with the sanitarium. *Mount Sinai Year Book, 1946.* 30. This was similar to the Denver sanitarium. See William Toll, "Gender and the Origins of Philanthropic Professionalism: Seraphine Pisko at the National Jewish Hospital," *Rocky Mountain Jewish Historical Notes* 11 (Winter–Spring 1991): 6–8.

120. Members in Los Angeles contributed twenty-two hundred dollars, and fourteen hundred dollars was raised from members outside of Los Angeles. "Beginnings of the Jewish Consumptive Relief Association," 123. Vorspan and. Gartner, *Jews of Los Angeles*, 176. Rogers, "Story of the City of Hope."

121. "The City of Hope Story," in Malamut, *Southwest Jewry*, 3:82.

122. Fischel, "Spirit of Duarte," 27.

123. The Los Angeles Women's Auxiliary was credited with being "a mighty bulwark to the movement." Shulman, "California Consumptives' Relief Association," 38.

124. Sharlip, "My Memoirs," 127, 110, 113.

125. "The Family Warner," in *Golden Book: Los Angeles Sanatorium*, 23.

126. Seattle did not have a City of Hope auxiliary, but instead affiliated with Denver. In 1900, members of the NCJW's Seattle section were required to contribute twenty-five cents to the Denver hospital yearly. NCJW, Seattle Section, "History," 8.

127. Other structures that completed the complex included a commissary, medical and dental clinics, a bathhouse, an open-air theater, a hospital, a recreation hall, a laboratory, nurses' quarters, physicians' quarters, a laundry, a library, and the New York Hospital, the largest building.

128. Vera Slifman Brownstein, interview with Leah Hecht, February 21, 1978, 22, Oregon Jewish Museum. Another version is that the Portland Builders started when a Los Angeles woman visited Portland and spoke of the City of Hope during a card game. "Portland Builders," in City of Hope, *Silver Jubilee: The City of Hope* (Los Angeles: City of Hope, 1939), 164. It is possible that there were two groups that merged.

129. "Our Auxiliaries," in *Golden Book: Los Angeles Sanatorium*, 63.

130. Lowenstein, *Jews of Oregon*, 145.

131. Jacqueline B. Williams, "If I Am Only for Myself, What Am I? Two Successful Jewish Women's Organizations in King County" (ca. 2000), 17 (copy in possession of the authors). Williams's essay was later published in Mary C. Wright, ed., *More Voices, New Stories: King County, Washington's First 150 Years* (Seattle: Pacific Northwest Historians Guild / University of Washington Press, 2002).

132. Their support is described in the quotation by Rebecca J. Gradwohl, "The Jewess in San Francisco," *American Jewess* 4, no. 1 (1896): 10–12.

133. Michael E. Engh, *Frontier Faiths: Church, Temple, and Synagogue in Los Angeles, 1846–1888*

(Albuquerque: University of New Mexico Press, 1992), 79; Catherine Ann Curry, "Public and Private Education in San Francisco: The Early Years, 1851–1876," in Guarneri and Alvarez, *Religion and Society*, 319–24.

134. Barbara Kirshenblatt-Gimblett, "The Moral Sublime: Jewish Women and Philanthropy in Nineteenth-Century America," in *Writing a Modern Jewish History: Essays in Honor of Salo W. Baron*, ed. Barbara Kirshenblatt-Gimblett (New York: Jewish Museum, 2006), 42.

135. Karen S. Wilson, "'A Directing Spirit': Sarah Newmark and Jewish Benevolence in Nineteenth Century Los Angeles" (paper presented at the Western Jewish Studies Association conference, Long Beach, Calif., March 19, 2006).

136. Newmark, *Sixty Years* (1970 ed.), 660. Beverly Gordon, *Bazaars and Fair Ladies: The History of the American Fundraising Fair* (Knoxville: University of Tennessee Press, 1998).

137. Wilson, "Directing Spirit," 7–8.

138. See Scott, *Natural Allies*, 160–65.

139. By-Laws of the Women's Educational and Industrial Union of San Francisco, incorporated January 22, 1891, Bancroft Library.

140. Women's Educational and Industrial Union, Third Annual Report, 1891–92, Bancroft Library.

141. See chapter 1.

142. When Solomons was president, financial support came from Levi Strauss, the Hass Bros., and the Alaska Commercial Company and from other prominent Jewish families. This funding vanished when Solomons left the union. The ethnic composition of union students/clients is not available.

143. More than two decades later, during World War I, Peixotto organized California's first training program for social work.

144. See Selina Solomons, *How We Won the Vote in California: A True Story of the Campaign of 1911* (San Francisco: New Woman Publishing, n.d.).

145. On the recruiting of women for synagogue charitable work and on Kaufman Kohler, see Sarna, *American Judaism*, 142–51.

146. Toll, *Ethnic Middle Class*, 103; Rogow, Gone to Another Meeting, 59.

147. Naomi W. Cohen, *Encounters with Emancipation: The German Jews in the United States, 1830–1914* (Philadelphia: Jewish Publication Society of America, 1984), 115.

148. "The Helpers," Eureka Benevolent Society Collection, box 1, folder 2, Western Jewish History Center.

149. It was founded about the same time as Henry House in New York, which officially became a settlement house in 1895. "JWA—Lillian Wald-Henry Settlement," Jewish Women's Archive, August 10, 2008, http://jwa.org/exhibits/wov/wald/lw4.html.

150. "President's Report," "Temporary Relief Committee," "Employment Department," in *First Annual Report of the Emanu-El Sisterhood. Third Annual Report of the Emanu-El Sisterhood for Fiscal Year 1896–97* (San Francisco, 1897), 11, 17.

151. Kathleen D. McCarthy, *Noblesse Oblige: Charity and Cultural Philanthropy in Chicago, 1849–1929* (Chicago: University of Chicago Press, 1982), 11; Carson, *Settlement Folk*, 51–52; Mary Ellen Richmond, *The Good Neighbor in the Modern City* (Philadelphia: Lippincott, 1908), 99–101; Robert A. Woods and Albert J. Kennedy, *The Settlement Horizon: A National Estimate* (New York: Russell Sage Foundation, 1922), 88.

152. *Third Annual Report of the Emanu-El Sisterhood*, 21.

153. Eustace Peixotto, "A Brief History of the Columbia Park Boys' Club," June 23, 1926, Peixotto Family Papers.

154. *Third Annual Report of the Emanu-El Sisterhood*, 34; Eustace Peixotto, "The Columbia Park Boys' Club: An Analysis," n.d., Peixotto Family Papers.

155. Margaret Slattery, *The Girl in Her Teens* (Philadelphia: Sunday School Times Company, 1910), 4, 68.

156. *Third Annual Report of the Emanu-El Sisterhood*, 30.

157. Minutes, February 4, 1914, Emanu-El Sisterhood for Personal Service Collection, Western Jewish History Center.

158. Caroline Sahlein, letter to the editor, *Emanu-El*, April 9, 1916, quoted in Voorsanger, *Western Jewry*, 32.

159. For further discussion, see Toll, "Gender, Ethnicity, and Jewish Settlement Work," 291–306.

160. *Jewish Progress (San Francisco)*, August 16, 1895, 4; Litman, *Ray Frank Litman*, 53.

161. Rogow, *Gone to Another Meeting*, 113.

162. Toll, *Ethnic Middle Class*, 56, 57.

163. Bogen, *Jewish Philanthropy*, 261.

164. Minutes, April 8, 1901; October 17, 1901; November 6, 1901, NCJW, Portland Section, Oregon Jewish Museum.

165. Toll, *Ethnic Middle Class*, 61.

166. Lowenstein, *Jews of Oregon*, 139.

167. NCJW, Seattle Section, "History"; "Formative Meeting," accession no. 2089-29, box 1, folder 1, NCJW, Seattle Section.

168. NCJW, Seattle Section, "History," 3.

169. Minutes of the Executive Committee, May 6 and June 20, 1901, NCJW, Seattle Section; Minutes of the Regular Meeting, March 8 and April 12, 1906, NCJW, Seattle Section.

170. NCJW, Seattle Section, "History," 20–21. Rabbi Koch spent time at the settlement house observing the religious school and within a short time married one of the teachers, Cora Dinkelspiel.

171. Ibid.

172. This was two years before the NCJW founded a section in Los Angeles, although Vorspan and Gartner consider it to be a council project. Vorspan and Gartner, *Jews of Los Angeles*, 146.

173. Ibid. For a discussion of the origins of western immigrants, see chapter 3.

174. A 1959 retrospective article noted that women started the section even though they risked "the disapproval of husbands, many of whom felt that it was unwomanly of their wives to become clubwomen." "A Half Century: National Council of Jewish Women, Los Angeles Section, 1909–1959," *Western States Jewish History* 37, no. 2 (2004): 150.

175. Ibid., 151.

176. However, by 1930 these activities were given over to the Federation of Jewish Charities, which ran them as the Social Alliance and Girls' Home. The federation remained the prominent organization in the city, with both men and women serving in leadership roles.

177. A connection to the founding generations was Evelyn Aronson Margolis, a section board member (1903–6) and national board member (1905–27). Rogow, *Gone to Another Meeting*, 232.

178. William Toll, "A Quiet Revolution: Jewish Women's Clubs and the Widening Female Sphere, 1870–1920," *American Jewish Archives* 41, no. 1 (1989): 17–18. Leibo, "Out the Road," 99, 105.

179. Minutes, November 8 and 28, 1900, NCJW, San Francisco Section, Western Jewish History Center. The section's real innovation came through the Philanthropic Committee, as Peixotto led her group to read the English Poor Laws, modern theories of charity, and factory legislation designed to improve the working conditions of women and children, as well as her own analysis of immigration. See Jessica Peixotto, *The French Revolution and Modern French Socialism* (New York: Thomas Y. Crowell, 1901); Peixotto, "Relief Work of the Associated Charities," Peixotto Family Papers; Minutes, November 8, 1900; May 6, 1901; January 16, 1902; October 17, 1902, NCJW, San Francisco Section.

180. Blanche Blumauer, "Council of Jewish Women in Portland—1905," *Western States Jewish Historical Quarterly* 9, no. 1 (1976): 19 (originally published in the *Jewish Times and Observer* [San Francisco], February 17, 1905).

181. Toll, *Ethnic Middle Class*, 58.

182. Blumauer, "Council of Jewish Women in Portland," 19.

183. Bogen, *Jewish Philanthropy*, 266.

184. Minutes, July 5, 1902, NCJW, Portland Section.

185. Quoted in Alissa Schwartz, "Americanization and Cultural Preservation in Seattle's Settlement House: A Jewish Adaptation of the Anglo-American Model of Settlement Work," *Journal of Sociology and Social Welfare* 36, no. 3 (1999): 36.

186. NCJW, Seattle Section, "History," [page markings unclear]; Lowenstein, *Jews of Oregon*, 141.

187. Roza R. Willer, "The History of Jewish Social Work in Portland" (student paper, Portland School of Social Work, June 1923), 25, Oregon Jewish Museum.

188. 1919–20 Report, NCJW, Seattle Section. The Workmen's Circle was an ardent foe of Bolsheviks.

189. For example, the YMCA in Tacoma, Washington, offered night Americanization classes. Van Nuys, *Americanizing the West*, 36.

190. Gayle Gullett, "Women Progressives and the Politics of Americanization in California, 1915–1920," *Pacific Historical Review* 64, no. 1 (1995): 73.

191. The national organization stressed teaching English to "mitigate the gap between first genera-

tion children and their parents." See Rogow, *Gone to Another Meeting*, 134, 148. For discussion on the effects of Americanization on parents and children, see Bogen, *Jewish Philanthropy*, 249.

192. Schwartz, "Americanization and Cultural Preservation," 35.

193. Willer, "Jewish Social Work in Portland," 16.

194. Ibid.

195. NCJW Seattle Section, "History."

196. Willer, "Jewish Social Work in Portland," 14.

197. Miriam Atkins, oral history, July 22, 1974, transcript, 15, Oregon Jewish Museum.

198. Rogow, *Gone to Another Meeting*, 135.

199. Eisenberg, "Immigrants, Ethnics, and Natives," 12.

200. Ibid., 13; Gertrude Feves, oral history, May 27, 1975, transcript, 6, Oregon Jewish Museum.

201. Eisenberg, "Immigrants, Ethnics, and Natives," 10.

202. Miriam Heller Stern, "Ladies, Girls, and Mothers: Defining Jewish Womanhood at the Settlement House" (ca. 2002), 4, Western Jewish History Center; published in the *Journal of Jewish Education* 69, no. 2 (2003): 22–34.

203. Constitution and By-Laws, 1902, Emanu-El Sisterhood for Personal Service, Western Jewish History Center, quoted in Stern, "Ladies, Girls, and Mothers," 3.

204. Bella Lilienthal, "President's Report," in *Tenth Annual Report of the Emanu-El Sisterhood for Personal Service* (San Francisco, 1904), 8, quoted in Stern, "Ladies, Girls, and Mothers," 6–7.

205. Gordon DeLeon, interview transcript, quoted in Cone, Droker, and Williams, *Family of Strangers*, 94. "The secretary of the Board called to mind an exceptionally kindly woman living in San Francisco who might be persuaded to fill the bill and make her home at the Settlement House." NCJW, Seattle Section, "History," 22.

206. DeLeon, quoted in Cone, Droker, and Williams, *Family of Strangers*, 94.

207. "First Resident Worker," in NCJW, Seattle Section, "History," 23.

208. Mrs. Emar Goldberg, "First Report of Settlement Work," in NCJW, Seattle Section, "History," 25.

209. Ibid.

210. Schwartz, "Americanization and Cultural Preservation," 41.

211. "Report of Settlement House, C.J.W. 1913," in NCJW, Seattle Section, "History."

212. Anna L. Homes, "Report of Committee of Philanthropy, 1916–1917," in NCJW, Seattle Section, "History," [page numbers are not always marked].

213. William Toll, "Pioneering: Jewish Men and Women of the American West," in *Creating American Jews: Historical Conversations about Identity*, ed. Karen S. Mittelman (Philadelphia: National Museum of American Jewish History / Brandeis University Press, 1998), 35.

214. Lowenstein, *Jews of Oregon*, 141.

215. Ida Loewenberg, quoted in Willer, "Jewish Social Work in Portland," 15.

216. Trachtenberg, oral history, 36.

217. "The Economist Turned Advocate—Edward Thomas Devine," Professional Social Work Centennial, 1898–1998, National Association of Social Workers, *NASW News*, April 1998, http://www.socialworkers.org/profession/centennial/devine.htm.

218. Annual Report to the Board of Directors, Pacific Hebrew Orphan Asylum and Home Society, 1878, quoted in Kahn, *Jewish Voices*, 233. Levy served as president and executive officer of the home for more than forty years; he was also one of the founders of kindergartens in the Pacific states.

219. Ibid.

220. Ibid.

221. Stern, "Ladies, Girls, and Mothers," 8.

222. A similar view was held by the Christian women of San Francisco's Chinese Mission Home, who believed that "courtship, marriage, and domestic service" equaled the "Christian Home." Pascoe, *Relations of Rescue*, 148.

223. For a brief summary of changes in the numbers of women working and their new employment structure, see Cott, *Grounding of Modern Feminism*, 22–24.

224 Judy Yung, *Unbound Feet: A Social History of Chinese Women in San Francisco* (Berkeley: University of California Press, 1995), 200. At the end of the course the women were assured jobs paying at least a minimum wage.

225. Mary Ann Irwin, "Plumbing a Mystery: The Emanu-El Sisterhood for Personal Service Confronts Prostitution" (paper presented to the Western Association of Women Historians, Berkeley, Calif., June 2003) (in the possession of Ava F. Kahn). Judge Marcus Cauffman Sloss, a coauthor of the California juvenile court bill, was with his wife, Hattie, a patron of the Emanu-El Sisterhood Home and a member of the NCJW. The women attending the sessions may have become aware of one Jewish girl who became a prostitute after leaving the Hebrew Orphan Asylum. Philip Bird, "Child Dependency with Particular Reference to Conditions in San Francisco" (master's thesis, Department of Economics, University of California, Berkeley, 1910), cited in Irwin, "Plumbing a Mystery."

226. Rogow, *Gone to Another Meeting*, 136.

227. Irwin, "Plumbing a Mystery."

228. "Emanu-El Sisterhood: Annual Report of Head Worker," in *Twelfth Annual Report of the Federation of Jewish Charities* (San Francisco, 1921), 84–85; Toll, "Feminization of the Heroic," 202–10.

229. Stern, "Ladies, Girls, and Mothers," 10.

230. *Who's Who among the Women of California*, 1922 (San Francisco: Security Publishing, 1922), http://www.calarchives4u.com/women/whotxt/189-213.htm.

231. Toll, "Feminization of the Heroic," 207.

232. Stern, "Ladies, Girls, and Mothers," 12.

233. "Half Century," 152.

234. Hamburger Home, "A Report Submitted by the Survey Division L.A. Community Welfare Federation to the Joint Committee of the Council of Social Agencies and the Budget Committee of the Los Angeles Community Welfare Federation on the Study of Housing Facilities for Single and Unattached Women" (March 23, 1934), 1, 15a, American Jewish Archives.

235. "Half Century," 153.

236. Diner, "Political Tradition," 62.

237. Lowenstein, *Jews of Oregon*, 169.

238. Helen Winkler, Department of Immigration Aid, NCJW, to Mrs. L. M. Stern, President, Seattle Section, NCJW, March 1, 1918, box 1, folder 6, NCJW, Seattle Section.

239. Rogow, *Gone to Another Meeting*, 138. The council employed speakers of Yiddish and other European languages.

240. Winkler to Stern, March 1, 1918.

241. NCJW, Seattle Section, "History," [pages unnumbered, approximately 29, 44].

242. Like chapters in other cities, the society helped settle immigrants, or, if their destination was farther east, its members assisted them with their travel. Although men were members of the society, their wives did the washing and cooking for the immigrants. Cone, Droker, and Williams, *Family of Strangers*, 96–97.

243. Winkler to Stern, March 1, 1918. The Hebrew Immigrant Aid Society was organized by Eastern European immigrant men, while NCJW was run by elite women, so conflicts of authority on class as well as gender lines had surfaced. See Diner, "Political Tradition," 63.

244. Diner "Political Tradition," 63.

245. One letter from the Joint Distribution Committee, dated January 6, 1921 requested the council to have a man cable them three hundred dollars to pay for transportation before the "applicants" passport expired. Director of the Transmission Bureau, Joint Distribution Committee, New York, to Mrs. William Mittelberger, box 1, folder 3, NCJW, Seattle Section.

246. NCJW, Seattle Section, "History," 43 1/2.

247. Toll, *Ethnic Middle Class*, 36. In Los Angeles the Hebrew Benevolent Society sent funds to the "Southern Relief Fund after the Civil War." Wilson, "Citizens of Los Angeles," 62.

248. For an excellent discussion on this process, see Mary McCune, "Formulating the 'Women's Interpretation of Zionism': Hadassah Recruitment of Non-Zionist American Women, 1914–1930," in *American Jewish Women and the Zionist Enterprise*, ed. Shulamit Reinharz and Mark A. Raider (Waltham, Mass.: Brandeis University Press, 2005), 89–111.

249. Laura Berch, "Our Roots," accession no. 2092-6, box 1, Hadassah, Berch Papers, University of Washington Archives.

250. Wachtin, oral history, 11–12. Women in Los Angeles also took on similar sewing projects for Hadassah. See the *B'nai B'rith Messenger*, May 14, 1926.

251. NCJW, Seattle Section, "History," 42.

252. *B'nai B'rith Messenger*, February 12, 1926; June 25, 1926. Having moved recently to Los Angeles from San Francisco, it was natural for Lipsitch to foresee and

then implement a regional organization for the Jewish Consumptive Relief Association.

253. Toll, *Ethnic Middle Class*, 57.

254. An excellent example of this process is Wilson's comparison of the 1855 and 1918 mission statements of the Hebrew Benevolent Society and the Jewish Aid Society. The benevolent society emphasized the "holy cause of Benevolence," while the Jewish Aid Society emphasized "prevent[ing] poverty wherever possible." Wilson, "Citizens of Los Angeles," 70.

5. CONSOLIDATION, INTEGRATION, AND DIVERGENCE DURING THE INTERWAR YEARS

Epigraph. Description of Congregation Herzl's Junior Guild in Seattle in the 1930s, Harry Ash, oral history, 1983, Jewish Community Oral History Project, University of Washington Archives.

1. For example, in December of 1941, the Temple De Hirsch bulletin noted that a group of Quaker youth had attended services, and the Rabbi had addressed the local Quaker meeting during a Sunday service. *Temple Tidings (Seattle)*, December 26, 1941, box 14, Temple De Hirsch records, University of Washington Archives.

2. Herzl, an Orthodox congregation founded in 1906, became Conservative in the late 1920s.

3. Cone, Droker, and Williams, *Family of Strangers*, 221; Seattle Jewish Fund correspondence, box 1, folders 7–8, Kaplan Papers. Kaplan served as chair in the fund's inaugural year.

4. Cone, Droker, and Williams, *Family of Strangers*, 83. A list of all of the past presidents of the lodge, together with their pictures, was printed in 1925. Interestingly, all are listed as past presidents of Lodge No. 503, the consolidated lodge, suggesting an effort to de-emphasize the separate histories of the various lodges. Photograph, Presidents of Seattle B'nai B'rith Lodge No. 503, box 1, folder 2, Kaplan Papers.

5. For example, in 1912, both Koch's and Kaplan's lodges participated in the Golden Potlatch Seattle picnic. Golden Potlatch Seattle program, July 19, 1912, box 2, folder 2, Kaplan Papers.

6. Letters of recognition, box 1, folder 24, Kaplan Papers, and accession no. 1759, box 1, Samuel Koch

Papers, University of Washington Archives.

7. Arthur Goren, *The Politics and Public Culture of American Jews* (Bloomington: Indiana University Press, 1999), 4.

8. Sarna, *American Judaism*, chap. 5. In addition to Goren, *Politics and Public Culture*, see Gulie Ne'eman Arad, *America, Its Jews, and the Rise of Nazism* (Bloomington: Indiana University Press, 2000), chap. 3; and Henry Feingold, *A Time for Searching: Entering the Mainstream, 1920–1945* (Baltimore: American Jewish Historical Society / Johns Hopkins University Press, 1992).

9. See the discussion of Los Angeles's growth patterns in chapter 3.

10. *Jewish Transcript (Seattle)*, February 3, 1928; March 2, 1928; February 15, 1929.

11. *B'nai B'rith Messenger (Los Angeles)*, May 4, 1928.

12. *Jewish Transcript*, June 20, 1930; May 23, 1930; August 8, 1930; August 15, 1930; August 22, 1930.

13. *Jewish Transcript*, March 21, 1930.

14. *B'nai B'rith Messenger*, January 13, 1928; February 24, 1928; March 2, 1928; April 6, 1928; May 18, 1928; *Jewish Transcript*, January 3, 1930.

15. Zarchin, *Glimpses of Jewish Life*, 133–34.

16. *Jewish Transcript*, April 18, 1930; May 2, 1930.

17. *B'nai B'rith Messenger*, January 27, 1928.

18. *B'nai B'rith Messenger*, May 16, 1930; *Jewish Transcript*, May 23, 1930.

19. Felicia Herman, "Jewish Leaders and the Motion Picture Industry," in Kahn and Dollinger, *California Jews*, 99–100.

20. *Jewish Transcript*, January 24, 1930.

21. *B'nai B'rith Messenger*, April 6, 1928.

22. Solomon Prottas to Jonah Wise, November 21, 1919, box 1, folder 5, Prottas Papers.

23. Correspondence, 1917–47, folder 2, Prottas Papers. Sam Prottas served as Seattle Council president of the Jewish National Fund from 1942 to 1946.

24. See the discussion of the consolidation movement in chapter 2.

25. Marc Dollinger, *Quest for Inclusion: Jews and Liberalism in Modern America* (Princeton, N.J.: Princeton University Press, 2000), 93.

26. Feingold, *Time for Searching*, 59.

27. Vorspan and Gartner, *Jews of Los Angeles*, 151, 218.

28. Lowenstein, *Jews of Oregon*, 156; Toll, *Ethnic Middle Class*, 131–32.

29. The various past presidents are pictured in a 1925 photograph. Presidents of Seattle B'nai B'rith Lodge No. 503.

30. Lowenstein, *Jews of Oregon*, 156–60.

31. Ibid., 194.

32. *Emanu-El (San Francisco)*, January 15, 1926; February 21, 1930. This group included the lawyer I. M. Golden and the bankers Harold Zellerbach and Philip Lilienthal, both from pioneer families.

33. Louis Blumenthal, "YMHA and YWHA, San Francisco History, 1877–1954," *Western States Jewish History* 36, no. 4 (2004): 302.

34. Ibid., 309–10.

35. Sophia M. Robison, ed., *Jewish Population Studies* (New York: Conference on Jewish Relations, 1943), 172. Also see Shelly Tenenbaum, "Community Self-Help: San Francisco Jews and the Great Depression," *Jewish Journal of Sociology* 45, nos. 1–2 (2003): 36.

36. Elaine Leeder, *The Gentle General: Rose Pesotta, Anarchist and Labor Organizer* (Albany: State University of New York Press, 1993), 57.

37. Figures for 1907 and 1927 are from Weissbach, "Eve of Mass Migration," 84. Figures for 1938 are from Robison, *Jewish Population Studies*, 162.

38. Lowenstein, *Jews of Oregon*, 190.

39. The 1922 figures are from Midler, "Neighborhood Survey"; the 1930 figures are from Cohn, "Residential Patterns," 34, 43.

40. Cohn, "Residential Patterns," 43.

41. Franco, Behar, de Leon, and Nieder all mention this phenomenon in their oral histories; see also Charles Alhadeff, oral history, May 1982, Jewish Community Oral History Project, University of Washington Archives. It is also noted in Cone, Droker, and Williams, *Family of Strangers*, 179.

42. Tenenbaum, "Community Self-Help," 34–45.

43. Vorspan and Gartner, *Jews of Los Angeles*, 195–96.

44. Tenenbaum, "Community Self-Help," 36–37.

45. Williams, "If I Am Only for Myself," 2, 8–9.

46. Jewish Welfare Service, 1932 report, quoted in Williams, "If I Am Only for Myself," 10.

47. Williams, "If I Am Only for Myself," 10.

48. Cone, Droker, and Williams, *Family of Strangers*, 221–22, 228, 231.

49. Bikur Cholim, *Synagogue Tribune (Seattle)*, February 1935, accession no. 2450-001, box 4, Congregation Bikur Cholim Machzikay Hadath Collection, University of Washington Archives.

50. Ash, oral history; the oral histories of both Glazer and Rubin mention joining the temple.

51. This practice is documented in several Seattle oral histories, including those of Franco, Capeloto, and Asia. A chapter of Alpha Epsilon Pi, which welcomed Sephardim, was established at the University of Washington in 1947. Soon after, the other Jewish fraternities began to welcome them. Marianne R. Sanua, *Going Greek: Jewish College Fraternities in the United States, 1895–1945* (Detroit: Wayne State University Press, 2003), 157, 382n29.

52. Driesen, interview. Rabbi Berkowitz came from a leading family of American Reform rabbis. His uncles, Joseph Krauskopf and the elder Henry Berkowitz, were two of the first graduates of Hebrew Union College. See Nodel, *Ties Between*, 131.

53. Narell, *Our City*, 9.

54. Ibid., 383.

55. Fred Rosenbaum, "Zionism versus Anti-Zionism," in Rischin and Livingston, *Jews of the American West*, 116–35; and John Livingston, introduction to Rischin and Livingston, *Jews of the American West*, 20–22, 120–24.

56. Thomas Kolsky, "Jews against Zionism: The American Council for Judaism, 1942–1948" (Ph.D. diss., George Washington University, 1986), app. D. Kolsky's list of key ACJ activists includes members of the West's most prominent Jewish families: from Los Angeles, Joseph Loeb and Jack Skirball; from San Francisco, Monroe Deutsch, Lloyd Dinkelspiel, Daniel Koshland, Samuel Lilienthal, Grover Magnin, Marcus and Hattie Sloss, and J. D. Zellerbach; from Portland, Aaron Frank, Max Hirsch, and Mrs. Julius Meier; and from Seattle, Morton Schwabacher and Alfred Shemanski.

57. Irving Reichert, "One Reform Rabbi Replies to Ludwig Lewisohn" (January 11, 1936), in *Judaism and the American Jew: Selected Sermons and Addresses*

(San Francisco: Grabhorn Press, 1953), 133.

58. Rosenbaum, "Zionism versus Anti-Zionism," 123.

59. Narell, *Our City*, 381. She also notes that some Zionist members resigned from the congregation.

60. Zarchin, *Glimpses of Jewish Life*, 221–22; Rosenbaum, *Visions of Reform*, 123–24. An oral history in which Mrs. Reuben (Rose) Rinder discusses her role in Hadassah is available at the Western Jewish History Center.

61. Rosenbaum, *Visions of Reform*, 198.

62. Rosenbaum, "Zionism versus anti-Zionism," 120, 123–24.

63. Rosenbaum, *Free to Choose*, 108.

64. Oakland Jewish Community Center scrapbooks, 1935–45, Alameda-Contra Costa County Jewish Organization Records, Western Jewish History Center.

65. *Temple Tidings*, January 16, 1942, Temple De Hirsch Collection, University of Washington Archives.

66. *B'nai B'rith Messenger*, January 20, 1928.

67. *B'nai B'rith Messenger*, September 17, 1937, 3.

68. For example, Reichert's critique of the proposal to form a Jewish army in Palestine was printed in the *San Francisco Chronicle* on February 27, 1942, and the statement of non-Zionist Reform rabbis appeared there on October 9, 1942. For an example of pro-Zionist coverage, see *Emanu-El*, special Hanukkah edition, December 12, 1941, 1.

69. Fred Rosenbaum, "Cataclysm" (unpublished manuscript, December 2006), 30.

70. Bikur Cholim, *Synagogue Tribune*, June 1935.

71. Bikur Cholim, *Synagogue Tribune*, February 1935; Bikur Cholim, Board Minutes, July 1942, Congregation Bikur Cholim Machzikay Hadath Collection.

72. Bikur Cholim correspondence files, Congregation Bikur Cholim Machzikay Hadath Collection.

73. Goldberg, "Jewish Spirit," 54.

74. Eisenberg, "Transplanted to the Rose City," 92–93.

75. Goldberg, "Jewish Spirit," 55.

76. Eisenberg, "Beyond San Francisco," 318.

77. *American Israelite (Cincinnati)*, February 28, 1901, 3.

78. Goldberg, "Jewish Spirit," 52.

79. *Jewish Transcript*, January 30, 1930.

80. Bikur Cholim, *Synagogue Tribune*, February 1935.

81. Cone, Droker, and Williams, *Family of Strangers*, 227.

82. Levine's name appears, along with Wohlgelernter's, on the emergency committee's letterhead in 1944. Correspondence, February 7, 1944, box 1, folder 8, Congregation Bikur Cholim Machzikay Hadath Collection. Levine remained officially neutral on Zionism, but his writings reveal that he was sharply critical of Jewish nationalism at the time. See, e.g., Raphael Levine, "A Pattern of Adjustment for the American Jew," accession no. 2352-002, box 4, and Levine, oral history, 1975, transcript, accession no. 2352-005, box 19, Rabbi Raphael Levine Papers, University of Washington Archives.

83. *B'nai B'rith Messenger*, February 3, 1928; January 10, 1930; March 28, 1930; May 2, 1930; June 30, 1930.

84. Levine, oral history.

85. Telegrams, Reichert and Dinkelspiel to Franklin D. Roosevelt, January 22, 1938; Reichert to Abba Hillel Silver, January 23, 1938, Irving Reichert Papers, Western Jewish History Center.

86. Rosenbaum, "Cataclysm," 22n10.

87. Ibid., 31n12. One member recalled that the Zionist Organization of America chapter was so small that "you could count the members . . . on two hands." Quoted in Natalie Weinstein, "Conflict between Pro- and Anti-Zionists Polarized Bay Area Jewry Fifty Years Ago," *J.: The Jewish News Weekly of Northern California (San Francisco)*, April 24, 1998, http://www.jewishsf.com/content/2-0-/module/displaystory/story_id/8549/edition_id/162/format/html/displaystory.html.

88. Phillips, "Challenge of Family," 20–21.

89. Vorspan and Gartner, *Jews of Los Angeles*, 203–5. See also Elliott, "Jews of Boyle Heights," 1–10. Estimates of the Jewish population of Boyle Heights vary, with the figure put at thirty-five thousand in 1940. See George J. Sanchez, "'What's Good for Boyle Heights Is Good for the Jews': Creating Multiracialism on the Eastside during the 1950s," *American Quarterly* 56, no. 3 (2004): 635.

90. Phillips, "Challenge of Family," 20.

91. Vorspan and Gartner, *Jews of Los Angeles*, 203–4.

92. Ibid., 214.

93. Hershey Eisenberg, oral history, December 18, 2000, transcript, 9, Boyle Heights Oral History Project, Japanese American National Museum, Los Angeles. This interview, and many others from this project, are quoted in John Esaki, producer, *Crossroads: Boyle Heights* (Los Angeles: Japanese American National Museum, 2002), video.

94. Leo Frumkin, oral history, December 19, 2001, transcript, 6–7, Boyle Heights Oral History Project.

95. Quoted in Elliott, "Jews of Boyle Heights," 7.

96. Sanchez, "What's Good for Boyle Heights," 635. Sanchez states that in 1940 the Jewish community numbered approximately thirty-five thousand, the Mexican community fifteen thousand, and the Nikkei (Japanese American) community five thousand.

97. Einbinder, *Clinton Street*, 128.

98. Fred Okrand, oral history, January 22, 2001, transcript, 13–14, Boyle Heights Oral History Project.

99. Shana Beth Bernstein, "Building Bridges at Home in a Time of Global Conflict: Interracial Cooperation and the Fight for Civil Rights in Los Angeles, 1933–1954" (Ph.D. diss., Stanford University, 2003), 72–73; Daniel Hurewitz, *Bohemian Los Angeles and the Making of Modern Politics* (Berkeley: University of California Press, 2007), 151–60.

100. Toll, "Acclimatizing Fashion."

101. Alkow became the chief fund-raiser for the Zionist Organization of America in the Pacific Coast region. Jacob Alkow, *In Many Worlds* (New York: Shengold Publishers, 1985), 32, 44.

102. Gerald Sorin, "Rose Pesotta in the Far West: The Triumphs and Travails of a Jewish Woman Labor Organizer," in "Jewish Women of the American West," ed. Gladys Sturman and David Epstein, special issue, *Western States Jewish History* 35, nos. 3–4 (2003): 204–5.

103. For a detailed explanation of how the moguls accumulated chains of movie theaters, managed distribution, and moved into film production, see Thomas Schatz, *The Genius of the System: Hollywood Film Making in the Studio Era* (New York: Pantheon, 1988), 4–12.

104. Steve J. Ross, *Working Class Hollywood, Silent Film, and the Shaping of Class in America* (Princeton,

N.J.: Princeton University Press, 1998), 3–12.

105. Lary May, *Screening out the Past: The Birth of Mass Culture and the Motion Picture Industry* (Chicago: University of Chicago Press, 1980), 188–90.

106. Lary May, *The Big Tomorrow: Hollywood and the Politics of the American Way* (Chicago: University of Chicago Press, 2000), 59.

107. Schatz, *Genius of the System*, 4–11, 21–28, 60, 80; Aubrey Solomon, *Twentieth Century Fox: A Corporate and Financial History* (Metuchen, N.J.: Scarecrow Press, 1988), 3–4, 9. The key role of the distribution of films in cementing the studio system is emphasized in Vorspan and Gartner, *Jews of Los Angeles*, 132. On land speculation, see William Churchill DeMille, *Hollywood Saga* (New York: E. P. Dutton, 1939), 87. For wage rates, see Murray Ross, *Stars and Strikes: Unionization of Hollywood* (New York: Columbia University Press, 1941), 6–7. In 1939, the studios employed between 27,500 and 33,600 people each week producing films. See Leo B. Rosten, *Hollywood: The Movie Colony, the Movie Makers* (New York: Harcourt Brace, 1941), 4, 107.

108. The social snobbery of the old Jewish elite is presented in Gabler, *Empire of Their Own*, 275–77. On the involvement of the moguls in philanthropy, see chapter 4.

109. *B'nai B'rith Messenger*, March 26, 1926; April 2, 1926; June 15, 1928; June 22, 1928; January 10, 1930; January 24, 1930; February 7, 1930. *Scribe (Portland)*, January 10, 1930.

110. Edgar Magnin, *The Warner Murals in the Wilshire Boulevard Temple, Los Angeles, California* (Los Angeles: Wilshire Boulevard Temple, 1974).

111. *B'nai B'rith Messenger*, January 13, 1928; Charles Higham, *Merchant of Dreams: Louis B. Mayer, M.G.M., and the Secret Hollywood* (New York: D. I. Fine, 1993), 78; Schulberg, *Moving Pictures* 191, 203.

112. Schatz, *Genius of the System*, 131, 136.

113. Michael E. Birdwell, *Celluloid Soldiers: The Warner Brothers Campaign against Nazism* (New York: New York University Press, 1999), 1–2, 18–19.

114. Joel Kotkin, *Tribes: How Race, Religion, and Identity Determine Success in the New Global Economy* (New York: Random House, 1992), 61.

115. See, e.g., Feingold, *Time for Searching*, 2; and

Sarna, *American Judaism*, chap. 5. On nativism in general in this period, see John Higham, *Strangers in the Land: Patterns of American Nativism, 1860–1925* (1955; reprint, New York: Atheneum, 1986), chap. 10.

116. For example, Feingold characterizes the period from 1920 to 1945 as "the story of the children and grandchildren of the eastern European Jews." Feingold, *Time for Searching*, xvi.

117. Ibid., 189.

118. Ibid., 198.

119. Dollinger, *Quest for Inclusion*, 42.

120. Ibid., 55–59.

121. According to Leonard Dinnerstein, the University of Washington was the one western university that did have quotas affecting Jewish admissions. Leonard Dinnerstein, *Anti-Semitism in America* (New York: Oxford University Press, 1994), 86. On the founding dates of chapters of Jewish fraternities, see Sanua, *Going Greek*, app. A and B.

122. *Emanu-El*, March 27, 1936.

123. Jewish Welfare Federation Records (San Francisco), 79B box 31, Western Jewish History Center.

124. Rosenbaum, *Free to Choose*, 91, 96.

125. Oakland Jewish Community Center scrapbook, 1930s.

126. Lowenstein, *Jews of Oregon*, 173.

127. Ash, oral history, 42.

128. "Racial Restrictive Covenants," 1926–48, Seattle Civil Rights and Labor History Project, University of Washington, http://depts.washington.edu/civilr/covenants.htm. A list of restrictive covenants on this Web site includes covenants from three different neighborhoods (Beverly Park, Ballard / Sunset Hill, and Broadmoor) excluding "Hebrews," among dozens of Seattle neighborhoods with racial restrictions. The majority of these covenants targeted Asians ("Japanese," "Chinese," "Asiatics," "Malays," and "Mongolians") and African Americans ("Africans" and "Negroes"). Many simply stated that the neighborhood was restricted to "whites" or "Caucasians"—a restriction that did not apply to Jews, whose status as whites was not questioned.

129. Levine's perception was colored by his own sensitivity to the issue: he came to Seattle from a London congregation, had lived through the Blitz, and was on an ADL-sponsored speaking tour about anti-Semitism and Nazism when he was offered Temple De Hirsch's pulpit. Autobiographical notes, box 1, Levine Papers.

130. *Emanu-El*, January 17, 1936.

131. Yoon K. Pak, *Wherever I Go, I Will Always Be a Loyal American: Schooling Seattle's Japanese Americans during World War II* (New York: RoutledgeFalmer, 2002), 76, chap. 4.

132. Bikur Cholim, *Synagogue Tribune*, June 1935.

133. Asia, oral history, 15.

134. Wilson, "Citizens of Los Angeles," 6.

135. Quoted in Vorspan and Gartner, *Jews of Los Angeles*, 135.

136. Mike Davis, *City of Quartz: Excavating the Future in Los Angeles* (New York: Verso 1990), 116. While Davis, who treats this issue only briefly, dates the problem to the turn of the century, Wilson and Vorspan and Gartner point to a gradual increase, with these practices becoming particularly prominent in the 1920s and 1930s. Wilson, "Citizens of Los Angeles"; Vorspan and Gartner, *Jews of Los Angeles*.

137. Wilson's thesis documents the ways in which elite families weathered the dramatic changes in Los Angeles and maintained both their business interests and a level of influence in the city. Wilson, "Citizens of Los Angeles."

138. Vorspan and Gartner, *Jews of Los Angeles*, 205. Wilson's analysis of the officers and directors of the chamber of commerce from 1888 to 1921 suggests a policy of "token acceptance," with only one Jewish individual serving in most of these years. Wilson, "Citizens of Los Angeles," 50.

139. Wilson, "Citizens of Los Angeles," 75.

140. Vorspan and Gartner, *Jews of Los Angeles*, 200.

141. The *B'nai B'rith Messenger* for January 30 and August 1, 1930, refers to Judges Elias Rosencrantz and Harry Holzer.

142. Davis, *City of Quartz*, 102.

143. Henry Schwartz, "The Silver Shirts: Anti-Semitism in San Diego," *Western States Jewish History* 25, no. 1 (1992): 54; Birdwell, *Celluloid Soldiers*, 154–60.

144. Schwartz, "Silver Shirts," 55.

145. The records of the Los Angeles Jewish Community Committee (later known as the Community Relations Council), including its reports on local fascist and anti-Semitic groups, are available at the Urban Archives

Center, Delmar T. Oviatt Library, California State University, Northridge.

146. Schwartz, "Silver Shirts," 58. On the political connections of the Silver Shirts, see Jim Miller, "Just Another Day in Paradise? An Episodic History of Rebellion and Repression in America's Finest City," in Mike Davis, Kelly Mayhew, and Jim Miller, *Under the Perfect Sun: The San Diego Tourists Never See* (New York: New Press, 2003), 199–200.

147. *Emanu-El*, April 3, 1942.

148. Vorspan and Gartner, *Jews of Los Angeles*, 205.

149. *B'nai B'rith Messenger*, May 30, 1930.

150. *B'nai B'rith Messenger*, September 17, 1937, 1. The domestic stories were on a Senate Foreign Relations Committee investigation of an alleged Nazi conspiracy in America and on the New York trial of an anti-Semitic propagandist.

151. Kenneth C. Burt, "The Birth of the Jewish Labor Committee" (paper presented at "Building Bridges to Our Communities: Yesterday, Today, Tomorrow," Jewish Labor Committee Western Region, Seventieth Annual Recognition Awards Brunch program, Century City, Calif., Sunday, May 23, 2004).

152. Alkow, *In Many Worlds*, 35–41.

153. Rosenbaum, *Architects of Reform*, 89.

154. For a detailed account of the incident, see Herman, "Jewish Leaders," 98–100. See also Louis Newman's column, "Telling It in Gath," *Scribe*, November 25, 1927.

155. *Scribe*, December 23, 1927.

156. *Scribe*, December 9, 1927.

157. Herman, "Jewish Leaders," 102; Stuart Svonkin, *Jews against Prejudice* (New York: Columbia University Press, 1999), 16. The groups' anti-Nazi activities are detailed in Eisenberg, *Cry Down Injustice*, chap. 4.

158. Dollinger, *Quest for Inclusion*, 42.

159. *Scribe*, September 26, 1919, 1.

160. Rosenbaum, *Free to Choose*, 96–100.

161. Letter from Oakland Commission on Americanism to Israel Golden Gate B'nai B'rith Lodge, Oakland, Calif., January, 29, 1940, Commission on Americanism file, Israel Golden Gate Lodge records, Western Jewish History Center.

162. Lowenstein, *Jews of Oregon*, 186–87.

163. *Scribe*, September 28, 1928.

164. Rosenbaum, *Visions of Reform*, 149.

165. *Jewish Transcript*, May 19, 1930.

166. Herman, "Jewish Leaders," 100. Also see Rosenbaum, *Visions of Reform*, chap. 5.

167. Ellen Eisenberg, "Civil Rights and Japanese American Incarceration," in Kahn and Dollinger, *California Jews*, 110–22.

168. Irving Reichert, "The New Year and Nazi Terror," in *Judaism and the American Jew*, 118–22.

169. Buerge and Rochester, *Roots and Branches*, 162–63. The Centralia Affair of 1919 was a violent clash between antiradicals and Industrial Workers of the World activists.

170. Svonkin, *Jews against Prejudice*, 13.

171. *Scribe*, November 3, 1922.

172. William Issel, "Jews and Catholics against Prejudice," in Kahn and Dollinger, *California Jews*, 128.

173. Edgar Magnin, "Labels That Are Libels," *B'nai B'rith Messenger*, February 27, 1942, 1.

174. Zarchin, *Glimpses of Jewish Life*, 134.

175. Bernstein, *Building Bridges at Home*, 155, 94. See also Eisenberg, *Cry Down Injustice*, chap. 4, epilogue.

176. Issel, "Jews and Catholics," 123.

177. Dalin, "Jewish and Non-Partisan Republicanism," 124.

178. On the national role of Nelson, see the *Scribe*, February 22, 1929.

179. Lowenstein, *Jews of Oregon*, 170; Nodel, *Ties Between*, 157.

180. For discussion of this phenomenon nationally, see the work of Stuart Svonkin and Marc Dollinger. Dollinger argues that this interfaith movement emerged in the 1930s, while Svonkin sees it as a product of the World War II–era. Dollinger, *Quest for Inclusion*, chap. 3; Svonkin, *Jews against Prejudice*, 18.

181. Dollinger, *Quest for Inclusion*, 61.

182. See the discussion of this incident in chapter 1.

183. Burt, "Birth of the Jewish Labor Committee."

184. B'nai B'rith District Grand Lodge No. 4, "Americanization Program," 1940, Western Jewish History Center.

185. Issel, "Jews and Catholics," 125.

186. On the General Jewish Council, see Dollinger, *Quest for Inclusion*, 55–59.

187. Reichert, "New Year and Nazi Terror."

6. JEWS OF THE WESTERN SUN BELT, 1945–1980

Epigraph. Rabbi Louis Newman, "Telling It in Gath," *Scribe (Portland)*, November 11, 1927.

1. Richard M. Bernard and Bradley R. Rice, eds., introduction to *Sunbelt Cities: Politics and Growth since World War II* (Austin: University of Texas Press, 1983), 1–30.

2. Lansky lived in Miami and had interests in casinos in Havana. See Dennis Eisenberg, Uri Dan, and Eli Landau, *Meyer Lansky: Mogul of the Mob* (New York: Paddington Press, 1979), 225–26; and Robert Lacey, *Little Man: Meyer Lansky and the Gangster Life* (Boston: Little, Brown 1991), 150–52.

3. Alan Balboni, "Southern Italians and Eastern European Jews: Cautious Cooperation in Las Vegas Casinos, 1940–1967," *Nevada Historical Society Quarterly* 38 (Fall 1995): 153–60. For a clear account of the way Jewish gangsters turned bootlegging, the illegal lottery, prostitution, and offtrack betting into "organized crime," see Robert A. Rockaway, *But He Was Good to His Mother: The Lives and Crimes of Jewish Gangsters* (Jerusalem: Gefen Publishing House, 2000).

4. Lacey, *Little Man*, 150–52. On the importance of economic infrastructure and the Hoover Dam, see M. Gottdiner, Claudia C. Collins, and David R. Dickens, *Las Vegas: The Social Production of an All-American City* (Malden, Mass.: Blackwell, 1999), 14–15.

5. William F. Roemer, Jr., *War of the Godfathers: The Bloody Confrontation between the Chicago and New York Families for Control of Las Vegas* (New York: Donald I. Fine, 1990), 66, 84.

6. On the elevation of Lapidus to an architectural icon because of his work on Florida hotels, see Sydney LeBlanc, *Twentieth Century American Architecture: A Traveler's Guide to Two Hundred Twenty-two Key Buildings* (New York: Whitney Library of Design 1996), 97. Sally Denton and Roger Morris, *The Money and the Power: The Making of Las Vegas and Its Hold on America* (New York: Vintage Books, 2001), 150–69.

7. Hal K. Rothman, *Neon Metropolis: How Las Vegas Started the Twenty-first Century* (New York: Routledge, 2003), 309.

8. By September 2003, Adelson had filed for bankruptcy. See "Fortune Lost to Bad Investments: Adelson Seeks Bankruptcy Shield," *Los Angeles Business Journal*, September 29, 2003, http://www.highbeam.com/doc/1G1-108883156.html.

9. Davis, Mayhew, and Miller, *Under the Perfect Sun*, 87–88.

10. See, e.g., Gerald Nash, *The American West Transformed: The Impact of the Second World War* (Lincoln: University of Nebraska Press, 1985), 25–29; Bradford Luckingham, *Phoenix: The History of a Southwestern Metropolis* (Tucson: University of Arizona Press, 1989), 155; and Roger W. Lotchin, "The City and the Sword through the Ages and the Era of the Cold War," in *Essays on Sunbelt Cities and Recent Urban America*, ed. Raymond Mohl (College Station: Texas A&M Press, 1990), 90–107.

11. Rockaway, *But He Was Good*, 47.

12. Powell, "Shlomo Bardin's 'Eretz' Brandeis," 171.

13. David Biale, "Between Los Angeles and Berkeley: Memoirs of a California Jewish Historian," *Judaism* 44, no. 4 (1995), http://findarticles.com/p/articles/mi_m0411/is_n4_v44/ai_17884745/print.

14. Powell, "Shlomo Bardin's 'Eretz' Brandeis," 177.

15. Deborah Dash Moore, "Inventing Jewish Identity in California: Shlomo Bardin, Zionism, and the Brandeis Camp Institute," in *National Variations in Jewish Identity: Implications for Jewish Education*, ed. Steven M. Cohen and Gabriek Horencyzk (Albany: State University of New York Press, 1999), 201–2, 211, 213. Moore even characterizes Bardin as an "entrepreneur" and illustrates his versatility in shifting the cultural content to appeal to a broader audience, more than two-thirds of whom by 1971 were women.

16. Powell, "Shlomo Bardin's 'Eretz' Brandeis," 177–83.

17. In 1944, the city government established a Human Rights Commission to address racial issues. See Hurewitz, *Bohemian Los Angeles*, 197–99, 215.

18. For an assessment of civil rights coalition building in Los Angeles from the 1930s through the early 1950s, see Bernstein, "Building Bridges."

19. Deborah Dash Moore, *To the Golden Cities: Pursuing the American Jewish Dream in Miami and Los Angeles* (New York: Free Press, 1994), 133–40. Weiner married entertainment lawyer Eugene Wyman and has been known ever since as Roz Wyman. Roybal's campaign obtained substantial financial and voting support from Jews and labor organizations. See Kenneth C. Burt, "Edward Roybal's Election to the LA City Council Marked the Birth of Latino Politics in California," *Public Affairs Report* 43, no. 1 (2002), http://www.igs.berkeley.edu/publications/par/spring2002/roybal.htm.

20. Bernard and Rice, introduction to *Sunbelt Cities*, 1–30.

21. Comparative data on migration of Jews to and from different regions of the United States are provided in detail in Phillips, "Challenge of Family," 17–28.

22. Gary R. Mormino, *Land of Sunshine, State of Dreams: A Social History of Modern Florida* (Gainesville: University Press of Florida, 2005), 126. For a description of the place of retired Jews in the post-1950s history of South Florida, see Mormino, 16–17, 128–30. By 2000, two of every three Jews and one of every two Italians who lived in the South lived in Florida.

23. Ibid., 131.

24. On the mood of the aggressive, technologically advanced economic growth that motivated regional leaders in 1945, see Nash, *American West Transformed*, 212–16.

25. Moore, *To the Golden Cities*, 23–24.

26. For city statistics, see U.S. Bureau of the Census, *Statistical Abstract of the United States, 1988; 108th Edition* (Washington, D.C.: Government Printing Office, 1987), 32–33, table 38. Los Angeles's Jewish population of 535,000 was almost as large as Chicago's (269,000) and Philadelphia's (330,000) combined. See *The American Jewish Year Book, 1970* (Philadelphia: Jewish Publication Society, 1970), 71:348–51.

27. Bruce Phillips, "Los Angeles Jewry: A Demographic Portrait," in *The American Jewish Year Book, 1986* (Philadelphia: Jewish Publication Society, 1986), 86:126–27.

28. Ibid., 141.

29. John P. Schmal, "Edward Roybal Was a Pioneer," *LatinoLA*, October 27, 2005, http://www.latinola.com/story.php?story=2941.

30. Deborah Dash Moore and Dan Gebler, "The Ta'am of Tourism," *Pacific Historical Review*, May 1999, 205–6; George J. Sanchez, comments in "Regionalism: The Significance of Place in American Jewish Life," roundtable, with William R. Ferris, Deborah Dash Moore, John Shelton Reed, Theodore Rosengarten, and George J. Sanchez, *American Jewish History* 93, no. 2 (2007): 125.

31. The open geography of the sprawling valley, still holding in the 1950s many square miles of wheat fields, covered an area the size of Chicago. Moore, *To the Golden Cities*, 23–24.

32. Greg Hise, *Magnetic Los Angeles: Planning the Twentieth Century Metropolis* (Baltimore: Johns Hopkins University Press, 1997) 191, 195, 206.

33. Vorspan and Gartner, *Jews of Los Angeles*, 276–77.

34. Bob Colacello, "Eli Broad's Big Picture," *Vanity Fair*, December 2006, 328; Claudia H. Deutsch, "The Tishman Empire: The Rise, Fall, and Rise of a Construction Business," *New York Times*, July 24, 1994; "Joseph Eichler," http://wwweichlerforsale.com/Joseph_Eichler (accessed July 25, 2008).

35. Vorspan and Gartner, *Jews of Los Angeles*, 235–36; Anderson School of Business, University of California, Los Angeles, "Eli Broad Shares His Philosophy of Business and Leadership with the Anderson Community," Media, May 12, 2002, http://www.anderson.ucla.edu/x4518.xml.

36. Edna Bonacich and Richard P. Appelbaum, *Behind the Label: Inequality in the Los Angeles Apparel Industry* (Berkeley: University of California Press, 2000), 31, 140–47.

37. In 1994, as the manufacture of textiles and clothing continued to grow and as airplane and aerospace manufacture declined because of cutbacks in federal defense orders, the garment industry supplanted transportation equipment to become the largest manufacturing employer in Los Angeles County. Jonathan Bowles, "The Empire Has No Clothes," Center for an Urban Future, February 29, 2000, 15, http://www.nycfuture.org/images_pdfs/pdfs/Empire%20has%20No%20Clothes%2000.pdf; Bonacich and Appelbaum, *Behind the Label*, 35.

38. Schatz, *Genius of the System*, 4; David L. Clarke,

"Improbable Los Angeles," in Bernard and Rice, *Sunbelt Cities*, 281.

39. Michael Eisner with Tony Schwartz, *Work in Progress* (New York: Random House, 1998), 52–53, 56–67, 72–76, 117, 140–42.

40. Eisner, *Work in Progress*, 96–98, quotation on 101; Joseph McBride, *Steven Spielberg: A Biography* (New York: Simon and Schuster, 1997), 12–13, 110–11, 135, 163–64, 310–12.

41. McBride, *Steven Spielberg*, 21.

42. Tom Tugend, "Why Aren't Jews Giving to Jews?" *Jewish Journal of Greater Los Angeles*, June 27, 2003, http://www.jewishjournal.com/home/preview. php?id=10744. One such project is the exhibit "Jewish Life in the American West: Generation to Generation," organized in 2002–3 by the Autry Museum of Western Heritage in Los Angeles.

43. Ben Hecht, *A Guide for the Bedeviled* (New York: Charles Scribner's Sons, 1944), 202, 211.

44. Birdwell, *Celluloid Soldiers*, 154–75.

45. See the discussion of Hollywood anticommunism in May, *Big Tomorrow*, 196–211. May notes that blacklisted performers and writers found work in Europe.

46. The board of regents of the University of California devised its own loyalty oath for its employees in 1949. For a brief summary, see Cathy Cockrell, "University Revisits Controversial California Loyalty Oath," *Berkeleyan*, October 13, 1999, http://berkeley.edu/news/berkeleyan/1999/1013/loyalty.html.

47. Victor S. Navasky, *Naming Names* (New York: Penguin Books, 1981), 78–96; Moore, *To the Golden Cities*, 194–97, 253. The California loyalty oath was rescinded in 1967. See John C. Caughey, "Farewell to California's 'Loyalty' Oath," *Pacific Historical Review* 38, no. 2 (1969): 123–28.

48. Moore, *To the Golden Cities*, 249–53.

49. Bernstein, "Building Bridges," 155–58. See also Eisenberg, *Cry Down Injustice*, epilogue.

50. Sanchez, remarks in "Regionalism" roundtable, 124–25.

51. See George J. Sanchez, *Becoming Mexican American: Ethnicity, Culture, and Identity in Chicano Los Angeles, 1900–1945* (New York: Oxford University Press, 1993), 73–75.

52. David J. Leonard, "'The Little Fuehrer Invades Los Angeles': The Emergence of a Black-Jewish Coalition after World War II," *American Jewish History* 92, no. 1 (2004): 96–98; Bernstein, "Building Bridges," 110–11, 245. The work of the communist-led Civil Rights Congress is described in Hurewitz, *Bohemian Los Angeles*, 218–28.

53. In September 1947, the Community Service Organization invited the executive secretary of the CRC to serve as the only non–Mexican American on its advisory board. See Bernstein, "Building Bridges," 244. Coalitions across racial boundaries with Mexicans in Los Angeles coincided with similar coalition building and activism with African American organizations in Eastern cities, especially in New York. Building both coalitions was part of a struggle with the Communist Party for leadership of ethnic communities. See Cheryl Greenberg, *Troubling the Waters: Black-Jewish Relations in the American Century* (Princeton, N.J.: Princeton University Press, 2006), 114–19, 169–70.

54. Burt, "Edward Roybal's Election." On the moderate goals of the Community Service Organization and its compatibility with the Jewish CRC, see Bernstein, "Building Bridges," 241–43, 256.

55. On the construction of a communist political culture, its origins in Boyle Heights, and its subsequent relationship to artistic support networks in Silver Lake, see Hurewitz, *Bohemian Los Angeles*, 151–228.

56. Moore, *To the Golden Cities*, 197–201; Bernstein, "Building Bridges," 202, 212.

57. Los Angeles Public Library, "A Brief Benjamin Franklin Library Branch History," http://www.lapl.org/branches/hist/01-h.html (accessed July 25, 2008).

58. Vorspan and Gartner, *Jews of Los Angeles*, 255; Moore, *To the Golden Cities*, 211.

59. Fred Massarik, "A Report on the Jewish Population of Los Angeles" (Los Angeles: Jewish Community Council, January 1953), 11, 111; Shevitz, "Jewish Space and Place in Venice," 69–73.

60. Samuel Dinin, "My Educational Credo," in *Judaism and the Jewish School*, ed. Judah Pilch and Meir Ben-Horin (New York: Bloch, 1966), 319–22.

61. University of Judaism, "History, University of Judaism," http://www.ajula.edu/Content/ContentUnit. asp?CID=141&u=525&t=0 (accessed July 25, 2008).

62. Moore, *To Golden Cities*, 72–73, 78, 118, 126, 133–40.

63. Farrel Broslawsky, "Lives without Passion," in *The San Fernando Valley: Past and Present* (Los Angeles: Pacific Rim Research, 1986), 196.

64. "History," Milken Community High School, http://www.milkenschool.org/history.aspx (accessed July 25, 2008).

65. David Finnigan, "Chasen Forging New Path at Leo Baeck," *Jewish Journal of Greater Los Angeles*, January 16, 2004, http://www.jewishjournal.com/community_briefs/article/chasen_forging_new_path_at_leo_baeck_20040116/.

66. Fred Massarik, "A Study of the Jewish Population of Long Beach, Lakewood, and Los Alamitos" (Long Beach, Calif.: Jewish Community Federation, 1962), 26, table 19; 34, table 23; 38, table 27.

67. Caryn Aviv and David Shneer, "Temples of American Identity: Jewish Museums in Los Angeles," in Aviv and Shneer, *New Jews*, 80.

68. Aviv and Shneer, "Temples of American Identity," 81. The grants were supported by former governor Gray Davis and his chief of staff, Lynn Schenk, the daughter of Holocaust survivors and a founding member of Congregation Beth Am in San Diego. See Micah Sachs, "Right-Hand Woman," *San Diego Jewish Journal*, October 2003, http://www.sdjewishjournal.com/stories/xarchive.php?id=534.

69. Tom Tugend, "Rites Launch Israel Tolerance Museum," *Jewish Journal of Greater Los Angeles*, May 7, 2004.

70. Ibid. To engage its student audiences, the Museum of Tolerance has borrowed technologies from the movie industry to make visitors "participants" in the genocides it documents. See Aviv and Shneer, "Temples of American Identity," 82–83.

71. Aviv and Shneer, "Temples of American Identity," 90.

72. The story is told with a mordant edge in Davis, *City of Quartz*, 114–25.

73. Tugend, "Why Aren't Jews Giving to Jews." Broad's emergence as the key philanthropist for medicine and art in Los Angeles and elsewhere is outlined in Colacello, "Eli Broad's Big Picture," 324–30, 379–86.

74. Vorspan and Gartner, *Jews of Los Angeles*, 245.

75. Bonacich and Appelbaum, *Behind the Label*, 114.

76. The three men were joined in 1982 by Mel Levine (Santa Monica and Venice), a University of California, Berkeley, graduate who had gained recognition by becoming active in Jewish communal affairs. See Kurt F. Stone, "Berman, Howard Lawrence; Levine, Meldon Edises; Waxman, Henry Arnold," in *The Congressional Minyan: The Jews of Capitol Hill* (New York: KTAV, 2000), 30–34, 301–3, 512–16.

77. Raphael J. Sonenshein, *Politics in Black and White: Race and Power in Los Angeles* (Princeton, N.J.: Princeton University Press, 1993), 187–88. Sonenshein (20) argues that this coalition rested on *ideological* grounds—support for policies to combat discrimination—but also had material benefits for both groups.

78. On the events in Watts, see Gerald Horne, "Black Fire: 'Riot' and 'Revolt' in Los Angeles, 1965 and 1992," in *Seeking El Dorado: African Americans in California*, ed. Lawrence de Graaf, Kevin Mulroy, and Quintard Taylor (Los Angeles: Autry Museum of Western Heritage, 2001), 377–404.

79. On initial Jewish settlement in the upper reaches of South-Central Los Angeles, see Mark Wild, *Street Meeting: Multiethnic Neighborhoods in Early Twentieth Century Los Angeles* (Berkeley: University of California Press, 2005), 33.

80. Sonenshein, *Politics in Black and White*, 55–88, 104; see also Davis, *City of Quartz*, 140–43.

81. Fred Sigel, *The Future Once Happened Here* (San Francisco: Encounter Books, 1997), 156–58.

82. Raab, "No City like San Francisco," 372.

83. In 1964, Rabbi Fine was appointed a charter member of San Francisco's Human Rights Commission. See Rosenbaum, *Architects of Reform*, 147.

84. Raab, "No City like San Francisco," 376.

85. Rosenbaum, *Architects of Reform*, 159–65.

86. Julie Gruenbaum Fax, "Courage and Innovation, and at Eighty, Rabbi Harold Schulweis Plans to Keep Going," *Jewish Journal of Greater Los Angeles*, April 1, 2005, http://www.jewishjournal.com/articles/item/courage_and_innovation_20050404/.

87. Temple Sinai (Reno, Nev.), "Temple History," http://templesinai-reno.com/aboutus/history/ (accessed July 25, 2008). Rabbi Gumbiner had been Temple Sinai's rabbi in the 1940s and retained contact with the

temple. In the early 1970s, he returned twice a month to officiate at Shabbat services.

88. David Burner, *Making Peace with the Sixties* (Princeton, N.J.: Princeton University Press, 1996), 37–39.

89. Ibid., 44. See the lengthy description of the free speech movement in an interview of Jackie Goldberg, who subsequently had a long career as a teacher, as an elected member of the board of the Los Angeles Unified School District and of the state legislature, and as an advocate for gays and lesbians. "Interview with Jackie Goldberg," http://www.gwu.edu/~nsarchiv/coldwar/interviews/episode-13/goldberg2.html (accessed July 25, 2008).

90. William Rorabaugh, *Berkeley at War: The 1960s* (New York: Oxford University Press, 1989), 25; "Interview with Jackie Goldberg."

91. On the Jewish base of the California Democratic Council in Los Angeles, see Sonenshein, *Politics in Black and White*, 47.

92. *Humanity: An Arena of Critique and Commitment*, No. 2 (Berkeley, Calif.: National Association of College and University Chaplains, December 5, 1964), http://content.cdlib.org/ark:/13030/kt067n97c2. Rabbi Gumbiner was a member of the publication's editorial committee.

93. Clayborne Carson, *In Struggle: SNCC and the Black Awakening of the 1960s* (Cambridge, Mass.: Harvard University Press, 1981), 266–69.

94. Dollinger, "Counterculture," 154–61.

95. Rabbi Gumbiner received a Berkeley Citation (the forty-first person to do so) at about the same time as did wealthy San Francisco Jewish philanthropists Daniel Koshland and Harold Zellerbach, who had also been supporters of Rabbi Fine. See "UC Berkeley Awards," University Relations, http://awards.berkeley.edu/pdf/Berkeley_Citation.pdf.

96. The son of department store owners in Oakland, Magnes aspired to intellectual rather than entrepreneurial excellence, and in the 1890s he enrolled at Hebrew Union College in Cincinnati. After a brief career as associate rabbi at New York's Temple Emanu-El and as head of the city's "Kehillah experiment," Magnes immigrated to Palestine in 1923 and became the first chancellor of the Hebrew University in Jerusalem. For a summary of

Magnes's career, see Arthur Goren, ed., introduction to *Dissenter in Zion: From the Writings of Judah Magnes* (Cambridge, Mass.: Harvard University Press, 1982), 3–57.

97. Seymour Fromer, interview by Elinor Mandelson, September 14, 1981, Western Jewish History Center, Judah L. Magnes Museum, Berkeley, Calif.

98. Biale, "Between Los Angeles and Berkeley."

99. For an early assessment of Ginsberg and Alan Watts that sets them into the Beat scene stretching from New York to San Francisco and apparently nowhere in between, see Theodore Roszak, *The Making of a Counter Culture: Reflections on the Technocratic Society and Its Youthful Opposition* (Garden City, N.Y.: Anchor Books), 124–54. Ferenc Morton Szasz notes that only in the 1960s in intellectual circles did Asian religions like Buddhism and Native American worldviews achieve moral parity with Christianity. See Szasz, *Religion in the Modern American West*, xiii–xv, 194–98.

100. The general background and career of Carlebach is traced in Sarna, *American Judaism*, 345–49.

101. The personal charm in winning "converts" is explained in David Margolis, "Seeing Shlomo: A Bittersweet Remembrance of My Teacher, Rabbi Shlomo Carlebach," August 2007, http://www.davidmargolis.com/article.php?id=64&cat_cc=&cat_fp=3. Allegations that Carlebach's idea of outreach to women led to violations of their person in the permissive San Francisco atmosphere are discussed in Sarah Blustain, "A Paradoxical Legacy: Rabbi Shlomo Carlebach's Shadow Side," *Lilith* 23, no. 1 (1998), http://rickross.com/reference/lubavitch12.html.

102. Yaakov Ariel, "Hasidism in the Age of Aquarius: The House of Love and Prayer in San Francisco, 1967–1977," *Religion and American Culture: A Journal of Interpretation* 13, no. 2 (2003): 139–49.

103. Ibid., 152.

104. For a broad sketch of the Pacific region as a distinctive religious realm because of the exchange with East Asia, see Maffly-Kipp, "Eastward Ho," 127–48.

105. Lori Epstein, "Renewal Rabbi Taught at Aquarian Minyan," *Jewish Bulletin of Northern California*, September 4, 1998; Aleza Goldsmith, "Local Sweat Lodge Is Cleansing Ritual for Holy Days," *Jewish Bulletin of Northern California*, September 29, 2000;

Noma Faingold, "'Soulmates' Are Hired as Co-leaders at Aquarian Minyan," *Jewish Bulletin of Northern California*, February 27, 1998; Betsy Kaufman, "Singing Rabbis Together Again," *Jewish Review (Portland)*, June 1, 2004; Aquarian Minyan Web site, http://www.aquarianminyan.org/.

106. Michael E. Staub, *Torn at the Roots: The Crisis of Jewish Liberalism in Postwar America* (New York: Columbia University Press, 2002), 287–88.

107. A *havurah* might best be understood as a meeting of friends for spiritual purposes.

108. See, e.g., the brief discussion in Michael Lerner, *Jewish Renewal: A Path to Healing and Transformation* (New York: Harper Perennial, 1995), 29.

109. "Biographical Notes on Rabbi Lerner," *Tikkun*, http://www.tikkun.org/rabbi_lerner/bio (accessed July 25, 2008).

110. Joe Eskenazi, "Organized Religion Thriving in 'Bezerkeley,'" *J.: Jewish News Weekly of Northern California*, October 14, 2005, http://www.jewishf.com/content/2-0-/module/displaystory/story_id/27278/format/html/displaystory.html.

111. On the relative stagnation especially of Portland after the war, see Carl Abbott, "Regional City and Network City: Portland and Seattle in the Twentieth Century," *Western Historical Quarterly* 23, no. 3 (1992): 305–6. Portland in particular lacked even a four-year state college until the 1960s, because of opposition from the state universities in Corvallis and Eugene. Gordon B. Dodds, *The College That Would Not Die: Portland State University, 1946–1996* (Portland: Oregon Historical Society Press, 2000), 36.

112. "Bond Drive Nets Dollars," *Oregonian (Portland)*, Sunday ed., June 25, 1972, 4; clipping provided by the American Jewish Archives. James McCann, *A Study of the Jewish Community in the Greater Seattle Area* (Seattle: Jewish Federation of Greater Seattle, 1979), 6, 8.

113. Their parallel careers were the subject of a documentary, *The Three Rabbis*, produced by Oregon Pubic Television in 2005.

114. Rabbi Joshua Stampfer, interview with Shirley Tanzer, February 28, 1980, Oregon Jewish Museum.

115. Rabbi Emanuel Rose, interview with Shirley Tanzer, March 10, 1981, Oregon Jewish Museum.

116. Stampfer, interview.

117. Rose, interview; Stampfer, interview.

118. Joel Crohn, *Ethnic Identity and Marital Conflict: Jews, Italians, and WASPs* (New York: American Jewish Committee, 1986); William Toll, "Intermarriage and the Urban West: A Religious Context for Cultural Change," in Rischin and Livingston, *Jews of the American West*, 174–85.

119. Stampfer, interview.

120. Ibid.

121. Rose, interview.

122. Shaarei Torah, "Our History, Shaarei Torah," http://www.shaareitorah.org/about.html (accessed July 25, 2008). The Portland Jewish Academy was relocated to the Mittleman Jewish Community Center. See "MJCC/ PJA Remodeling Begins April 13," *Jewish Review*, April 15, 2006, 5.

123. Judge Solomon, born in South Portland in 1906, was nominated as the first Jewish federal district judge in Oregon by President Harry Truman in 1950. Solomon served until his death in 1987, longer than any federal district judge in Oregon history. See Harry H. Stein, *Gus Solomon: Liberal Politics, Jews, and the Federal Courts* (Portland: Oregon Historical Society Press, 2006).

124. Cone, Droker, and Williams, *Family of Strangers*, 254–57.

125. New zoning required that many of the new office towers include space for retail stores at the street level and apartments above the offices. See "A New Kind of City," *New Yorker*, October 21, 1985, 49–50.

126. On his return to Oregon, Goldschmidt was employed by one of Oregon's most dynamic new companies, Nike, and was associated with the movement to attract high-tech firms to the state. In 1987, when Oregon was beginning to recover from a major recession, he was elected governor. His political career abruptly ended in 1991, however, with suspicions, later confirmed, of sexual misconduct. See "Governor Neil Goldschmidt," *Gubernatorial History in Oregon*, Oregon Historical Society, http://www.ohs.org/education/focus/governor_neil_goldschmidt.cfm (accessed July 25, 2008).

127. McCann, *Jewish Community*, 31.

128. Cone, Droker, and Williams, *Family of Strangers*, 251, 264, 276; McCann, *Jewish Community*, 53.

129. McCann, *Jewish Community*, 16, 35–36, 74.

130. Michele Rosen, "Stroum Jewish Community Center of Greater Seattle," updated March 2008, http://www.historylink.org/essays/output.cfm?file_id=104; Lee Micklin, "Samuel Stroum, (1921–2001)," August 2001, http://www.historylink.org/essays/output.cfm?file_id=3516.

131. Phillips, "Los Angeles Jewry," 158.

132. Ibid., 157–58.

133. Jewish population estimates can be tracked in "Jewish Population Estimates of Selected Cities, 1950," 71; "Jewish Population in the United States, 1970," 348; and "Jewish Population in the United States, 1980," in *The American Jewish Year Book, 1980* (Philadelphia: Jewish Publication Society, 1980), 81:175.

134. Benjamin N. Brook, *Tucson: The Building of a Jewish Community* (Tucson: Bloom Southwest Jewish Archives, University of Arizona, 1992), 14–15.

135. See Luckingham, *Phoenix*, 258–62.

136. In Seattle, McCann measured "household heads" rather than men and found that 78 percent of this smaller group in the nineteen to forty-five age cohort had also earned at least undergraduate degrees. These findings suggest that no matter where Jews coming west settled, they were the beneficiaries of a national trend toward high college completion. McCann, *Jewish Community*, 62; Bruce A. Phillips and William S. Aron, "The Phoenix Jewish Population Survey," typescript, September 1983, 21, 24, 26 (in possession of William Toll).

137. Phillips and Aron, "Phoenix Jewish Population Survey," 21, app., table 12a.

138. McCann, "Jewish Community," 65.

EPILOGUE: ASPIRING
TO NATIONAL LEADERSHIP

Epigraph. Robert Goldblum, "Gambling on the Jewish Future: Is the Boomtown in the Nevada Desert a Model for Jewish Life in the Twenty-first Century?" *Jewish Week (New York)*, June 17, 2004.

1. Scholars have observed that "in the 1970s and 1980s, Los Angeles became the West Coast anchor of American Jewish museum culture." Aviv and Shneer, *New Jews*, 79, 98–99.

2. Peter Schrag, *California: America's High Stakes Experiment* (Berkeley: University of California Press, 2006), 40.

3. Edward W. Soja, "Los Angeles, 1965–1992: From Crisis-Generated Restructuring to Restructuring-Generated Crisis," in *The City: Los Angeles and Urban Theory at the End of the Twentieth Century*, ed. Allen J. Scott and Edward W. Soja (Berkeley: University of California Press, 1996), 442–44.

4. Edward W. Soja and Allen J. Scott, "Introduction to Los Angeles: City, and Region," in Soja and Scott, *City*, 12.

5. Roger Waldinger and Michael Lichter, "Anglos: Beyond Ethnicity?" in *Ethnic Los Angeles*, ed. Roger Waldinger and Mehdi Bozorgmehr (New York: Russell Sage Foundation, 1996), 427–29. Chinese and Japanese Angelenos parallel this transition in niche concentration and in social and economic mobility.

6. The concept of edge cities, and their distinctive differences from residential suburbs, is explained in Joel Garreau, *Edge Cities: Life on the New Frontier* (New York: Anchor Books / Doubleday, 1991), 3–15, 265–342.

7. Tom Tugend, "CSUN Exemplifies the Changing Face of 'Jewish Studies,'" *Jewish Journal*, August 17, 2007, http://www.jewishjournal.com/home/print.php?id=18055; Deborah Moon, "PSU's Judaic Studies Grows Faster than Planners Dreamed," *Jewish Review,* September 15, 2007, 12.

8. Bob Young, "Still Going, but Where?" *Willamette Week (Portland)*, December 16, 1998. On how African American and Latino politicians, as well as Jews before them, judiciously divided the political geography of Los Angeles County into "safe" ethnic districts, see Harold Myerson, "The Delicate Balance of Black and Brown," Opinion, *Los Angeles Times*, June 24, 2007. Peter Savodnik, "A Party Divided?" *Los Angeles Times*, May 14, 2006, http://articles.latimes.com/writers/peter-savodnik.

9. James D. Besser describes grassroots efforts in cities across the country, including Los Angeles and San Francisco, an inclusion made initially in San Francisco and Los Angeles. See James D. Besser, "Filling the Void on Domestic Issues," *Jewish Week*, January 5, 2007.

10. Soja and Scott, "Introduction to Los Angeles," 12; Soja, "Los Angeles," 441. The crucial role of the

transportation infrastructure, and especially the port, in building the new economic base of Los Angeles—with no apparent Jewish influence—is explained in Erie, *Globalizing L.A.*, 4–11.

11. Waldinger and Lichter, "Anglos," 435.

12. James P. Allen and Eugene Turner, *The Ethnic Quilt: Population Diversity in Southern California* (Northridge: Center for Geographical Studies, California State University, Northridge, 1997), 70; Joel Kotkin and Erika Ozuna, *The Changing Face of the San Fernando Valley*, 2002, 15–18, http://publicpolicy.pepperdine.edu/davenport-institute/reports/changing-face/.

13. Wendy J. Madnick, "Conejo Valley Hit by Growing Pains," *Jewish Journal*, April 25, 2003, http://www.jewishjournal.com/community_briefs/article/conejo_valley_hit_growing_pains_20030425. Note that the rabbis interviewed for this article in 2003 were no longer at those institutions when the following listing was consulted in 2007. See Jewish Family Service, Ventura County, "Congregations of Ventura County," http://www.cipcug.org/minkin/jfs/congregations.htm (accessed August 14, 2008).

14. Sonenshein, *Politics in Black and White*, 148–51.

15. Wendy J. Madnick, "The Final Push," *Jewish Journal of Greater Los Angeles*, November 1, 2002. Republicans also appeal to Jewish immigrants from Russia and Iran, who support President George Bush's foreign policy. See Jill Stewart, "GOP Shifts, Pursues Immigrant Votes," *Jewish Journal of Greater Los Angeles*, October 22, 2004. Jews were also prominent in a

16. Ellen Jaffe-Gill, "Rabbi Geller Honored," *Jewish Journal*, May 25, 2001, http://www.jewishjournal.com/community_briefs/article/rabbi_geller_honored_20010525/; Wendy J. Madnick, "Where We Were," *Progressive Jewish Alliance*, April 26, 2002, http://www.pjalliance.org/article.aspx?ID=189&CID=20. Were," *Progressive Jewish Alliance*, April 26, 2002, http://www.pjalliance.org/article.aspx?ID=189&CID

17. Congregation Kol Ami, "About Congregation Kol Ami," http://www.kol-ami.org/about/index.html (accessed July 25, 2008).

18. Robert Gottlieb, Mark Valliantos, Regina M. Freer, and Peter Drier, *The Next Los Angeles: The Struggle for a Livable City* (Berkeley: University of California Press, 2006), 152–53.

19. Ralph J. Sonenshein, "City of L.A. Report Card: Mayor Villaraigosa and the Jewish Community at Mid-term," *Jewish Journal*, June 8, 2007, http://www.jewishjournal.com/home/print.php?id=17772. The class background of elite Mexican Americans building bridges with Yaroslavsky is quite different from that of those who negotiated with the CRC in 1947. See Bernstein, *Building Bridges*, 247–53. Ethnic coalitions also include negotiations with African Americans. See Harold Meyerson, "The Delicate Balance of Black and Brown," Opinion, *Los Angeles Times*, June 24, 2007, M1, M8.

20. Aviv and Shneer, "Temples of American Identity," 105.

21. Bernard Weinraub, "Travel Advisory: Jewish History Museum Opening in Los Angeles," *New York Times*, April 21, 1996.

22. Gene Lichtenstein, "L.A. Museums: Saved by the Jews," *Jewish Journal of Greater Los Angeles*, August 16, 2002.

23. Joel Kotkin, "Jews Stick to Their Turf," *Jewish Journal*, January 3, 2003, http://www.joelkotkin.com/ReligionTJJ%20Jews%20stick%20to%20Their%20Turf.htm.

24. "Regionalism" roundtable, 127.

25. Steven J. Gold, *The Israeli Diaspora* (Seattle: University of Washington Press, 2002), 38.

26. Naama Sabar, *Kibbutzniks in the Diaspora*, translated from the Hebrew by Chaya Naor (Albany: State University of New York Press, 2000), 1. Sabar notes that through the late 1980s Israeli secular society faced a dilemma: "how to create a non-assimilating Jewish Zionist self-identity, while remaining open to the world at large and even influencing it" (x).

27. Gold, *Israeli Diaspora*, 189.

28. United Jewish Communities, "Israelis in the United States: Reconciling Estimates with NJPS," http://www.ujc.org/page.aspx?id=46358 (accessed July 6, 2007). See also Tom Tugend, "From Mulholland, to the Freeway, to the Ocean, White with Foam . . . God Bless the Valley Hills, the Jews New Home," *Jewish Journal*, http://www.jewishjournal.com.forums/viewthread/1294 (accessed January 12, 2007). Tugend notes the difficulty in obtaining accurate population data. See also Gold, *Israeli Diaspora*, 17, 23, 33, 54.

29. Gold, *Israeli Diaspora*, 168–69, 178, 215.

30. Different sources cite different statistics for the Iranian population of southern California. The general range is from three hundred thousand to as many as six hundred thousand, with the Iranian Jewish émigrés and their offspring estimated at perhaps thirty thousand. See Heather Catherine Orr, "Tehrangeles: L.A., the Iranian Expatriate Capital Abroad," *Persian Journal*, August 19, 2004, http://www.Iranians.ws/cgi-bin/iran_news/exec/viewcgi/2/3382/printer; Tara Bahrampour, "Persia on the Pacific," *New Yorker*, November 10, 2003, http://newyorker.com/archive/2003/11/10/031110fa_fact?currentPage=6; Mehdi Bozorgmehr, Claudia Der-Martirosian, and Georges Sabagh, "Middle Easterners: A New Kind of Immigrant," in Waldinger and Bozorgmehr, *Ethnic Los Angeles*, 352. Jews remaining in Iran are estimated to be about thirty thousand. See Robin Wright, *The Last Great Revolution: Turmoil and Transformation in Iran* (New York: Vintage Books, 2001), 207.

31. Most Russian Jewish émigrés settled in New York City, while the majority of those coming to the Pacific Coast settled in the San Francisco area. See Kevin Starr, *Coast of Dreams: California on the Edge, 1990–2003* (New York: Knopf, 2004), 176. Estimates of the number of Russian émigrés in Los Angeles are also greatly exaggerated. See Stewart, "GOP Shifts, Pursues Immigrant Votes."

32. Martin Kasindorf, "Beverly Hills Will Have First Iranian-Born Mayor in USA," *USA Today*, http://usatoday.printthis.clickability.com/pt/cpt?action=cp&title=BE (accessed July 17, 2007).

33. As early as 1984, 13 percent of the white students at Beverly Hills High School were classified as Persian. See Michael Leahy, "Beverly Hills High in the 1980s," in *Hard Lessons: Senior Year at Beverly Hills High School* (Boston: Little, Brown, 1988), posted on Eighties Club, http://eightiesclub.tripod.com/id132htm; Joel Kotkin, "Welcome to the Casbah," *American Enterprise*, January–February 1999, http://www.taemag.com/issues/articleid.16921/article_detail.asp.

34. Gold, *Israeli Diaspora*, 85.

35. Shoshanah Feher, "From the Rivers of Babylon to the Valleys of Los Angeles: The Exodus and Adaptation of Iranian Jews," *Gatherings in Diaspora: Religious Communities and the New Immigration*, ed. R. Stephen Warner and Judith G. Wittner (Philadelphia: Temple University Press, 1998), 74. Edna Bonacich and Richard P. Appelbaum report that they were told by public relations officials that Asians and Iranians do not support general communal charities like the Cedars-Sinai Hospital. Bonacich and Appelbaum, *Behind the Label*, 117. Younger professionals educated in America have formed an organization to deal with intergenerational problems of identity conflict that face most immigrant groups but whose existence older heads of families among Persian Jews seem to deny. The International Judea Foundation / SIAMAK was founded in 1979, at first to help émigrés find jobs, apartments, and general counseling on their adjustment to living in America. See Feher, "From the Rivers of Babylon," 76–78, 82–83.

36. "Jimmy Delshad, Mayor," http://*www.delshad.com/Mambo/index.php?option+com_content&task=view&id=11&Itemid=33* (accessed October 12, 2008).

37. Michael Aushenket, "Marching to a New Magbit," *Jewish Journal of Greater Los Angeles*, June 13, 2002, http://www.jewishjournal.com/community_briefs/article/marching_to_a_new_magbit_20020614/ (accessed July 2, 2009).

38. Judy Siegel-Itzkovich, "Los Angeles Group Donates $3.2 Million for Terror Victims," *Jerusalem Post*, June 8, 2002; Nelson Moussazadeh, "Combating Electoral Complacency in Israel: A New Vision for Electoral Reform in Israel," *Yale Israel Journal*, Summer 2005.

39. Sabah Soomekh, "Tehrangeles: Capital, Culture, and Faith among Iranian Jews" (paper presented at the "Religious Pluralism in Southern California" conference, University of California, Santa Barbara, May 9, 2003). For the ambiguous feelings among Jews in Iran through 2000, see Wright, *Last Great Revolution*, 208–12.

40. Kotkin, "Jews Stick to Their Turf."

41. Gene Lichtenstein, "The Mideast Comes to LA," *Jewish Journal of Greater Los Angeles*, April 19, 2002, http://www.pjalliance.org/article.aspx?ID=191&CID=20.

42. David Brindley, "A Big Picture Guy," *Prism*, April 2001, http://www.prism-magazine.org/april01/guy.cfm. Samueli and his wife, Susan, also ventured into the world of professional sports team ownership by buying the Anaheim Mighty Ducks from the Disney

Corporation in 2005. See "Henry and Susan Samueli Reach an Agreement to Buy the Mighty Ducks of Anaheim from the Walt Disney Company," *Disney Corporate*, http://corporate.disney.go.com/news/corporate/2005/2005_0225_mightyducks.html. *Forbes* magazine estimates the Samuelis' net worth in 2006 at two billion dollars. See "The 400 Richest Americans: #160, Henry Samueli," September 21, 2006, http://www.forbes.com/lists/2006.

43. Karen Alexander, "Move over, Los Angeles," *Jewish Journal of Greater Los Angeles*, August 31, 2001, http://wwwjewishjournal.com/community_briefs/article/move_over_los_angeles_20010831; Ilena Schneider, "Jewish in OC," *Jewish Journal of Greater Los Angeles*, April 28, 2000.

44. Phillips, "Challenge of Family," 22; United Jewish Federation of San Diego County, "Jewish Community's Strategic Plan."

45. Some of the buildings, designed by the world-renowned Jewish architect Louis Kahn, were opened in 1963, and the campus was completed in 1967. See Salk Institute for Biological Studies, "Jonas Salk," *http://www.salk.edu/jonassalk* (accessed October 12, 2008); "Salk Institute Gets $30 M, Its Largest Donation Ever," *North County Times*, November 18, 2003, http://www.nctimes.com/articles/2003/11/18/business/news.

46. California Institute for Telecommunications and Information Technology, "Academics and Industry Leaders Honor Irwin Jacobs at UCSD Symposium," October 20, 2003, http://www.calit2.net/newsroom/article.php?id=305. Davis, Mayhew, and Miller, *Under the Perfect Sun*, 131. Trudy E. Bell, "The Quiet Genius of Andrew J. Viterbi," *Bent of Tau Beta Pi*, Spring 2006, 20; Matt Welch, "Birth of a Blueprint: Profile Internet Father, Leonard Kleinrock," *Zone News*, January 2000, http://mattwelch.com/ZoneSave/Kleinrock.htm.

47. Congregation Beth Israel, San Diego, "History," http://www.cbisd.org/about/history.shtml (accessed July 25, 2008). Its old building downtown was eventually acquired by Conservative Ohr Shalom Synagogue, which caters to newly arriving Spanish-speaking Jews. See Donald H. Harrison, "A Tour of Jewish San Diego," *Jewish News of Greater Phoenix*, June 25, 2004, http://www.jewishaz.com/jewishnews/040625/sandiego.shtml.

48. Jews also began settling between the San Diego State area and Poway, along Interstate 15. See United Federation of San Diego County, "Jewish Community's Strategic Plan."

49. "Population Booms," *Jewish News of Greater Phoenix*, December 6, 2002.

50. The federal government in the 1960s subsidized the Southern Nevada Water Project to make this development possible. See Gottdiner, Collins, and Dickens, *Las Vegas*, 20–21.

51. Denton and Morris, *Money and the Power*, 352–61.

52. The shift from one level of financing to another from 1980 through 2000 is summarized in two essays in Hal K. Rothman and Mike Davis, eds., *The Grit beneath the Glitter: Tales from the Real Las Vegas* (Berkeley: University of California Press, 2002): Hal K. Rothman, "Colony, Capital, and Casino: Money in the Real Las Vegas," 75 –78, and Eugene Moehring, "Growth, Services, and the Political Economy of Gambling in Las Vegas, 1970–2000," 326–30.

53. Michael Green, "The Jews," in *The Peoples of Las Vegas: One City, Many Faces*, ed. Jerry L. Simich and Thomas C. Wright (Reno: University of Nevada Press, 2005), 168; Davis, Mayhew, and Miller, *Under the Perfect Sun*, 87. Las Vegas Jewry also had its respectable characters, like the journalistic crusader and clandestine Haganah supplier, Hank Greenspun, as well as the Federal Bureau of Investigation's chief local sleuth, Joseph Yablonsky, who also contributed to the synagogues. See Hank Greenspun, with Alex Pelle, *Where I Stand: The Record of a Restless Man* (New York: David McKay, 1966), 80–122. On Greenspun and Yablonsky, see Denton and Morris, *Money and the Power*, 59–74, 332–44.

54. Steve Friess, "Oy Vegas! Sin City Gets Kosher," *Boston Globe*, April 4, 2004, http://www.boston.com/news/nation/articles; quotation in Goldblum, "Gambling on the Jewish Future."

55. Joe Eskenazi, "Bay Area's Growing Jewish Scene," June 16, 2005, http://www.ynetnews.com/articles/O,7340,L-3098911,00.html.

56. See Edward Epstein, "Lantos the Master Storyteller, Communicator," *SFGate*, January 1, 2007, http://sfgate.com/cgi-bin/article.cgi?file=lcla/2007/01/01/

MNGBDNB8MF1.DTL&type=printable. Lantos died on February 11, 2008.

57. Milk was assassinated, along with Mayor George Moscone, on November 27, 1978, by former supervisor Dan White. See Joshua Schuster, "Slain S.F. Supervisor Milk Eulogized at Sha'ar Zahav," *J.: The Jewish News Weekly of Northern California*, November 27, 1998, *http://www.jewishsf.com/content/2-0-/module/displaystory/story_id/10065/edition_id/192/format/html/displaystory.html*.

58. By 2002, the federation had formed the first Gay and Lesbian Division in the country, with a gay psychotherapist as its full-time paid staff member. See Dan Pine, "A Twenty-five-Year Retrospective," *Keshet Ga'avah*, 2003, http://www.glbtjews.org/article.php3?id_article=199; and Aleza Goldsmith, "San Francisco Federation Creates New Division For Gays," http://www.pass.to/newsletter/ANewDivisionForGays.htm (accessed July 25, 2008).

59. Eskenazi, "Organized Religion Thriving."

60. Joe Eskenazi, "Have Demographers Undercounted Jews in the West?" *J.: The Jewish News Weekly of Northern California*, October 18, 2002, http://www.jewishsf.com/content/2-0-/module/displaystory/story_id/190866/format/html/edition_id/386/displaystory.html.

61. Ibid.

62. One prominent East Coast Jewish demographic has conceded that prior approaches to the study of intermarriage have taken an unnecessarily narrow view of the lives of the individuals under study. "We sociologists have designed our research to focus mainly on individual identity in a family vacuum, obtaining survey information about one respondent rather than from all family members." Calvin Goldscheider, *Studying the Jewish Future* (Seattle: University of Washington Press, 2004), 31.

63. Though Tobin may have been over-inclusive in his count of western Jews, a 2004 survey of Jews in the San Francisco Bay Area organized by Bruce Phillips confirmed to some degree Tobin's projections, since the Jewish population in San Francisco and in the counties to its south and north had almost doubled since 1986, to more than four hundred thousand. Eskenazi, "Bay Area's Growing Jewish Scene." Surveys of Phoenix and San Diego in 2002 included all members of households that contained a Jewish adult, though counting toward the Jewish total only those persons who identified as such. See United Federation of San Diego County, "Jewish Community's Strategic Plan"; Leisah Namm, "Population Booms: Phoenix Ranks as Thirteenth Largest Jewish Community in Nation," *Jewish News of Greater Phoenix*, December 6, 2002, http://www.jewishaz.com/jewishnews/02106/booms.shtml. On Tobin's career and his critique of traditional American Jewish demography, see Ben Harris, "Gary Tobin, Head of S.F.-based Institute for Jewish and Community Research, Dies at 59," http://www.jweekly.com/article/full/38492/gary-tobin-head-of-s.f.-based-institute-for-jewish-community-research-dies/ (accessed July 7, 2009).

64. Tom Tugend, "Firing of Regional ADL Leader Shocks L.A. Jews," *J.: The Jewish News Weekly of Northern California*, January 4, 2002, http://www.jewishsf.com/content/2-0-/module/display/story_id/17472/format/html/edition_id/346/displaystory. See also James D. Besser, "AJ Congress Completing Sharp Turn to Right," *Jewish Alliance for Law and Social Action*, November 14, 2003, http://www.jewishalliance.org/news2/james_besser.htm.

65. Tugend, "Firing of Regional ADL Leader."

66. David Lehrer, telephone interview with William Toll, June 15, 2006. The importance of coalitions based on religious communities in creating cohesiveness in a city is emphasized in Michael E. Engh, "At Home in Heteropolis: Understanding Postmodern L.A.," *American Historical Review* 105, no. 4 (2000): 1681.

67. Abraham Foxman, telephone interview with Ellen Eisenberg, May 31, 2006.

68. Rob Eshman, "A Fistful of Scholars," *Jewish Journal of Greater Los Angeles*, December 2, 2005, http://www.jewishjournal.com/home/print.php?id=15043.

BIBLIOGRAPHY

PERIODICALS

Allgemeine Zeitung des Judenthum (Leipzig)
American Hebrew News
American Israelite (Cincinnati)
Berkeley Daily Planet
B'nai B'rith Messenger (Los Angeles)
Daily Alta California (San Francisco)
Daily Evening Herald (Marysville, Calif.)
Daily Standard (Portland)
Emanu-El (San Francisco)
Fortune
Forward (New York)
Hebrew (San Francisco)
J.: The Jewish News Weekly of Northern California
Jerusalem Post
Jewish Bulletin (San Francisco)
Jewish Immigration Bulletin (New York)
Jewish Journal of Greater Los Angeles
Jewish Messenger (New York)
Jewish News of Greater Phoenix
Jewish Progress (San Francisco)
Jewish Times (San Diego)
Jewish Times and Observer (San Francisco)
Jewish Transcript (Seattle)
Jewish Week (New York)
Los Angeles Business Journal

Los Angeles Daily Star
Los Angeles Times
New York Times
Occident (Philadelphia)
Oregonian
Overland Monthly (San Francisco)
San Diego Jewish Journal
San Francisco Call
San Francisco Chronicle
San Francisco City Directory, 1879, 1910
Scribe (Portland)
Weekly Gleaner (San Francisco)

MANUSCRIPT COLLECTIONS

American Jewish Archives, Cincinnati
    Congregation Emanu-El [Spokane]
    Hamburger Home Collection
    Jacob Nieto Papers
    Temple Beth Israel [Tacoma]
    Jacob Voorsanger Papers
American Jewish Historical Society, New York and
    Newton Center, MA
    Industrial Removal Office Records
    Stephen S. Wise Papers

Bancroft Library, University of California, Berkeley
Bailey Gatzert Dictation, H. H. Bancroft Collection
Bernard Goldsmith Dictation, H. H. Bancroft
Collection
Simon Lubin Papers
Peixotto Family Papers
Japanese American National Museum, Los Angeles
Boyle Heights Oral History Project, transcripts
Jewish Women's Archive
Ray Frank Collection
Weaving Women's Words (Seattle)
Oregon Historical Society, Portland
Ben Selling Papers
Oregon Jewish Museum, Portland
Congregation Beth Israel (Portland)
Jewish Old People's Home Collection
National Council of Jewish Women (Portland
Section)
Eugene Nudelman, "The Family of Joseph
Nudelman"
Shirley Tanzer Oral History Collection
Roza R. Willer, "The History of Jewish Social Work
in Portland"
Rocky Mountain Jewish Historical Society, Denver
Sanatorium (1914, 1918)
University of Oregon Archives, Eugene
President's Office Correspondence
President's File [Prince Lucien Campbell]
University of Washington Archives, Seattle
Elazar Behar Papers
Laura Berch Papers
Joseph Cohen Papers
Congregation Bikur Cholim Machzikay Hadath
Collection
Congregation Herzl Collection
Jewish Community Oral History Project
Jewish Family and Children Services Papers
Jacob Kaplan Papers
Rabbi Samuel Koch Papers
Rabbi Raphael Levine Papers
National Council of Jewish Women (Seattle Section)
Sam Prottas Papers
Clara Gordon Rubin Papers
Seattle Hebrew Benevolent Society Collection
Temple De Hirsch Collection

*Urban Archives Center, Delmar T. Oviatt Library,
California State University, Northridge*
Jewish Family Service of Los Angeles Collection
Los Angeles Jewish Community Committee
Collection
*Western Jewish History Center, Judah L. Magnes
Museum, Berkeley, Calif.*
Alameda Contra Costa Jewish Organizations
Collection
B'nai B'rith District Grand Lodge No. 4
County Jewish Organization Records
Emanu-El Sisterhood for Personal Service Collection
Eureka Benevolent Society Collection
Federation of Jewish Charities (San Francisco)
Hebrew Free Loan Association (San Francisco)
Israel Golden Gate Lodge, B'nai B'rith (Oakland)
Jewish Welfare Federation Records (San Francisco)
Mount Zion Hospital Collection
National Council of Jewish Women (San Francisco
Section)
Oakland Jewish Community Center, in Alameda–
Contra Costa
Ohabai Shalom Collection
Petaluma Jewish Community Oral History Project
Irving Reichert Papers
San Francisco Jews of Eastern European Origin,
1880–1904: A Community Oral History Project
of the American Jewish Congress and the Judah L.
Magnes Memorial Museum
Fanny Sharlip Collection
Sherith Israel Collection

ORAL HISTORIES

Alhadeff, Charles, University of Washington Archives
Ash, Harry, University of Washington Archives
Asia, Benjamin "Bud," University of Washington
Archives
Atkins, Miriam, Oregon Jewish Museum
Behar, Elazar, University of Washington Archives
Berch, Laura, University of Washington Archives
Brandt, Ruth Fujii, Japanese American National
Museum
Brownstein, Vera Slifman, Oregon Jewish Museum

Capeloto, Mary, University of Washington Archives

Cherney, Lilian Gertrude, Western Jewish History Center

de Leon, Tillie, University of Washington Archives

Durkheimer, Sylvan, Oregon Jewish Museum

Eisenberg, Hershey, Japanese American National Museum

Ets-Hokin, Rose Harman, Western Jewish History Center

Feves, Gertrude, Oregon Jewish Museum

Franco, Albert, University of Washington Archives

Fromer, Seymour, Western Jewish History Center

Frumkin, Leo, Japanese American National Museum

Glazer, Edward, University of Washington Archives

Heppner, Fannie, Western Jewish History Center

Holzman, Lena Kleinberg, University of Washington Archives

Katz, Max, University of Washington Archives

Krems, Nathan, University of Washington Archives

La Pove, Jean Braverman, Western Jewish History Center

Nieder, Bailey, University of Washington Archives

Okrand, Fred, Japanese American National Museum

Rich, Raye, Western Jewish History Center

Rinder, Rose, Western Jewish History Center

Rose, Rabbi Emanuel, Oregon Jewish Museum

Rosenfeld, Miriam, Oregon Jewish Museum

Rubin, Clara Gordon, University of Washington Archives

Rucker, B. Wallace, University of Washington Archives

Silverstone, Rachel, University of Washington Archives

Solomon, Vivian Dudune, Western Jewish History Center

Soren, David, Western Jewish History Center [Petaluma Collection]

Stampfer, Rabbi Joshua, Oregon Jewish Museum

Stein, Claire Olosoroff, Japanese American National Museum

Trachtenberg, Gladys, Oregon Jewish Museum

Wachtin, Sonia Myers, University of Washington Archives

Wilson, Atoy Rudolf, Japanese American National Museum

INTERVIEWS

Driesen, Felice Lauterstein, interview with Ellen Eisenberg, November 11, 1997

Foxman, Abraham, telephone interview with Ellen Eisenberg, May 31, 2006

Lehrer, David, telephone interview with William Toll, June 15, 2006

GOVERNMENT DOCUMENTS

New Odessa Community, Articles of Incorporation (December 31, 1883), Records of Land Purchases and Incorporation, Douglas County, Oregon

Seattle Naturalization Records, 1907–14

U.S. Census, 1870, 1880, 1900, 1910, 1920, 1930

BOOKS, JOURNALS, AND OTHER MATERIAL

Abbott, Carl. "Regional City and Network City: Portland and Seattle in the Twentieth Century." *Western Historical Quarterly* 23, no. 3 (1992): 293–322.

Abrams, Jeanne E. *Blazing the Tuberculosis Trail: The Religio-ethnic Role of Four Sanatoria in Early Denver.* Denver: Colorado Historical Society, 1991.

———. "Chasing the Cure in Colorado." In Rischin and Livingston, Jews of the American West, 92–115.

———. *Jewish Women Pioneering the Frontier Trail: A History in the American West.* New York: New York University Press, 2006.

Adatto, Albert. "Sephardim and the Seattle Sephardic Community." Master's thesis, University of Washington, 1939.

Alkow, Jacob. *In Many Worlds.* New York: Shengold Publishers, 1985.

Allen, James P., and Eugene Turner. *The Ethnic Quilt: Population Diversity in Southern California.* Northridge: Center for Geographical Studies, California State University, Northridge, 1997.

American Jewish University [formerly University of Judaism]. "History." http://www.ajula.edu/Content/ContentUnit.asp?CID=52&u=525&t=0 (accessed July 25, 2008).

The American Jewish Year Book. Vols. 51–93. Philadelphia: Jewish Publication Society, 1950–92.

The American Jewish Year Book, 2000. New York: American Jewish Committee, 2000.

The American Jewish Yearbook, 5675 [1914–1915]. Philadelphia: Jewish Publication Society, 1914.

The American Jewish Yearbook, 5701 [1940–1941]. Philadelphia: Jewish Publication Society, 1941.

Anderson School of Business, UCLA. "Eli Broad Shares His Philosophy of Business and Leadership with the Anderson Community." Media, May 12, 2002. http://www.anderson.ucla.edu/x4518.xml.

Angell, Norman. After All: The Autobiography of Norman Angell. London: Hamish Hamilton, 1951.

Arad, Gulie Ne'eman. America, Its Jews, and the Rise of Nazism. Bloomington: Indiana University Press, 2000.

Ariel, Yaakov. "Hasidism in the Age of Aquarius: The House of Love and Prayer in San Francisco, 1967–1977." Religion and American Culture: A Journal of Interpretation 13, no. 2 (2003): 139–65.

Auerbach, Eveline Brooks. Frontier Reminiscences of Eveline Brooks Auerbach. Edited and with an introduction by Annegret S. Ogden. Berkeley, Calif.: Friends of the Bancroft Library, 1994.

Averbach, Alvin. "San Francisco's South of Market District, 1850–1950: The Emergence of a Skid Row." California Historical Quarterly 52 (Fall 1973): 197–223.

Aviv, Caryn, and David Shneer. New Jews: The End of the Jewish Diaspora. New York: New York University Press, 2005.

———. "Temples of American Identity: Jewish Museums in Los Angeles." In Aviv and Shneer, New Jews, 72–106.

Bahrampour, Tara. "Persia on the Pacific." New Yorker, November 10, 2003.

Balboni, Alan. "Southern Italians and Eastern European Jews: Cautious Cooperation in Las Vegas Casinos, 1940–1967." Nevada Historical Society Quarterly 38 (Fall 1995): 153–73.

Baron, Salo W., and Jeannette M. Baron. "Palestinian Messengers in America, 1849–79: A Record of Four Journeys." Jewish Social Studies 5, no. 2 (1943): 115–62; no. 3 (1943): 225–85.

Barth, Gunther. Instant Cities: Urbanization and the Rise of San Francisco and Denver. New York: Oxford University Press, 1975.

Bauman, Mark K. "Southern Jewish Women and Their Social Service Organizations." Journal of American Ethnic History 22, no. 3 (2003): 34–78.

———. The Southerner as American: Jewish Style. Cincinnati: American Jewish Archives, 1996.

Bauman, Mark K., and Bobbi Malone, eds. Introduction to "Directions in Southern Jewish History." Special issue, American Jewish History 85, no. 3 (1997): 191–93.

Baur, John E. The Health Seekers of Southern California, 1870–1900. San Marino, Calif.: Huntington Library, 1959.

Bean, Walton. Boss Ruef's San Francisco: The Story of the Union Labor Party, Big Business, and the Graft Prosecution. Berkeley: University of California Press, 1952.

Bell, Trudy E. "The Quiet Genius of Andrew J. Viterbi." Bent of Tau Beta Pi, Spring 2006.

Benjamin, I. J. Three Years in America, 1859–1862. 2 vols. Translated by Charles Reznikoff. Philadelphia: Jewish Publication Society of America, 1956.

Bernard, Richard M., and Bradley R. Rice, eds. Sunbelt Cities: Politics and Growth since World War II. Austin: University of Texas Press, 1983.

Bernstein, Shana Beth. "Building Bridges at Home in a Time of Global Conflict: Interracial Cooperation and the Fight for Civil Rights in Los Angeles, 1933–1954." Ph.D. diss., Stanford University, 2003.

Biale, David. "Between Los Angeles and Berkeley: Memoirs of a California Jewish Historian." Judaism 44, no. 4 (1995). http://findarticles.com/p/articles/mi_m0411/is_n4_v44/ai_17884745/print.

Birdwell, Michael E. Celluloid Soldiers: The Warner Brothers Campaign against Nazism. New York: New York University Press, 1999.

Bloom, Sol. The Autobiography of Sol Bloom. New York: G. P. Putnam's Sons, 1948.

Blumauer, Blanche. "Council of Jewish Women in Portland—1905." Western States Jewish Historical Quarterly 9, no. 1 (1976): 19–20.

Blumenthal, Louis. "YMHA and YWHA, San Francisco History, 1877–1954." *Western States Jewish History* 36, no. 4 (2004): 290–322.

Blustain, Sarah. "A Paradoxical Legacy: Rabbi Shlomo Carlebach's Shadow Side." *Lilith* 23, no. 1 (1998). http://rickross.com/reference/lubavitch12.html.

Bogen, Boris. *Jewish Philanthropy: An Exposition of Principles and Methods of Jewish Social Service in the United States.* New York: Macmillan, 1917.

Bonacich, Edna, and Richard P. Appelbaum. *Behind the Label: Inequality in the Los Angeles Apparel Industry.* Berkeley: University of California Press, 2000.

Bonadio, Felice *A. A. P. Giannini: Banker of America.* Berkeley: University of California Press, 1994.

Bowles, Jonathan. "The Empire Has No Clothes." Center for an Urban Future, February 29, 2000. http://www.nycfuture.org/content/reports/report_view.cfm?repkey=55.

Bozorgmehr, Mehdi, Claudia Der-Martirosian, and Georges Sabagh. "Middle Easterners: A New Kind of Immigrant." In Waldinger and Bozorgmehr, *Ethnic Los Angeles,* 345–78.

Brechin, Gray. *Imperial San Francisco: Urban Power, Earthly Ruin.* Berkeley: University of California Press, 1999.

Brook, Benjamin N. *Tucson: The Building of a Jewish Community.* Tucson: Bloom Southwest Jewish Archives, University of Arizona, 1992.

Broslawsky, Farrel. "Lives without Passion." *The San Fernando Valley: Past and Present.* Los Angeles: Pacific Rim Research, 1986.

Buerge, David, and Junius Rochester. *Roots and Branches: The Religious Heritage of Washington State.* Seattle: Church Council of Greater Seattle, 1988.

Burlison, Robert A. "Samuel Fox: Merchant and Civic Leader in San Diego, 1886–1939." *Journal of San Diego History* 26, no. 1 (1980). http://www.sandiegohistory.org/journal/80winter/fox.htm.

Burner, David. *Making Peace with the Sixties.* Princeton, N.J.: Princeton University Press, 1996.

Burt, Kenneth C. "Edward Roybal's Election to the LA City Council Marked the Birth of Latino Politics in California." *Public Affairs Report* 43, no. 1, 2002. http://www.igs.berkeley.edu/publications/par/spring2002/roybal.htm.

Carson, Clayborne. *In Struggle: SNCC and the Black Awakening of the 1960s.* Cambridge, Mass.: Harvard University Press, 1981.

Carson, Mina. *Settlement Folk, Social Thought, and the American Settlement Movement, 1885–1930.* Chicago: University of Chicago Press, 1990.

Caughey, John C. "Farewell to California's 'Loyalty' Oath." *Pacific Historical Review* 38, no. 2 (1969): 123–28.

Chang, Edward T., and Jeannette Diaz-Veizades. *Ethnic Peace in the American City: Building Community in Los Angeles and Beyond.* New York: New York University Press, 1999.

City of Hope. *Silver Jubilee: The City of Hope.* Los Angeles: City of Hope, 1939.

Clar, Reva. "First Jewish Woman Physician of Los Angeles." *Western States Jewish Historical Quarterly* 14, no. 1 (1981): 66–75.

———. "Jewish Acculturation in California's San Joaquin Valley: A Memoir." *Western States Jewish History* 19, no. 1 (1986): 55–64.

———. "The Jews of Los Angeles: Urban Pioneers Los Angeles Jewry—a Chronology." 2005. http://flatiron.sdsc.edu/projects/jla/main.php?page_id=37.

Clar, Reva, and William M. Kramer. "Chinese-Jewish Relations in the Far West: 1850–1950; Part 2." *Western States Jewish History* 21, no. 2 (1989): 132–53.

———. "The Girl Rabbi of the Golden West." *Western States Jewish History,* pt. 1, vol. 18, no. 2 (1986): 99–111; pt. 2, vol. 18, no. 3 (1986): 223–36; pt. 3, vol. 18, no. 4 (1986): 336–51.

———. "Julius Eckman and Herman Bien: The Battling Rabbis of San Francisco." *Western States Jewish Historical Quarterly,* pt. 2, vol. 15, no. 3 (1983): 232–53; pt. 3, vol. 15, no. 4 (1983): 341–59.

Clarke, David L. "Improbable Los Angeles." In Bernard and Rice, *Sunbelt Cities: Politics and Growth since World War II,* 268–308.

Cleland, Robert Glass, and Frank B. Putnam. *Isaias W. Hellman and the Farmers and Merchants Bank.* San Marino, Calif.: Huntington Library, 1965.

Cline, Scott. "Creation of an Ethnic Community: Portland Jewry, 1851–1866." *Pacific Northwest Quarterly* 76, no. 2 (1985): 52–60.

———. "The Jews of Portland, Oregon: A Statistical

Dimension, 1860–1880." *Oregon Historical Quarterly* 88, no. 1 (1987): 4–25.

Cockrell, Cathy. "University Revisits Controversial California Loyalty Oath." *Berkeleyan*, October 13, 1999. http://berkeley.edu/news/berkeleyan/1999/1013/loyalty.html.

Cohen, Benjamin Louis. "Constancy and Change in the Jewish Family Agency of Los Angeles, 1854–1979." Diss., University of Southern California, 1972.

Cohen, Naomi W. *Encounter with Emancipation: The German Jews in the United States, 1830–1914*. Philadelphia: Jewish Publication Society of America, 1984.

Cohen, Nathan, ed. *The Los Angeles Riots: A Socio-Psychological Study*. New York: Praeger, 1970.

Cohn, Lori Etta. "Residential Patterns of the Jewish Community of the Seattle Area, 1910–1980." Master's thesis, University of Washington, 1982.

Colacello, Bob. "Eli Broad's Big Picture." *Vanity Fair*, December 2006, 324–30, 379–86.

Cone, Molly, Howard Droker, and Jacqueline Williams. *Family of Strangers: Building a Jewish Community in Washington State*. Seattle: University of Washington Press, 2003.

Congregation Beth Israel of San Diego. "History." 2002–8. http://www.cbisd.org/about/history.shtml.

Cott, Nancy F. *The Grounding of Modern Feminism*. New Haven, Conn.: Yale University Press, 1987.

Crohn, Joel. *Ethnic Identity and Marital Conflict: Jews, Italians, and WASPs*. New York: American Jewish Committee, 1986.

Curry, Catherine Ann. "Public and Private Education in San Francisco: The Early Years, 1851–1876." In Guarneri and Alvarez, *Religion and Society*, 319–32.

Dalin, David G. "Jewish and Non-Partisan Republicanism in San Francisco, 1911–1963." In Rischin, *The Jews of the West: The Metropolitan Years*, 108–32. Berkeley, Calif.: American Jewish Historical Society / Western Jewish History Center, 1979.

D'Ancona, David A. *A California-Nevada Travel Diary of 1876*. Edited by William M. Kramer. Santa Monica, Calif.: Norton B. Stern, 1975.

Danziger, Gustav A. "The Jew in San Francisco: The Last Half Century." *Overland Monthly*, April 1895, 381–410.

Davis, Mike. *City of Quartz: Excavating the Future in Los Angeles*. New York: Verso, 1990.

Davis, Mike, Kelly Mayhew, and Jim Miller. *Under the Perfect Sun: The San Diego Tourists Never See*. New York: New Press, 2003.

Decker, Peter R. *Fortunes and Failures: White-Collar Mobility in Nineteenth-Century San Francisco*. Cambridge, Mass.: Harvard University Press, 1978.

DeMille, William Churchill. *Hollywood Saga*. New York: E. P. Dutton, 1939.

Denton, Sally, and Roger Morris. *The Money and the Power: The Making of Las Vegas and Its Hold on America*. New York: Vintage Books, 2001.

Diner, Hasia R. *The Jews of the United States, 1654–2000*. Berkeley: University of California Press, 2004.

———. "A Political Tradition? American Jewish Women and Political History." In *Jews and Gender: The Challenge to Hierarchy*, edited by Jonathan Frankel, 54–69. Oxford: Oxford University Press, 2000.

———. *A Time for Gathering: The Second Migration, 1820–1880*. Baltimore: Johns Hopkins University Press, 1992.

Diner, Hasia R., and Beryl Lieff Benderly. *Her Works Praise Her*. New York: Basic Books, 2002.

Dinin, Samuel. "My Educational Credo." In *Judaism and the Jewish School*, edited by Judah Pilch and Meir Ben-Horin, 318–22. New York: Bloch, 1966.

Dinnerstein, Leonard. *Anti-Semitism in America*. New York: Oxford University Press, 1994.

———. "From Desert Oasis to the Desert Caucus." In Rischin and Livingston, *Jews of the American West*, 136–63.

Dodds, Gordon B. *The College That Would Not Die: Portland State University, 1946–1996*. Portland: Oregon Historical Society Press, 2000.

Dollinger, Marc. "The Counterculture." In Kahn and Dollinger, *California Jews*, 154–66.

———. *Quest for Inclusion: Jews and Liberalism in Modern America*. Princeton, N.J.: Princeton University Press, 2000.

Downey, Lynn. "Levi Strauss Invented Western Work Clothes for Miners, Cowboys, and Engineers." In *The American Frontier: Opposing Viewpoints*, edited by Mary Ellen Jones, 272–76. San Diego, Calif.: Greenhaven Press, 1994.

Einbinder, Gershon [Chaver Paver]. *Clinton Street and Other Stories.* Translated by Henry Goodman. New York: YKUF, 1974.

Eisenberg, Dennis, Uri Dan, and Eli Landau. *Meyer Lansky: Mogul of the Mob.* New York: Paddington Press 1979.

Eisenberg, Ellen. "Beyond San Francisco: The Failure of Anti-Zionism in Portland, Oregon." *American Jewish History* 86, no. 3 (1998): 309–22.

——. "Civil Rights and Japanese American Incarceration." In Kahn and Dollinger, *California Jews*, 110–22.

——. "Fellow Whites or Fellow Minorities? Ethnic Identity and Responses to Prejudice among Jewish Oregonians." Paper presented at the conference "Through the Prism of Race and Ethnicity: Re-imagining the Religious History of the American West," Arizona State University, Tempe, March 2006.

——. *The First to Cry Down Injustice? Western Jews and Japanese Removal during WWII.* Lanham, Md.: Rowman and Littlefield, 2008.

——. "From Cooperative Farming to Urban Leadership." In Kahn, *Jewish Life in the American West*, 113–31.

——. "Immigrants, Ethnics, and Natives: Jewish Women in Portland, 1910–1940." Paper presented at the Western Jewish Studies Association conference, Seattle, March 1999.

——. *Jewish Agricultural Colonies in New Jersey.* Syracuse, N.Y.: Syracuse University Press, 1990.

——. "Transplanted to the Rose City: The Creation of East European Jewish Community in Portland, Oregon." *Journal of American Ethnic History* 19, no. 3 (2000): 82–97.

Eisenberg, Matthew J. "The Last Pioneers in Alaska." *Western States Jewish History* 24, no. 1 (1991): 51–73.

Eisner, Michael, with Tony Schwartz. *Work in Progress.* New York: Random House, 1998.

Elazar, Daniel J. *Community and Polity: The Organizational Dynamics of American Jewry.* Philadelphia: Jewish Publication Society, 1980.

Elliott, Wendy. "The Jews of Boyle Heights, 1900–1950: The Melting Pot of Los Angeles." *Southern California Quarterly* 78, no. 1 (1996): 1–10.

Engh, Michael E. "At Home in Heteropolis: Understanding Postmodern L.A." *American Historical Review*, 105, no. 4 (2000): 1676–81.

——. *Frontier Faiths: Church, Temple, and Synagogue in Los Angeles, 1846–1888.* Albuquerque: University of New Mexico Press, 1992.

Erie, Steven P. *Globalizing L.A.: Trade, Infrastructure, and Regional Development.* Stanford, Calif.: Stanford University Press, 2004.

Ernst, Eldon G. "American Religious History from a Pacific Coast Perspective." In Guarneri and Alvarez, *Religion and Society*, 3–39.

——. "The Emergence of California in American Religion's Historiography." *Religion and American Culture: A Journal of Interpretation* 11, no. 1 (2001): 31–52.

Esaki, John, producer. *Crossroads: Boyle Heights.* Video. Los Angeles: Japanese American National Museum, 2002.

Eskanazi, Joe. "Bay Area's Growing Jewish Scene." Ynetnews, June 3, 2005, http://ynetnews.com.

Ethington, Philip J. *The Public City: The Political Construction of Urban Life in San Francisco, 1850–1900.* Cambridge: Cambridge University Press, 1994.

Etulain, Richard W. "Visions and Revisions: Recent Interpretations of the American West." In *Writing Western History: Essays on Major Western Historians*, edited by Richard W. Etulain, 335–58. Albuquerque: University of New Mexico Press, 1991.

Eulenberg, Julia Niebuhr. "Jewish Enterprise in the American West: Washington, 1853–1909." Ph.D. diss., University of Washington, 1996.

Feher, Shoshanah. "From the Rivers of Babylon to the Valleys of Los Angeles: The Exodus and Adaptation of Iranian Jews." In *Gatherings in Diaspora: Religious Communities and the New Immigration*, edited by R. Stephen Warner and Judith G. Wittner, 71–94. Philadelphia: Temple University Press, 1998.

Feingold, Henry. *A Time for Searching: Entering the Mainstream, 1920–1945.* Baltimore: American Jewish Historical Society / Johns Hopkins University Press, 1992.

Ferris, Marcie Cohen, and Mark I. Greenberg, eds. *Jewish Roots in Southern Soil: A New History.* Hanover,

N.H.: University Press of New England / Brandeis University Press, 2006.

Finestein, Israel. *Jewish Society in Victorian England.* Portland, Ore.: Vallentine Mitchell, 1993.

Fitzgerald, O. P. *California Sketches.* Nashville: Southern Methodist Publishing House, 1881.

Flamm, Jerry. *Good Life in Hard Times: San Francisco in the '20s and '30s.* San Francisco: Chronicle Books, 1999.

Fogelson, Robert. *The Fragmented Metropolis: Los Angeles, 1850–1930.* Cambridge, Mass.: Harvard University Press, 1967.

Fradkin, Philip L. *The Great Earthquake and Firestorms of 1906.* Berkeley: University of California Press, 2005.

Francaviglia, Richard V. *Believing in Place: A Spiritual Geography of the Great Basin.* Reno: University of Nevada Press, 2003.

Frankiel, Sandra Sizer. *California's Spiritual Frontiers: Religious Alternatives in Anglo-Protestantism, 1850–1910.* Berkeley: University of California Press, 1988.

Friedlander, Jonathan, and Anita Colby. "Jews." In *Irangeles: Iranians in Los Angeles*, edited by Ron Kelley, 99–107. Berkeley: University of California Press, 1993.

Friman, Axel. "Two Swedes in the California Goldfields: Allvar Kullgren and Carl August Modh, 1850–1856." *Swedish-American Historical Quarterly* 34, no. 2 (1983): 102–30.

Gabler, Neal. *An Empire of Their Own: How the Jews Invented Hollywood.* New York: Crown, 1988.

Garreau, Joel. *Edge Cities: Life on the New Frontier.* New York: Anchor Books / Doubleday, 1991.

Gelfand, Mitchell Brian "Chutzpah in El Dorado: Social Mobility of Jews in Los Angeles." Ph.D. diss., Carnegie Mellon, 1981.

Giannini, Attilio H. "Financial Aspects." In *The Story of the Films*, edited by Joseph P. Kennedy, 78–85. Chicago: A. W. Shaw, 1927.

Glanz, Rudolf. *The Jews in American Alaska, 1867–1880.* New York: F. Maliniak, 1953.

———. *The Jews of California: From the Discovery of Gold until 1880.* New York: Southern California Jewish Historical Society, 1960.

Glassberg, David. "Making Places in California." In *Sense of History: The Place of the Past in American Life*, 167–202. Amherst: University of Massachusetts Press, 2001.

Glazier, Jack. *Dispersing the Ghetto: The Relocation of Jewish Immigrants across America.* Ithaca, N.Y.: Cornell University Press, 1998.

Gold, Steven J. *The Israeli Diaspora.* Seattle: University of Washington Press, 2002.

Goldberg, Deborah. "Jewish Spirit on the Urban Frontier: Zionism in Portland, 1901–1941." B.A. thesis, Reed College, 1982.

Goldberg, Robert. *Barry Goldwater.* New Haven, Conn.: Yale University Press, 1995.

Goldman, Karla. "In Search of an American Judaism." In Gurock and Raphael, *Inventory of Promises*, 137–50.

Goldscheider, Calvin. *Studying the Jewish Future.* Seattle: University of Washington Press, 2004.

Goldstein, Eric. *The Price of Whiteness: Jews, Race, and American Identity.* Princeton, N.J.: Princeton University Press, 2006.

Goldstein, Sidney. "Profile of American Jewry: Insights from the 1990 National Jewish Population Survey." In *American Jewish Year Book, 1992*, 93:77–173.

Gordon, Beverly. *Bazaars and Fair Ladies: The History of the American Fundraising Fair.* Knoxville: University of Tennessee Press, 1998.

Gordon, Linda. *The Great Arizona Orphan Abduction.* Cambridge, Mass.: Harvard University Press, 1999.

Goren, Arthur, ed. Introduction to *Dissenter in Zion: From the Writings of Judah Magnes.* Cambridge, Mass.: Harvard University Press, 1982.

———. *New York Jews and the Quest for Community: The Kehillah Experiment, 1908–1922.* New York: Columbia University Press, 1970.

———. *The Politics and Public Culture of American Jews.* Bloomington: Indiana University Press, 1999.

Gottdiner, M., Claudia C. Collins, and David R. Dickens. *Las Vegas: The Social Production of an All-American City.* Malden, Mass.: Blackwell, 1999.

Gottlieb, Robert, Mark Valliantos, Regina M. Freer, and Peter Drier. *The Next Los Angeles: The Struggle for a Livable City.* Berkeley: University of California Press, 2006.

Green, Michael. "The Jews." In *The Peoples of Las*

Vegas: One City, Many Faces, edited by Jerry L. Simich and Thomas C. Wright, 164–83. Reno: University of Nevada Press, 2005.

Greenberg, Cheryl. *Troubling the Waters: Black-Jewish Relations in the American Century.* Princeton, N.J.: Princeton University Press, 2006.

Greenberg, Erik. "Peter 'Pete' Kahn: Los Angeles Jewish Leader, 1878–1952." *Western States Jewish History* 38, no. 1 (2005): 17–43.

Greenspun, Hank, with Alex Pelle. *Where I Stand: The Record of a Restless Man.* New York: David McKay, 1966.

Guarneri, Carl, and David Alvarez. *Religion and Society in the American West.* Lanham, Md.: University Press of America, 1987.

Gullett, Gayle. "Women Progressives and the Politics of Americanization in California, 1915–1920." *Pacific Historical Review* 64, no. 1 (1995): 71–94.

Gurock, Jeffrey S., and Marc Lee Raphael, eds. *An Inventory of Promises: Essays on American Jewish History; In Honor of Moses Rischin.* Brooklyn, N.Y.: Carlson, 1995.

"A Half Century: National Council of Jewish Women, Los Angeles Section, 1909–1959." *Western States Jewish History* 37, no. 2 (2004): 149–60.

Harris, Victor. "The Beginning of Los Angeles' First Jewish Hospital." *Western States Jewish Historical Quarterly* 8, no. 2 (1976): 136–38.

Harrison, Donald H. *Louis Rose: San Diego's First Jewish Settler and Entrepreneur.* San Diego, Calif.: Sunbelt Publications, 2005.

Hasson, Aron. "The Los Angeles Rhodeslie Sephardic Community." *Western States Jewish History* 28, no. 4 (1996): 383–95.

———. "A Rhodesli Register of Los Angeles Pioneers and a Sourcebook for Rhodseli Scholarship." *Western States Jewish History* 28, no. 4 (1996): 397–415.

———. "The Sephardic Jews of Rhodes in Los Angeles." *Western States Jewish Historical Quarterly* 6, no. 4 (1974): 241–54.

Hatfield, Henry R. "Jessica Blanche Peixotto." In *Essays in Social Economics in Honor of Jessica Blanche Peixotto*, 5–14. Berkeley: University of California Press, 1935.

Hebrew Sheltering and Immigrant Aid Society of America. "Report of the Sixth Annual Meeting." *Jewish Immigration Bulletin (New York)* 5, no. 3 (1915).

Hecht, Ben. *A Guide for the Bedeviled.* New York: Charles Scribner's Sons, 1944.

Herman, Felicia. "Jewish Leaders and the Motion Picture Industry." In Kahn and Dollinger, *California Jews*, 95–109.

———. "Sisterhoods of Personal Service." In *Jewish Women in America: An Historical Encyclopedia*, edited by Paula Hyman and Deborah Dash Moore, 1264–66. New York: Routledge, 1998.

Higham, Charles. *Merchant of Dreams: Louis B. Mayer, M.G.M., and the Secret Hollywood.* New York: D. I. Fine, 1993.

Higham, John. *Send These to Me.* Baltimore: Johns Hopkins University Press, 1984.

———. *Strangers in the Land: Patterns of American Nativism, 1860–1925.* 1955. Reprint, New York: Atheneum, 1986.

Hise, Greg. "Industry and Imaginative Geographies." In *Metropolis in the Making: Los Angeles in the 1920s*, edited by Tom Sitton and William Deverell, 13–44. Berkeley: University of California Press, 2001.

———. *Magnetic Los Angeles: Planning the Twentieth Century Metropolis.* Baltimore: Johns Hopkins University Press, 1997.

Hofstadter, Richard. *The Age of Reform: From Bryan to F.D.R.* New York: Knopf, 1955.

Horne, Gerald. "Black Fire: 'Riot' and 'Revolt' in Los Angeles, 1965 and 1992." In *Seeking El Dorado: African Americans in California*, edited by Lawrence de Graaf, Kevin Mulroy, and Quintard Taylor, 377–404. Los Angeles: Autry Museum of Western Heritage, 2001.

Hurewitz, Daniel. *Bohemian Los Angeles and the Making of Modern Politics.* Berkeley: University of California Press, 2007.

Irwin, Mary Ann. "Plumbing a Mystery: The Emanu-El Sisterhood for Personal Service." Paper presented to the Western Association of Women Historians, Berkeley, Calif., June 2003.

Issel, William. "'Citizens outside the Government': Business and Urban Policy in San Francisco and Los Angeles, 1890–1932." *Pacific Historical Review* 57, no. 2 (1988): 117–45.

——. "Jews and Catholics against Prejudice." In Kahn and Dollinger, *California Jews*, 123–34.

Issel, William, and Robert W. Cherny. *San Francisco, 1865–1932: Politics, Power, and Urban Development.* Berkeley: University of California Press, 1986.

Jackson, W. Turrentine. "Portland: Wells Fargo's Hub for the Pacific Northwest." *Oregon Historical Quarterly* 86, no. 3 (1985): 229–67.

Jacobson, Matthew Frye. *Whiteness of a Different Color.* Cambridge, Mass.: Harvard University Press, 1998.

Jewish Genealogical Society of Los Angeles. "A Jewish Presence in Los Angeles." Timeline. *Roots–Key: Newsletter of the Jewish Genealogical Society of Los Angeles* 23, nos. 2–3 (2003). http://home.earthlink.net/~nholdeneditor/timelinea.htm.

"Jewish Population Estimates of Selected Cities." In *American Jewish Year Book, 1950,* 51:71–73.

"Jewish Population in the United States." In *American Jewish Year Book, 1970,* 71:344–53.

"Jewish Population in the United States, 1980." In *American Jewish Year Book, 1980,* 81:170–82.

Jones, Jacqueline. *The Dispossessed: America's Underclass from the Civil War to the Present.* New York: Basic Books, 1992.

Kahn, Ava F. Introduction to *Incidents of Travel and Adventure in the Far West with Colonel Fremont's Last Expedition,* by Solomon Nunes Carvalho. Lincoln: University of Nebraska Press, 2004.

——, ed. *Jewish Life in the American West.* Los Angeles: Autry Museum of Western Heritage / University of Washington Press, 2002. Repr. Heyday Books, 2004.

——. *Jewish Voices of the California Gold Rush: A Documentary History, 1849–1880.* Detroit: Wayne State University Press, 2002.

——. "Looking at America from the West to the East, 1850–1920s." In Kahn, *Jewish Life in the American West,* 13–31.

Kahn, Ava F., and Marc Dollinger, eds. *California Jews.* Hanover, N.H.: University Press of New England / Brandeis University Press, 2003.

Kahn, Ava F., and Ellen Eisenberg. "Western Reality: Jewish Diversity during the 'German' Period." *American Jewish History* 92, no. 4 (2004): 455–79.

Kahn, Ava F., and Glenna Matthews. "One Hundred Twenty Years of Women's Activism." In Kahn and Dollinger, *California Jews,* 143–53.

Kahn, Judd. *Imperial San Francisco: Politics and Planning in an American City, 1897–1906.* Lincoln: University of Nebraska Press, 1979.

Kahn, Peter M., Louis L. Silverberg, and Ben Tyre, eds. *Who Is Who in Sponsoring Mount Sinai Hospital and Clinic: Annual Directory.* Los Angeles: Associated Organizations of Los Angeles, 1945.

Kann, Kenneth. *Comrades and Chicken Ranchers: The Story of a California Jewish Community.* Ithaca, N.Y.: Cornell University Press, 1993.

Katz, Virginia. "The Ladies' Hebrew Benevolent Society of Los Angeles in 1892." *Western States Jewish Historical Quarterly* 10, no. 2 (1978): 157–58.

Kaufman, David. "Early Synagogue Architecture." In Kahn and Dollinger, *California Jews,* 40–56.

Kertzer, David I. *The Kidnapping of Edgardo Mortara.* New York: Vintage Books, 1997.

Killen, Patricia O'Connell, and Mark Silk, eds. *Religion and Public Life in the Pacific Northwest: The None Zone.* Walnut Creek, Calif.: AltaMira Press, 2004.

Kirshenblatt-Gimblett, Barbara. "The Moral Sublime: Jewish Women and Philanthropy in Nineteenth-Century America." In *Writing a Modern Jewish History: Essays in Honor of Salo W. Baron,* edited by Barbara Kirshenblatt-Gimblett, 36–56. New York: Jewish Museum, 2006.

Koepplin, Leslie W. *A Relationship of Reform: Immigrants and Progressives in the Far West.* New York: Garland, 1990.

Kohut, Rebekah. *My Portion (An Autobiography).* New York: Thomas Seltzer, 1925.

Kolsky, Thomas. "Jews against Zionism: The American Council for Judaism, 1942–1948." Ph.D. diss., George Washington University, 1986.

——. *Jews against Zionism: The American Council for Judaism, 1942–1948.* Philadelphia: Temple University Press, 1990.

Korn, Bertram Wallace. *American Jewry and the Civil War.* Marietta, Ga.: R. Bemis, 1995.

——, ed. *A Bicentennial Festschrift for Jacob Rader Marcus.* Waltham, Mass.: American Jewish Historical Society, 1976.

——. "Jewish 'Forty-Eighters' in America." In *Event-*

ful Years and Experiences: Studies in Nineteenth Century American Jewish History, 1–26. Cincinnati: American Jewish Archives, 1954.

Kotkin, Joel. *Tribes: How Race, Religion, and Identity Determine Success in the New Global Economy.* New York: Random House, 1992.

——. "Welcome to the Casbah." *American Enterprise.* January–February 1999. http://www.taemag.com/issues/articleid.16921/article_detail.asp.

Kramer, William M. *Sephardic Jews in the West Coast States.* Vol. 2, *Los Angeles.* Los Angeles: Western States Jewish History Association, 1996.

——. "Solomon Nunes Carvalho Helped in Founding the Los Angeles Jewish Community." *Western States Jewish History* 28, no. 4 (1996): 327–36.

Kramer, William M., and Reva Clar. "Michael G. Solomon (1868–1927): Rabbi and Lawyer of Los Angeles." *Western States Jewish Historical Quarterly* 14, no. 1 (1981): 3–29.

——. "Rabbi Edgar F. Magnin and the Modernization of Los Angeles Jewry." *Western States Jewish History* 19, no. 3 (1987): 233–51.

Kramer, William M., Stanley Schwartz, and Laurel Schwartz, eds. *Old Town, New Town: An Enjoyment of San Diego Jewish History.* Los Angeles: Western States Jewish History Association, 1994.

Kramer, William M., and Norton B. Stern. "Early California Associations of Michel Goldwater and His Family." *Western States Jewish Historical Quarterly* 4, no. 4 (1972): 173–96.

——. "A Search for the First Synagogue in the Golden West." *Western States Jewish Historical Quarterly* 7, no. 1 (1974): 3–20.

——. "Sephardic Founders of the Los Angeles Community: Samuel K. and Joseph I. Labatt." *Western States Jewish History* 28, no. 4 (1996): 337–45.

——. "The Study of Los Angeles Jewish History: An Analytical Consideration of a Major Work." *Western States Jewish Historical Quarterly* 3, no. 1 (1970): 38–58.

Kraut, Alan M., and Deborah A. Kraut. *Covenant of Care: Newark Beth Israel and the Jewish Hospital in America.* New Brunswick, N.J.: Rutgers University Press, 2007.

Lacey, Robert. *Little Man: Meyer Lansky and the*

Gangster Life. Boston: Little, Brown, 1991.

Lamb, Blaine. "Jews in Early Phoenix, 1870–1920." *Journal of Arizona History* 18, no. 3 (1977): 299–318.

LeBlanc, Sydney. *Twentieth Century American Architecture: A Traveler's Guide to Two Hundred Twenty-two Key Buildings.* New York: Whitney Library of Design 1996.

Leeder, Elaine. *The Gentle General: Rose Pesotta, Anarchist and Labor Organizer.* Albany: State University of New York Press, 1993.

Leibo, Steven. "Out the Road: The San Bruno Avenue Jewish Community of San Francisco, 1901–1968." *Western States Jewish Historical Quarterly* 11, no. 2 (1979): 99–110.

Leonard, David J. "'The Little Fuehrer Invades Los Angeles': The Emergence of a Black-Jewish Coalition after World War II." *American Jewish History* 92, no. 1 (2004): 81–102.

Leonoff, Cyril Edel. "Pioneer Jewish Merchants of Vancouver Island and British Columbia." *Canadian Jewish Historical Society Journal* 8, no. 1 (1984): 12–43.

Lerner, Michael. *Jewish Renewal: A Path to Healing and Transformation.* New York: Harper Perennial, 1995.

Levinson, Robert E. *The Jews in the California Gold Rush.* New York: KTAV, 1978; reprint, Berkeley, Calif.: Commission for the Preservation of Pioneer Jewish Cemeteries and Landmarks of the Judah L. Magnes Museum, 1994.

——. "The Jews of Eugene, Oregon." *Western States Jewish History* 30, no. 1 (1997): 41–62.

——. "Julius Eckman and the Weekly Gleaner: The Jewish Press in the Pioneer American West." In *A Bicentennial Festschrift for Jacob Rader Marcus*, 323–40. Waltham, Mass.: American Jewish Historical Society, 1976.

Levitin, Joseph. "Mount Zion of San Francisco: The History of a Hospital." Unpublished manuscript, Western Jewish History Center, Judah L. Magnes Museum, Berkeley, Calif., ca. 1975.

Levy, Daniel. "Letters about the Jews of California: 1855–1858." *Western States Jewish Historical Quarterly* 3, no. 2 (1971): 86–112.

Levy, Harriet Lane. *920 O'Farrell Street: A Jewish Girl-*

hood in Old San Francisco. Berkeley, Calif.: Heyday
Books, 1996.

Limerick, Patricia. *The Legacy of Conquest: The Unbro-
ken Past of the American West.* New York: Norton,
1987.

Lissak, Rivka S. *Pluralism and Progressivism: Hull
House and the New Immigrants, 1890–1919.* Chicago: University of Chicago Press, 1989.

Litman, Simon. *Ray Frank Litman: A Memoir.* New
York: American Jewish Historical Association, 1957.

"Los Angeles' Little Cutters." *Fortune* 31 (May 1945):
134–39.

Lotchin, Roger W. "The City and the Sword through
the Ages and the Era of the Cold War." In *Essays on
Sunbelt Cities and Recent Urban America,* edited
by Raymond Mohl, 87–124. College Station: Texas
A&M Press, 1990.

"Louis Fleischner." *Oregon Native Son* 1, no. 1 (1899):
346–47.

Lowenstein, Steven. *The Jews of Oregon, 1850–1950.*
Portland: Jewish Historical Society of Oregon, 1987.

Lubove, Roy. *The Professional Altruist: The Emergence
of Social Work as a Career, 1880–1930.* New York:
Atheneum, 1969.

Luckingham, Bradford. *Phoenix: The History of a
Southwestern Metropolis.* Tucson: University of
Arizona Press, 1989.

MacColl, E. Kimbark. *The Growth of a City: Power
and Politics in Portland, Oregon, 1915 to 1950.* Portland, Ore.: Georgian Press, 1979.

MacColl, E. Kimbark, with Harry Stein. *Merchants,
Money, and Power: The Portland Establishment,
1843–1913.* Portland, Ore.: Georgian Press, 1988.

Mack, Gerstle. *1906: Surviving San Francisco's Great
Earthquake and Fire.* San Francisco: Chronicle
Books, 1981.

MacPhail, Elizabeth R. *The Influence of German Immigrants on the Growth of San Diego.* San Diego: San
Diego Historical Society, 1986.

Maffly-Kipp, Laurie F. "'Eastward Ho!' American
Religion from the Perspective of the Pacific Rim." In
Retelling U.S. Religious History, edited by Thomas
Tweed, 127–48. Berkeley: University of California
Press, 1997.

———. *Religion and Society in Frontier California.* New
Haven, Conn.: Yale University Press, 1994.

Magnin, Edgar. *The Warner Murals in the Wilshire
Boulevard Temple, Los Angeles, California.* Los
Angeles: Wilshire Boulevard Temple, 1974.

Malamut, Joseph L. "The Mount Sinai Hospital Story."
In *Southwest Jewry: An Account of Jewish Progress
and Achievement in the Southland,* edited by Joseph
L. Malamut, 89–94. Los Angeles: Los Angeles Jewish
Institutions and Their Leaders, 1957.

Marcus, Jacob Rader. *To Count a People: American
Jewish Population Data, 1585–1984.* Lanham, Md.:
University Press of America, 1990.

Markens, Isaac. *The Hebrews in America.* New York,
1888.

Massarik, Fred. "A Report on the Jewish Population
of Los Angeles." Jewish Community Council, Los
Angeles, January 1953.

———. "A Study of the Jewish Population of Long Beach,
Lakewood, and Los Alamitos." Jewish Community
Federation, Long Beach, Calif., 1962.

May, Lary. *The Big Tomorrow: Hollywood and the
Politics of the American Way.* Chicago: University of
Chicago Press, 2000.

———. *Screening out the Past: The Birth of Mass Culture
and the Motion Picture Industry.* Chicago: University
of Chicago Press, 1980.

McBride, Joseph. *Steven Spielberg: A Biography.* New
York: Simon and Schuster, 1997.

McCann, James. *A Study of the Jewish Community in
the Greater Seattle Area.* Seattle: Jewish Federation
of Greater Seattle, 1979.

McCarthy, Kathleen D. *Noblesse Oblige: Charity and
Cultural Philanthropy in Chicago, 1849–1929.* Chicago: University of Chicago Press, 1982.

McCune, Mary. "Formulating the 'Women's Interpreta-
tion of Zionism': Hadassah Recruitment of Non-
Zionist American Women, 1914–1930." In *American
Jewish Women and the Zionist Enterprise,* edited
by Shulamit Reinharz and Mark A. Raider, 89–111.
Waltham, Mass.: Brandeis University Press, 2005.

Mead, Rebecca J. *How the Vote Was Won: Suffrage in
the United States, 1868–1914.* New York: New York
University Press, 2004.

Menuhin, Moshe. "Jewish Communal Education in San
Francisco in 1926." *Western States Jewish History*

21, no. 2 (1989): 99–102. Originally published in *Jewish Education News*, March 1926.

Meyer, Martin A. *Western Jewry.* San Francisco: Emanu-El, 1916.

Micklin, Lee. "Samuel Stroum, (1921–2001)." August 2001. http://www.historylink.org/essays/output.cfm?file_id=3516.

Miller, Jim. "Just Another Day in Paradise? An Episodic History of Rebellion and Repression in America's Finest City." In *Under the Perfect Sun: The San Diego Tourists Never See*, by Mike Davis, Kelly Mayhew, and Jim Miller, 159–262. New York: New Press, 2003.

Moehring, Eugene. "Growth, Services, and the Political Economy of Gambling in Las Vegas, 1970–2000." In Rothman and Davis, *Grit beneath the Glitter*, 73–98.

Moore, Deborah Dash. *B'nai B'rith and the Challenge of Ethnic Leadership.* Albany: State University of New York Press, 1981.

———. "Inventing Jewish Identity in California: Shlomo Bardin, Zionism, and the Brandeis Camp Institute." In *National Variations in Jewish Identity: Implications for Jewish Education*, edited by Steven M. Cohen and Gabriek Horencyzk, 201–22. Albany: State University of New York Press, 1999.

———. *To the Golden Cities: Pursuing the American Jewish Dream in Miami and Los Angeles.* New York: Free Press, 1994.

Moore, Deborah Dash, and Dan Gebler. "The Ta'am of Tourism." *Pacific Historical Review* 68, no. 2 (1999): 193–212.

Mormino, Gary R. *Land of Sunshine, State of Dreams: A Social History of Modern Florida.* Gainesville: University Press of Florida, 2005.

Moynihan, Ruth Barnes. *Rebel for Rights: Abigail Scott Duniway.* New Haven, Conn.: Yale University Press, 1983.

Narell, Irena. *Our City: The Jews of San Francisco.* San Diego, Calif.: Howell-North Books, 1981.

Nash, Gerald. *The American West Transformed: The Impact of the Second World War.* Lincoln: University of Nebraska Press, 1985.

Navasky, Victor S. *Naming Names.* New York: Penguin Books, 1981.

Newmark, Harris. *Sixty Years in Southern California, 1853–1913.* Edited by Maurice H. Newmark and Marco R. Newmark. New York: Knickerbocker Press, 1916. 4th ed., Los Angeles: Zeitlin and Ver Brugge, 1970.

Newmark, Helen. "A Nineteenth Century Memoir." *Western States Jewish Historical Quarterly* 6, no. 3 (1974): 204–18.

Newmark, Leo. *California Family Newmark: An Intimate History.* Santa Monica, Calif.: Norton B. Stern, 1970.

Newmark, Marco R. "Wilshire Boulevard Temple: Congregation B'Nai B'Rith." *Historical Society of Southern California Quarterly* 38, no. 2 (June 1956): 167–84.

Nodel, Rabbi Julius J. *The Ties Between: A Century of Judaism on America's Last Frontier.* Portland, Ore.: Temple Beth Israel, 1959.

Ogden, Kate Nearpass. "California as Kingdom Come." In *Art of an American Icon: Yosemite*, edited by Amy Scott. Los Angeles: Autry National Center, 2006.

Olin, Spencer C., Jr. "European Immigrant and Oriental Alien: Acceptance and Rejection by the California Legislature of 1913." *Pacific Historical Review* 35 (1966): 303–15.

Orr, Heather Catherine. "Tehrangeles: L.A. the Iranian Expatriate Capital Abroad." *Persian Journal*, August 19, 2004. http://www.iranian.ws/cgi-bin/iran_news/exec/view.cgi/2/3382.

Ostroff, Manning. "The Story behind the Story: Our Auxiliaries." In *Golden Book: Los Angeles Sanatorium, 1913–1933; Twentieth Anniversary Edition.* Los Angeles: Los Angeles Sanatorium and Expatients Home, 1934, 15, 59.

Pacific Hebrew Orphan Asylum and Home Society. *Annual Report.* San Francisco: self-published, 1878.

Pak, Yoon K. *Wherever I Go, I Will Always Be a Loyal American: Schooling Seattle's Japanese Americans during World War II.* New York: RoutledgeFalmer, 2002.

Pascoe, Peggy. *Relations of Rescue: The Search for Female Moral Authority in the American West, 1874–1939.* New York: Oxford University Press, 1990.

Peixotto, Jessica. *The French Revolution and Modern*

French Socialism. New York: Thomas Y. Crowell, 1901.

Pesotta, Rose. *Bread upon the Waters*. Edited by John Nicholas Beffel. Ithaca, N.Y.: ILR Press, 1987.

Phillips, Bruce. "The Challenge of Family, Identity, and Affiliations." In Kahn and Dollinger, *California Jews*, 17–28.

———. "Los Angeles Jewry: A Demographic Portrait." In American Jewish Year Book, 1986, 87:126–95.

Polier, Justine Wise, and James Waterman Wise. *The Personal Letters of Stephen Wise*. Boston: Beacon, 1956.

Pomeroy, Earl. *The Pacific Slope: A History of California, Oregon, Washington, Idaho, Utah, and Nevada*. Seattle: University of Washington Press, 1965.

Powell, Bruce. "Shlomo Bardin's 'Eretz' Brandeis." In Kahn and Dollinger, *California Jews*, 151–84.

Quinn, D. Michael. "Religion in the American West." In *Under an Open Sky: Rethinking America's Western Past*, edited by William Cronon, George Miles, and Jay Gitlin, 145–66. New York: Norton, 1992.

Raab, Earl. "There's No City like San Francisco." *Commentary* 10, no. 4 (1950): 369–78.

Rafael, Ruth Kelson. *Continuum—a Selective History of San Francisco Eastern European Jewish Life, 1880–1940*. Berkeley, Calif.: Western Jewish History Center, Judah L. Magnes Memorial Museum, 1977.

Raphael, Marc Lee. "Beyond New York: The Challenge to Local History." In Rischin and Livingston, *Jews of the American West*, 48–65.

———. "Rabbi Jacob Voorsanger of San Francisco on Jews and Judaism: The Implications of the Pittsburgh Platform." *American Jewish Historical Quarterly* 63, no. 2 (1973): 185–203.

Rasmussen, Louis J. *San Francisco Ship Passengers Lists*. Colma, Calif.: San Francisco Historical Records, 1970.

"Regionalism: The Significance of Place in American Jewish Life." Roundtable, with William R. Ferris, Deborah Dash Moore, John Shelton Reed, Theodore Rosengarten, and George Sanchez. *American Jewish History* 93, no. 2 (2007).

Reichert, Irving. *Judaism and the American Jew: Selected Sermons and Addresses*. San Francisco: Grabhorn Press, 1953.

Reynolds, L. G. "Historic Recollections of Congregation Sinai." In *The Burning of a Mortgage: An Historic Record of Congregation Sinai*. Los Angeles: Congregation Sinai, 1945.

Riche, Aaron. "Zionism in Los Angeles on Its Twenty-fifth Anniversary." *Western States Jewish History* 23, no. 1 (1990): 31–34. Originally published in Jewish National Fund of Los Angeles, *Jubilee Number 1902–1927*, edited by George Saylin (1927).

Richmond, Mary Ellen. *The Good Neighbor in the Modern City*. Philadelphia: Lippincott, 1908.

Rischin, Moses. "The Jewish Experience in America." In Rischin and Livingston, *Jews of the American West*, 26–47.

———. *The Jews of the West: The Metropolitan Years*. Berkeley, Calif.: American Jewish Historical Society / Western Jewish History Center, 1979.

Rischin, Moses, and John Livingston, eds. *Jews of the American West*. Detroit: Wayne State University Press, 1991.

Robison, Sophia M., ed. *Jewish Population Studies*. New York: Conference on Jewish Relations, 1943.

Rochlin, Harriet, and Fred Rochlin. *Pioneer Jews: A New Life in the Far West*. Boston: Houghton Mifflin, 1984.

Rockaway, Robert A. *But He Was Good to His Mother: The Lives and Crimes of Jewish Gangsters*. Jerusalem: Gefen Publishing House, 2000.

Roemer, William F., Jr. *War of the Godfathers: The Bloody Confrontation between the Chicago and New York Families for Control of Las Vegas*. New York: Donald I. Fine, 1990.

Rogers, Barbara S. "To Be or Not to Be a Jewish Hospital?" *Western States Jewish Historical Quarterly* 10, no. 3 (1978): 195–201.

Rogers, Barbara S., and Stephen M. Dobbs. *The First Century: Mount Zion Hospital and Medical Center, 1887–1987*. San Francisco: Mount Zion Hospital and Medical Center, 1987.

Rogers, Bonnie. "The Founders: The Story of the City of Hope." April 2003. http://home.earthlink.net/~nholdeneditor/City%20of%20Hope.htm.

Rogoff, Leonard. "Is the Jew White? The Racial Place of the Southern Jew." In "Directions in Southern Jewish

History." Special issue, *American Jewish History* 85, no. 3 (1997): 195–230.

Rogow, Faith. *Gone to Another Meeting.* Tuscaloosa: University of Alabama Press, 1993.

Rohrbacher, Stefan. "From Württemberg to America: A Nineteenth-Century German-Jewish Village on Its Way to the New World." *American Jewish Archives* 41, no. 2 (1989): 143–71.

Rorabaugh, William. *Berkeley at War: The 1960s.* New York: Oxford University Press, 1989.

Rosen, Michele. "Stroum Jewish Community Center of Greater Seattle." Updated March 2008. http://www.historylink.org/essays/output.cfm?file_id=104.

Rosenbaum, Fred. *Architects of Reform: Congregational and Community Leadership, Emanu-El of San Francisco, 1849–1980.* Berkeley, Calif.: Western Jewish History Center, Judah L. Magnes Memorial Museum, 1980.

——. *Free to Choose: The Making of a Jewish Community in the American West; The Jews of Oakland, California, from the Gold Rush to the Present Day.* Berkeley, Calif.: Judah L. Magnes Memorial Museum, 1976.

——. *Visions of Reform: Congregation Emanu-El and the Jews of San Francisco 1849–1999.* Berkeley, Calif.: Judah L. Magnes Memorial Museum, 2000.

——. "Zionism versus Anti-Zionism." In Rischin and Livingston, *Jews of the American West,* 116–35.

Rosenthal, Marcus. "The Jewish Immigration Problem." *Western States Jewish Historical Quarterly* 6, no. 4 (1974): 278–89. Originally published in *Emanu-El,* February 24, 1905.

Ross, Murray. *Stars and Strikes: Unionization of Hollywood.* New York: Columbia University Press, 1941.

Ross, Steve J. *Working Class Hollywood, Silent Film, and the Shaping of Class in America.* Princeton, N.J.: Princeton University Press, 1998.

Rosten, Leo B. *Hollywood: The Movie Colony, the Movie Makers.* New York: Harcourt Brace, 1941.

Roszak, Theodore. *The Making of a Counter Culture: Reflections on the Technocratic Society and Its Youthful Opposition.* Garden City, N.Y.: Anchor Books.

Rothman, Hal K. "Colony, Capital, and Casino: Money in the Real Las Vegas." In Rothman and Davis, *Grit beneath the Glitter,* 307–34

——. *Neon Metropolis: How Las Vegas Started the Twenty-first Century.* New York: Routledge, 2003.

Rothman, Hal K., and Mike Davis. *The Grit beneath the Glitter: Tales from the Real Las Vegas.* Berkeley: University of California Press, 2002.

Saalfeld, Lawrence J. *Forces of Prejudice in Oregon, 1920–1925.* Portland, Ore.: Archdiocesan Historical Commission, 1984.

Sabar, Naama. *Kibbutzniks in the Diaspora.* Translated from the Hebrew by Chaya Naor. Albany: State University of New York Press, 2000.

Sanchez, George J. *Becoming Mexican American: Ethnicity, Culture, and Identity in Chicano Los Angeles, 1900–1945.* New York: Oxford University Press, 1993.

——. "'What's Good for Boyle Heights Is Good for the Jews': Creating Multiracialism on the Eastside during the 1950s." *American Quarterly* 56, no. 3 (2004): 633–61.

Sandberg, Neil C. *Jewish Life in Los Angeles: A Window to Tomorrow.* Lanham, Md.: University Press of America, 1986.

Sanua, Marianne R. *Going Greek: Jewish College Fraternities in the United States, 1895–1945.* Detroit: Wayne State University Press, 2003.

Sarna, Jonathan D. *American Judaism: A History.* New Haven, Conn.: Yale University Press, 2004.

——. "The Jews of Boston in Historical Perspective." In *The Jews of Boston,* edited by Jonathan D. Sarna and Ellen Smith, 3–21. Boston: Jewish Philanthropies of Greater Boston, 1995.

Sarna, Jonathan D., and Nancy H. Klein. *The Jews of Cincinnati.* Cincinnati: Center for the Study of the American Jewish Experience, Hebrew Union College–Jewish Institute of Religion, 1989.

Schatz, Thomas. *The Genius of the System: Hollywood Film Making in the Studio Era.* New York: Pantheon Books, 1988.

Schmal, John P. "Edward Roybal Was a Pioneer." *LatinoLA,* October 27, 2005. http://www.latinola.com/story.php?story=2941.

Schrag, Peter. *California: America's High Stakes Experiment.* Berkeley: University of California Press, 2006.

Schulberg, Budd. *Moving Pictures: Memories of a Hollywood Prince.* New York: Stein and Day, 1981.

Schwartz, Alissa. "Americanization and Cultural Preservation in Seattle's Settlement House: A Jewish Adaptation of the Anglo-American Model of Settlement Work." *Journal of Sociology and Social Welfare* 36, no. 3 (1999): 25–47.

Schwartz, Henry. "The Silver Shirts: Anti-Semitism in San Diego." *Western States Jewish History* 25, no. 1 (1992), 52–60.

Schweitzer, Jane. "The Russian Jewish Immigration and Rabbi Jacob Voorsanger." *Western States Jewish History* 17, no. 2 (1985): 137–43.

Scott, Anne Firor. *Natural Allies: Women's Associations in American History.* Urbana: University of Illinois Press, 1991.

Selznick, Gertrude J., and Stephen Steinberg. *The Tenacity of Prejudice: Anti-Semitism in Contemporary America.* New York: Harper and Row, 1969.

Shevitz, Amy Hill. *Jewish Communities on the Ohio River: A History.* Lexington: University Press of Kentucky, 2007.

——. "Jewish Space and Place in Venice." In Kahn and Dollinger, *California Jews*, 65–76.

Shulman, Leon. "The California Consumptives' Relief Association: A Historical Sketch." *Sanatorium: Official Organ of the Jewish Consumptives' Relief Society (Denver)* 7, no. 2 (1913): 38–39.

Sigel, Fred. *The Future Once Happened Here.* San Francisco: Encounter Books, 1997.

Sitton, Tom, and Deverell, William, eds. *Metropolis in the Making: Los Angeles in the 1920s.* Berkeley: University of California Press, 2001.

Slattery, Margaret. *The Girl in Her Teens.* Philadelphia: Sunday School Times Company, 1910.

Soden, Dale E. "Contesting the Soul of an Unlikely Land: Mainline Protestants, Catholics, and Reform and Conservative Jews in the Pacific Norwest." In *Religion and Public Life in the Pacific Northwest: The None Zone*, edited by Patricia O'Connell Killen and Mark Silk, 51–78. Walnut Creek, Calif.: AltaMira Press, 2004.

Soja, Edward W. "Los Angeles, 1965–1992: From Crisis-Generated Restructuring to Restructuring-Generated Crisis." In *The City: Los Angeles and Urban Theory at the End of the Twentieth Century*, edited by Allen J. Scott and Edward W. Soja, 426–62. Berkeley: University of California Press, 1996.

Solomon, Aubrey. *Twentieth Century Fox: A Corporate and Financial History.* Metuchen, N.J.: Scarecrow Press, 1988.

Solomons, Selina. *How We Won the Vote in California: A True Story of the Campaign of 1911.* San Francisco: New Woman Publishing, n.d..

Sonenshein, Raphael J. *Politics in Black and White: Race and Power in Los Angeles.* Princeton, N.J.: Princeton University Press, 1993.

Soomekh, Sabah. "Tehrangeles: Capital, Culture, and Faith among Iranian Jews." Paper presented at the "Religious Pluralism in Southern California" conference, University of California, Santa Barbara, May 9, 2003. http://www.religion.ucsb.edu/projects/newpluralism/tehrangeles.doc.

Sorin, Gerald. "Rose Pesotta in the Far West: The Triumphs and Travails of a Jewish Woman Labor Organizer." In "Jewish Women of the American West," edited by Gladys Sturman and David Epstein. Special issue, *Western States Jewish History* 35, nos. 3–4 (2003): 201–10.

——. *A Time for Building: The Third Migration, 1880–1920.* Baltimore: Johns Hopkins University Press, 1995.

Soule, Frank, John H. Gihon, and James Nisbet. *The Annals of San Francisco; containing a summary of the history of California and a complete history of its great city: to which are added, biographical memoirs of some prominent citizens.* New York: Appleton, 1855.

Stampfer, Rabbi Joshua. *Pioneer Rabbi of the West: The Life and Times of Julius Eckman.* Portland, Ore.: self-published, ca. 1988.

Starr, Kevin. *Coast of Dreams: California on the Edge, 1990–2003.* New York: Knopf, 2004.

Staub, Michael E. *Torn at the Roots: The Crisis of Jewish Liberalism in Postwar America.* New York: Columbia University Press, 2002.

Stein, Harry H. *Gus Solomon: Liberal Politics, Jews, and the Federal Courts.* Portland: Oregon Historical Society Press, 2006.

Stern, Miriam Heller. "Ladies, Girls, and Mothers:

Defining Jewish Womanhood at the Settlement House." *Journal of Jewish Education* 69, no. 2 (2003): 22–34.

Stern, Norton B. "Jews in the 1870 Census of Los Angeles." *Western States Jewish Historical Quarterly* 9, no. 1 (1976): 71–86.

———. "Myer Joseph Newmark: Los Angeles Civic Leader." *Western States Jewish Historical Quarterly* 2, no. 3 (1970): 136–71.

Stern, Norton B., and William M. Kramer. "Jewish Padre to the Pueblo: Pioneer Los Angeles Rabbi Abraham Wolf Edelman." *Western States Jewish Historical Quarterly* 3, no. 4 (1971): 193–226.

———. "The Major Role of Polish Jews in the Pioneer West." *Western Jewish States Historical Quarterly* 8, no. 4 (1976): 326–44.

Stone, Kurt F. *The Congressional Minyan: The Jews of Capitol Hill.* Hoboken, N.J.: KTAV, 2000.

Stuppy, Laurence. "Henry H. Lissner, M.D.: Los Angeles Physician." *Western States Jewish Historical Quarterly* 8, no. 3 (1976): 209–16.

Svonkin, Stuart. *Jews against Prejudice* (New York: Columbia University Press, 1999).

Szasz, Ferenc Morton. *Religion in the Modern American West.* Tucson: University of Arizona Press, 2000.

Takaki, Ronald. *Strangers from a Different Shore: A History of Asian Americans.* Boston: Little, Brown, 1989.

Taylor, Graham. *Pioneering on Social Frontiers.* Chicago: University of Chicago Press, 1930.

Temple Sinai (Reno, Nev.). "Temple Sinai History." http://www.templesinai-reno.com/aboutus/history/ (accessed July 25, 2008).

Tenenbaum, Shelly. "Community Self-Help: San Francisco Jews and the Great Depression." *Jewish Journal of Sociology* 45, nos. 1–2 (2003): 34–45.

Toll, William. "Acclimatizing Fashion: Jewish Inventiveness on the Other (Pacific) Coast, 1850 to 1940." In *A Perfect Fit: The Garment Industry and American Jewry.* Lubbock: Texas Tech University Press, forthcoming.

———. "Ethnicity and Stability: The Italians and Jews of South Portland, 1900–1940." *Pacific Historical Review* 54, no. 2 (1985): 161–89.

———. "The Feminization of the Heroic: Ethel Feineman and Professional Nurture." In *Crisis and Reaction: The Hero in Jewish History*, edited by Menachem Mor, 199–216. Omaha, Neb.: Creighton University Press, 1995.

———. "Fraternalism and Community Structure on the Urban Frontier: The Jews of Portland, Oregon—a Case Study." *Pacific Historical Review*, August 1978, 369–403.

———. "From Domestic Judaism to Public Ritual." In *Women and American Judaism*, edited by Pamela S. Nadell and Jonathan D. Sarna, 128–47. Hanover, N.H.: University Press of New England / Brandeis University Press, 2001.

———. "Gender and the Origins of Philanthropic Professionalism: Seraphine Pisko at the National Jewish Hospital." *Rocky Mountain Jewish Historical Notes* 11 (Winter–Spring 1991): 1–9.

———. "Gender, Ethnicity, and Jewish Settlement Work in the Urban West." In Gurock and Raphael, *Inventory of Promises*, 291–306.

———. "Intermarriage and the Urban West: A Religious Context for Cultural Change." In Rischin and Livingston, *Jews of the American West*, 164–89.

———. "Jewish Families and the Intergenerational Transition in the American Hinterland." *Journal of American Ethnic History* 12, no. 2 (1993): 3–34.

———. *The Making of an Ethnic Middle Class.* Albany: State University of New York Press, 1982.

———. "Pioneering: Jewish Men and Women of the American West." In *Creating American Jews: Historical Conversations about Identity*, edited by Karen S. Mittelman, 24–37. Philadelphia: National Museum of American Jewish History / Brandeis University Press, 1998.

———. "A Quiet Revolution: Jewish Women's Clubs and the Widening Female Sphere, 1870–1920." *American Jewish Archives* 41, no. 1 (1989): 7–26.

———. "A Regional Context for Pacific Jewry, 1880 to 1930." In *The Columbia History of Jews and Judaism in America*, edited by Marc Lee Raphael, 217–45. New York: Columbia University Press, 2008.

———. "They Built a New Home." In *The Historical Scribe*, 1–2. Portland: Jewish Historical Society of Oregon, 1980.

———. "Voluntarism and Modernization in Portland

Jewry: The B'nai B'rith in the 1920s." *Western Historical Quarterly* 10, no. 1 (1979): 21–38.

United Jewish Federation of San Diego County. "The Jewish Community's Strategic Plan." http://sandiego. ujcfedweb.org/content_display.html (accessed July 25, 2008).

U.S. Census Bureau. *Census of Religious Bodies: 1926*. Vol. 1. Washington, D.C.: Government Printing Office, 1930.

Van Nuys, Frank. *Americanizing the West: Race, Immigrants, and Citizenship, 1890–1930*. Lawrence: University Press of Kansas, 2002.

Voorsanger, A. W., ed. *Western Jewry: An Account of the Achievements of the Jews and Judaism in California*. San Francisco: Emanu-El, 1916.

Voorsanger, Jacob. "The Beginning of the First Jewish Hospital in the West." *Western States Jewish Historical Quarterly* 8, no. 2 (1976): 99–101. Originally published in Emanu-El, January 1, 1897.

Vorspan, Max, and Lloyd P. Gartner. *History of the Jews of Los Angeles*. Philadelphia: Jewish Publication Society, 1970.

Waldinger, Roger, and Mehdi Bozorgmehr. *Ethnic Los Angeles*. New York: Russell Sage Foundation, 1996.

Waldinger, Roger, and Michael Lichter. "Anglos: Beyond Ethnicity?" In Waldinger and Bozorgmehr, *Ethnic Los Angeles*.

Walsh, James P. "Abe Ruef Was No Boss: Machine Politics, Reform, and San Francisco." *California Historical Society Quarterly* 51 (Spring 1972): 3–16.

Warner, Sam Bass. *The Urban Wilderness: A History of the American City*. New York: Harper and Row, 1972.

Weissbach, Lee Shai. "East European Immigrants and the Image of Jews in the Small-Town South." *American Jewish History* 85, no. 3 (1997): 231–62.

——. "The Jewish Communities of the United States on the Eve of Mass Migration." *American Jewish History* 78, no. 1 (1988): 79–108.

——. *Jewish Life in Small-Town America: A History*. New Haven, Conn.: Yale University Press, 2005.

White, Richard. *"It's Your Misfortune and None of My Own": A New History of the American West*. Norman: University of Oklahoma Press, 1991.

Wiebe, Robert H. *The Search for Order, 1877–1920*.

Westport, Conn.: Greenwood Press, 1980.

Wild, Mark. *Street Meeting: Multiethnic Neighborhoods in Early Twentieth Century Los Angeles*. Berkeley: University of California Press, 2005.

Willer, Roza R. "The History of Jewish Social Work in Portland." Student paper, Portland School of Social Work, June 1923. Oregon Jewish Museum, Portland.

Williams, Jacqueline B. "If I Am Only for Myself, What Am I? Two Successful Jewish Women's Organizations in King County." In *More Voices, New Stories: King County, Washington's First 150 Years*, edited by Mary C. Wright. Seattle: Pacific Northwest Historians Guild / University of Washington Press, 2002.

——. "Was It Strictly Kosher? Washington State, 1889–1937." *Western States Jewish History* 36, no. 3 (2004): 225–36.

Wilson, Karen S. "Citizens of Los Angeles: Jewish Families and the Naissance of the Metropolis." Master's thesis, Hebrew Union College–Jewish Institute of Religion, 2003.

——. "'A Directing Spirit': Sarah Newmark and Jewish Benevolence in Nineteenth Century Los Angeles." Paper presented at the Western Jewish Studies Association conference, Long Beach, Calif., March 19, 2006.

Women's Educational and Industrial Union of San Francisco. *Third Annual Report*. San Francisco: self-published, 1891–92.

Woods, Robert A., and Albert J. Kennedy. *The Settlement Horizon: A National Estimate*. New York: Russell Sage Foundation, 1922.

Wright, Gavin. *Old South, New South: Revolutions in the Southern Economy since the Civil War*. New York: Basic Books, 1986.

Wright, Robin. *The Last Great Revolution: Turmoil and Transformation in Iran*. New York: Vintage Books, 2001.

Yung, Judy. *Unbound Feet: A Social History of Chinese Women in San Francisco*. Berkeley: University of California Press, 1995.

Zarchin, Michael. *Glimpses of Jewish Life in San Francisco*. 2nd ed. Berkeley, Calif.: Judah L. Magnes Museum, 1964.

INDEX

Page numbers in *italics* refer to illustrations

A

Abraham, Y., 25

Abrams, Jeanne E., 118

accommodationist response, 178, 180

accommodations for Jewish students, 175

Addams, Jane, 119, 133–34

Adelson, Mervyn, 186, 196

Adelson, Sheldon, 221

Adler, B., 25, 229n49

affiliation rate, low, 13–14, 210–11

affirmative action, 199

African Americans, 6–7, 175, 193, 198, 246n152

Agoura Hills, CA, 216

Ahavai Shalom, Portland: arson attack on, 101; founding of, 34–35; Neveh Zedek and, 96, 206; Poseners in, 96; Russian immigrants and, 97

Ahavath Achim, Portland, 100, 206

Ahmanson, Howard, 198

AIDS, 222

Aiken, Miriam, 140

Alaska, 19, 23, 82

Alaska Commercial Company, 23, 113

Albany, OR, 63

alien land laws, 102, 247n156

Alinsky, Saul, 193

Alkow, Jacob, 169, 178, 262n101

America, Sadie, 134

American Council for Judaism (ACJ), 162, 162–63, 165, 179, 260n56

Americanization, 77, 107, 108, 136, 139, 139, 140

American Jewish Committee, 179, 180, 184, 219

American Jewish University (University of Judaism), 195

Americans for Israel and Torah (AMIT), 149

Am Olam movement, 10, 82

Angell, Norman, 58

Anglos, Jews perceived as, 7

Anti-Defamation League (ADL), 174, 175, 178, 180, 183–84, 223

anti-Semitism: exclusion from clubs, 51, 154; in interwar period, 155, 173, 174–77; lesser in West, 7; in Northeast and South, 246n147; responses to, in interwar period, 177–84; Ruef scandal and, 67–68, 102, 240n101; stance against offensive portrayals, 146–47, 177–78; student protests over Smith, 193; "whiteness" and, 6–7, 78, 100–102. *See also* residential restrictions

anti-Zionist movements, 95, 162–63, 245n111. *See also* American Council for Judaism

Aptheker, Bettina, 200

Aquarian Minyan, Berkeley, 204, 205

Archibald, Harry, 69

Arizona State University, 221

Arizona Territory, 60

Arlozoroff, Chaim, 156

Ash, Harry, 175

Ashkenazim and Sephardim, relations between, 76, 97–100, 159, 160–61. See also Eastern European immigrants

Asian immigrants, 49, 102, 175, 246n152, 263n128

Associated Charities of Los Angeles, 125

Avat Shalom, Los Angeles, 100

B

balls, 39

banking, 53–55, 66

Bank of America, 55

Bank of Italy, 54–55

Bardin, Shlomo, 14, 186–87, 218, 265n15

Barnett, Aaron, 60

Baron de Hirsch Fund, 147

Bauman, Mark K., 4–5, 225n3, 226n8

Bavaria, 20

Beerman, Leonard, 195–96

Behar, Elazar, 98

Beilenson, Anthony C., 198

Bellingham, WA, 86–87

benevolent societies: overview, 116–17; Los Angeles, 41–42, 117; newcomers and, 125; Portland, 42; role of, 39; San Francisco, 32, 39–41, 42, 72–73, 117, 133; Seattle, 117; Sonora, 31, 32, 41, 44; women's organizations, 42

Benjamin, I. J., 33, 42, 232n133

Beral, Linda, 219

Berch, Laura, 95

Berg, Charles F., 72

Berger, Elmer, 163

Berkeley, 200–203, 211, 222

Berkeley Citation (University of California), 202, 269n95

Berkowitz, Henry J., 155, 161, 184, 260n52

Berman, Howard, 198

Berris, Dora, 125

Berry, William, 208–9

Beth Abraham, Oakland, 200

Beth Am, Seattle, 209–10

Beth El, Los Angeles, 87–88, 89–90, 97

Beth Israel, Berkeley, 222

Beth Israel, La Jolla (originally San Diego), 220

Beth Israel, Los Angeles, 87. *See also* Kehal Adath Beth Israel, Los Angeles

Beth Israel, Portland: arson attack on, 101; Bavarians in, 96; founding of, 34; in postwar period, 206–7; rabbis of, 64; reforms, 35–36; regional relationships, 155; social divisions and, 161; Zionism and, 165

Beth Israel, San Diego, 61

Beth Israel, San Francisco, 28, 56

Beth Israel, Tacoma, 63

Beth Israel Hospital, Newark, 252n67, 252n69

Beth Israel Hospital and Clinic Association, Los Angeles, 127

Beth Jacob, Oakland, 9, 90

Beth Shalom, Las Vegas, 221

Beth Shalom, San Francisco, 166

Bettelheim, Albert (Aaron), 28, 53

Bettelheim, Rebekah, 53, 236n23

Beverly Hills, 154, 169, 218

Biale, David, 202

Bible classes, 137

Bichor Cholim, San Jose, 56, 237n42

Bien, Herman, 21, 34, 228n26

Bierstadt, Albert, 12

Bikur Cholim, Seattle: diverse membership of, 95; occupations of members, 103; Orthodoxy and, 88–89; rabbis of, 156, 161; Sephardim and, 97–98; Zionism and, 153, 164. *See also* Chevrah Bikur Cholim, Seattle

Bikur Cholim Hospital, Los Angeles, 127

Billikopf, Jacob, 144

birth control, 142

Bisno, Julius, *115*

Blackman, Abraham, 44

black power, 202

Bloch, Sadie, 142

Block, Benjamin, 60

Blumauer, Blanche, 117, 132, 135, 137, 149, 165

Blumauer, Hattie Fleischner, 101

Blumauer, Sigmund, 35

Blumauer, Sol, 101

Blumenthal, William, 69

B'nai B'rith, Order of: consolidation of lodges, 63–64, 69–70, 158; District Grand Lodge No. 4, San Francisco, 43, 51, 69, 117–18, 156, 183; as fraternal organization, 42–43; Hebrew school in Los Angeles, 109; newcomers and, 52, 96; in Portland, 64; Portland community center, 70; regional connections, 156–57; Seattle Lodge No. 503, *152*, 153; Selling and, 51; services for immigrants, 105–6; stance against anti-Semitism, 146–47; welfare federation and, 73. *See also* Pacific Hebrew Orphan Asylum

B'nai B'rith Congregation (later Wilshire Boulevard Temple), Los Angeles: Beth El and, 97, 232n133; Edelman at, 37–38; Goldwater and, 32; hospital and, 125–26; rabbis of, 63–64, 136, 155; Wilshire Blvd. building, 171, 172; Zionism and, 165. *See also* Magnin, Edgar

B'nai B'rith Messenger (Los Angeles), 157, 170–71

boardinghouses, kosher, 25

Bogen, Boris, 73, 127, 135, 253n99

Bouskila, Daniel, 223

Bowron, Fletcher, 187

Boxer, Barbara, 215

boycott of German goods, 181, 183–84

neighborhoods, Jewish: Boyle
neighborhoods, Jewish (cont.)
    Heights, Los Angeles, 90, 91, 154,
    166–69, 189, 192–95, 261n89;
    Central District, Seattle, 91; East-
    ern European immigrants and,
    90–93; Fillmore, San Francisco,
    92, 93; San Bruno, 106–7, 109;
    South Portland, 100, 107, 115,
    137, 158, 159, 164
Nelson, Roscoe, 183
Nemerovsky, David, 71, 245n120
Neuberger, Maureen, 209
Neuberger, Richard, 209
Neustadter, Ben, 165
Nevada Bank, 53–54
Nevada City: kosher in, 32
Neveh Shalom, Portland, 206
Neveh Zedek, Portland, 87, 96, 97,
    206; choir, 13, 13
Newman, Louis, 52, 70, 73, 110,
    156, 157; as community spokes-
    man, 178, 179, 180
Newmark, Harris, 36, 59, 126,
    236n17
Newmark, Helen Levinson, 29
Newmark, J. P., 36
Newmark, Joseph: family arrival
    in San Francisco, 23; as leader
    in Los Angeles, 36–37, 38, 131,
    234n171
Newmark, Myer, 23
Newmark, Rosa, 131
Newmark, Rosa Levy, 23
Newmark, Sarah, 131
New Odessa, OR, 82
newspapers: anti-Semitism cover-
    age, 175, 177; migration stimu-
    lated by, 21; offensive portrayals
    of Jews in, 146–47; regional
    ties and, 43–44, 157; Zionism
    and, 163–64. See also specific
    newspapers
New York: relocation from, 86
New York Tolerance Center, 196

Nicaragua isthmus, 24
Nieto, Jacob, 49; 1906 earthquake
    and, 66, 240n96; anti-Semitism
    and, 68, 178; career of, 47–49;
    Educational Alliance, 47, 56, 91;
    on hospital outreach, 251n45; on
    insularity, 5–6; Jewish Educa-
    tional Society, 58; regional ties
    and, 157; stained glass window
    and, 12; status and, 51; Zionism
    and, 110
Northeast: racial concerns in, 6
Norton, Isaac, 128
Nudelman, Fanny, 10–11
Nudelman, Joseph, 9–11, 11, 12, 89

O

Oakland: Eastern European immi-
    grants to, 79, 80–81; economic
    opportunities in, 103; Orthodox
    congregations in, 90; population
    trends in, 211; in postwar period,
    200; welfare federation in, 72;
    Zionism and, 163
Oakland Commission on American-
    ism, 179
Oakland Jewish Community Center,
    174–75, 179
Ogden, Kate Nearpass, 12
Ohabai Shalome, San Francisco:
    Ahavai Shalom and, 34; beauty
    of, 56; Eckman at, 230n71; estab-
    lishment of, 28
Ohabai Zion (Friends of Zion) soci-
    eties, 42
Ohaveth Sholum, Seattle: Gatzert
    and, 9
Ohr Shalom, San Diego, 274n47
Okrand, Fred, 168–69
Older, Fremont, 68
Old People's Home (San Francisco),
    67
Olympia, WA, 39, 117

Orange County, CA, 219–20
Oregon: Jewish population of,
    226n22; smaller communities in,
    58–60. See also Portland
Oregon Native Son, 246n152
Oregon Trail, 22, 23
Organization for Jewish Coloniza-
    tion in Russia (ICOR), 179
orphanages: Jewish Orphans Home
    of Southern California, 250n20;
    Pacific Hebrew Orphan Asylum,
    40, 43, 67, 113, 118, 144, 149
orphans, teenage female, 143–47
Orthodoxy: Los Angeles congrega-
    tions, 81, 88–90, 127; Oakland,
    90; Portland congregations, 87,
    89; San Francisco congregations,
    28–29, 93, 109; Seattle congre-
    gations, 81, 88–90, 159; Zion-
    ism and, 95, 153, 164. See also
    reforms and Reform Judaism;
    specific congregations
Ostrynski, B., 156

P

Pacht, Isaac, 193
Pacific Hebrew Orphan Asylum, 40,
    43, 67, 113, 117–18, 144, 149
Painted Woods, North Dakota, 75,
    76
Panama Canal, 101, 143
Panama isthmus, 23–24
Parzen, Herbert, 108, 111
Pascoe, Peggy, 119
Passover Seder, 144, 146
paternalism, 106
Peace and Progress Society, Los
    Angeles, 100
Peixotto, Eustace, 133
Peixotto, Jessica, 67, 132, 136–37,
    256n179
Peixotto, Sidney, 133
Peltzman, Nettie, 194

Persian immigrants, 218–19, 273n30
Pesotta, Rose, 169
Petaluma, CA, 83, 93–95, 94
Phelan, James D., 68, 240n101
philanthropy: overview, 113–16, 149–50; 1906 earthquake and, 65–68; B'nai B'rith consolidation and, 69–70; casino owners and, 186; Depression and, 160; foundation for, 116–18; hospitals, 120–30; men's roles in, 150; movie industry and, 191; museum funding, 217; national and world charities, 148–49; secular, in Los Angeles, 198; settlement houses, 106–7, 109, 132–43; teenage female orphans, 143–47; welfare federations, 70–73; women and professionalization of, 118–20; women in non-Jewish organizations, 130–32; women's activism and, 68–69. *See also* benevolent societies; B'nai B'rith, Order of
Phillips, Bruce, 189, 275n63
Phoenix, AZ, 211–12, 221, 275n63
Pirnazar, Nahid, 223
Pissis, Emile, 12
Pittsburgh Platform, 110, 151
P'nai Or (Face of Light), 204
Poker Flat, CA, 30–31
Poles: at B'nai B'rith, Los Angeles, 37
Policar, Jacob, 76
"Polish" origins, 34–35
political leadership. *See* civic and political leadership and activism
population trends: 1880 statistics, 59; in interwar period, 159; National Jewish Population Survey, 222–23; in postwar period, 189, 194, 206, 207, 209–10, 211–12; recent, 221–22, 223, 275n63; in San Francisco, 19, 52, 159
Portland: civic leadership in, 61; development of community

in, 33–36; Eastern European immigrants to, 75, 79, 80–81, 87, 96; Frank in, 9, 134; growth of Jewish community in, 21; Mosler's Bakery, 85; NCJW section in, 117, 135; Nudelmans in, 10–11; Orthodox congregations, 89; Pacific Fish Co., 84; in postwar period, 206–9; religious education in, 107–8; Selling and, 49–51; Sephardim in, 100; working conditions in, 106; Zionism in, 111. *See also specific congregations*
Portland Builders of Health, 130
Portland Committee on Relief of Jewish War Sufferers, 71
Portland Hebrew School, 95, 107–8
Portland Jewish Academy, 208
Poseners (Prussians), 34–35, 37, 78, 96–97
Poway, CA, 221
Prag, Mary Goldsmith. *See* Goldsmith, Mary (later Prag)
Preminger, Otto, 192
Prinz, Joachim, 204
Progressive Movement, 119–20
Protestants: anti-discrimination campaign, 183; anti-Semitism and, 236n16; ecumenical work with, 52, 64, 151, 180, 202; female moral authority and, 119; hospitals of, 120; Jewish charities and, 41, 71; Los Angeles leadership and, 154, 176, 198–99; migrations of, 81, 95, 125, 175; Mortrara affair and, 44; philanthropy and, 131; religious diversity and, 19, 44; suffrage movement and, 69; unions and, 65; women revivalists, 9
Prottas, Solomon, 110–11, 157
Prussians (Poseners), 34–35, 78, 96–97
public protests, 183

Q

Quakers, 259n1
QUALCOM, 220
Quinn, D. Michael, 7

R

Raab, Earl, 25, 199–200
rabbinical authority, isolation from, 25
race relations: interracial coalitions, 192–94, 198–99, 216; in Western region, 6; "whiteness" and, 6–7, 100–102, 246n148
Radical Jewish Union, 202
Ragins, Sanford, 196
Raiders of the Lost Ark (film), 191
Raphael, Marc Lee, 5
real estate financing and construction, 190
Red scare, 137–38
reforms and Reform Judaism: Beth Israel, Portland, 34, 35–36; Bikur Cholim, Seattle, and struggles over, 88–89; B'nai B'rith, Los Angeles, 37–38; Emanu-El, San Francisco, 27–28; network of rabbis, 155–56; of Russian congregations in Portland, 12–13; Sherith Israel, San Francisco, 27; Zionism and, 110, 162–63, 165. *See also specific Reform congregations*
Reichert, Irving, 162–63, 164, 165–66, 180–81, 182, 184, 249n214
Reinstein, S., 53
religious diversity: 1926 statistics, 235n5; and lack of dominant culture, 19; secularism, 14, 227n31; Sunday closing laws, 51, 235n15; on wagon trains, 22; in West, 7. *See also* Catholics; Protestants

Selling, Ben, 49, 50; business of, 59; Free Loan Society and, 245n120; fund-raising and, 71; immigrant assistance and, 106; life of, 49–51; school bill and, 247n154; wedding anniversary notice, 156; Wise and, 64

Selling, Caroline, 32, 49

Selling, Laurence, 50

Selling, Philip, 32, 35, 49

Selling, Tillie Hess, 50, 135, 156

Sephardic Communidad, Los Angeles, 100

Sephardic Talmud Torah, 97

Sephardim: Congregation Herzl, Seattle, and, 161; immigration of, 76–77, 78; Seattle community and separation from Ashkenazim, 97–100, 99; Temple De Hirsch, Seattle and, 159, 160–61

settlement houses, 106–7, 109, 132–43. *See also* Emanu-El Sisterhood for Personal Service; Neighborhood House, Portland

Shaaray Tefila, Los Angeles, 88

Shaarei Torah, Portland (First Street Shul), 87, 89, 206, 208

Sha'ar Zahav, San Francisco, 222

Shabbat services in homes in Los Angeles, 36

Shafer, Julius, 82, *152*

Sharlip, Ben, 83

Sharlip, Fanny Jaffe, 83, 130

Shenberg, Hyman, 171

Sherith Israel, San Francisco: 1906 earthquake and, 66; establishment of, 26–27; first marriage at, 32; first services, location of, 229n53; Goldwater and, 32; Polish *minhag*, 27; Poseners in, 96; reforms, 27; stained-glass windows, 3, 12, 227n27

Shevitz, Amy Hill, 81–82

ships, migration by, 21, 23, 24, 74

Shloss, Morris, 26

Shoah oral history project, 191

shochetim (ritual slaughterers): certification of, 25, 27–28; Goldsmith, 16; in Los Angeles, 36, 37; in Nevada City, 32, 34; in San Francisco, 26, 229n49

Shomrai Shaboth (Keepers of the Sabbath), San Francisco, 28–29

Shreiber, Emanuel, 63

Sickels, W. K., 91, 92

Siegel, Benjamin "Bugsy," 185–86

Sieroty, Mrs., 156

Silicon Valley, 14, 211, 222

Silver, Abba Hillel, 165–66

Silverman, Yair, 222

Silver Shirt movement, 174, 176

Silverstone, Rachel, 82

Simon, Joseph, 50, 61, 68

Sinai, Los Angeles, 87, 88, 219

Sinai, Reno, 268n87

Sinai (First Hebrew Congregation), Oakland, 9, 56, 72, 237n42

Sisters of Charity, 131, 251n36

Sisters of Presentation, 131

Skirball Cultural Center, 217

Sloss, Hattie, 149

Sloss, Louis, 22–23, 46, 144

Sloss, M. C., 71, 144

smaller communities: benevolence in, 118; buildings and rabbis in, 62–63; civic leadership in, 58–62; Eastern European immigrants and, 79

Smith, Gerald L. K., 193

social clubs, 42, 51, 236n17

social divisions in interwar period, 159–62

Social Hygiene Society of Portland, 236n18

socialist movements, 103, 168–69

social justice, 47, 132, 183, 196, 200, 204–5, 217

social networking, 40, 42–44

social welfare, 52. *See also* benevolent societies; philanthropy

social workers, 114, 119, 132, 142, 249n2

sojourns, 75–76, 77–78, 81–82, 85–86

Solis-Cohen, David, 236n16, 245n120

Solomon, Gus, 209, 270n123

Solomon, Moses ("Michael"), 87–88

Solomon, Vivian Dudune, 106–7, 109

Solomons, Hannah, 131–32, 134, 255n142

Solomons, Lucius L., 87, 150

Solomons, Selina, 132

Sonenshein, Raphael J., 268n77

Sonora, CA, 31–32, 41, 44

Soren, David, 93

Soto-Michigan Center, 193, 194

South African Jews, 220

southern Jews, 4–5

South Portland: Hebrew School in, 137, 164; migration out of, 158, 159; Neighborhood House in, 107, 115; Sephardim and, 100

Spector (rabbi), 156

Spielberg, Steven, 191

Spivak, Charles, 128

Spokane, 9, 62, 63

sportswear industry, 14

Spreckels, Rudolph, 68

Stampfer, Joshua, 206, 208

steamships, 23–24, 30

Steinbock, Hyman, 62

Stephen S. Wise Temple, Los Angeles, 195–96

step migration, 95

Stern, William, 174, 179

Strauss, Charles, 60

Strauss, Levi, 53

Stroum, Althea, 210

Stroum, Samuel, 210

student radicalism and protests, 193,